AMERICAN DISCORD

Conflicting Worlds: New Dimensions of the American Civil War

T. Michael Parrish, Series Editor

AMERICAN DISCORD

THE REPUBLIC AND ITS PEOPLE IN THE CIVIL WAR ERA

EDITED BY MEGAN L. BEVER
LESLEY J. GORDON AND
LAURA MAMMINA

Louisiana State University Press
Baton Rouge

Published with the assistance of the University of Alabama's Charles G. Summersell Chair of Southern History and the Frances J. Summersell Center for the Study of the South.

Published by Louisiana State University Press

Designer: Michelle A. Neustrom
Typeface: Sentinel

"Christian Paternalism and Racial Violence: White and Black Baptists in Texas during the Civil War Era," by T. Michael Parrish, first appeared, in different form, in *Texas Baptist History* (2015), and is published here with the permission of the Texas Baptist Historical Society.

Portions of "Newspaper Advertisements and American Political Culture, 1864–1865" first appeared in chapter 3 of *Marketing the Blue and Gray: Newspaper Advertising and the American Civil War,* by Lawrence A. Krieser Jr., and are used by permission of the publisher.

Portions of "Fires at the Battles of Chancellorsville and the Wilderness" first appeared in chapter 3 of *The Battle of the Wilderness in Myth and Memory: Reconsidering Virginia's Most Notorious Civil War Battlefield,* by Adam H. Petty, and are used by permission of the publisher.

Library of Congress Cataloging-in-Publication Data

Names: Bever, Megan L. (Megan Leigh), 1984– editor. | Gordon, Lesley J. (Lesley Jill), editor. | Mammina, Laura, editor.
Title: American discord : the Republic and its people in the Civil War era / edited by Megan L. Bever, Lesley J. Gordon, and Laura Mammina.
Description: Baton Rouge : Louisiana State University Press, [2020] | Series: Conflicting worlds: new dimensions of the American Civil War | Includes index.
Identifiers: LCCN 2019041538 (print) | LCCN 2019041539 (ebook) | ISBN 978-0-8071-6969-8 (cloth) | ISBN 978-0-8071-7374-9 (pdf) | ISBN 978-0-8071-7373-2 (epub)
Subjects: LCSH: United States—History—Civil War, 1861–1865—Social aspects. | United States—History—Civil War, 1861–1865—Influence.
Classification: LCC E468.9 .A465 2020 (print) | LCC E468.9 (ebook) | DDC 973.7/1—dc23
LC record available at https://lccn.loc.gov/2019041538
LC ebook record available at https://lccn.loc.gov/2019041539

The paper in this book meets the guidelines for permanence and durability of the Committee on Production Guidelines for Book Longevity of the Council on Library Resources. ∞

CONTENTS

vii Foreword, *by Gary W. Gallagher*

1 Editors' Introduction: The Mundane and the Sublime

5 **PART I Enemies Must Be Defined: Party Politics
   and Political Culture**

7 Northern Temperance Reformers, Slavery, and the Civil War
   MEGAN L. BEVER

22 Debating Black Manhood: The Northern Press Reports
   on the 54th Massachusetts at Fort Wagner
   GLENN DAVID BRASHER

45 Newspaper Advertisements and American Political Culture,
   1864–1865
   LAWRENCE A. KREISER JR.

60 The White Horse or the Mule: Lincoln in Civil War Music
   CHRISTIAN McWHIRTER

77 **PART II Rippling Effects: Political and Military Conflicts**

79 Acts of War: The Southern Seizure of Federal Forts and Arsenals,
   1860–1861
   RACHEL K. DEALE

99 Contaminated Water and Dehydration during the Vicksburg Campaign
   LINDSAY RAE PRIVETTE

116 Fires at the Battles of Chancellorsville and the Wilderness
   ADAM H. PETTY

131 United States Colored Troops and the Battle of the Crater
   A. WILSON GREENE

Contents

150   Domesticity in Conflict: Union Soldiers, Southern Women,
      and Gender Roles during the American Civil War
      LAURA MAMMINA

172   An Elusive Freedom: Black Women, Labor, and Liberation
      during the Civil War
      CHARITY RAKESTRAW AND KRISTOPHER A. TETERS

187   **PART III A Thermidorean Reaction: Reconstruction
      and Counterrevolution**

189   Christian Paternalism and Racial Violence: White and Black
      Baptists in Texas during the Civil War Era
      T. MICHAEL PARRISH

208   Deriding the Democracy: The Partisan Humor of David Ross Locke
      DANIEL J. BURGE

223   Reconstruction and Historical Allusion
      T. ROBERT HART

236   Sherman and Grant: Different Men and Different Memoirs
      JOHN F. MARSZALEK

250   The Evolution of the Public Memory of the Hamburg Massacre
      KEVIN L. HUGHES

269   Acknowledgments

271   Contributors

275   Index

FOREWORD

I was delighted to be asked to contribute a brief foreword to this book honoring George C. Rable. I have known Professor Rable quite well for a number of years and consider him a much-valued friend—though, I hasten to add, our friendship developed after I had formed a very high opinion of his scholarship. That opinion has grown ever more positive over the past twenty-five years.

George Rable's first two books—*But There Was No Peace: The Role of Violence in the Politics of Reconstruction* (1984) and *Civil Wars: Women and the Crisis of Southern Nationalism* (1989)—reflected his ability to combine sound research in a wealth of primary materials, sophisticated analysis, and strong literary skills. I used both in courses and found them to be excellent tools to inspire lively and productive debate. I will not dwell on what I consider to be the many virtues of these books—both of which anticipated major shifts in the field—beyond stating that my admiration for them prompted me to ask Rable to give a lecture in 1993 at a conference devoted to the campaign of Fredericksburg. He subsequently contributed an essay to a collection I edited titled *The Fredericksburg Campaign: Decision on the Rappahannock* (1995). His piece discussed the ways in which civilians and soldiers in the United States and the Confederacy sought to come to terms with the seemingly senseless slaughter at Fredericksburg.

During the period that involved the conference and book of essays on Fredericksburg, I sought to convince Professor Rable to publish his book-length manuscript, then in progress, on the political culture of the Confederacy in a series I edited. He agreed, and *The Confederate Republic: A Revolution against Politics* (1994) more than met my very high expectations. I do not believe any other scholar has treated this subject more deftly or with a better command of the sources, and the book soon became, and has remained, the clear standard on the topic.

Rable's next book, *Fredericksburg! Fredericksburg!*, also appeared in the series. This pathbreaking study achieved a thorough, and highly unusual, blending of the military and nonmilitary dimensions of a major Civil War campaign. Indeed, Professor Rable remains one of the few scholars who consistently attempts to explore questions within the broadest context of civilian and military influences, and his work on Fredericksburg represents an ambitious effort to examine a "military" topic within an expansive framework that employs the tools of intellectual, social, political, and military history. *Fredericksburg! Fredericksburg!,* a most deserving winner of the 2002 Lincoln Prize, fits squarely within a humanistic tradition, something quite unusual in the genre of "battle" books. I believe it stands as a model for how such topics should be addressed in the future.

I had the good fortune to work with Professor Rable on a third major project. His prizewinning *God's Almost Chosen Peoples: A Religious History of the American Civil War* (2010) added new luster to his already superior reputation. It appeared as the fourth title in "The Littlefield History of the Civil War Era," a sixteen-volume series I coedit with T. Michael Parrish. It is remarkable that no academic scholar previously had undertaken a full-blown examination of Civil War religion, and the field of Civil War studies benefited immensely from seeing this glaring void in the literature filled. Based on meticulous research in unpublished materials as well as printed literature, the book combines in pleasing proportion descriptive passages, analysis, and synthesis. It set a very high bar in every way, immediately became the obvious first title to read on the topic (matching *The Confederate Republic* in that respect), and surely will inspire a great deal of additional work.

It must be evident that I consider George Rable to be one of the premier scholars in the field of Civil War–era history. He is widely admired and frequently cited by his peers. To a degree highly unusual in our time of narrow specialization, he has made major contributions to the literatures on political, social, women's, military, and religious history of the nineteenth-century United States. He has been consistently productive in a field that offers unusual potential for scholars to reach a lay as well as an academic audience. Professor Rable has made the most of that potential. His many prizes and presidency of the Society of Civil War Historians attest to his reputation among scholars, and the success of *Fredericksburg! Fredericksburg!,* which was a selection of the History Book Club, underscores the fact that his writings have found a lay audience.

Throughout our friendship, I have found George to be generous, supportive of fellow scholars in his field (senior and junior), willing to render more than his share of professional service, and possessed of an understated sense of humor that serves him well in a number of forums. He personifies the very best of our profession.

Gary W. Gallagher
John L. Nau III Professor in the History
   of the American Civil War Emeritus
University of Virginia

AMERICAN DISCORD

Editors' Introduction

The Mundane and the Sublime

I n the prologue to his award-winning 2002 book, *Fredericksburg! Fredericksburg!,* George Rable explained that he sought to write a new kind of campaign history by merging the "old" and "new," thus offering a "new understanding of a battle." He added: "It requires a blending of the everyday and the spectacular, the mundane and the sublime." "It means," Rable wrote, "treating the people involved as full human beings."

Rable's long and prolific career as a historian, teacher, and mentor speaks to his desire to treat everyone—students, colleagues, and his subjects—as "full human beings." He possesses an uncanny ability to mix the old and the new, the mundane and the sublime, creating some of the most significant scholarship of the past three decades. In these pages, our contributors seek to follow his example and legacy. His contemporaries and former students write about well-known campaigns and famous military leaders but also less well-known subjects like water contamination at Vicksburg and the contested memory of the Hamburg Massacre during Reconstruction. Rable's scholarly footprint is a large one, and one that will be indelible to future students of the war. Perhaps, though, the most important part of his legacy is his refusal to be confined by simplistic labels or categories: he is a historian of the Civil War and Reconstruction era writ large. In seeking to understand the war and its aftermath, this volume seeks to follow his lead, delving deeply into the past and thinking expansively about its implications for today.

American Discord: The Republic and Its People in the Civil War Era begins, fittingly, with an assessment of Rable's scholarship by his longtime colleague Gary W. Gallagher. In his foreword, Gallagher observes that in addition to close and careful research, Rable has "anticipated major shifts in the field." His ability to be pathbreaking undoubtedly comes from his focus on (and his deep familiarity with) the sources. And Rable's work is always meticulously researched. This is no small feat for someone who has written on so many different topics, from the violence of Reconstruction to a single Civil War campaign to religion and Confederate women.

In the spirit of Rable's eclectic interests, this volume moves to cover a wide range of topics and themes. We have arranged the essays into three sections, each of which follows a more or less thematic narrative that takes readers through the sectional crisis, the war, and on into Reconstruction. The sections are loosely organized around the following topics: party politics and political culture, political and military conflicts, and Reconstruction and counterrevolution.

Readers familiar with Rable's work will notice the similarities between these essays and the themes he explores not only in *The Confederate Republic* but also in his more recent studies, *God's Almost Chosen Peoples* and *Damn Yankees!* Our collection begins with a look at American political culture in the 1860s. These essays reveal Americans—specifically northerners—entering the decade largely uninterested in political compromise. Focused on the perceived moral superiority of their politics, both Democrats and Republicans created an atmosphere (which the war certainly exacerbated) in which they viewed their political opponents as villains working on behalf of the devil. In addition to surveying the rancorous political culture, part I builds on Rable's work by continuing to flesh out the ways in which white supremacy was woven into the political fabric of the North. Both Republicans and Democrats considered their opposition's views on slavery and emancipation as signs of moral depravity.

The second section, which examines the war from the battlefield, continues these themes of internal conflict, lack of compromise, and the political forms of white supremacy. As Rable has done in *Fredericksburg! Fredericksburg!* and *Civil Wars*, these essays conceive of battle broadly, considering its environmental effects and how the war shaped the lives of the soldiers and civilians caught in its midst. And they reveal the pervasiveness of internal conflict as Confederates attempted to determine how to secede or as Union commanders disagreed over how to use African American troops in battle, and as civilians— whether southern white women or "contraband" African American women— attempted to redefine and enlarge the boundaries of domestic ideology and citizenship. While the war may have blurred boundaries between battle and home or civilian and soldier, the chaos of the war ultimately prompted Americans to grasp for familiar gender and racial hierarchies.

Chaos and internal division continued as the war ground to a close and the political culture of Reconstruction was every bit as acrimonious as it was in the early 1860s. Former Confederates decried the barbarity of their Yankee conquerors, comparing their own plight to that of French conservatives overrun by

Jacobins. Republicans portrayed Democrats as backward rubes in need of civilizing. But while the essays in the third section highlight Americans' continued reliance on hyperbolic rhetoric, they demonstrate that their commitment to white supremacy was in flux by the end of the war. In fact, the acceptance of emancipation was central to Republicans' conception of what it meant to be civilized, educated, and reconstructed. Even so, these essays share an emphasis with *But There Was No Peace* (and, recently, *Damn Yankees!*) in insisting that the backlash against black equality was often fervent and violent. As historians know well, former Confederates rejected outright—in the press, in their churches, and through extralegal violence—any attempts to solidify freedom through political rights, integration, and land redistribution. And yet, as the foregoing sections reveal, the conflicts created by the war were not simply sectional but internal. As Reconstruction ended, politicians sought to mold the meaning of the war to suit their own ambitions. Union generals penned memoirs—at times combative ones—to solidify their place in history. Confederate politicians connected themselves to the extralegal violence of Reconstruction in order to establish their white supremacist bona fides with southern white voters.

Overall, *American Discord* embraces a multifaceted view of the war and its aftermath, attempting to capture, as Rable has for decades, the myriad complicated experiences of the human beings who experienced the conflict. The many interpersonal and interconnected struggles that occurred within the Union and the Confederacy shaped people's individual and collective responses to the war. But these essays also reveal the extent to which Rable's work has profoundly reshaped the fields of Civil War and Reconstruction studies. All of these scholarly inquiries begin with the premise that ordinary human beings and their experiences matter—that the dynamics among family, friends, and enemies have not only local consequences but often sweeping national consequences as well. The mundane and the sublime have become knitted together. We dedicate *American Discord* to one of the masters in the field of Civil War history whose scholarly imprint will be enduring for future generations of students and scholars. But we also hope that this volume, showcasing Rable's students and his colleagues, contributes to the ongoing historiographical debates he helped lead and sustain.

ENEMIES MUST BE DEFINED

Party Politics and Political Culture

War itself requires no little hatred. There must be enemies, and those enemies must be defined, denounced, and defeated.
  —George C. Rable, *Damn Yankees!* (2015), 2

That slavery roiled the religious and political waters should have caused no great surprise, but there were several ironies. Northerners portrayed the slave power as an aggressive force hell bent on stamping out civil and religious liberty—a mirror image of southern diatribes against Yankee political preachers. Extremism quite literally bred extremism.
  —George C. Rable, *God's Almost Chosen Peoples* (2010), 30

A s George Rable observes in his most recent works, mid-nineteenth-century partisan rancor became intensely uncompromising in the wake of sectional conflict and war. These first four essays build on these themes as they explore American political rhetoric, noting the extremism both between and within the North and South. Northern Democrats and Republicans, as well as northerners and southerners, fought bitterly over white supremacy and black equality as well as over the war, the Union, and the future of the nation.

Perhaps none of the essays illustrates these themes more clearly than Megan L. Bever's "Northern Temperance Reformers, Slavery, and the Civil War." According to Bever, temperance reformers (much like their abolitionist acquaintances) grew tired of making moral compromises for the sake of political peace. This lack of interest in compromise continued throughout the war, as Lawrence A. Kreiser Jr. ("Newspaper Advertisements and American Political Culture") and Christian McWhirter ("The White Horse or the Mule") demonstrate. Gimmicks like advertisements and songs increased rather than allayed partisan hostilities, and portraying the opposition as idiotic proved essential to increasing enthusiasm for one's own cause.

Behind the partisan rancor ran a conviction that compromising with the opposition was immoral. Temperance reformers are perhaps the most blatant example of this sentiment because they insisted that saving the Union must involve legislation to prohibit alcohol, thus preventing drunken ruin on a national scale. Yet perhaps more ominous is the way that these reformers understood the problem of slavery. Rather than opposing slavery wholeheartedly, teetotalers were often only concerned with abolition when it directly facilitated their own crusade against alcohol. Still, temperance reformers did not hold a monopoly on hyperbolic imagery. According to Kreiser, Democrats warned voters that Lincoln's reelection would cause the United States to "sink into despotism" and would bring "universal anarchy and ultimate RUIN!" In their campaign music, Peace Democrats took the warnings even further, suggesting that Lincoln was in cahoots with the devil. Similar to Rable's own observations, Americans connected their politics to a larger moral cause, thus enabling—and even necessitating—them to vilify the opposition.

As extreme as Democrats and Republicans' penchant for consigning their political opponents to the pits of hell might seem, they saved their most virulent rhetoric for expressions of white supremacy. While McWhirter points out that after January 1863, popular songs in the North—particularly those authored by African Americans—celebrated Lincoln's role as emancipator, Democrats ridiculed the president's antislavery actions. Kreiser, likewise, argues that Democrats used blatantly racist imagery to play on fears of black equality and to stir up enthusiasm among voters. And Glenn David Brasher's "Debating Black Manhood" illustrates that northern support for emancipation fell well short of a commitment to racial equality. Arming black men was controversial in the wartime North, and some in the northern press hesitated to fully celebrate black soldiers even after the 54th Massachusetts bravely stormed Fort Wagner. As Brasher makes clear, some Democratic papers at least initially covered the 54th's performance at Fort Wagner sympathetically, but only because the Lincoln administration continued to pay black soldiers less than white soldiers, demonstrating that the North had not fully accepted black equality. Ultimately, these essays portray extreme partisan rancor as well as the wide variety of issues that animated white and black northerners and southerners. No one could quite agree which was most important—white supremacy versus black equality or individual rights versus federal power—or which national sin, slavery or intemperance, most urgently required addressing. The war had not raised these questions, but it also failed to resolve them.

Northern Temperance Reformers, Slavery, and the Civil War

MEGAN L. BEVER

I n December 1860, the American Temperance Union (ATU) rejoiced at the election of Abraham Lincoln and Hannibal Hamlin, both of whom were "thorough temperance men." From the perspective of John Marsh, the editor of the *Journal of the American Temperance Union: And the New-York Prohibitionist* (*JATU*), supporters of temperance from all over the United States—regardless of "politics or . . . local interest"—should "look up and be thankful that there is one placed at the helm who will, never, through the wine bottle, lose his reckoning and run our noble steamer into Dundrum Bay." That Lincoln was a teetotaler was of upmost importance to the temperance community. They believed firmly that there was "not safety to any government," nor was there "permanent prosperity to any people, but in the temperance principle."[1] For the United States to prosper, the entire nation needed to embrace total abstinence. In fact, many members of the New York–based ATU were convinced that temperance was the primary issue of the 1860 presidential election. When southern subscribers to the *Journal* balked at its endorsement of the Republican ticket, ATU president Marsh believed that southerners would quickly calm down and continue to "stand bravely for the temperance flag as the only flag of the Free."[2] After all, Lincoln, Hamlin, and the Republican Party offered them the best chance to achieve their main political goal, which, of course, was prohibition.

With the benefit of hindsight, it would seem that northern temperance reformers were wildly out of step with the major political debates that engrossed the American public during the 1860 presidential campaign. Contrary to Marsh's optimism, southern temperance reformers insisted that the movement's alignment with the Republican Party was absurd. While most Americans focused on debates over the expansion of slavery into the territories during the 1850s, the temperance community remained obsessed with ridding the United States of the liquor traffic. Even as the sectional crisis erupted into secession and war, northern temperance reformers remained preoccupied with the problem of drunkenness. For these reformers, saving the Union became inextricably linked to prohibition. Because of this, they monitored slavery's demise closely. On one level, reformers firmly opposed slavery and believed that, like intemperance, it threatened national well-being. But in their view, emancipating the slaves was only the first step toward saving the Union. Reformers insisted that rum was the most harmful evil facing the nation and that the emphasis on ending chattel slavery was a distraction. Drunkenness, in their minds, had caused the sectional crisis to erupt into war, and in order to save the nation, prohibition, not simply emancipation, had to be enacted.

The connection between temperance and antislavery reform that appeared in the *JATU* reveals how temperance reformers understood the fight for the Union. Historians of reform have identified the war as a pivotal point for the temperance community. Specifically, Holly Berkeley Fletcher argues that the movement became more concerned with the national community than individual drunks during the 1860s. Looking closely at how reformers spoke of "saving the Union" builds on her findings.[3] For teetotalers, saving the Union was not a new concept in 1861. Antebellum reformers, steeped in evangelical beliefs, believed that they were on a crusade to save their nation from vice (and from hell) in order to protect the integrity of the political system and to usher in the millennium.[4] During the secession crisis and war, temperance advocates became convinced that sobriety was a key to the Union's survival.

This idea of saving the Union has in recent years recaptured the attention of historians. Gary Gallagher has demonstrated that the idea of the Union could exist independently of other war aims, though other scholars have argued that ending slavery and saving the Union often went hand in hand even before the Emancipation Proclamation.[5] Temperance reformers—like most evangelicals—understood the fight for the Union in providential terms. Salvation, for them, required reforming the soul of the nation, not just preserving the Constitution and the political system. The war, for them, was a holy crusade.[6] To be certain, there were many reformers who were members of both the temperance and abolitionist movements. But reformers whose primary concern was fighting the liquor traffic did not always believe that slavery was the sin most threatening the nation. In fact, they initially believed that the hullabaloo surrounding slavery and its expansion was a distraction from the real crisis—drunkenness. Early in the war they came to view slavery and intemperance as twin evils. After the Emancipation Proclamation was issued, reformers turned their full attention back to intemperance, labeling it a national sin worse than chattel slavery. They argued that in order to save the Union—both politically and religiously—Americans needed to sober up.

The pages of the *JATU* reveal how reformers linked slavery, prohibition, and saving the Union. Although published in New York, the *JATU* reprinted articles and reports from temperance publications across the northern and western states. Membership in the American Temperance Union was on the decline in the 1850s and 1860s (in part because Americans were not consuming as much alcohol). The movement had counted more than a million followers in the antebellum decades, about 12 percent of the free US population. As many temperance societies and publications petered out during the war, the *JATU* persisted and even reached Union soldiers, thousands of whom read its contents.[7] Nevertheless, Americans who supported prohibition and perceived drunkenness to be the greatest calamity facing the United States in the 1860s were, admittedly, a minority. Still, because prohibition would emerge as a powerful political force in the decades following the Civil War, the ATU's understanding of the conflict is important for understanding the changes taking place within the temperance movement.

For members of the ATU, the fight to save the soul of the nation in many ways began decades before the 1860s, when they embarked on their political crusade to rid their communities of the demon rum. In the antebellum decades, membership in the temperance and abolitionist movements overlapped significantly, but northern temperance advocates sometimes remained quiet about slavery so as not to offend their southern counterparts.[8] During the sectional crisis and the war, however, white northern temperance reformers became increasingly vocal about slavery—both because they were concerned about its evil and because they were angry about its distraction from temperance. By the 1850s, when the United States as a whole became engrossed in a fight over the expansion of slavery into the territories, temperance reformers were preoccupied with a different battle: prohibition laws. In 1851, the state of Maine passed prohibition. By 1855, twelve additional northern and midwestern states had followed suit. Prohibition sentiment was even more widespread. In all states north of the Ohio River, prohibition found support among Democrats and Whigs, even if the states did not vote to go dry. Despite prohibition's seeming popularity, the issue proved divisive in both political parties—neither was willing to fully incorporate prohibition into its platform for fear that it would alienate proliquor voters. As the second party system collapsed over slavery's expansion, prohibitionists continued to find themselves without a party firmly devoted to their priorities (although they tended to vote American, Free-Soil, and, eventually, Republican). They grew exasperated, believing that any compromise on the liquor question acquiesced to sin.[9] Compounding their frustration was the fact that by the late 1850s, a series of court cases struck down portions of the various state laws, and most early supporters lost their zeal for prohibition when they realized that it was simply unenforceable. Hard-line supporters of prohibition, however, doubled down and became angry when the Republican Party refused to incorporate support for prohibition into its state and national platforms in the 1850s. From the perspective of John Marsh and others, prohibition was being sidelined in favor of building a large antislavery coalition. They did not understand that, regardless of the slavery question, prohibition had simply lost public support.[10]

Understanding how prohibitionists perceived the political climate of the 1850s is essential for explaining how they interpreted slavery as it related to their antiliquor crusade. In July 1860, James Black of Lancaster, Pennsylvania, anticipated that the end of the presidential election would bring about "an active movement against the Liquor Traffic." Black argued that the passing of the Kansas-Nebraska Act in 1854 (rather than the 1854 decision of the Massachusetts Supreme Court, in *Fisher v. McGirr*, which had ruled components of the state's prohibition law unconstitutional) had stymied the antiliquor crusade.[11] Black believed that northerners were consumed with fear of "Slavery aggression" on the part of southerners. If Lincoln won, he assumed, the political threat of slavery would subside. After November, surely "the arrested labor will re-commence with vigor in the States that have not adopted the principle of *prohibition,* and the States which have that principle embodied in their law, will also see to a better enforcement of it than now exists." As Black saw it, there was "no other evil in our midst . . . so burdensome and afflictive" as the liquor traffic because it threatened all families.[12]

Reformers took the stance that alcohol posed the greatest threat to Americans, but even before the war began, they understood their crusade to be linked to abolitionism—legislatively and morally. Both abolitionists and prohibitionists targeted state and federal laws they believed sanctioned sin (slavery and drunkenness). What prohibitionists wanted in the late 1850s was for their states to take a moral stance against alcohol by eliminating it. As prohibition was repealed state by state, it had been replaced by a series of license laws that regulated the selling and consumption of liquor. These license laws, from the perspective of temperance reformers, represented the states' implicit approval of drinking. A reverend Mr. Hawley of Cazenovia, New York, explained that license laws were "wicked" because they took "advantage of man's natural reverence for law, and thus, through a false standard for his conscience enlists him on the side of crime." As a matter of comparison, Hawley pointed to slavery, another sin that had been protected by law for centuries. Referring to slavery "as a licensed curse," Hawley argued that the law's condoning of slavery caused "the criminal and his victim [to be] seen through a false medium, and the moral judgment is grossly perverted, and Satan triumphs."[13] In other words, members of the American Temperance Union were profoundly uncomfortable with laws that sanctioned—in their minds—sins. More importantly, they believed that the state should have the power to regulate morality.

After the Republican Party won the presidency in 1860, northern temperance reformers prepared to pick up their prohibition crusade, rejoicing that the election had most assuredly put the slavery question to rest. "What Next?," asked the *JATU* in December 1860. Certainly, it would be "a revival of the Temperance Cause."[14] The "political excitement" of the election had passed, explained the editors of the *Templars' Magazine,* and there was "nothing of general interest to engross the public." It was time for temperance men to fill that void, now that the distraction of the campaign season had ended.[15] It was time for churches to take a stand in favor of prohibition, which was "a moral, a Christian enterprise." And it was time for the state to "help . . . by getting out of our way" and "by coming directly to our aid."[16]

When the secession crisis, not temperance reform, became the issue engrossing the public in the months following the election, temperance reformers' anger toward the Republican Party and the abolitionist movement erupted. In December 1860, reformers in Boston decried that their state legislature had implored them to "wait till we have knocked off the shackles in Southern climes . . . ;—see that wife in the Sunny South whose husband is toiling under the beautiful Palmetto tree,—we must first give liberty to him." With the reference to the lovely palmetto trees, reformers seemingly wanted to emphasize that the toll inflicted by southern chattel slavery was not as severe as the toll inflicted by the liquor traffic. They went further, though, explaining that they could not "understand it, that while there is such an indignation through all the North against Southern slavery, there should be almost none at all against the rum power, which is binding at least fifty, if not an hundred thousand, husbands, fathers, and sons in the rum-seller's chains."[17] As the secession crisis gathered steam, temperance advocates continued to implore the Republican Party to "oppose the slavery of rum" by supporting prohibitory laws. As one reformer of Jefferson County, New York, explained in 1861, "The evils of secession, and even permanent separation, are incomparably less than those inflicted by our present license laws."[18] In contending that the liquor trade threatened national well-being more seriously than slavery or the ripping apart of the states, he was not alone among prohibitionists.

The *JATU* lashed out at secessionists and liquor dealers with even more fervor than it critiqued Republicans. Reformers regularly articulated the threat of the "rum power" in much the same way that antislavery northerners referred to the Slave Power. It is clear that prohibitionists believed that the rum power (read: liquor sellers) threatened the nation's democratic institutions. This notion had existed for decades among reformers. If representative self-government were going to succeed, it needed sober voters and sober men holding office. Mixing liquor and the ballot paved the way for corruption and degradation.[19] Reverend John Marsh (editor of the *JATU*), in a January 1860 article entitled "Saving the Union," acknowledged the brewing sectional hostilities but reminded his fellow teetotalers that they had been working a long time to save the Union from a drunken Congress. Liquor was fueling the political fires in Washington, including the debate over slavery's expansion, and Marsh predicted that if there were "fighting and bloodshed . . . King Alcohol will have much to do with it."[20] One New Yorker, C. A. Hammond, was more specific about the ways that liquor was fueling sectional tensions. In early 1861, he reminded his fellow reformers that it was "the rum and rowdy power" that had "been making a characteristic demonstration of devotion to the kindred curse of slavery, by sending out their forces to mob down free speech against that national pet 'Institution.'" Rum, he intimated, had been fueling the violent attacks against abolitionists in the North.[21] In February 1861, the *JATU* labeled "the uprising and rebellion of our brethren at the South . . . A WHISKEY REBELLION; because whiskey flows freely . . . whenever men are congregated for agitation, discussion or extreme action."[22] Drunkenness, in other words, was causing the violence, discord, and threats to the Constitution. From the perspective of Marsh and others, the best method for saving the Union was to save the population from the sin of intemperance. Sobriety would allow the United States to remain at peace.[23]

Temperance reformers' concern for the soul of the nation only increased when the secession crisis devolved into civil war. It was bad enough, from their perspective, that rum had interfered with the political process. But in the summer of 1861, reformers believed that conflict would expand the threat of drunkenness to the nation. Specifically, they worried that the threat of vice in camps would bring about the ruin of the Federal army, and they cautioned young men "to beware of the enemy of appetite." Believing that rum could be just as deadly as the rebels, reformers set to work raising money to distribute thousands of tracts and tried to get soldiers to sign temperance pledges.[24] Their concerns did not dissipate at any point during the war. When it came to intoxicated officers, reformers feared that habitual drunkenness could bring the patriotic young men to "dangerous and fatal courses."[25] Reformers were not simply worried that young soldiers were sinning when they imbibed (although that was certainly part of their fear). They believed that "Generals" who relied on "the bottle for stimulus or base gratification" would "not unfrequently become, in the hour of greatest peril, utterly incapable of discharging their high trust."[26] Quite literally, reformers thought, alcohol would cause the Union army to lose the war by making them poor fighters. Furthermore, advocates of prohibition were certain that concern over soldiers' behavior and performance would cause more Americans to join their legislative crusade against alcohol. How could anyone object to prohibitory laws at a time when the fate of the nation rested with an army of drunks? Temperance reformers believed that more Americans would see the problems with license laws when the fate of the Union was at stake.[27]

This fear that drunken armies would hasten the Union's ruin colored temperance reformers' understanding of the war, and it shaped their framing of the slavery question. Reformers wanted to end slavery in order to end the war because the war made intemperance worse. As such, they themselves were filled with abolitionist fervor during the war's early years. As they had during antebellum decades, northern temperance reformers argued that slavery violated God's laws and chastised white southerners for perpetuating slavery by persuading the federal government to protect the institution. That the nation as a whole had benefited economically from the system of slavery for decades did not keep some northern reformers from lambasting southern slaveholders. As a Wisconsin newspaper explained in 1861, the "North, by abandoning the evil, has not only cleansed her own skirts from the guilt, but acquired the right to condemn in others that sin" of slavery.[28] Others admitted that the North had been the "accomplice of the South" in the past and that they themselves had "submitted" so as not to jeopardize the temperance cause. After southerners seceded, however, New York's temperance community no longer felt compelled to offer any defense of the institution of slavery. As these reformers understood it, white southerners had seceded to protect slavery. Secession threatened the nation by causing a war. And reformers believed that "slavery must perish" in order for the nation to be saved.[29]

Reformers had never denied that slavery was a moral evil, but temperance activists argued that drunkenness and the liquor traffic created an equal—if not more severe—threat to national well-being. Referring to the "two giant sins" and "the twin scourges" of the nation, reformers likened drunkenness to the "kindred curse of slavery" and referred to the United States as a "rum and slave benighted country."[30] On one level, temperance rhetoric simply named slavery and drunkenness as the causes of the war—it was drunkards who harassed abolitionists, and it was drunkards who had seceded.[31] But on another level, temperance reformers offered a larger critique of American society—particularly American economic development—when they linked the sins of slavery and drunkenness. The liquor traffic, reformers insisted, was as immoral as the slave trade. In at least one instance, the *JATU* went so far as to link the origins of the trades, pointing out that the "slave dealers . . . c[a]me on to their coasts with rum to buy men for horrid bondage."[32] Comparing the rum trade with the African slave trade, reformers argued that while the slave trade brought "subjection," the rum trade brought "disorder and crime."[33] Both the slave and rum trade were exploitative and antithetical to the goals of a free-labor society. Both traffics also thwarted reformers' millennialist goals. Temperance activists, then, made it clear that they were fighting to rid the country of both vices in order to bring about a more perfect nation.[34]

By linking the evils of chattel slavery and drunkenness, temperance reformers, who interpreted the war in millennial terms, understood the conflict as a crusade to free the nation from all forms of sin. Activists even went beyond simply labeling slavery and intemperance the "twin scourges" of the land. They declared that drunkenness itself was a form of slavery, and they insisted—as the Bostonians had during the secession crisis—that this slavery was much worse than the slavery that existed in the southern states. James Brewster of New Haven, Connecticut, explained that while "there are four millions of human beings held in bondage" in the South, "a much larger number of persons, are under bondage to a great evil . . . that of intemperance." From his point of view, the comparison of evils was not simply an issue of numbers, either. Brewster argued that "because slavery does not involve a moral wrong on the part of the slaves; because it is involuntary" it was not as immoral—at least from the enslaved person's perspective—as intemperance. Drunkenness was "voluntary throughout, involving moral guilt and depravity, both with the vendor and the receiver."[35] In the 1860s, Brewster's fellow reformers would have undoubtedly engaged him in a lively debate over whether "the receiver" acted as voluntarily as "the vendor," as most reformers put the blame for intemperance on the trafficker rather than the drunk.

Nevertheless, Brewster's use of the imagery of the bondage of slavery to describe habitual drunkenness would have been familiar; referring to an individual as being a "slave to the habit" still exists as a way to describe addiction or vice, including intoxication. Antebellum temperance reformers were particularly fond of this image, using it often to describe alcohol's victims (as they perceived them).[36] The idea that intoxication robbed an individual—in most cases, a man—of control over his actions had taken root in the decades preceding the Civil War. In an era of economic growth, men needed to be sober in order to succeed as industrious, hardworking, independent individuals. Therefore alcohol could ruin a man and destroy his family.[37] Throughout the war, reformers continued with this reasoning, arguing that the "slaves of a blind and foolish custom" lost their "individuality," and while drunkards may have initially "lacked the moral element to . . . shield them from temptation," the blame for their plight rested with alcohol itself and, more importantly, with "Satan's vilest slaves—the grogsellers," who "hunted and enticed" young men.[38] Because sheer greed led liquor dealers to do Satan's bidding, temperance reformers believed that only prohibitory laws would put an end to the traffic. Moral suasion was not always successful. Excise laws worsened the problem. Legal prohibition was necessary to rescue "slaves" from the chains of rum and rum sellers.

Early in the war, members of the American Temperance Union were content to fight against the twin evils of liquor and slavery. But because they were intently focused on their own goal—prohibition—reformers reacted to Lincoln's preliminary Emancipation Proclamation in the fall of 1862 with great interest. Primarily, they expressed joy that slavery was finally out of their way. Responding to the proclamation in October, the editors of the *JATU* exclaimed: "And now if slavery is dead and the Republic is to rise to life of freedom and justice, let us who are engaged in a warfare against that other enemy of God and man, take courage and press on in the conflict. . . . Now is the time to drive out and crush that other horrid traffic, which is a traffic in the souls and bodies of men."[39] Selling liquor once again took center stage as the nation's greatest sin.

While emancipation had been a moral victory and a necessary war measure, temperance reformers remained convinced that alcohol itself prolonged the war and threatened the ability of the Union to prevail. Citing slavery as the root cause of the war, reformer C. S. Nichols exclaimed in 1862 that the "slave rebellion has slain its thousands, but this heaven-denounced and God defying rum rebellion its hundreds of thousands!"[40] Other reformers shared his concerns. "How can God be for us amid all the drunkenness and profanity prevalent among us?" asked the journal's editor.[41] The war—just like the sectional crisis of the 1850s—caused "the danger and guilt of intemperance [to be] lost sight of." While Americans were "struggling to save the country in its peril, we have lost sight of the greater obstacle to our success, and the greatest evil under which the land mourns."[42] Victory and the preservation of the Union required God's blessing, and emancipating the slaves alone was not enough. The liquor trade had to be abolished because saving the Union required saving the souls of the Union's citizens, specifically by sobering them up.

On this crusade, temperance reformers believed that Lincoln's Emancipation Proclamation helped their cause. If slavery and drunkenness were related national sins, getting rid of one (slavery) surely provided clues for eradicating the other (drunkenness). As historian Gaines Foster has argued persuasively, the abolition of slavery was a watershed moment for American moral reformers. From their perspective, it appeared that the federal government was finally willing to throw its weight behind moral causes. This left reformers, in general, and prohibitionists, specifically, ready once again to fight their righteous crusades in the legislatures and the courts.[43] This line of reasoning emerged in the pages of the *JATU* quickly after the Emancipation Proclamation took effect. In March 1863, reformers were certain that the "power that will destroy slavery will destroy rum. The power that will emancipate millions from cruel taskmasters, will emancipate millions from more cruel rumsellers." Americans had risen up to defend their country and free the enslaved. This momentum, reformers believed, would carry over to prohibition.[44] By emerging as "the nation's greatest foe," by "endangering and bringing certain ruin upon the nation's army of defense," the liquor traffic became more alarming. Marsh hoped that within the context of war, "all complaints of prohibitory law as unconstitutional and an interference with the liquor dealers' rights" would be "rendered contemptible."[45] Surely Americans who had previously thought that drinking was a private choice would be convinced that drunken soldiers endangered the welfare of the entire nation.

In other words, with slavery being eradicated, temperance reformers could devote the remainder of the war to their crusade against intoxication. And they conflated the spiritual salvation of the Union with the literal preservation of the nation. Temperance reformers, with the help of the Union army, were "fight[ing] for the American Union" (July 1863) and for the "maintenance of the Union" (September 1865).[46] And, to temperance reformers, to preserve the Union meant also to preserve liberty and the Declaration of Independence.[47] Anticipating the war's end in the summer of 1864, John Marsh explained why drunkenness was antithetical to liberty. "A nation of drunkards must be a nation of slaves," he warned, and thus temperance reformers (and Americans) needed to work toward a national future free of intoxicating drinks.[48] Sobriety would lead to liberty for all American citizens.

In May 1865, temperance reformers celebrated the end of the war, marking it as "one of the great eras in the world's history, from which is to be dated some of the most important movements toward millennium." Northerners had shown that they were willing to sacrifice everything in order "to save the nation, to break the yoke of rebellion, and to redeem four millions of human beings from the yoke of servitude." Yet the struggle was not over because intemperance continued to drag "fifty thousands" of Americans to poverty, crime, and insanity.[49] Union victory had preserved the nation, but for temperance reformers, the task of saving the country was still incomplete. As Connecticut governor William Alfred Buckingham put it in September 1865, "The rebellion has shown us the power of law—let it be exercised on the side of Temperance."[50] By the late 1860s, temperance reformers, still riding the momentum and hope embedded in emancipation, had formed a national Prohibition Party because they believed that the federal government had emerged from the war with enough power to rid their nation of rum.[51] Yet, in 1865, reformers were only cautiously optimistic. Demon rum retained the power to "curse this nation more than slavery ever cursed it" because "intemperance, which is the slavery of the soul, is infinitely worse than chattel slavery."[52] If liquor were not eradicated quickly, the Union might face future calamities even greater than the ones it had just survived.

Notes

1. *Journal of the American Temperance Union: And the New-York Prohibitionist* (hereafter *JATU*) 24 (December 1860): 184.

2. "Our Southern Brethren," *JATU* 25 (February 1861): 25.

3. Holly Berkley Fletcher, *Gender and the American Temperance Movement of the Nineteenth Century* (New York: Routledge, 2008), 58–78.

4. Clifford S. Griffin, *Their Brothers' Keepers: Moral Stewardship in the United States, 1800–1865* (New Brunswick, NJ: Rutgers University Press, 1960), 81–98.

5. Gary W. Gallagher, *The Union War* (Cambridge, MA: Harvard University Press, 2011); for scholarship on the evolving conceptions of "Union," as well as its relationship to slavery and emancipation both during and after the war, see James Oakes, *Freedom National: The Destruction of Slavery in the United States, 1861–1865* (New York: W. W. Norton, 2013); Melinda Lawson, *Patriot Fires: Forging a New American Nationalism in the Civil War North* (Lawrence: University Press of Kansas, 2002); Chandra Manning, *What This Cruel War Was Over: Soldiers, Slavery, and the Civil War* (New York: Alfred A. Knopf, 2007); David W. Blight, *Race and Reunion: The Civil War in American Memory* (Cambridge, MA: Belknap Press of Harvard University Press, 2001); Barbara A. Gannon, *The Won Cause: Black and White Comradeship in the Grand Army of the Republic* (Chapel Hill: University of North Carolina Press, 2011); John R. Neff, *Honoring the Civil War Dead: Commemoration and the Problem of Reconciliation* (Lawrence: University Press of Kansas, 2005).

6. In this way, temperance reformers fit into the war as framed by religious historians such as George C. Rable and David Goldfield. See George C. Rable, *God's Almost Chosen Peoples: A Religious History of the American Civil War* (Chapel Hill: University of North Carolina Press, 2010); and David Goldfield, *America Aflame: How the Civil War Created a Nation* (New York: Bloomsbury, 2011).

7. It is difficult to find hard data to determine how many subscribers the *JATU* had in the 1860s. Millions of temperance pamphlets, tracts, and periodicals circulated throughout the Northeast in the antebellum decades, and the American Temperance Society and American Temperance Union had more than a million members in their heydays. See W. J. Rorabaugh, *The Alcoholic Republic: An American Tradition* (Oxford: Oxford University Press, 1979), 197–202; Jack S. Blocker, *American Temperance Movements: Cycles of Reform* (Boston: Twayne, 1989), 14. Blocker's numbers are for membership in the ATU and do not include Americans who joined the Washingtonian or Sons of Temperance movements. Clifford Griffin estimates that thousands of Union troops read the *JATU* while serving in the ranks; see *Their Brothers' Keepers*, 247. Frank Luther Mott lists the *JATU* as the only temperance journal to publish throughout the Civil War, but he does not provide subscriber information for the journal or any other temperance publication; see Mott, *A History of American Magazines, 1741–1930* (Cambridge, MA: Belknap Press of Harvard University Press, 1938), 2:210.

8. Fletcher, *Gender and the American Temperance Movement*; Ronald G. Walters, *American Reformers, 1815–1860* (New York: Hill and Wang, 1978); Griffin, *Their Brothers' Keepers*.

9. Ian R. Tyrrell, *Sobering Up: From Temperance to Prohibition in Antebellum America, 1800–1860* (Westport, CT: Greenwood, 1979), 260–269. Prohibition had less support in southern states, but it is worth noting that many southerners joined the antiliquor crusade in some form or fashion. Ian R. Tyrrell, "Drink and Temperance in the Antebellum South: An Overview and Interpretation," *Journal of Southern History* 48 (November 1982): 485–510; Ellen Eslinger, "Antebellum Liquor Reform in Lexington, Virginia: The Story of a Small Southern Town," *Virginia Magazine of History and Biography* 99 (April 1991): 163–186; Douglas W. Carlson, "'Drinks He to His Own Undoing': Temperance Ideology in the Deep South," *Journal of the Early Republic* 18 (Winter 1998): 659–691; Bruce E. Stewart, "'This County Improve in Cultivation, Wickedness, Mills, and Still': Distilling and Drinking in Antebellum Western North Carolina," *North Carolina Historical Review* 83 (October 2006): 447–478; Bruce E. Stewart, "Select Men of Sober and Industrious Habits," *Journal of South-*

ern History 73 (May 2007): 289–322; Bruce E. Stewart, "'The Forces of Bacchus Are Fast Yielding': The Rise and Fall of Anti-Alcohol Reform in Antebellum Rowan County, North Carolina," *North Carolina Historical Review* 87 (July 2010): 310–338.

10. Tyrrell, *Sobering Up*, 290–309.

11. Ibid., 290.

12. "Mr. Delavan has forwarded to us the following letter from James Black, Esq., of Pennsylvania, for publication, which we give with pleasure, Lancaster, Pa, 25, July, 1860," *JATU* 24 (September 1860): 130.

13. "Letter from Rev. Mr. Hawley—State Agent, Cazenovia, December 2, 1859," *JATU* 24 (January 1860): 12.

14. "What Next?," *JATU* 24 (December 1860): 184.

15. *Templars' Magazine* (Cincinnati) quoted in *JATU* 24 (December 1860): 188.

16. "What Next?," *JATU* 24 (December 1860): 184.

17. "Boston, December 11, 1860," *JATU* 25 (February 1861): 24.

18. "Remarks of Hon. Mr. Bell, of Jefferson County, New York, In the Senate, February 21st, on the concurrent resolutions proposing to prohibit the Liquor Traffic by constitutional enactment," *JATU* 25 (April 1861): 51.

19. Bruce Dorsey, *Reforming Men and Women: Gender in the Antebellum City* (Ithaca, NY: Cornell University Press, 2002), 14–28; Jed Dannenbaum, *Drink and Disorder: Temperance Reform in Cincinnati from the Washingtonian Revival to the WCTU* (Urbana: University of Illinois Press, 1984), 106–155; for fear of "rum power," see 131.

20. "Saving the Union," *JATU* 24 (January 1860): 11.

21. C. A. Hammond, "The 'Higher Law' in New York, Petebboro, N.Y. Feb. 4, 1861," *Higher Law* 1 (February 28, 1861): 67. (This was a weekly newspaper not solely devoted to temperance.) According to Benjamin Sevitch, an antiabolitionist riot in Utica, New York, in 1835 may have been fueled by alcohol. See "The Well-Planned Riot of October 21, 1835: Utica's Answer to Abolitionism," *New York History* 50 (July 1969): 257.

22. *JATU* 25 (February 1861): 25.

23. It was not simply that liquor incidentally fueled the violence of the already corrupt proslavery faction. Reformers believed that an increasingly organized rum power "controlled the elections" in northern states and that "each political party feared to curb its power." Liquor dealers' associations had been forming since the 1850s to advocate for regulations that secured the interests of distillers and merchants. Advocates of prohibition believed that it was this special interest—the rum power—that undercut the will of the people (prohibition) in favor of license laws. See "A Scrap of History," *JATU* 24 (August 1860): 113. See also Tyrrell, *Sobering Up*, 296–297.

24. "War Items: Michigan Soldiers," *JATU* 25 (June 1861): 90; see also *JATU* 25 (June 1861): 88; "Tracts for the Army," *JATU* 25 (June 1861): 96 (packages of one thousand tracts could be sent for free to a quartermaster of a regiment, or they could be sent by express for two dollars); "Growth of Intemperance," *JATU* 28 (March 1864): 36.

25. "The Drunken Officer," *JATU* 27 (December 1863): 186.

26. "A Nation's Call," *JATU* 27 (May 1863): 65–66.

27. Rev. John Marsh, D.D., "Twenty-Eighth Anniversary," *JATU* 28 (June 1864): 83; for secondary material on the problem of drunkenness in the Union army see Griffin, *Their Brothers' Keepers*; Bell Irvin Wiley, *The Life of Billy Yank: The Common Soldier of the Union* (Indianapolis: Bobbs-

Megan L. Bever

Merrill, 1951); Rable, *God's Almost Chosen Peoples*; Steven J. Ramold, *Baring the Iron Hand: Discipline in the Union Army* (DeKalb: Northern Illinois University Press, 2010).

28. Henrietta Costolo, "Communication: Pleasant Hill, PA, December 17, 1860," *JATU* 25 (January 1861): 7; "Slavery at the North & South," *Higher Law* 1 (January 9, 1861): 10.

29. From the *Gasparin*, "Costliness of Human Progress," *JATU* 26 (December 1862): 177; J. W. Love, "A Subscriber Offended," *JATU 26* (July 1862): 106.

30. P. Osterhaut, "Correspondence: Schoharie, Oct. 9, 1861," *JATU* 25 (November 1861): 163–164; *JATU* 26 (March 1862): 40; Love, "A Subscriber Offended," 120; C. A. Hammond, "The 'Higher Law' in New York, Petebboro, N.Y. Feb. 4, 1861," *Higher Law* 1 (February 28, 1861): 67.

31. Hammond, "The 'Higher Law,'" 67; "Gubernatorial Election," *JATU* 26 (November 1862): 169.

32. Love, "A Subscriber Offended," 105–106. Rorabaugh has pointed out this connection between the slave trade and the rum trade in antebellum temperance literature; see Rorabaugh, *Alcoholic Republic*, 214–215; Robert H. Abzug has noted this as well in *Cosmos Crumbling: American Reform and the Religious Imagination* (New York: Oxford University Press, 1994), 81–104.

33. "Twenty-Fourth Anniversary: Report," *JATU* 25 (June 1861): 82.

34. "Gubernatorial Election," 169.

35. Letter from James Brewster of New Haven, October 14, 1862, *JATU* 26 (November 1862): 165.

36. The specific phrase "slave to the habit" appears multiple times throughout the war in the *JATU*. See "Stimulant and Irritant," *JATU* 24 (March 1860): 41; "Quiet Workers for Temperance," *JATU* 28 (May 1864): 71; George W. Bungay, "Mustered Out—Now Look Out," *JATU* 29 (June 1865): 93.

37. Fletcher, *Gender and the American Temperance Movement*; Walters, *American Reformers*; Elaine Frantz Parsons, *Manhood Lost: Fallen Drunkards and Redeeming Women in the Nineteenth-Century United States* (Baltimore: Johns Hopkins University Press, 2003).

38. "Dash Away the Ruby Cup," *JATU* 28 (April 1864): 54; Rev. S. Barrows, "The Relations of the Ministry to the Temperance Reforms," *JATU* 27 (November 1863): 163. Drunkards are also compared to the insane and to women and children—all dependent and helpless—in the journal; see Rev. John Marsh, D.D. (editor), "Important Inquiry Answered: A sermon for Connecticut, preached by request in the Centre Church, New Haven, the Sabbath evening previous to the Annual Meeting of the State Temperance Society, Nov. 16," *JATU* 24 (January 1860): 1; Albert Conkling, "Correspondence: Conkingville, Saratoga, Co., N.Y., October 23, 1861," *JATU* 25 (November 1861): 165.

39. "Wonderful Workings of Providence: President's Proclamation: Liberty to the Enslaved," *JATU* 26 (October 1862): 152.

40. C. S. Nichols, "A Solemn Fact," *JATU* 26 (November 1862): 164.

41. *JATU* 26 (November 1862): 168.

42. "Address of Hon. S. C. Pomeroy, U.S. Senator from Kansas," *JATU* 27 (June 1863): 85.

43. Gaines M. Foster, *Moral Reconstruction: Christian Lobbyists and the Federal Legislation of Morality, 1865–1920* (Chapel Hill: University of North Carolina Press, 2002). While Foster focuses on a number of postwar reform movements, Holly Berkeley Fletcher focuses on the temperance movement itself. Like Foster, Fletcher also views the war as a pivotal moment for prohibition because it refocused the goals of reformers and made them more nationalistic. See Fletcher, *Gender and the American Temperance Movement*, 58–78.

44. *JATU* 27 (March 1863): 40.

45. Marsh, "Twenty-Eighth Anniversary," 83.

46. *JATU* 27 (March 1863): 40; "Fifth National Temperance Convention: Second Day Proceedings," *JATU* 29 (August 1865): 122; American Temperance Union, "The Sick Soldier, Thoughts of Home: A New Tract for the Army," *JATU* 27 (July 1863): 101; "A SHORT AND POINTED TEMPERANCE SPEECH," (from *Zion's Herald*), *JATU* 29 (September 1865): 144.

47. "A SHORT AND POINTED TEMPERANCE SPEECH," 144.

48. Marsh, "Twenty-Eighth Anniversary," 84.

49. "Address to the People of the United States," *JATU* 29 (May 1865): 72.

50. "A SHORT AND POINTED TEMPERANCE SPEECH," 144.

51. Foster, *Moral Reconstruction*, 27–46. It is interesting to note, however, that temperance reformers still did not find a comfortable home in either the Republican or Democratic Party in the postwar decades. See Paul Kleppner, *The Third Electoral System, 1853–1892* (Chapel Hill: University of North Carolina Press, 1979), 240–257.

52. "A Word to Ministers" (from *Zion's Herald*), *JATU* 29 (September 1865): 135.

Debating Black Manhood

The Northern Press Reports on the 54th Massachusetts at Fort Wagner

GLENN DAVID BRASHER

Popular Civil War interpretation holds that the 54th Massachusetts regiment's July 18, 1863, attack on Fort Wagner led northerners to accept African Americans as soldiers, increasing the number of black regiments recruited into service. Further, the regiment's valiant but doomed effort helped turn northern opinion in favor of emancipation as a tool for saving the Union. Perhaps still the most frequently assigned Civil War text in college classrooms, James McPherson's classic *Battle Cry of Freedom* emphatically claims, "Anti-abolitionism and racism . . . lost potency" after the Wagner attack. More recent works of historical synthesis, such as Elizabeth R. Varon's *Armies of Deliverance*, offer more nuanced but somewhat similar assessments. Yet the highly partisan newspaper coverage of the event reveals that northerners bitterly contested the regiment's effectiveness. Further, that dispute, and especially the treatment of the regiment's prisoners, added fuel to the volatile question of racial equality and African American citizenship.[1]

* * * *

At the start of the war, African American men wanted to enlist in the US Army, but the government refused. The 1857 Dred Scott decision ruled that blacks were not citizens, affirming what most state laws had long established. Because blacks were thus essentially noncitizens, many whites felt the nation was not theirs to defend, also insisting blacks could not be good soldiers because they did not possess "manly" qualities. Nineteenth-century coverture laws defined women as dependent, needing men's protections. Thus, culturally, the ideal of strong, autonomous males contrasted with that of dependent women and children. Antebellum language reflected this inequality, as "men" were self-reliant, protecting and shepherding dependents. Because African American men did not possess citizenship rights allowing them to be autonomous patriarchs, whites perceived black men as lacking manhood.[2]

Even in free states, proslavery arguments added to this emasculation, insisting African Americans were inferiors needing a master's protection and guidance. Further, as one white abolitionist explained, many northern whites despised "the Negro because he is not an insurgent, for the Anglo-Saxon would certainly be so in his case." Culturally, popular minstrel shows featuring ignorant and dependent black characters reinforced these perceptions. Ironically, many abolitionists unwittingly added to the stereotype, painting blacks as simple, kindhearted stoics, loyal despite mistreatment. Abolitionists used such characterizations to create sympathy for long-suffering blacks, yet in doing so perpetuated perceptions about the lack of manliness in African Americans.[3]

Still, by summer 1862 a faltering military situation led many white northerners to decide it was necessary for blacks to aid the Union effort in some form. Congress authorized the president to enlist the runaway slaves of rebels in any military service "for which they may be found competent." Most viewed this as endorsing the use of African Americans as laborers only. Lest anyone think such services elevated blacks to the status of "men" deserving citizenship, their compensation purposely indicated otherwise. Blacks were paid three dollars less per month than white soldiers, with another three deducted for clothing.[4]

The Emancipation Proclamation later specifically encouraged black enlistment as soldiers, yet many still felt they should be limited to garrison and fatigue duty. Democrats objected to African American soldiers altogether, insisting their existence would increase southern hostility, making a negotiated peace impossible. Further, fighting alongside black troops would demoralize whites, slowing enlistments. Lastly, Democrats insisted black troops would be the first step toward black equality. While many Radicals did hope for that outcome, Republicans generally downplayed the possibility.[5]

Massachusetts governor John Andrew, however, did not. The Radical Republican was determined his Bay State would produce the first African American regiment recruited in the North, openly asserting that blacks should fight not just to strike at slavery but to establish their citizenship. Turning to the antislavery community for the regiment's leadership, he chose Robert Gould Shaw as commander, an officer who had led troops in significant combat and was the son of two of Massachusetts's most prominent abolitionists.[6]

With Shaw aboard, Andrew leaned on the abolitionist community for funds

and recruiting. Some African Americans complained because only white officers would lead the regiment and because blacks would be fighting for a country that did not recognize their citizenship. In response, recruiters touted the
chance to prove African American manhood, demonstrating the injustice of denying black citizenship. Blacks "should not stand aloof from [the war] and say
they [have] no country," one recruiter exhorted a Chicago gathering. "We have
a country and should fight for it." He presciently predicted black troops would
be involved in an attack on Charleston. If the seedbed of secession "should fall
by the hands of the colored people, Negro blood would immediately rise two
or three hundred percent" in people's estimation. Further, a white recruiter
explained to a Boston gathering, "If the Union lives, it will live with equal
races. . . . [If] you have done your duty . . . you will stand on the same platform as
the white race."[7]

The most famous recruiter was Frederick Douglass. Speaking across the
North, he insisted that once African American men were in uniform it would
be impossible to deny their citizenship. The *New York World* reported on one
of his recruitment pitches in which "he demanded for the Negro the most perfect civil and political equality" and "predicted that the American people will
soon be eager to receive Negroes as citizens." A public letter Douglass wrote appeared widely in newspapers. "Liberty won by white men," he asserted, "would
lose half its luster." Douglass cajoled African American men to enlist for the
"welfare of your country" but also for "every aspiration which you cherish for
the freedom and equality of yourself and your children." In another diatribe
published in his *Douglass Monthly*, the renowned African American leader
claimed the political and cultural emasculation of black men had caused many
to rate themselves "less than [they] are." Thus "You owe it to yourself and your
race to rise from your social debasement and take your place among the soldiers of your country, a man among men."[8]

Even more blunt was John S. Rock, a black activist from Boston, who re-
cruited soldiers by provocatively paraphrasing from the words of Chief Justice
Roger Taney's Dred Scott decision. Armed African Americans in military service,
Rock declared, would be a power "which white men will be bound to respect."[9]

* * * *

The message worked. Throughout March and April 1863, a stream of recruits
came to the regiment's training camp in Readville, Massachusetts. Most were

free blacks drawn to the message of manhood and citizenship, but some were runaway slaves or the children of runaways. Among the first recruits of what was soon designated the 54th Massachusetts Volunteer Infantry was William Carney, an escaped slave; Lewis and Charles Douglass, two of Frederick Douglass's sons; and James Caldwell, Sojourner Truth's grandson.

"The regiment attracts considerable attention," noted James Gooding, one of the first recruits who wrote for his hometown *New Bedford Mercury,* "if judged by the number of visitors we have." The 54th Massachusetts immediately drew attention from newspapers across the North. "All [the men have] been supplied with uniforms," a Michigan paper observed, "and have assumed quite a soldierly appearance." A Vermont paper reported, "There is among [the regiment] a pride in their organization; they are strong, active men having confidence in themselves and their officers."[10]

Newspapers were not the only ones taking note. "We had several officers out to take a look at the men," Shaw noted, "[and] they all went away very much pleased. Some were very skeptical about it before, but say, now, that they shall have no more doubts of negroes making good soldiers." Indeed, even a Minnesota Democratic paper reported that army "officers speak warmly of their men. They are obedient, steady, and learn the drill with great readiness."[11]

Much of the credit goes to Shaw, insisting on high physical fitness standards, strict discipline, and stern punishments. Yet the 54th's best asset was that its soldiers understood that "every black man and woman," as the *Anglo-African* asserted, "feels a special interest in the success of this regiment." Further, the men knew the war was destroying slavery, making it imperative for blacks to deliver the death blows. If slavery were to "die without the aid of our race to kill it," Gooding explained, "language cannot depict ... the scorn ... that will be heaped upon us." The *Anglo-African* was more blunt: "We would be ranked with the most cowardly of men." Therefore, Gooding claimed, "It seems that most every man in the regiment vies with each other in excellence in whatever they undertake."[12]

The dedication paid off. All "visitors have been surprised to find a remarkably fine body of men," the *Boston Daily Advertiser* reported, "and have come away from the camp ... with strong confidence that [the regiment] will do well." Thus, as Governor Andrew remarked, even in its "brief history of camp life" the 54th was already accomplishing its most important goal: demonstrating "the manly character ... of the colored citizens" enlisted in the regiment.[13]

Nevertheless, the Democratic press mocked the 54th Massachusetts. The

Boston Pilot, for example, odiously opined, "Negroes on the march will be smelled 10 miles distant." The *Boston Courier* fabricated a recruitment speech given in a "cellar." Using minstrel dialect, the paper suggested the regiment's existence challenged white northern manhood and promoted black citizenship. "White folks is all skeered," the fictional black recruiter proclaimed, "and now dey calls on us to save de nation. Bredren is we ekal to do it? Yes, fellah citizens, is twenty-five tousan' niggers more'n tree hund' tousan' white men?" Meanwhile, the *New York World* was outraged by a Republican editorial expressing hope that the 54th would not see combat until they had enough weapons training. The paper criticized the "negrophilists of Massachusetts" for loving "the negro with a love passing the love of woman." The editors insisted, no "public journal ever urged that any one of [the white regiments] be retained in camp to save them from the horrors and perils of the battle-field."[14]

Despite the detractors, on May 18, the regiment received its colors in a ceremony newspapers reported as "impressive and interesting." A crowd estimated at over one thousand listened as Governor Andrew declared, "Today we recognize the right of every man . . . to be a MAN and a citizen." The soldiers of the regiment fight "not for themselves alone," he insisted, but also for their race. Their military service would refute "the foul aspersion that they [are] not men," proving African Americans deserved citizenship rights.[15]

On May 28, the regiment arrived in Boston, marching to Battery Wharf while a crowd as large as twenty thousand watched. "No regiment has collected so many thousands as the fifty-fourth," one Boston paper reported. "Vast rows lined the street where the regiment was to pass." A Washington paper observed, "The men were dressed in regular United States uniforms, splendidly equipped, headed by a full band of colored musicians. The regiment made a magnificent appearance." Perhaps most striking of all, a correspondent noted in a report reprinted in many northern papers, was that "in all respects, except that they have only white officers, men of this regiment are placed on an equality with those of any other new regiment." Whether they could maintain that equality, the reporter opined, "depends upon themselves."[16]

* * * *

Unfortunately, the regiment's first action in the field garnered negative press coverage. The military assigned the 54th Massachusetts to the Department of the South (which included coastal South Carolina and Georgia), pairing them with another black regiment, the 2nd South Carolina. Composed of freed slaves, the less-well-trained regiment was led by Colonel James Montgomery, one of John Brown's cohorts in Kansas. On June 9, the regiments went on a supply raid into the small town of Darien, Georgia. Finding it practically deserted, Montgomery ordered the soldiers to take all useful supplies and then to burn the town. Dutifully, the soldiers set Darien ablaze.[17]

The action bothered Shaw, mainly because "I am not sure that it will not harm very much the reputation of black troops." Southern papers quickly reported the "atrocity" committed by "Yankee vandals," exaggerating the details. As Shaw feared, northern papers soon picked up the story as well. African American papers like *Douglass Monthly* only indifferently noted that "the town was destroyed," but even Republican papers like the *New-York Tribune* issued a mild rebuke. The Democratic press was harsher. The *New York Journal of Commerce*, for example, reported that "from one end of the country to the other" there were protests "against the monstrous vindictiveness" unleashed by the black troops. The paper decried the leading of a regiment "into a peaceful village, whence all the men have gone," letting loose "the work of robbery and fire." Because only women remained to resist, the paper depicted the 54th's actions as unmanly. Soon criticisms came from even the faraway *Times* of London. Over the next few weeks, Shaw hoped for a way to counteract the bad press.[18]

Prospects brightened in July when the military sent the regiment to augment US forces gathering for operations against Charleston, assigning them to James Island, one of the small islands ringing the city. On July 16, about 900 Confederates attacked 250 of the 54th's men on picket duty. The black troops gave the rebels "a warmer reception than they had expected," Gooding boasted in the *New Bedford Courier*. Confederates forced back the regiment, but they rallied, fighting a perfectly executed delaying action that saved a white regiment. The skirmish received scant newspaper attention, but Union commanders praised the 54th. "The best disciplined white troops could have fought no better," division commander Alfred H. Terry told the *New-York Tribune*. Gooding was most pleased by the praise of other enlisted men. "When a regiment of white men gave us three cheers as we were passing them, it shows that we did our duty as men."[19]

Soon after, brigade commander General George C. Strong summoned Shaw to Morris Island on July 18. Because of its performance on James Island, the 54th would be included in a large-scale assault that evening. Taking Charleston required capturing Fort Sumter, but this required negating the sandy forts on the islands ringing the harbor. Most essential was Fort Wagner. Naval artillery pummeled the Confederate stronghold for a week, but infantry would have to attack. Strong asked Shaw if the 54th could lead. Answering with an affirmative, the colonel felt that if his regiment played a prominent role in Charleston's capture it might help accomplish all they were fighting for: emancipation, manhood, and citizenship.[20]

That evening, Gooding noted, "We were marched up past our batteries, amid the cheers of the officers and soldiers." Shaw stopped for a moment to speak to Edward L. Pierce, a friend who wrote for the *New-York Tribune*, had close access to Union headquarters and thus had a perfect viewing spot on a nearby knoll. Shaw then took his position at the regiment's head.

Soon, General Strong rode up and reportedly shouted to the 54th, "Is there a man here who thinks himself unable to sleep in that fort to-night?" The men shouted back "No!" After Strong rode away, Shaw gave a last exhortation to his soldiers, summing up their higher objective: "I want you to prove yourself men."[21]

* * * *

It was a full three days before news of the 54th's fate emerged in newspapers. Southern sheets were the first to report, with the *Richmond Enquirer* succinctly and accurately noting on July 21, "The bombardment of battery Wagner . . . was terrific. . . . At dark the enemy numbering 10 regiments made a determined assault on our works. After a desperate struggle . . . they were repulsed with heavy loss. We captured over 200 prisoners, including some black troops."[22]

This was all the public knew until six days after the attack when the *Charleston Mercury* offered an account based on reports from rebel officers. Northern newspapers doubted its veracity but reprinted the *Mercury*'s story. The *New York Herald* surmised it more likely that Union troops had captured Charleston, labeling the reported Union loss "a great canard." It was not until nine days after the attack that northern newspapers finally had detailed accounts. Over the next few days, newspapers provided the bloody details, criticized the assault's planning, but praised the African American troops.[23]

Having watched from his perch, Shaw's friend Edward L. Pierce provided the *New-York Tribune* with an exceptional account that Republican, Democratic, and African American newspapers widely reprinted. Noting the "terrible shower of shot and shell," greeting the troops after Shaw led them forward,

Pierce watched the men advance "along the narrow beach for more than half a mile before [reaching] the fort, exposed every step to . . . fire in front from the heavy guns and . . . the massed musketry of Fort Wagner, and still more terrible enfilading fire from Fort Sumter."[24]

The *New York Times* noted that when the soldiers were within two hundred yards of the fort, they "gave a fierce yell." Despite the "murderous reception" of artillery and small-arms fire, Pierce detailed how the regiment continued through the abatis as the rebels hit them with "grape and canister . . . hand grenades, and . . . almost every other murderous implement of modern warfare." Still, the *Times* observed, "The gallant negroes . . . plunged on" and into a ditch "containing 4 feet of water," gaining the fort's parapet. Accounts vary, but Shaw clearly then went down in a hail of gunfire while rallying his men forward.[25]

Pierce saw the rebels become furious at the sight of black troops "and neglect all else for a moment in attacking the negroes." The fight became a savage hand-to-hand struggle in the dark, illuminated by musket flashes and artillery bursts. Reporters praised the 54th for standing firm. Pierce felt the men proved their manliness when "fighting in that deadly breach till almost every officer had fallen and three hundred of its men lay dead."[26]

The *New York Herald* opined, "The Fifty-fourth fought very bravely. They had numerous invitations to become prisoners . . . but they declined . . . for the terrors of bondage . . . were worse than those of death. . . . The rebels attacked them with a cry of 'No quarter,' and they accepted the condition of the fight. Several fell pierced by many bullets while fighting singly with half a dozen rebels." One black soldier "bayoneted an officer who was leading a squad of men, and then gave a thrust which wounded a sergeant just as he was falling." The reporter witnessed one soldier "whose arm had been shot off, [bring] his musket off the field in the other hand, carrying it until he fell down and bled to death." Indeed, "Individual instances of heroism in the contest were numerous." Sergeant William Carney managed to grab the colors, and, as the *New York Times* observed, "he stood nobly on the glacis with his flag, endeavoring to rally the men." He then planted the flag, the African American *Christian Recorder* claimed, "right where [General Strong] told them to plant it."[27]

When supporting regiments arrived, Union forces maintained a position in the fort for close to an hour, but it was futile. By the time the men heard the retreat, nearly ever commissioned officer in the 54th was shot. Despite grievous wounds, Carney brought the regimental flag back from the fort and was cheered when he announced, "Boys, the old flag never touched the ground."[28]

Along with the violent details, papers provided short biographies of Shaw, praising Governor Andrew's selection. "How well that choice was justified," the *Tribune* opined, as Shaw led "the best disciplined regiment that ever left the state." The *Cleveland Morning Leader* noted, "Col. Shaw formed the regiment, and drilled it so excellently that its discipline was always counted as among the best." Sadly, the paper reported, "The country has lost . . . a tried and skillful soldier."[29]

Nevertheless, while the northern press lavished praise on the regiment's white leader, it did not exceed that heaped upon the black soldiers. The *Boston Herald*, for example, noted that despite being "the object of the most severe attack of the day," the men "behaved exceedingly well." In an editorial reprinted in papers across the country, the *New York Times* praised "the gallant negroes" and their "gallant Col. Shaw," and related Carney's heroic retrieval of the colors (an action later earning the Congressional Medal of Honor). Perhaps the most notable and widely seen editorial was the *New York Herald*'s. Their reporter admitted he had been a critic of black troops, but changed his mind. "I must do this regiment the credit of fighting bravely and well." Even if they were "darkeys," he maintained, "the Massachusetts negro regiment is evidently made of good stuff."[30]

Pierce's praise was the most generous. "Let it be remembered," he proclaimed, "that this colored regiment . . . was put at the head of a storming column" in the "utmost test of courage and of soldierly qualities." Yet they "gave the most splendid and most terrible proof of [their] heroism; fighting in a deadly breach until almost every officer had fallen and 300 of [their] men dead." A blurb appearing in numerous papers subtlety hinted the men proved themselves equal to white soldiers. "They fought heroically and only retreated when the rest [of the white troops] did." Northern papers even passed around a "gleaning" from the *Savannah Republican* begrudgingly acknowledging the 54th had fought well. "Willing to do justice to a brave foe," the rebel paper noted, "it may be added that a more daring assault has not been made on either side since the commencement of the war."[31]

* * * *

Two days after the battle, Pierce visited the 54th's wounded, and papers across the North widely reprinted his report. He noted that while the 54th's men grieved over "Father" Shaw and fallen friends, they were determined to persist.

Despite their wounds, the men indicated they would not quit fighting "till the last rebel be dead," or until "all our people get their freedom."[32]

But while casualties did not damper their ardor, the men received a crushing blow just two weeks after the attack, learning the government intended to pay them only ten dollars per month. This problem had haunted the regiment since training camp but now seemed especially egregious. When recruited they were told they would receive the same pay as white soldiers, thirteen dollars per month. The government's stated reason for paying less, however, was that African American regiments had enlisted under the 1862 Militia Act authorizing black laborers at ten dollars per month. But the men of the 54th were not laborers; they were soldiers striving for equal treatment and citizenship. Taking less pay would acknowledge an inferior status. In reaction to this indignity, the men refused any pay, even after Massachusetts tried to make up the difference by pitching in the other three dollars per month. Had the men accepted this seemingly reasonable accommodation, it would acknowledge dependency on the patriarchy of white men. Their heroism had garnered lofty praise, yet the nation still seemed intent on denying their full manhood.[33]

The pay dispute lingered for months, as the abolitionist and African American communities created charities to support the men's dependents. It was hardly enough, further challenging each soldier's sense of his own manhood. Family members and other supporters deluged the government with letters begging for equal pay, yet the issue received little attention from the northern press. One exception was a letter Gooding wrote to Lincoln appearing in the *New Bedford Courier*. The soldier humbly asked "Your Excellency" for equal treatment. African Americans "have done a Soldier's Duty. Why can't we have a Soldier's pay?" Another critique came from Frederick Douglass's *Monthly*. The famed abolitionist insisted that the pay difference was especially loathsome because, unlike whites, blacks were "fighting for principle." The colored soldier, he noted, "strikes for manhood and freedom."[34] Douglass soon took his case directly to Lincoln.

"Fred[erick] Douglass was in Washington yesterday for the first time in his life," an Indiana newspaper reported in early August. "He had interviews with the president and Secretary of War, connected with the business of Negro recruiting." In this legendary meeting between the famed runaway slave and the president, Douglass raised the issue of pay disparity. He could no longer assert the government gave equal treatment to black soldiers, he argued, hindering his recruiting. Douglass later claimed Lincoln was sympathetic but explained the pay disparity was necessary at the moment to get whites to accept black troops.[35]

If the president was correct, it helps explain why the Democratic press did not initially refute reports of the 54th's soldierly qualities, as the pay difference indicated the government did not embrace black equality. Attuned to newspaper editorials, Lincoln was keenly aware of public opinion and only moved slowly ahead of it. He understood many were not ready to equate a white man with a black man, even in pay. Lincoln's sentiments reveal the real reason for the lower pay, perhaps explaining why most Republican papers remained silently uncritical of the policy.

The pay disparity did not end Douglass's recruiting efforts, nor the 54th's dedication. "Do not forget," a *New York Times* letter to the editor noted while calling for equal compensation, "the colored soldiers are not fighting for pay." Their objectives were higher, and "they will not lose this, their first chance, to vindicate their right to be called and treated as men."[36]

* * * *

Yet, while the pay dispute remained largely out of the headlines, the treatment of the 54th Massachusetts's prisoners of war quickly grabbed the nation's attention, opening up questions about black equality that the pay disparity seemingly kept covered. Soon the issue affected the assessment of the regiment's performance during the battle, largely because of what it indicated about their entitlement to citizenship rights.

At the end of July, the *New-York Tribune* reported on a meeting between Union and Confederate officers to discuss burial of the Fort Wagner dead and prisoner exchanges. The rebels assured they had attended to the burials, but expressed "much indignation," the *Tribune* reported, because "Negro troops [had been] in the front on the night of the assault." Apparently, the paper mocked, "They desire to be killed by white men and not by 'stolen' slaves." The rebels claimed the white prisoners would be "well treated." Yet while admitting "the Fifty-fourth Massachusetts fought well, [they] say all the prisoners captured from that regiment will be sold into slavery."[37]

Southern papers unapologetically confirmed this news. The *Charleston Mercury* reported the Confederate military turned the 54th's prisoners over to state authorities to determine their fate. The rebel government had long claimed they would enslave black POWs and now seemed ready to fulfill the threat. "We cannot, of course," the *Mercury* opined, "pit ourselves against Negroes; we cannot ignore and belie our own social organization." In response to such reports, the *New York Herald* insisted, "Serious complications are likely to arise from the barbarous treatment by the rebels of Negro soldiers who fall into their hands." If the rebels start "selling at auction all Negro soldiers captured . . . retaliation is inevitable."[38]

This prediction proved accurate. Just three days after papers first reported the rebels were not exchanging the 54th's prisoners, Lincoln responded with an Order of Retaliation. "It is the duty of every government," the president proclaimed, "to give protection to its *citizens*, of whatever class, color, or condition, and especially to those who are duly organized as soldiers in the public service." Thus he ordered that for every black soldier sold into slavery, a white POW held by the Union would be sentenced to hard labor.[39]

Days later, a widely reprinted Republican editorial on Lincoln's order appeared in northern papers, noting the problem was not just with the 54th: "The colored troops, of whom we have many thousands in the service, have hitherto, apparently been treated as outside the protection of the government." The editor praised Lincoln's action: "This order . . . puts [the black troops] in this respect, just where they should be, on an equality with the other troops in the service." *Douglass Monthly* also praised Lincoln's actions yet lamented that the victory came at such great cost: "It really seems that nothing of justice, liberty or humanity can come to us except through tears and blood."[40]

Meanwhile, the popular *Harper's Weekly* magazine amplified these calls for equal treatment of black soldiers. Praise of the 54th filled newspapers at the same time as reported attacks on African Americans during the infamous New York Draft riots. Noting that black soldiers had been heralded for their performance at battles such as Port Hudson in Louisiana, *Harper's* especially noted that at Fort Wagner "the colored regiment from Massachusetts . . . was placed in the front, and sacrificed itself to make way for the white troops that followed." The editors pointed out that even the *New York Herald*, "prejudiced as they admit they had been about the employment of negro troops," were "forced to admit that they never saw better fighting done than was done by the colored regiments at Charleston" and elsewhere.[41]

Claiming that naturalized Irishmen had sparked the New York riot, *Harper's* noted the irony of Irish citizens attacking blacks at the same moment black noncitizens were bravely serving the country. Accusing certain politicians and newspapers of fomenting the home front violence, *Harper's* noted that "at the very hour when Negroes were pouring out their blood like water on the slopes of Fort Wagner" naturalized foreigners "tried to exterminate the negro race in New York."[42]

"Such contrasts are rare," *Harper's* opined, suggesting the Irish, despite their citizenship, had shown themselves less praiseworthy than blacks. "Where . . . have the Irish, as a race, won so clear a gratitude of the people of the United States" as blacks had recently? Further, while anti-Irish prejudices had long existed, they seem to have "died out," but the same was not true of antiblack sentiment. *Harper's* insisted racial animosity should have been "squelched . . . when the colored soldiers died at Port Hudson and Fort Wagner." The editors predicted the result of the contrast between the Irish rioters and black troops would be that employers would now hire blacks instead of Irishmen.[43]

Thus, less than two weeks after the country learned of the 54th Massachusetts' praiseworthy conduct in the Wagner attack, high profile demands were coming for African Americans to be treated on par with white men, if not in pay, at least in regard to employment and prisoner exchanges. Was this not a prelude to calls for black citizenship, just as the men of the regiment hoped to achieve? Northern Democrats quickly saw it that way and therefore now began questioning the performance of the 54th Massachusetts.

* * * *

Back on July 28, the Washington *Evening Star* was one of the first northern papers to report, "Stories are flying around . . . that but for the frightened Fifty-Fourth Massachusetts (negro) regiment we would have carried the Fort." Before Lincoln's retaliation order and the *Harper's* story, however, the only papers providing negative assessments of the regiment were mostly southern. The *Charleston Courier*, for example, claimed the regiment was "first drenched with whiskey, and then told to go forward." Once the bullets and shrapnel flew, white soldiers behind the regiment told "every negro that faltered [they] would be shot down or run through with a bayonet."[44]

Drunkenness claims were echoed by other southern papers. The *Richmond Enquirer*, for example, reported the black troops that attacked Wagner "were drunk at the time, and the remnant not killed can not be made to fight again." Further, the paper claimed that the few men in the 54th who were runaway slaves "want to come home."[45] Thus black courage came from the bottle, not manhood, and black soldiers wished they could resume their dependence on the white race.

After Lincoln's retaliation order and the *Harper's* story, northern Democratic papers picked up these dubious southern reports. Additionally, as the *Milwaukee News* bemoaned under the headline "More Negro Equality," Democrats insisted Lincoln's retaliation order declared, "in substance that Negroes are the equals of white men." In a similar diatribe, an Ohio paper criticized the *New-York Tribune* and other papers that had printed Edward L. Pierce's reports praising the 54th, charging that he characterized black soldiers as superior to whites. "Having found that the Negroes, after being drilled as soldiers, do not drop their arms and skedaddle, or lie down on their backs and cry for mercy," Republican papers "are now asserting that they are the best soldiers in the Army." Further, the Democratic paper criticized Republicans for ignoring the white regiments involved in the Wagner and Port Hudson attacks, while "the Negroes are exalted as demi-gods" with "superhuman bravery."[46]

Turning to the controversial *Harper's Weekly* editorial, the editors complained, black soldiers "have been engaged in but two or three fights" and have "in no way distinguish[ed] themselves more than the white soldiers." It was unfair to credit them "over a class of our fellow [Irish] citizens, who . . . [have] furnished [thousands] of our brave soldiers, and some of the best officers in the service."[47]

A widely shared editorial by the Democratic *Buffalo Courier* further cast doubt on the 54th's performance. The paper printed a statement purporting to be from "a [Union] officer in the Army before Charleston" who insisted, "The stories about the [54th's] splendid fighting are 'all in my eye.'" During the Wagner assault, "they ran away as fast as they could, and came near demoralizing the whole attacking force." Soon, "over a thousand of them came straggling down to the south end of the island, and before morning there were at the hospital and dock over three hundred of them not hurt in the least."[48]

The *Chicago Times* leveled the most vicious attack in another widely circulated editorial. The paper had warned the president "that the employment of Negro soldiers would cause the war to assume features of atrocity," which the possible enslavement of black POWs and Lincoln's retaliation order had now unleashed. "It were folly to suppose that the rebels can recognize negroes as soldiers . . . [affording] them the same rights which they afford to" white men. Thus, the president's "pompous order" would "not save the unfortunate darkeys." Further, "A negro is not equal to a white soldier, and Mr. Lincoln cannot change the law of nature so that the negro will become so." The editors crit-icized his "flippant language" and "virtual assertion . . . that every worthless darkey is as good in every respect as . . . a noble [white] soldier." Insisting white troops would loathe their commander in chief for equalizing them with black men, the editors felt Lincoln should quickly "disband his regiment of 'shades,'" using blacks only for manual labor.[49]

More succinct was a Pennsylvania paper: "One of the greatest outrages ever offered to people on earth," the editors asserted, "has been that of the Lincoln administration, in uniforming and arming Negro troops and demanding their equal consideration with the volunteer citizen soldiery of the Republic! Oh! The offense is rank! It smells to heaven!"[50]

The Republican press quickly responded, with the *Chicago Tribune* leading the way. Less than a week after the Democratic *Chicago Times* unleashed its scathing invective, the Republican paper printed "a plea for the colored race," insisting African American troops should be praised for their "fidelity" to the Union cause. "They ask only the chance to prove their manhood," the paper opined, and had in fact "establish[ed] their claim to be recognized as men." Scolding the "Copperhead press," the editors wondered how the nation would survive "if we persist in denying the most ordinary of rights to this persecuted race?" In words meant to provoke, the *Tribune* radically professed, "We have no fear of Negro equality, nor of the debasement of the northern blood."[51]

As for the 54th Massachusetts, the *Tribune*'s editors declared it "an atro-cious libel" to denigrate their performance at Fort Wagner. "Nothing could be meaner than the attempts to rob them of their well earned laurels." Noting the Democratic press had leaned on an anonymous assessment by an alleged offi-cer, they continued, "The falsity of this mean and atrocious attack is demon-strated by every account . . . from an authentic source. Official and non-official accounts . . . all unite in saying that the negroes fought bravely."[52]

To fortify the case, the editors presented a letter from Lieutenant Colo-nel A. C. Hamlin, a US Army medical inspector, written from South Carolina to Massachusetts senator Henry Wilson. "Knowing that you feel an interest in the fate of the Fifty-Fourth Massachusetts," the doctor wrote, "I . . . assure you that slander will not affect the reputation of that regiment in the two battles" they recently fought. At Fort Wagner, "I saw them march along to the assault as steadily . . . as the most veteran of the battalion [and] plunge bravely into the terrible abyss of death." That they fought manfully is attested to by "the long list of the wounded," and "the fact of sixty being captured within the fort."

The Democratic newspapers might deny the mettle of the regiment, the doctor exerted, but it was even "admitted to me by the rebels under the flag of truce." Further, Hamlin concluded, "I can testify that they bore their wounds with the fortitude of the most determined veterans, and that they died as nobly."[53] Reprinted in newspapers across the North, Hamlin's letter was more credible than anything the Democrats offered to denigrate the regiment.

Days later, the president entered the discussion. Two weeks after the Wagner assault, he had informed General Grant that he believed black troops were "a resource which if vigorously applied now will soon close the contest." Now in late August, as newspapers debated the performance of the 54th Massachusetts, Lincoln wrote a letter to be read at a political rally in his hometown of Springfield, Illinois. Addressing his critics on several issues, he noted many were "dissatisfied with me about the negro." Defending the Emancipation Proclamation, he turned to black troops, insisting that army commanders who had delivered "our most successes" in the field, and who were men who "never had any affinity for Abolitionism," nevertheless now agree that "the colored troops constitute the heaviest blow yet dealt the rebellion." These were "purely . . . military opinions" apart from "party politics," he insisted. "I submit these opinions as being entitled to some weight against the objections often urged that emancipation and the arming of blacks are unwise as military measures."[54]

The power of the A. C. Hamlin letter, and especially Lincoln's, brought a temporary lull to the debate, but Democrats were not ready to concede. While the *Chicago Tribune* praised blacks for not using their weapons to lash out in "bloody revenge" against all whites, a Pennsylvania Democratic newspaper alleged that rumors abounded about black troops killing southern civilians. The newspaper criticized the president's desire for more black troops, insisting that if the government recruited more of "Lincoln's newborn citizens of African descent," there would be massacres all over the South.[55]

* * * *

Soon the debate fueled the rhetoric of the 1863 state and local elections. After Union successes at Gettysburg, Vicksburg, and Chattanooga, the positive war news favored Republicans, so Democrats made emancipation the central issue, insisting the conflict might already be over if it were not for the Emancipation Proclamation. Without it, the South might be open to peace talks, Democrats argued, refusing to see emancipation and black troops as military necessities.[56]

In their opinion, there must be some other reason why the Republicans were insisting on black troops—and they concluded it was the party's embrasure of racial equality.

To prove the point, a Pennsylvania paper provided a lesson in recent history, insisting that praise of black troops was the next step in the Republican Party's "long pre-determined deep design" to bring about equality. First, "[Secretary of State William] Seward ... gave passports to Negroes as 'American citizens,'"; then, "at the insistence of [Massachusetts senator Charles] Sumner, a Negro was recognized as minister from Hayti." Next, "the Emancipation Proclamation was issued ... [and] Negroes were enlisted." Most recent, the president's retaliation order referred to blacks as "citizens," regardless of color, and called for their equal treatment. In this manner, "successive steps were taken towards the accomplishment" of their ultimate goal. The paper warned, "The next argument will be, those who fight shall vote." The purpose of praising black troops, the editor surmised, was to argue, "negro troops are the equal of white soldiers" in order to then conclude that "negro voters are the equal of a white freeman." Make no mistake, the editors charged, the Republican Party's "design is negro suffrage [and] equality." Referring to the state's upcoming gubernatorial election, the paper entreated "the people of Pennsylvania ... to pronounce their decision on the question."[57]

Ohio also faced a gubernatorial election, and the *Cincinnati Enquirer* likewise alleged Republicans were using the success of black troops to push for racial equality. As proof, the paper pointed to a resolution adopted by the Massachusetts Republican state convention. "*Resolved,*" it read, "the policy of employing colored soldiers is wise and just, and should ... be liberalized by putting such soldiers *on a perfect equality with whites* as to rights and compensation."[58] This would be followed, the Democratic paper insisted, by calls for racial equality in all things. The *Enquirer* asked Ohio voters to remember, "A vote for Democrats ... is a vote for the supremacy of your race."[59]

Ultimately, the election results were more about recent Union military successes, as Republicans retained the governorships of Ohio and Pennsylvania and gained in state and local offices everywhere except New Jersey. Democrats fretted about their losses, painting them as a triumph for racial equality. Radical Massachusetts is now "leading the Republican flock," the *Cincinnati Enquirer* insisted, and will soon press Congress for "a perfect equality of the Negro soldier with the white." This meant "making officers of Negroes for white soldiers to lift up their caps to, and means, when the war is over, the introduction of Negroes into the jury-boxes, the family tenement houses of the poor—in short a *perfect equality*."[60]

Ebullient about their victory, Republicans mocked the constant Democratic harangues about race. "Negro Equality," an Illinois paper asserted, "doubtless our readers have heard that expression before. There is not a Democratic paper in the country but what daily or weekly—and generally *weakly*—gives its subscribers a homily on the dangers of Negro Equality." During the recent campaigns it had been "a powder . . . shot a great many times." Democrats, the editors opined, "have frightened many timid voters" with it in the past, but the election results demonstrate the cry of "nigger equality" as a "political trick has lost its magical influence." It is now "about 'played out' in the free states."[61]

Unfortunately, this was far from true.

* * * *

Despite the election results, in the fall of 1863 the 54th's morale plummeted. Perhaps because Republicans feared Democrats would use the pay issue against them in the elections as they had Lincoln's retaliation order, the regiment still had not received full pay. In October, they refused the ten dollars again, as their brigade commander, Colonel James Montgomery (the officer that burned Darien), angrily lectured them in words fit for a Democratic paper. "You ought to be glad to pay for the privilege to fight, instead of squabbling about money," he told them. Furthermore, they were not equal to whites: "You are a race of slaves. A few years ago your fathers worshipped snakes and crocodiles in Africa." He went so far as to insist that black facial features were proof of inferior blood, and argued that if they really wanted to improve their race "the lightest of you must marry the blackest women."[62]

These words shocked the men. When George E. Stephens, a soldier in the regiment and correspondent for the *Anglo-African Weekly*, reported on the speech, newspapers picked up his article, which appeared even in the faraway *Burlington (IA) Hawkeye*. There was a predictable split between the different northern papers on Montgomery's comments. Many abolitionists and African American papers published Stephens's response: "For what are we to be grateful?" he wrote. "Here the white man has grown rich on our unpaid labor. . . . I think it is a question of repentance on his part instead of gratitude on ours." Now that the elections were over, some Republican papers finally started to help the 54th's case for equal pay by running more details about William Carney's retrieval of the US flag during the battle, printing the story as "an instance of heroism in a negro soldier that deserves to go into history."[63]

In response, on November 22 an Ohio Democratic paper reported that the Department of the South's commander, General Quincy Gilmore, had no faith in black troops after the Fort Wagner repulse, intending to use them from now on only for fatigue duty. The *New York Times* quickly disproved the allegation by publishing a letter from Gilmore himself. Yet the assertion seemed true to the regiment, as Stephens wrote home that the 54th had become a group of "ditchers." Sadly, he wrote, "The spade and shovel is their only implement of warfare." Despite the fame they had won and the role they played in changing the image of black troops, he described the regiment as being "in a state of demoralization."[64]

That the 54th seemed doomed to fatigue duty thrilled Democratic newspapers, and near the end of 1863 they went on the offensive again, claiming the praise the regiment received had now proven to be false news. A Democratic paper in Ohio's capital, for example, insisted Republicans had "manufacture[d] all kinds of false stories about the bravery and efficiency" of black troops. "We all remember the enormous accounts of the bravery of Colonel Shaw's regiment of Massachusetts negroes at Fort Wagner; how they stormed the fort and fell gloriously on the parapet, and a great deal more of the same sort." The editors insisted, "There was scarcely one word of truth in the whole account. The regiment never reached anywhere near the fort, and never stormed it at all." The paper then sarcastically addressed General Gilmore. "Don't bother worrying yourself about losing a battle by trusting to the Negro regiments," they advised. In fact, using them was a sure-fire way to increase his reputation. "Put them forward, and our word for it, the worst defeat you receive will be trumpeted as a glorious victory in which the blacks performed prodigies of valor never equaled by white soldiers." In fact, they argued, the general should choose troops with the darkest skin, because for the Republicans, the soldiers' "bravery is in exact proportion to their blackness."[65]

The editors turned back to their argument that the praise of black troops was a step in the direction of racial equality. "Bravery we know, is the first of all virtues," they opined. "Therefore if the Negroes make good fighters," the Republicans feel "they are fit to vote and hold office." Then, as a next step to creating an abolitionist "utopia," the Radicals would propose "to marry every black soldier to a white woman." The Democratic paper predicted Republicans, using black troops as proof of African American manhood and citizenship, would soon nominate a black man for president. Yet because they were sure to renominate Lincoln for the upcoming election, "We shall not be called upon to vote for a Negro President until 1868. . . . Why the abolitionists should put this off for another four years we really cannot understand. Better let us go the whole darkey at once."[66]

Clearly, Democrats were far from ready to concede the valor of the 54th Massachusetts and that of other African American troops. They continued to hammer Republicans with the issue in the next presidential election, an election Lincoln felt sure he would lose.

* * * *

By the end of 1863, officials worked out the prisoner exchange problem: the Confederacy refused to exchange black soldiers but would not enslave them. While this meant many blacks soon languished in prison camps (members of the 54th were among the first inmates at Andersonville), it also meant Confederate troops would not allow blacks to surrender, barbarically shooting them down instead. Such a fate befell some of the regiment's men in their next major engagement at Olustee, Florida. In part because of such outrages, once Grant became general in chief, he ended prisoner exchanges altogether, leading to overcrowded prisons on both sides.

Congress equalized pay in June 1864, and eventually the military did not confine the 54th to just fatigue duty. They gained national attention again because of their capable performance at Olustee. In the wake of the 54th's successes, the government aggressively recruited other black troops, most notably those in the Army of the James that participated in the Union's final siege of the Confederate capital, garnering fourteen Congressional Medals of Honor.

The 54th Massachusetts helped gain acceptance of black troops, equal treatment of prisoners (in theory), and equal pay, but were they successful in achieving their primary goal of earning recognition of their manhood and citizenship rights? While Lincoln's first Reconstruction proposal did not include racial equality, he did eventually suggest that black troops may have earned suffrage rights, just as Democrats had predicted he would. This proposal came in what turned out to be his last speech, directly leading to his assassination. Suffrage rights for some blacks was less than equality for all, but perhaps Lincoln would have slowly pushed for more, skillfully and manipulatively waiting for public opinion to catch up as it did on emancipation, black troops, and the pay issue.

Glenn David Brasher

We will never know if a slower pace by Lincoln would have achieved more lasting success than did the revolutionary efforts of congressional Radicals during Reconstruction, especially in a region in which whites continued to employ violence to maintain white supremacy. Even after slavery's demise, the bitter battle between Democrats and Republicans over the issue of black rights led to Reconstruction's failures, the subsequent Jim Crow era, continued pop cultural depictions of African Americans mirroring antebellum minstrel shows well into the twentieth century, and disproportionate incarceration of black men. Indeed, Americans largely forgot the Civil War services of black troops until Hollywood reintroduced the 54th Massachusetts to audiences in 1989 with the film *Glory*, cementing the image of the regiment's successful role in the recruitment of other black troops.

Are a black citizen's life and rights valued the same as those of a white citizen's? Sadly, even after the Thirteenth, Fourteenth, and Fifteenth amendments, valiant black service in every American war, the civil rights movement, and an African American presidency, the question still appears far from "played out." This seems especially true in an age when such issues as police brutality, voter registration, gerrymandering, immigration, and even the definition of patriotism all reveal that today's press and social media are perhaps just as rigidly partisan as were nineteenth-century newspapers.

Notes

1. James M. McPherson, *Battle Cry of Freedom: The Civil War Era* (New York: Oxford University Press, 1988), 686; Elizabeth R. Varon, *Armies of Deliverance: A New History of the Civil War* (New York: Oxford University Press, 2019), 275–282. See also Gary Gallagher and Joan Waugh, *The American War: A History of the Civil War Era*, 2nd ed. (State College, PA: Flip Learning, 2019), 102–104.

2. James Oliver Horton, "Defending the Manhood of the Race," in *Hope & Glory: Essays on the Legacy of the Fifty-Fourth Massachusetts Regiment*, ed. Martin H. Blatt, Thomas J. Brown, and Donald Yacovone (Amherst: University of Massachusetts Press, 2001), 8–14.

3. Ibid., 14.

4. Douglas R. Edgerton, *Thunder at the Gates: The Black Civil War Regiments That Redeemed America* (New York: Basics Books, 2016), 65.

5. Edgerton, *Thunder at the Gates*, 65.

6. Luis F. Emilio, *A Brave Black Regiment: The History of the 54th Regiment of Massachusetts Volunteer Infantry, 1863–1865* (Boston: Boston Book, 1891), 2–3; Russell Duncan, ed., *Blue-Eyed Child of Fortune: The Civil War Letters of Robert Gould Shaw* (Athens: University of Georgia Press, 1992), 285.

7. *Chicago Daily Tribune*, April 15, 1863; Emilio, *A Brave Black Regiment*, 14.

8. *Alexandria (VA) Gazette*, May 2, 1863; *Liberator* (Boston), March 18, 1863; *Douglass Monthly* (Rochester, NY), April 1863.

9. Horton, "Defending the Manhood of the Race," 20.

10. James Henry Gooding, *On the Altar of Freedom: A Black Soldier's Letters from the Front* (Amherst: University of Massachusetts Press, 1999), 11; *Hillsdale (MI) Standard*, March 24, 1863; *Burlington (VT) Free Press*, June 5, 1863.

11. Shaw, *Blue-Eyed Child of Fortune*, 309; *St. Cloud (MN) Democrat*, April 16, 1863.

12. George E. Stephens, *A Voice of Thunder: The Civil War Letters of George E. Stephens*, ed. Donald Yacovone (Urbana: University of Illinois Press, 1997), 31, 32; Gooding, *On the Altar of Freedom*, 11.

13. *Boston Daily Advertiser*, May 28, 1863; Emilio, *A Brave Black Regiment*, 26.

14. *Boston Pilot* quoted in *Liberator* (Boston), May 15, 1863; *Spirit of Democracy* (Woodsfield, OH), April 8, 1863; *Bedford (PA) Gazette*, May 8, 1863; *Daily Ohio Statesman* (Columbus), May 23, 1863.

15. *Rutland (VT) Weekly Herald*, May 21, 1863; Gooding, *On the Altar of Freedom*, 21.

16. Emilio, *A Brave Black Regiment*, 33; *Daily National Republican* (Washington, DC), May 28, 1863; *Burlington (VT) Free Press*, June 5, 1863; *Douglass Monthly* (Rochester, NY), June 1863.

17. Shaw, *Blue-Eyed Child of Fortune*, 341–342.

18. Ibid., 343; *Douglass Monthly* (Rochester, NY), August 1863; *Memphis Daily Appeal*, June 18, 1863; *Hartford County (MD) Intelligencer*, July 3, 1863; *Dollar Weekly Bulletin* (Maysville, KY), July 2, 1863; *Urbana (OH) Union*, July 15, 1863; *Indianapolis State Sentinel*, August 10, 1863.

19. Emilio, *A Brave Black Regiment*, 63; Gooding, *On the Altar of Freedom*, 37–38.

20. Gooding, *On the Altar of Freedom*, 72.

21. Ibid., 38; Emilio, *A Brave Black Regiment*, 73–78.

22. *Richmond Enquirer*, July 21, 1862.

23. *New York Herald*, July 26, 1862.

24. *New-York Tribune*, July 27, 1863.

25. Ibid.; *New York Times*, July 27, 1863.

26. *New-York Tribune*, July 27, 1863; *New York Times*, July 27, 1863.

27. *New York Herald*, July 27, 1863; *New York Times*, July 27, 1863; *Christian Recorder* (Philadelphia), August 22, 1863.

28. *New York Times*, July 28, 1863.

29. *New-York Tribune*, July 27, 1863; *Cleveland Morning Leader*, July 27, 1863.

30. *Boston Herald*, quoted in *Daily Green Mountain Freeman* (Montpelier, VT), July 29, 1863; *New York Times*, July 28, 1863; *New York Herald*, July 27, 1863.

31. *New-York Tribune*, July 27, 1863; *Cleveland Morning Leader*, July 28, 1863; *Savannah Republican*, quoted in *Weekly Perrysburg (OH) Journal*, July 29, 1863.

32. *New York Post*, quoted in *Boston Herald*, July 29, 1863.

33. Edgerton, *Thunder at the Gates*, 207–208.

34. Gooding, *On the Altar of Freedom*, 118–119; *Douglass Monthly* (Rochester, NY), August 1863.

35. Frederick Douglass, *The Life and Times of Frederick Douglass* (Hartford, CT: Park, 1881), 347–348.

36. *New York Times*, July 31, 1863.

37. *New-York Tribune*, July 27 1863.

38. *Richmond Dispatch*, August 17, 1863; *New York Herald*, July 27, 1863.

39. Abraham Lincoln, *The Collected Works of Abraham Lincoln*, 9 vols., ed. Roy P. Basler et al. (New Brunswick, NJ: Rutgers University Press, 1953–1955), 9:48–49. Emphasis added.

40. *Daily Green Mountain Freeman* (Montpelier, VT), August 3, 1863; *Douglass Monthly* (Rochester, NY), August 1863.

41. *Harper's Weekly*, August 8, 1863.

42. Ibid.

43. Ibid.

44. *Charleston Courier*, July 29, 1863.

45. *Savannah Republican*, quoted in *Yorkville (SC) Enquirer*, July 29, 1863; *Richmond Enquirer*, November 20, 1863.

46. *Milwaukee Times*, quoted in *Manitowoc (WI) Pilot*, August 7, 1863; *Spirit of Democracy* (Woodsfield, OH), August 12, 1863.

47. *Milwaukee Times*, quoted in *Manitowoc (WI) Pilot*, August 7, 1863; *Spirit of Democracy* (Woodsfield, OH), August 12, 1863.

48. *Buffalo Courier*, quoted in *Chicago Tribune*, August 28, 1863

49. *Chicago Times*, quoted in *Indiana State Sentinel* (Indianapolis), August 24, 1863.

50. *North Branch Democrat* (Tunkhannock, PA), October 7, 1863.

51. *Chicago Tribune*, August 28, 1863.

52. Ibid.

53. Ibid.

54. Lincoln, *Collected Works*, 9:65, 97–100.

55. *Chicago Tribune*, August 28, 1863; *Democrat and Sentinel* (Ebensburg, PA), September 16, 1863.

56. McPherson, *Battle Cry of Freedom*, 685.

57. *North Branch Democrat* (Tunkhannock, PA), September 16, 1863.

58. *Cincinnati Enquirer*, quoted in *Dollar Weekly Bulletin* (Maysville, KY), October 15, 1863.

59. *Ashland (OH) Union*, October 7, 1863.

60. McPherson, *Battle Cry of Freedom*, 687–688; *Cincinnati Enquirer*, quoted in *Dollar Weekly Bulletin* (Maysville, KY), October 15, 1863.

61. *Evansville (IN) Daily Journal*, November 9, 1863.

62. Stephens, *Voice of Thunder*, 47.

63. Stephens, *Voice of Thunder*, 47; *Chicago Daily Tribune*, November 6, 1863; *Cleveland Morning Leader*, November 12, 1863.

64. *Columbus Ohio Daily Statesman*, November 22, 1863; *New York Times*, November 27, 1863; Stephens, *Voice of Thunder*, 47.

65. *Columbus Ohio Daily Statesman*, November 22, 1863.

66. Ibid.

Newspaper Advertisements and American Political Culture, 1864–1865

LAWRENCE A. KREISER JR.

A s the campaign for the White House reached its final weeks during the autumn of 1864, Henry Hughes placed a notice in the *New York Herald*. The chairman of a local Democratic meeting, Hughes accused George Curtis, a possible delegate to the state convention in Albany, of "disloyalty to the party." Curtis reportedly had expressed doubts about the viability of George McClellan, a former Union general and the party's current presidential candidate, to win the election. Later that same day, in a letter to the editor, Curtis defended himself. Claiming that Hughes's advertisement had done him a "great injustice," he desired to make known his "true position." He fully supported McClellan and would "work, talk and vote" for the national ticket. He also assured his fellow party members that "those men who have inaugurated a crusade against me, that those who rely upon falsehood and calumny for success, will fail with an intelligent people."[1]

For Curtis to pen his letter immediately upon reading the *Herald* indicates his sense of outrage but, also, from the perspective of this essay, a reflection of the advertisements' importance to the daily lives of mid-nineteenth-century Americans. More northerners and southerners read a daily and weekly newspaper than at any other time yet in the nation's history, and they scoured the notices.[2] According to one contemporary observer, the advertising section had become "among the most important" pages of the newspaper. "No man really becomes acquainted even with the news of the day until he has thoroughly perused the advertisements," he explained. "They are the pulse and commerce of universal activity." Merchants, in turn, recognized the commercial opportunities. P. T. Barnum, one of the greatest salesmen of any age, exhorted store owners to promote their material wares in the so-called daily rag. "In a country like this, where nearly everybody reads, and where newspapers are issued and circulated in editions of five thousand to two hundred thousand," it would be a mistake to not run a notice. "A newspaper goes into the family and is read by wife and children," he declared, "as well as the head of house; hence hundreds and thousands of people may read your advertisement, while you are attending to your routine business."[3]

That attended business might have become too routine because, in their studies of the partisan press during the Civil War years, historians often mention the notices only in passing. In his award-winning study on the northern press, Harold Holzer argues that Abraham Lincoln mobilized editors and journalists to help win ultimate Union victory. More than his contemporaries, the president displayed a mastery of "political journalism as a means to earn and sustain voter support." In this deeply researched study, however, the announcements receive only a handful of references. Likewise, in her study on gender and antebellum political culture, Elizabeth Varon reminds her readers that newspapers themselves were a form of political advertisement. A contemporary observer might learn much about the political identity of a person simply by the newspaper he or she read. Yet to Varon, the notices, by comparison to the mastheads, remain in the background.[4]

What, then, might modern-day readers learn from the advertisements? A good deal, beginning with the blurring between the public and private boundaries in American political culture. That a fluid transition existed between the town square and the family parlor is a point made by Mark Neely in his recent study on material wares and partisanship. Americans decorated their homes with politically themed images, sculptures, and songbooks. He admits, however, that the corroborating documentary evidence is sometimes elusive. "Much of what we know about the home," he writes, "will have to come from inference from material culture and from other strategies of indirection."[5] Advertisements provide insight into these boundaries because they demonstrate how merchants attempted to find a profit in their election-year merchandise and how readers responded to the memorabilia. The notices also reveal that the sales pitches extended beyond the act of casting a ballot. Merchants were equally as quick to commercialize the assassination of Abraham Lincoln in April 1865 as they had been his reelection six months earlier.

Additionally, the sales announcements allowed the parties to make shorthand appeals to their readers. "Packaging the presidency," to use the words of Kathleen Hall Jamieson in her study on political advertising, had occurred since the early nineteenth century. In the first use of so-called image advertising, in 1840, the slogan "Tippecanoe and Tyler Too"—along with badges, pins, and banners featuring images of log cabins and hard cider—helped to carry William Henry Harrison to the White House. By the mid-1860s, Republicans and Democrats had extended their campaigns to the advertising columns. Perhaps the forerunners of today's political tweets, the parties distilled long-winded speeches and editorials into just a few words. The political spin was becoming, to the public mind, as important as the substance of the message.[6]

* * * *

By 1864, newspaper editors touted the political importance of their advertising columns that, for pennies a line, reached a large number of readers. The *New-York Tribune* proudly declared its circulation higher than "any other newspaper published in America or (we believe) in the world." The paper supported the Republican Party, but merchants might reach customers of any political background. The daily found its readers among the "large majority of schoolhouses and the decided minority of grog-shops." The *Philadelphia Ledger* had recently raised its subscription price, due to the increased cost of white paper. Store owners should not worry, however. The circulation and advertising of the Democratic paper "are larger now than at any period in the history of the establishment." The *Leavenworth Daily Conservative* abandoned any pretense of political neutrality in the sale notices. "The Republicans of Kansas should all advertise in the leading paper," the editor promised. "It will help your business."[7]

Merchants took advantage of the readership and announced a wide range of politically themed merchandise. They sold badges and other fashion accessories to wear to political rallies and parades. Supporters of the Democratic Party might buy a "Copperhead, or Badge of Liberty." A play upon the derisive name used for the party by its political opponents, the Copperhead was "made of pure copper, highly polished, and artistic." Voters who supported Lincoln might buy a silver-plated "Union League Badge." The badge also sold as a brooch for women who wanted to display their political sympathies. Democrats and Republicans alike might wear "Patriotic Medals"—the "only correct medallion likeness" of either of the presidential candidates—or hat cords in red, white, and blue to "Show Your Color!" Church and Clark, two merchants in San Francisco, induced partisans to literally light up the night. Their rockets, candles, and torches were "Sure to Bring Out All the Voters!"[8]

Contemporary observers used the political symbols to draw conclusions about the momentous issues of the presidential campaign. Pandering to racial stereotypes, Democrats ran a story about a "big negro" who seized a McClellan badge from a "lady's bosom" while she walked down the street. Rather than rushing to the woman's defense, Republican onlookers cheered and hooted. In a New Hampshire newspaper, a Union private wrote that he wore a Democratic pin on the morning of the election. His commanding officer told him to remove the trinket, or he would have to perform a "knapsack drill" until he died. The editor argued that only through such voter intimidation had Lincoln won re-election. Republicans countered by equating their badges with patriotism. A Michigan newspaper ran a story on a Union soldier who took leave from a military hospital to vote in Lansing. Wounded in the leg and "obliged to travel on crutches," the man "goes in for 'a vigorous prosecution of the war,' and wears a Lincoln badge." At a Republican rally in New England, a veteran argued that what political badge a soldier wore mattered less than his military uniform. The men in the army favored fighting the war through to Union triumph—a Republican campaign platform.[9]

Other merchants pulled from the headlines, blurring the distinction between the notices and the news. In the *Clearfield Republican*, a, despite the title, Democratic paper published in Pennsylvania, Frank Short announced:

TREMENDOUS VICTORY
GREATEST BATTLE ON RECORD
15,000 Killed and Wounded, and
30,000 taken Prisoners!
With Camp Equipage—And
70,000 Contrabands freed from the
BONDS OF SLAVERY!

The only negative to the Union triumph was that the former slaves were coming north "to 'eat out our substance,' and to wear out our shoes!" Shoppers should avoid the rush by visiting his footwear store, where he offered a wide selection and low prices. Readers might have found themselves primed for Short's advertisement after browsing reprinted speeches from the Democratic National Convention calling for reunion with slavery intact, and editorials decrying the continuation of the war for "abolitionist" aims.[10]

In Republican newspapers, merchants used a similar ploy. Following an editorial that encouraged voters in Tiffin, Ohio, to "Rally Round the Flag" and "Let the Cannon Roar," a tailor headlined his notice with "ATLANTA AND PETERSBURG." His material wares had little to do with the Union military operations in Georgia and Virginia; he simply wanted the association. That spring, in Washington, headlines in the *Evening Star* offered "Views from the South" and "News from Dixie." After the start of another Union offensive to capture Richmond and win the war, J. Cristadoro led an announcement for his patent medicine with "Heads that Rebel." He was not referring to the possible postwar fate of Jefferson Davis, Robert E. Lee, and other Confederate officials but to hair that had gone "against the rules of Taste or Beauty, in their color or in the loss of all their color." A few uses of his dye would restore a *"Beautiful Shade"* to any customers. In these newspapers, the advertisers were as quick to exploit the public's hunger for war-related news as the editors.[11]

Robert Thayer believed the issues of the election were so important that even children should be mobilized by reading *The Pioneer Boy and How He Became President*. Many youngsters had already seen, and in some cases experienced, the war's disruptions and sacrifices. As historian James Marten shows in his work on the Union home front, the fighting was appearing regularly in children's games and magazines by 1864. Publishers recognized that Thayer's readers were likely too young to vote but claimed the work taught important life lessons. "It shows what the qualities of honesty, industry, patience and perseverance will do for any boy who will try," described one notice. Another announcement asked parents to "BUY IT FOR YOUR BOY." Critics savaged the book as too simplistic. One reviewer scoffed that Thayer portrayed young Lincoln learning to write his name in the dirt as one of the great accomplishments in world history. However, Thayer had received an endorsement from Robert Todd Lincoln, the president's son, who claimed to be "very much pleased by the book." Thayer had been "singularly successful in avoiding errors, as I find I have, at some time, heard nearly every thing you narrate from a 'Reliable Gentleman.'" The younger Lincoln's praise boosted sales, and Thayer claimed a whopping nine thousand books ordered within a few months of the publication.[12]

Readers who wanted more information on McClellan and the Democratic platform had fewer options, because the party's convention did not meet until the end of summer. A former Union general, McClellan had authored several military titles that were still readily available. Because of the lateness of the campaign season, his political writings were only accessible in cheaply produced pamphlets. The letters and speeches of Clement Vallandigham, however, were reportedly having a "large sale." A vocal critic of emancipation and a former congressman, Vallandigham helped to shape the Democratic platform.

His *Record on Abolition, the Union, and Civil War* was "handsomely printed on good paper" and included a "very finely executed steel engraving." For those wanting a more intimate portrayal, a "biographical memoir" published by Vallandigham's brother also was for sale. The book was "of unusual value and interest; entirely authentic and reliable." According to the publishing company, Vallandigham was even more in demand than Lincoln. The memoir "is wanted everywhere, immediately by hundreds of thousands."[13]

A campaign chart drew negative attention to McClellan, by labeling him the "HERO OF ANTIETAM." Published by Charles Lubrecht, the lithograph included a colored picture of McClellan, a "sketch of his life," and excerpts from his acceptance letter for the presidential nomination. Lubrecht declared that the image "ought to decorate the wall of every Democratic voter." Republicans quickly protested that the Union soldiers were the real heroes of the fighting in western Maryland and turned their scorn upon the former general. A New York correspondent claimed that he had walked around much of Albany in the days before the election. "I can truthfully say," he wrote, "that every drunken or suspicious character, whom I have met, who expressed preferences at all, was in ecstasies over the 'hero of Antietam.'" Another correspondent claimed to have met a friend and longtime Democratic supporter in southern Illinois. The reporter told the man that three or four train cars had recently passed, full of soldiers shouting "unbounded enthusiasms for the hero of Antietam!" The friend replied that he had not heard such good news in some time. As they were preparing to say goodbye, the reporter commented that there was "'one thing I had like to have forgotten.'" The man leaned in, expecting a "still stronger evidence of the popularity of his candidate." The cheering men? They were *all rebel prisoners of war!*"[14]

A sampling of other campaign-related memorabilia also indicates the flexible boundaries between the political worlds of mid-nineteenth-century northerners. A steel engraving of Lincoln signing the Emancipation Proclamation was meant for display at home, because of its size and variety of framing options. As important to the publisher, the image was the "best and only correct likeness of this great man in existence." Another picture of the president was seemingly meant for a display hall because it was "full length." However, one critic suggested that potential customers pocket their money instead. The image was large, but Lincoln's face did not look as "as good as that on the Greenbacks." Hedging his bets, a book seller in Washington offered the "best stationary packages" emblazoned with images of McClellan and Lincoln. Potential letter writers might make their political leanings known even before they had jotted a word. In Pennsylvania, a Democratic paper offered an image of McClellan to hang in the family parlor. The engraving depicted the general turned politician on "his black horse on the battlefield of Antietam." Although the martial scene was impressive, the artwork made clear that the Democratic nominee was the "PEOPLE'S CHOICE FOR THE PRESIDENT OF THE UNITED STATES." At least one customer judged the engraving "very fine."[15]

The political memorabilia became perhaps too pervasive and, as 1864 deepened, some northerners grumbled that nowhere seemed free from the presidential campaign. A Pennsylvania editor was sorry that a religiously themed newspaper had given way to partisanship and worldly interests. Sermons and biblical lessons were replaced by "long winded, political articles and love stories." In Chicago, upon hearing talk about "the campaign" that summer, a reporter was shocked when people were discussing Lincoln and McClellan rather than the progress of the Union armies. A recent battle—"'our loss only some 3,000'"—was "instantly forgotten" in the political talk. That autumn, a Mr. Millington announced that he was postponing the opening of a dancing school in Gold Hills, Nevada, until after the election. To his mind, the "heads of the people are too full of politics to pay much attention to the 'light fantastic toe.'"[16]

Amid the hyper atmosphere, the political parties used the advertising columns to offer very different visions of the nation's future. By the war's fourth autumn, the Democrats claimed that only they supported "the Union and the Constitution." The Lincoln administration had trampled civil liberties through the enforcement of the military draft and the emancipation of the slaves in Confederate-held territories. "Shall we sink into despotism?" asked another Democratic announcement. The seemingly endless and bloody war continued only because the president and his political allies had gone well beyond the original war aim of preserving the Union. By 1864, the choice was clear. The Democrats offered "UNION! In an honorable, permanent and happy PEACE!" The Republicans offered "DRAFT! Universal anarchy and ultimate RUIN!"[17]

Open disagreement on the Democratic platform received advertisement in the *New York Sun*, an almost unprecedented occurrence, then or now. Moses Taylor announced that he was chairing the "Convention and Mass Meeting" of Democrats opposed to a negotiated peace with the Confederacy. He invited "all of the Democratic faith" who "retain their respect for the manhood and patriotism which animated the Democratic Party in the days of Jackson." This included anyone who "cannot endure the shame of seeing their country's flag lowered to a tottering foe ever ready to trample it in the dust." The goal was to remove the "degrading concession" announced at the national convention in Chicago that "'THE WAR' so nobly fought by our brave army and navy 'WAS A FAILURE.'" Another Democratic notice in the same paper attempted to patch over any differences by promising "Union, Harmony, and Victory!" Left for the reader to determine was whether this meant victory at the polls, on the battlefield, or both. The infighting made some party members nervous. On the day of the election, Democrats had to remind their comrades to "devote the day to save your country."[18]

Republicans had their disagreements on postwar policies toward the South, but they found ample room for unity in the battlefield successes of the Union army. Recent victories at Atlanta, Mobile, and the Shenandoah valley in Virginia headlined the notices for many campaign rallies. Other announcements highlighted the army officers invited to speak. Republicans now had the advantage of campaigning as the war turned decidedly in favor of the Union, and the language of their campaign announcements reflected a renewed military fervor. "Let our enemies see that patriots can and do appreciate Union victories whether they are won by bullets or ballots," thundered one notice. Another advertisement reminded voters that even if not a "soldier with a knapsack," they should be "in the field and . . . enlisted for the Union." As Republican voters went to the polls, they should remember to "Keep Your Eyes on That Flag . . . that today is waving over so many victorious fields."[19] The emphasis upon northern military successes allowed even many Democratic soldiers to cast their ballot for Lincoln. The president's reelection offered them the surest way home while also remaining true to the sacrifices made by their fallen comrades. Although not supportive of the abolitionist movement, these men recognized that a Republican triumph allowed them to not only end the war but, according to Chandra Manning, "end it right by eliminating slavery once and for all."[20]

The effectiveness of the notices in helping to form public opinion is found in other sections of the newspaper. Frederic Hudson, the managing editor of the *New York Herald*, admitted the many competing political claims sometimes made for confusing reading. Rather than throwing up their hands in frustration, potential voters should read the notices. "Let them study the eight or nine columns of political advertisements on another page," Hudson declared, "and glean such information there as may guide them aright." In early 1864, a Democratic paper fumed that Secretary of the Treasury Salmon Chase was using the advertising columns to further his own presidential ambitions. Chase had reportedly sent an "elaborate and extravagant puff" to a New York–based advertising agency with directions to insert the essay as a news story but pay for it as an advertisement. The paper judged the ploy a "novel mode" of disseminating "political advertising."[21]

Lincoln decisively won reelection, and advertisements for victory celebrations made clear the significance for the Union war effort. The president struck a conciliatory tone in his second inaugural address in March, famously urging "malice toward none; with charity for all." Notices for Republican bonfires and parades carried a more ominous message for any northern Democrat (or Confederate) reader hoping that the fighting might end in anything but the destruction of slavery and a complete Union victory. In Burlington, Iowa, an advertisement in the *Daily Hawk-Eye* rejoiced in the "glorious results" of the presidential election and the "crushing of the copper head party." Local Republicans were confident that the "great rebellion will soon go down in blood." Voters in central Pennsylvania purchased advertising space in the *Juniata Sentinel*, a weekly published in Mifflintown. "Victory! Union Forever! Father Abraham and Uncle Andy elected! No Compromise with Rebels!" As far away as Oregon Territory, Republicans hailed the reelection of Lincoln. The triumph of the president was the greatest of the many "Union Victories in 1864!" Now the final work of the Union was to "Push on the Column!"[22]

Politics remained in the advertising columns following the assassination of Lincoln that spring, when images of the martyred president flooded the northern market. Merchants emphasized the lifelike nature of the pictures as a way to mark the historical significance of the moment and to commemorate the fallen leader. William Rice advertised the "best likeness" of Lincoln that fit perfectly into a photographic album. He would mail it to "any part of the country" then under Federal control. Another photographer of course claimed that he had the "Finest Likeness of the Late President yet presented." Potential customers should not just take his word for it, but instead rely on the "judgment of [Lincoln's] widow and several intimate friends." There was about the picture that "indescribable something which assures even those who never saw Mr. Lincoln that it is a correct representation of his strong and good face." Other merchants touted their images of Lincoln as the "best steel engraving," a "splendid steel engraving," and of a "superior finish and most correct of any in circulation."[23]

Although not as numerous, images of John Wilkes Booth received a wide promotion. Card photographs of Booth were not uncommon in the Northeast prior to 1865, because of the actor's stage fame and good looks. They spread rapidly after the assassination, helped in part by the federal reward offered for his capture. One editor reminded his readers that a recently published image of the assassin "is said to be correct." Should any citizen recognize him, they should immediately "bring him to light" and claim the bounty. After Booth's death, the likenesses allowed people to see the man who had now become so infamous. A Massachusetts photographer offered a "splendid likeness of Booth, sitting or standing." He was so confident that northerners would want one of the two poses that agents selling the image "can easily make $5 a day." George Russell, a photographer in the Montana Territory, claimed to have "correct photographs" of the assassin. Individuals who "are anxious to see how the greatest scoundrel in America looked when living," should stop by his store. Other merchants advertised the "best likeness of Booth, the assassin, in existence" and the "most accurate picture of the assassin Booth."[24]

Such images played a key role in the trials of the supposed conspirators. Federal troopers recounted how they displayed photographs of Booth to local residents, as they pursued him into the countryside of northern Virginia. That might not have been very much help, one witness claimed, because the image was a "very poor one." She believed Booth was a "better looking man." In damaging evidence against Mary Surratt, one of the defendants, a Union captain claimed to have found images of Confederate officials at her boardinghouse. Even more incriminating, he discovered a photograph of Booth "hidden in the back of a little picture." That evidence was so shocking to some onlookers that local officials in Louisville, Kentucky, reportedly made it illegal for merchants to profit by selling any more of the assassin's images.[25]

In addition to the photographers, book dealers and other merchants attempted to commercialize the assassination. Publishers moved with remarkable speed. By late May, J. B. Hawley had released *The Assassination of President Lincoln*. The Cincinnati-based publisher declared that he had focused his "whole force and entire attention to bringing out a perfectly reliable record of the whole affair." No one should go without a copy. "Every American citizen—man, woman and child—will read it as an item of interest to-day, and which will pass into the annals of American history and be quoted as one of the greatest events, even to the most distant future." That summer, Linus Brockett published *The Life and Times of Abraham Lincoln*. The book ran 750 pages, with a "beautifully illuminated cover" and "fine engravings." The title reportedly had sold seventy-five thousand copies in the two months following its publication.

Agents who wanted to canvass for the book should move quickly, before more books flooded the market. The publisher crowed, "Much desirable territory remains uncanvassed. There is room for men of backbone." For those who simply wanted to mark time, a merchant in Buffalo appealed for agents to sell the "Lincoln watch." The lightweight timepiece "looks like silver" and sold for thirty-five cents. An ambitious young man might make up to $200 a day selling the watch at "Cattle Shows and Fairs." That might seem a high figure, but the merchant reminded readers that the Lincoln watch was the "greatest thing ever invented to sell." Other men and women might buy music written upon the death of Lincoln, as well as subscribe to a "monument fund" established in his honor.[26]

By the late spring, many northerners believed they had found evidence of complicity in the crime. They pointed to an advertisement that had run in an Alabama newspaper in late 1864 asking for donations to help assassinate Lincoln and other federal officials. With $1,000,000 in funds—payable to a "Box X" in Cahaba—the anonymous assassin promised not only to give the Confederacy "peace" but to "satisfy the world that cruel tyrants can not live in a 'land of liberty.'" Union newspapers soon republished the notice but with little commentary. One editor later explained that the offer seemed "mere braggadocio" rather than a legitimate threat. In late May, however, Federal officials arrested the man who had paid for the notice. A lawyer in Selma, George Washington Gayle, claimed that he had placed the advertisement only as a joke. Subsequent hearings cast doubt upon that as a line of defense, with one witness describing Gayle as "distinguished, even in Alabama, for his extreme views on the subject of slavery and the rebellion, and as an ardent supporter of the Confederacy."[27]

Gayle eventually received a presidential pardon but, in the spring of 1865, Frederick Frelinghuysen used the advertisement as an opening to condemn the Confederacy. Speaking at a public ceremony on April 19, the then attorney general of New Jersey argued that while the notice may have inspired Booth, the real killers of Lincoln were "Human Slavery and Rebellion against Freedom." According to Frelinghuysen, the slave system had cursed the nation since its beginnings. Now, while in "agonies of its dissolution," that system "has dealt a blow upon him, who, as God's instrument, . . . has vanquished it." The "other murder" was the "offspring" of slavery: the pride of slave owners to defy the democratic process. That "foul spirit" had caused them to rebel "without cause, and without the assignment of any cause, against the fairest and best government of the world." Any northerners who "would trace the crime to its proper source" must not point to the newspaper advertisement but "accept the truth that the murderers are the two foul powers" that he had named. The Union had effectively triumphed in the Civil War by the assassination of Lincoln but, as historian Caroline Janney has recently argued, national reconciliation would present its own battles.[28]

Later that same year, a novel by Dion Haco politicized the assassination notice even more extensively. *J. Wilkes Booth, the Assassinator of President Lincoln* recounted the crime from the actor's perspective. In the story, Booth and the fictional Larry McDonald, a member of the Knights of the Golden Circle, pen the newspaper notice (which Haco includes word-for-word). Several months later, on the night of the assassination, two of Booth's conspirators are talking inside Ford's Theater. When one of them expresses discouragement that no money had yet arrived from Confederate contributors, the other man corrects him. The point was to have the advertisement reprinted in northern newspapers. From that exposure, "sympathizers and friends North of the Potomac" had already contributed tens of thousands of dollars. "Only fancy a 'loyal newspaper' advertising gratuitously for funds to help us in killing off their vagabond leaders," he gloats. "Sharp as they appear to be they are as blind as a three day old kitten." Only three days after the republication of the announcement, "Our friends in Wall Street sent us all the profits they had made in their gold operations for a week, and it was no small sum either." Although intended as a plot device to explain where Booth had received his funding, Haco had foreshadowed some of the political battle lines of the postwar era. Republicans charged that the Democrats were a party of disloyalty and that the Copperheads and Knights of the Golden Circle had posed a serious internal threat to the Union war effort.[29]

Before the public's attention turned to the political battles of the Reconstruction years, Samuel Gardner, a longtime newspaper editor, wondered what politicians might learn from advertisers. A lot, he thought. In an essay titled "Style," he argued that the individuals who ran notices had really thought about their words and expressions "because it concerns them in the tenderest point, their pockets." Every line made a point, because every line cost money. "When tautology is an expensive sin, it is at once corrected," he asserted, "and repetition then becomes an unheard-of fault." Any reader might appreciate merchants' conciseness by placing their notices alongside "windy editorials" and, even more tedious, political speeches. He believed that members of Congress would become much more effective communicators if they were charged a small fee for everything from "gross expletives of language" to "outrageous

waste of good words, which convey no perceptible freight of ideas." He concluded that American democracy might work the best if politicians had to keep
the "fear of the reckoning of accounts, and not of critics, before their eyes."[30]

As Gardner acknowledged, the advertising columns had played a significant
role in the nation's political life. They had helped the parties to explain their
platform and to build a sense of political community. Amid the hype, the notices emphasized that individual voters had a simple choice in helping to shape
vastly different futures for the United States. Advertisers also recognized that
citizens' political engagement extended beyond the act of casting a ballot, as
significant as that was. They marketed a range of badges, biographies, and litho-
graphs. These wares sometimes drew a strong response from readers, from
Lincoln badges to the McClellan campaign chart. As the war drew to a close
in the spring of 1865, the notices even commercialized the president's assassination. Additionally, the public reaction to Gayle's announcement requesting
funds for the murder helped to shape some of the battles of the postwar era.
What guilt did slave owners bear in causing the war? Were Democrats traitors
to the nation? Americans would wrestle with these questions, but during the
war's last two years, the advertisements had demonstrated that they had fought
one another as fiercely in the political arena as on the battlefield.

Notes

1. *New York Herald*, September 12, 1864; George Curtis to the "Editor of the World," reprinted
in *Dayton (OH) Daily Empire*, September 19, 1864. The best overviews of the 1864 presidential
elections include John C. Waugh, *Reelecting Lincoln: The Battle for the 1864 Presidency* (New York:
Crown Publishers, 1997); and David E. Long, *The Jewel of Liberty: Abraham Lincoln's Re-Election
and the End of Slavery* (Mechanicsburg, PA: Stackpole Books, 1994).

2. Although the data are incomplete, one journalism historian argues that, by 1860, in urban areas, each family had access to 1.42 newspapers. That was an increase from 1.31 newspapers in 1850.
See Ted Curtis Smythe, "The Diffusion of the Urban Daily, 1850–1900," *Journalism History* 28, no.
2 (Summer 2002): 73–84. By 1860, about 3,700 newspapers were published on a regular basis. See
"Table 37—Newspapers and Periodicals in the United States in 1860," in Joseph C. G. Kennedy, *Preliminary Report on the Eighth Census, 1860* (Washington, DC: Government Printing Office, 1862),
211–213.

3. Joseph J. Belcher, "Newspaper Advertisements," *Harper's New Monthly Magazine* 33, no. 198
(November 1866): 781; P. T. Barnum, *The Humbugs of the World: An Account of Humbugs, Delusions,
Impositions, Quackeries, Deceits and Deceivers Generally, in All Ages* (New York: Carleton, 1866),
66; *Rowell's American Newspaper Directory* (New York: George P. Rowell, 1870), 2:82.

4. Harold Holzer, *Lincoln and the Power of the Press: The War for Public Opinion* (New York:
Simon and Schuster, 2014); Elizabeth R. Varon, "Tippecanoe and the Ladies, Too: White Women

and Party Politics in Antebellum Virginia," *Journal of American History* 82, no. 2 (September 1995): 494–521.

5. Mark E. Neely, *The Boundaries of American Political Culture in the Civil War Era* (Chapel Hill: University of North Carolina Press, 2005), 34. For a different perspective, that Americans were relatively unengaged with politics during the nineteenth century, despite impressive voter participation in national elections, see Glenn C. Altschuler and Stuart M. Blumin, *Rude Republic: Americans and Their Politics in the Nineteenth Century* (Princeton, NJ: Princeton University Press, 2000).

6. Kathleen Hall Jamieson, *Packaging the Presidency: A History and Criticism of Presidential Campaign Advertising*, 3rd ed. (New York: Oxford University Press, 1996). Jamieson describes the election of 1840 as the "first full-blown campaign," and a "national jamboree" with music, parades, and memorabilia. An excellent study on the use of political campaigns to reach an expanding electorate is Mark Renfred Cheatham, *The Coming of Democracy: Presidential Campaigning in the Age of Jackson* (Baltimore: Johns Hopkins University Press, 2018).

7. *Leavenworth (KS) Daily Conservative*, August 2, 1864; *Santa Fe (NM) Republican*, July 12, 1862. Prospectus of the *New-York Daily Tribune* and *Philadelphia Ledger* in *American Citizen* (Butler, PA), October 12, 1864; and *Ottawa (IL) Free Trader*, December 31, 1864. The *Santa Fe Republican* reminded its readers that it "is the only Union or National paper in New Mexico." Not only that, it "is the only paper published anywhere that circulates to any extent in this Territory."

8. *New York Caucasian*, May 2, 1863; *Long-Islander* (Huntington, NY), April 24, 1864; *Oregon Sentinel* (Jacksonville), November 5, 1864; *Evening Telegraph* (Philadelphia), July 8, 1864; *Quincy (IL) Herald*, October 7, 1864; *Gloucester (MA) Telegraph and News*, October 18, 1864; *Daily Alta California* (San Francisco), October 1, 1864.

9. *North Branch Democrat* (Tunkhannock, PA), November 2, 1864; *Farmer's Cabinet* (Amherst, NH), December 2, 1864; *Lansing (MI) State Republican*, October 5, 1864; *Rutland (VT) Weekly Herald*, November 3, 1864.

10. *Clearfield (PA) Republican*, September 14, 1864.

11. *Tiffin (OH) Weekly Tribune*, September 29, 1864; *Evening Star* (Washington, DC), May 2, May 3, and May 8, 1864.

12. *True Citizen* (New Britain, CT), August 5, 1864; *Chicago Daily Tribune*, September 22, 1863; *New-York Commercial Advertiser*, April 8, 1863; *Daily National Intelligencer* (Washington, DC), June 8, 1863; *Daily Green Mountain Freeman* (Montpelier, VT), June 8, 1863; *Civilian and Telegraph* (Cumberland, MD), June 11, 1863. On children during the Civil War era, see James A. Marten, ed., *Children and Youth during the Civil War Era* (New York: New York University Press, 2012); and Marten, *Children for the Union: The War Spirit on the Northern Home Front* (Chicago: Ivan R. Dee, 2004).

13. *Newark (OH) Advocate*, August 7, 1863; *Dawson's Fort Wayne (IN) Daily Times*, August 8, 1863; *Columbia Democrat and Bloomsburg (PA) General Advertiser*, November 12, 1864; *Clearfield (PA) Republican*, October 26, 1864; *Chicago Times*, August 24, 1863. Vallandigham also attracted attention in Confederate notices, with two merchants selling his speeches denouncing the Emancipation Proclamation. See *Southern Crisis* (Jackson, MS), February 4, 1863; and *Savannah (GA) Republican*, March 27, 1863.

14. *Daily National Intelligencer* (Washington, DC), September 20, 1864; "Albany Correspondence," *Western Reserve Chronicle* (Warren, OH), October 5, 1864; "That Cairo Regiment," *Marshall County Republican* (Plymouth, IN), October 13, 1864.

15. *Lewistown (PA) Gazette*, July 13, 1864; *Burlington (VT) Free Press*, September 16, 1864; *Chi-*

cago Daily Tribune, January 24, 1864; New York Herald, September 2, 1864; Cleveland Morning Leader, October 28, 1864; Star of the North (Bloomsburg, PA), September 28, 1864.

16. North Branch Democrat (Tunkhannock, PA), December 7, 1864; "The Campaign," Chicago Times, reprinted in Holmes County Farmer (Millersburg, OH), June 16, 1864; Gold Hill (NV) Daily News, November 2, 1864; Daily National Republican (Washington, DC), September 5, 1864.

17. Daily Ohio Statesman (Columbus), October 29, 1864; Erie (PA) Observer, October 27, 1864; McKean Democrat (Smethport, PA), January 9, 1864; Cambridge (MA) Chronicle, November 5, 1864.

18. Sun (New York), November 1, 1864; Elk Advocate (Ridgway, PA), November 5, 1864.

19. Delaware State Journal (Wilmington), October 25, 1864; Philadelphia Inquirer, November 3, 1864; Pittsburgh Daily Gazette and Advertiser, October 25, 1864; Eau Claire (WI) Daily Free Press, November 3, 1864; South Danvers Wizard (Peabody, MA), November 2, 1864.

20. Chandra Manning, What This Cruel War Was Over: Soldiers, Slavery, and the Civil War (New York: Alfred A. Knopf, 2007), 184. Offering a different perspective is Jonathan W. White, Emancipation, the Union Army, and the Reelection of Abraham Lincoln (Baton Rouge: Louisiana State University Press, 2014). White reminds his readers that, by his estimate, roughly 40 percent of Union soldiers did not vote for Lincoln, frustrated by the expansion of the nation's war aims.

21. New York Herald, November 30, 1863; Dayton (OH) Daily Empire, January 8, 1864.

22. Burlington (IA) Daily Hawk-Eye, January 5, 1865; Juniata Sentinel (Mifflintown, PA), November 9, 1864; Oregon Sentinel (Jacksonville), November 12, 1864.

23. Springfield (MA) Daily Republican, May 2 and May 15, 1865; Boston Evening Transcript, September 9, 1865; Portland (ME) Daily Advertiser, May 30, 1865; Illinois State Chronicle (Decatur), June 24, 1865; Christian Repository (Montpelier, VT), May 27, 1865. An excellent survey of the emotional reaction to the assassination is Martha Elizabeth Hodes, Mourning Lincoln (New Haven, CT: Yale University Press, 2015).

24. Manitowoc (WI) Pilot, April 28, 1865; Norfolk County Journal (Roxbury, MA), May 14, 1865; Montana Post (Virginia City), June 3, 1865; Woonsocket Patriot and Rhode-Island State Register, May 19, 1865; Goshen (IN) Democrat, May 10, 1865; Bedford (PA) Gazette, August 4, 1865.

25. New York Herald, May 17, 1865; Evening Star (Washington, DC), May 15, 1865; Ashtabula (OH) Weekly Telegraph, June 10, 1865.

26. Nashville Daily Union, May 30, 1865; Marshall (MI) Statesman, May 31, 1865; Indianapolis Daily Journal, August 18, 1865; Meriden Recorder (West Meriden, CT), July 14, 1865; Buffalo Express, July 27, 1865; Brooklyn Daily Eagle, July 17, 1865.

27. Chicago Daily Tribune, January 26, 1865; White Cloud Kansas Chief, April 27, 1865; "Million Dollars for Assassination," in The Assassination of President Lincoln and the Trial of the Conspirators, ed. Benn Pitman (Cincinnati, OH: Moore, Wilstach and Baldwin, 1865), 51.

28. Frederick T. Frelinghuysen, Obsequies of Abraham Lincoln, in Newark, N.J., April 19, 1865 (Newark, NJ: Daily Advertiser, 1865), 10–13. On northern claims that the slave system was responsible for the assassination of Lincoln, see Caroline E. Janney, Remembering the Civil War: Reunion and the Limits of Reconciliation (Chapel Hill: University of North Carolina Press, 2013), 55–62.

29. Dion Haco, J. Wilkes Booth, The Assassinator of President Lincoln (New York: T. R. Dawley, 1865), 43–45, 52–53.

30. Samuel Jackson Gardner, "Style," in Autumn Leaves (New York: Hurd and Houghton, 1865), 108–111.

The White Horse or the Mule

Lincoln in Civil War Music

CHRISTIAN McWHIRTER

As the Federal Writers' Project interviewed formerly enslaved African Americans in the late 1930s, a surprising musical thread began to appear. Responding to questions about Abraham Lincoln and Jefferson Davis, many of the interviewees recalled a common folk tradition. Amanda Oliver, then in Oklahoma, was typical. She admitted, "I can't say much 'bout Abe Lincoln" but she knew "he was a republican in favor of da cullud folk being free." However, she did remember a song:

> Lincoln rides a fine hoss,
> Jeff Davis rides a mule,
> Lincoln is de President,
> Jeff Davis is de fool.

Variations on this rhyme turn up repeatedly in the "slave narratives," with Lincoln and Davis interchangeably riding the horse (usually "fine" or "white") or the mule. That multiple interviewees referenced the song not only demonstrated its popularity but also that politics was a common and accepted musical subject.[1]

Indeed, music was one of the most effective ways to communicate political ideas during the Civil War. Songs like the "horse and mule" ditty were especially useful because their lyrics were flexible enough to accommodate different, even oppositional, political ideas. However, this particular song exposes another trend in Civil War music. Nothing personified the opposing sides so much as their respective leaders, and songs focusing on political and military figures practically became a subgenre of their own. This was certainly true for northern and southern songwriters, although the Union blockade ensured the North dominated this musical trend, as it did most others.

Thus it is no surprise that Lincoln dwarfs all other personalities as a wartime musical subject. More surprising, though, is how closely Lincoln songs reflect popular perceptions of the president. Even a small sampling of the music written from Lincoln's first presidential campaign to his assassination reveals an evolving public persona and an emerging American myth—both shaped by and reacting to the dramatic events of his time. What is more, this body of work shows this evolution more clearly than any other form of contemporary media.

This process started with the campaign songs of 1860, and many depict Lincoln as a mere caricature. A handful of simple attributes appear repeatedly, sometimes within the same piece. Lincoln's honesty recurs most frequently, but it is often depicted as a product of two specific traits: his age (he is "Old Abe" as often as "Honest Abe") and his western roots. "Honest Old Abe," attributed to "A Wide Awake," covers two of these bases in the title and a third in lines such as "But out on the wide rolling prairie / A tall Sucker has taken course." Similarly, "Old Abe's Visit to the White House" has him driving across the country to seize the capital:

> One Abr'am there was who lived out in the West,
> Esteemed by his neighbors the wisest and best,
> And you'll see him, on a time, if you follow my ditty,
> How he took a straight walk up to Washington City.[2]

The most common means of distributing these songs was pocket-sized songbooks without notation called songsters. One such volume, edited by the abolitionist Hutchinson Family Singers, featured a tune simply titled "Lincoln" that labels its subject "our Prairie King" and "the champion of the West." Indeed, despite its obvious anachronism, crowning Lincoln a frontier monarch had enough popularity that the *Wide-Awake Vocalist* applied it to an entire song: "Shout for the Prairie King." The ultimate goal was to portray Lincoln as incorruptible due to his scrupulous honesty and a purity of the soul from living outside of the corrupt, urban East. "Hurrah for Lincoln," from *The Republican Campaign Songster*, focuses almost exclusively on this idea in its remarkably unmusical second verse:

> Then, hurrah for ABRAHAM LINCOLN;
> 'Tis a glorious thing to think on
> He'll not wave, no! nor wink on
> Machinations and deceit;

Lobby schemes and treasury stealing
Find with him no "fellow feeling";
Haste he'll make their fraud revealing,
Justice at his hands they'll meet.[3]

Yet this portrayal of Lincoln as honest, wise, and pure conveyed only half of his public image. Songwriters also reveled in his supposed gruff masculinity—often tying it to his frontier background. The "Railsplitter" image dominated and became an indelible part of the Lincoln myth. These types of campaign songs attempted to transform Lincoln from a middle-class lawyer—with a now notorious childhood aversion to physical labor—to a rough-and-tumble workman, able to handle the crises of his era with practical common sense. For instance, "Then Put Away the Wedges and the Maul" characterizes him as a quintessential laborer:

There was an old hero, and they called him honest Abe,
And he lived out West, out West;
Work was his pleasure ever since he was a babe,
But now he's going to have a little rest.
. . . .
His fingers ain't so long as the one's in office now,
And he has two good eyes in his head;
A full set of brains, and an honest, manly brow.
Which things, of many others, can't be said.

In addition, Lincoln's height became a symbol of his moral and physical superiority. This proved especially useful when comparing him to the "Little Giant," Stephen A. Douglas, in tunes such as "The Taller Man Well Skilled" or in these lines from "High Old Abe Shall Win":

Hurrah hurrah! Did you hear the news?
At Baltimore they got the blues,
Because our leader is the best,
And tallest man in all the west.

Of course, Lincoln's determination and masculinity could also be put to blunter use. If Lincoln was a man of strength and accustomed to solving problems with tactile hard work, he was therefore capable of physical violence—especially against Democrats. The minstrel tune "Get Out de Way, You Little Giant" leaves little to the imagination:

> Old Abe is coming down to fight,
> And put de democrats to flight,
> He's coming wid de wedge and maul
> And he will split em one and all.[4]

All these themes (along with a reference to Lincoln's childhood poverty) came together in "Abe of Illinois," which appeared in at least three songsters:

> No! not for party—not for spoil
> Will he his gift employ,
> But for his country's good will toil,
> "Old Abe," of Illinois.
> Our hero once was short of pence,
> An humble farmer's boy,
> We *know* he'll teach us how to "fence—"
> "Old Abe," of Illinois.
> To fence the Union all around
> He'll work—he *will not toy*;
> The cause is earnest and profound,
> For Abe, of Illinois.[5]

Although Republican songwriters were willing to capitalize on various real, exaggerated, and fictional aspects of Lincoln's persona, his stance on abolition was mostly off limits. Slavery is almost entirely ignored in campaign songs—a remarkable omission given the number of abolitionists, most notably the Hutchinsons, involved in publishing and writing this music. When direct references are made, they usually illustrate Lincoln's opposition to the Democratic "slaveocracy" rather than the institution itself. "Lincoln, The Pride of the Nation," for instance, uses the word "slavery" but merely advocates avoiding its influence:

> There are lands where the millions are yearning
> For Freedom from Tyranny's chain;

For ours let our efforts be turning,
To shield her from Slavery's stain.

"Old Abe, The Rail-Splitter," on the other hand, praises Lincoln only for halting "This *spreading* of slavery—work of the devil," and requests

No more soil, which the brave, who are now in the grave,
Shed their blood from the grasp of oppression to save,
Must be turned into "commons" for men of black skin;
So the rails of "Old Abe" will the darkies fence in![6]

Judging by the number of extant copies and repeated publication in various songsters and songbooks, "Lincoln and Liberty" was the most popular of Lincoln's campaign songs. Part of its success may be that it incorporates almost all of the elements of Lincoln's other election songs, including their hesitant relationship with abolition. The middle verses illustrate this best, covering all the states Lincoln had called home, comparing him to King David in slaying the slave power (or Douglas specifically), and referencing his rail-splitting:

We'll go for the son of Kentucky—
The hero of Hoosierdom through;
The pride of the Suckers so lucky—
For Lincoln and Liberty too!

Our David's good sling is unerring,
The Slaveocrat's giant he slew;
Then shout for the Freedom-preferring—
For Lincoln and Liberty too!

They'll find what, by felling and mauling,
Our rail-maker statesman can do;
For the People are everywhere calling
For Lincoln and Liberty too![7]

This attempt to smooth out Lincoln's potentially radical edges became even more evident after he became president. Certainly, his public image evolved during the Civil War and emancipation became a central part of his legacy, but music about him was surprisingly devoid of these details. Furthermore, the idea of Lincoln as a gruff but wise frontiersman also faded. Instead, the period between Lincoln's two elections produced songs that mostly depict him as a traditional noble and wise leader. The most dominant expression of this trend was that of "father Abraham," the nation's paterfamilias. "Good Old Father Abraham," for instance, mobilizes Lincoln's paternal image in its title and chorus (with a split rail and ax on the cover to remind consumers of his 1860 persona). "Little Willie's Grave" plays off the idea of Father Abraham in a different sense, depicting Lincoln mourning the tragic death of his son Willie in 1862:

> Tender mother, glorious father,
> Keeping still our Nation true
> On the Constitution's mountain,
> Here the Nation weeps with you.

However, this trope found its greatest expression in the single most popular song about the president: "We Are Coming, Father Abra'am, 300,000 More." Most of the lyrics describe recruits responding to Lincoln's summer 1862 call for 300,000 volunteers. However, the repetition of the title phrase and popularity of the song made the label "Father Abraham" common cultural currency and probably did more to cement his paternal image than anything else.[8]

"We Are Coming" also highlights another element of wartime Lincoln songs: his association with the troops. In the context of the song, Lincoln is specifically "Father" to the recruits, not the nation as a whole. Soldiers embraced this connection and frequently sang "We Are Coming" and the Union's other major recruitment anthem, "The Battle Cry of Freedom," to Lincoln. As with his election music, this mirrored Lincoln's broader image as a wise, guiding hand, leading his troops to victory with nobility. Soldiers, in turn, built on the image of Lincoln in these recruitment anthems with their own improvised songs about their leader. A former slave recalled watching Union soldiers drill early in the war while singing:

> Lincoln's not satisfied,
> He wants to fight 'gain,
> All he got to do,
> Is hustle up his men.[9]

Emancipation did appear in some Lincoln songs, but its role was complex. The act split Lincoln's musical image and mostly accelerated a growing anti-Lincoln tradition, but there were a notable number of songs praising Lincoln for his proclamation. They arrived in late 1862 and early 1863 with titles such as "Uncle Abram, Bully for You!" ("Ho! the glorious proclamation, sounding grandly o'er the land; / Speaking to a joyful nation of her Jubilee at hand!"). Meanwhile, amateur songwriters crafted tunes for their friends and even Lincoln himself, such as one admirer who sent Lincoln an "Emancipation March" he wrote himself. Julia Ward Howe's "The Battle Hymn of the Republic" became part of this tradition too. Although it does not directly reference Lincoln and was written just over a year before the Emancipation Proclamation went into effect, its emancipationist content and late war popularity gave it a deep connection with Lincoln, especially in the decades following the war.[10]

Minstrelsy, however, became the main musical battlefield for ideas about emancipation—not surprising given the centrality of African Americans to the issue. Although a condescension for African American culture and intelligence was central to the genre, a small group of Civil War songwriters used it to generate sympathy for African Americans and their cause. Henry Clay Work was the most successful such songwriter and promoted emancipation with great success in several tunes. While he did not devote an entire piece to Lincoln himself, the president briefly appears in one of Work's most successful songs, "Kingdom Coming." The song equates Lincoln with the Union army through its "Linkum gumboats" and by depicting the military as an agent of liberty subtly links him with emancipation. Others who copied Work's style addressed Lincoln more directly, mostly by assuming the personae of African Americans eager to fight for the Union and destroy slavery. Chicago publisher H. M. Higgins's knockoff "Year of Jubilee or Kingdom Has Come" by "Sambo" explicitly praises Lincoln for emancipation and makes a pun about his height: "Abraham Lincoln and Emancipation, / De two tallest tings in dis tall nation." Another piece published by Higgins, "The Negro Emancipation Song," echoes Work by referencing "de Leinkum folks" and "de Leinkum sogers." "We'll Fight for Uncle Abe," cowritten by minstrel performer Fred Buckley, completed the cycle by having the minstrel performer take on the persona of an excited and willing African American soldier, especially in the chorus:

Rip, Rap, Flip, Flap,
Strap your knapsacks on your back

> For we're a gwine to Washington
> To fight for Uncle Abe.[11]

African Americans themselves proved eager to musically praise Lincoln for ensuring their freedom. Without access to the music publishing industry, their music is more obscure. However, there are several examples of pro-Lincoln songs by freedpeople, especially from the various Emancipation Day celebrations that occurred around January 1, 1863. Washington, DC, saw one of the largest such celebrations, which featured a large group of participants singing the blessings of those who helped defeat slavery, including these lines:

> And blessed be Abraham Lincoln,
> And the Union army too,
> May the choicest of Earth's blessings,
> Their pathways ever strew!

Later on, participants sang a new version of "Go Down Moses," substituting Lincoln for the eponymous biblical emancipator: "Go down, Abraham, away down in Dixie's land, / Tell Jeff. Davis to let my people go."[12]

Even before emancipation, Union soldiers noted how African Americans recognized Lincoln's potential to help eradicate slavery and began including him in their songs. This trend continued after the proclamation, albeit with a greater sense of familiarity and an accompanying diminishing reverence. The 54th Massachusetts Regiment's marching song, which described the unit bailing out the president, stands as a good example: "But Kentucky swore so hard and Old Abe he had his fears, / Till ev'ry hope was lost but the colored volunteers." Several white soldiers noted African Americans running to the roadside to praise Lincoln as the army made its way to Appomattox ("Bless God, Bless God, for Abram Lincoln's coming") and back to Richmond ("If you get dar befo' I do, / Tell Uncle Abe I's comin' too").[13]

These encouraging songs from minstrels and freedpeople aside, emancipation mostly enflamed the ire of anti-Lincoln northern songwriters. There had been some songs before emancipation—focusing on greenbacks or conscription—but emancipation pushed anti-Lincoln songwriters to new levels of virulence and sarcasm. This music mostly appeared in explicitly political songsters published by Democrats. The Lincoln that emerges in publications such as the *Copperhead Minstrel* (which is so over the top and apparently un-

ashamed of its eponymous moniker that it almost reads like Republican satire) is that of a funhouse mirror—with all the traits praised by Republicans
now inverted or made grotesque. Lincoln is callous, stupid, imperious, and a
race traitor. "Fight for the Nigger" presents a typically vicious, racially tinged
picture:

> Three cheers for honest Abe, he will be a great man yet,
> Tho' he's loaded us with taxes, and burdened us with debt;
> He often tell us little jokes while pocketing our pelf,
> And his last has made the nigger the equal of himself.

Emancipation, the draft, suspending habeas corpus, and adopting paper money
all stand as evidence of Lincoln's desperation due to his incompetent military
leadership. Conscription inspired particular rage inside and outside of the *Copperhead Minstrel*, as in frequent Lincoln critic Septimus Winner's "He's Gone
to the Arms of Abraham":

> The *draft* it was that took him,
> And it was a *heavy blow*,
> It took him for a Conscript,
> But he didn't want to go.[14]

In these Democrat songs, Lincoln cares nothing for the men he throws into
battle. Songwriters frequently depict themselves, or the ghosts of slain soldiers,
reminding Lincoln of the carnage his unjust and unnecessary war has created,
such as in this parody of "We Are Coming, Father Abra'am":

> We are coming, Abraham Lincoln,
> From mountain, wood, and glen;
> We are coming, Abraham Lincoln,
> With the ghosts of murdered men.
>
> Yes! We're coming, Abraham Lincoln,
> With curses loud and deep,
> That will haunt you in your waking,
> And disturb you in your sleep.

The ultimate end point of these criticisms was to compare Lincoln to Satan, or at least portray the two as in league with each other. "Old Abe and Old Nick" has the devil tempt Lincoln into becoming king of an America ruined by race mixing but ultimately punishing him in the afterlife ("Said the devil, make haste, I've no time to waste, / For Old Nick is waiting for you—you—you").[15]

Confederates, of course, wrote anti-Lincoln songs too, although they rarely matched the viciousness of Peace Democrats. Often, Confederate songwriters focused on Lincoln's supposedly incompetent military leadership—crowing over the Union army's repeated defeats in the field. "Where Are You Going, Abe Lincoln?" for instance, has Lincoln riding South on horses named for various commanders in the Eastern Theater, only to fall and return to a concerned Mary Lincoln each time. Given the limited nature of Confederate music publishing, it is no surprise that most of these songs borrow already popular melodies. The revival hymn "Happy Land of Canaan" and the Union anthem "John Brown's Body" (which also took its melody from a revival hymn) emerged as especially popular, if surprising, subjects for Confederate revision. With "Canaan," Confederates probably took comfort from placing criticisms of Lincoln and emancipation in the mouths of fictional slaves—also a reason for "Dixie's" immense popularity. An amateur contrafactum on "Canaan" exemplifies this by having the presumably enslaved singer repeat the common southern argument that slaves were better off than northern workers:

> Old Abe is talking bout de South,
> But he'd better shut his mouth
> Bout de Negroes on Southern plantations.
> They are better off by far
> Than the Northern poor folks are,
> For they always have a steady situation.

With "John Brown," it was surely satisfying co-opting a piece dedicated to the most infamous white abolitionist. Similarly, Confederates must have reveled in replacing Davis with Lincoln hanging from the fourth verse's "sour apple tree."[16]

However, Lincoln occupies a prominent, if anonymous, place in one of the Confederacy's most prominent anthems. "Maryland, My Maryland" does not name him, but its first line contains the only reference to Lincoln in a popular

Confederate song: "The despot's heel is on thy shore." This image of Lincoln as a despotic tyrant, both conquering and suppressing a noble but subjugated Maryland, establishes the tension for the entire piece. With such a limited number of Confederate songs, this brief but prominent reference would have resonated deeply with secessionist listeners and cemented Lincoln's status as a conquering tyrant.[17]

Anti-Lincoln songs ultimately found their most full-throated expression during the election of 1864. The level of hatred for Lincoln expressed by northern Democratic songwriters during the campaign is probably unmatched in the long subculture of anti-Lincoln rhetoric. As in the previous year, one of their main lyrical tactics was to invert Lincoln's positive popular image. Chief among these inversions was a reversal of Republican praise for Lincoln's western, working-class roots. Instead, Democrats portrayed him as an uneducated rube, mocking his fondness for crude jokes and minstrelsy in songs such as this awkward revision of "Yankee Doodle":

> Hurrah for our great President,
> The world never saw a bigger,
> In stature he is six feet three,
> And equal to a nigger,
> To tell a joke or split a rail
> And write a proclamation;
> We guess he is about a mile
> Ahead of all creation.

Even famed songwriter Stephen Foster took his shot in "Little Mac! Little Mac! You're the Very Man," with couplets such as "Democrats, Democrats do it up brown / Lincoln and his Niggerheads wont go down" and "Abraham the Joker soon will DISKIVER / We'll send him on a gun boat up Salt River." Lincoln's arrogance emerges as his most prominent feature, manipulating the war to serve his financial greed, imperial ambitions, and attraction to African Americans. Inevitably, Lincoln declares himself divine, as in "Five Hundred Thousand More," which sarcastically encourages conscripts to worship the president:

> I, gracious Master, semi-God,
> We ask thee to proclaim

To all Confed'rate States abroad
The horrors(!) of thy name.

"Abraham the Nigger King" (set to the tune of the hymn "He Shall Forever Reign") requests the same of freedpeople:

Come, "Darkies," tune your loftiest song,
And raise to "Abe" your joyful strain;
Worship and thanks to him belong,
Who reigns, and shall forever reign.[18]

Republicans published their own songsters and sheet music for 1864, but they took an opposite tactical position. In supporting Lincoln, they eschewed the specificity of Democrat songs or even their own party's from four years earlier. Just as Republicans expanded to rebrand themselves the Union party, so too did Lincoln become a generic leader to broaden his appeal. "Come Rouse Ye, Freemen," from *The Lincoln and Johnson Union Campaign Songster* completely reverses 1860's celebration of Lincoln's Republican loyalty, now equating him with "Washington and Jackson" and promising he "will not yield to party." The paternal image Lincoln developed during the war's first year continued (with Lincoln often appearing as "Father," "Uncle," or just "old") but now appeared alongside lyrics equating him with Union and perseverance. "Abraham, Our Abraham," for instance, challenged the "despot" opening of "Maryland, My Maryland":

To you we look in this dread hour,
Abraham, our Abraham.
Entrusted with a Nation's power,
Abraham, our Abraham,
To end the work so well begun
We'll stand by you till it is done,
Union and *Peace* by *Victory* won,
Abraham, our Abraham.

Republican campaign songwriters rarely mentioned George McClellan, but Democrats received their share of abuse, often referred to as Copperheads who are weak at best and treasonous at worst. "Come Rally, Freemen Rally" uses these labels while praising African American soldiers:

> Come, rally freemen, rally!
> We'll whip the copperheads,
> Hurrah boys! hurrah boys!
> And plant our noble banner
> Where Afrie's sons have bled.

Yet, as in 1860, such references to African Americans, slavery, or emancipation were rare in 1864. Only repeated uses of the melody for "John Brown's Body" introduced an emancipationist subtext.[19]

The pro-Lincoln image that emerged in the songs of 1864 largely matched that which has dominated public memory—a symbol of Union, victory, and occasionally emancipation. However, Lincoln's assassination broadened his image so thoroughly that it became nearly unrecognizable, even as he was increasingly revered. Musical memorials essentially robbed Lincoln of any defining features, casting him as a symbol of sacrifice and nationalism. A massive number of dirges and musical memorials appeared in the months after April 15, 1865, from every publishing house across the Union, and nearly all describe Lincoln in the broadest possible terms. Almost every northern songwriter of note wrote one, with a particularly prolific songwriter, Joseph W. Turner, providing at least four himself: "A Nation Weeps," "Live but One Moment," "Little Tad," and "The Assassin's Vision." Most of these songs have no lyrics, but those that do typically refer to Lincoln only as a leader. If they do highlight a specific aspect of his legacy, it is his restoration of the Union. "The Nation Is Weeping" is typical for simply providing mournful language and reference to victory:

> "Lincoln has fallen! the good and great!"
> Wail of a people in sorrow;
> "Martyr, we crown thee, at heaven's gate!"
> The song of the angels to-morrow.
> *Chorus*
> "Rest, rest, thy labor, done!"
> Dirge of a nation now weeping;
> Home, home, thy bright crown won,
> Fruit of a golden life reaping.

Indeed, Lincoln's appearance becomes his only distinguishing characteristic, as many of these pieces feature his portrait on the cover. With this, Lincoln became not just a symbol for Union but the embodiment of the concept itself. Like George Washington, whose actual personality is often subsumed by his public image as the indomitable father of our country, Lincoln in 1865 was another marble man.[20]

With time, this political deification of Lincoln lost some of its broadness, if not its stature. Popular representations of Lincoln now do not just recognize specific aspects of his personality and legacy; they celebrate them. It appears the Union Party Lincoln of 1864 had the most longevity, with emancipation gradually taking its place permanently alongside his other achievements. That it took emancipation so long to achieve that status is surprising, given its prominent role in the North's most popular songs of 1864 and 1865, especially "Marching through Georgia." Perhaps this is why so few wartime Lincoln songs remain popular today, as they reflect a different generation's perception of the man and his achievements. Regardless, Lincoln's image continues to evolve. That we can find so much of that evolution in songs from just the five most critical years of his life shows just how dynamic that image was in its time and what a critical role music played in shaping it.

Notes

1. All quotations from Federal Writers' Project interviews from Manuscript Division, Library of Congress, *Born in Slavery: Slave Narratives from the Federal Writers' Project, 1936–1938*, available at https://www.loc.gov/collections/slave-narratives-from-the-federal-writers-project-1936-to-1938/about-this-collection/. For the quoted slave song see "Interview with Amanda Oliver," *Oklahoma Narratives*, vol. 13, 231. For other examples, see "Interview with Maria Sutton Clements," *Arkansas Narratives*, vol. 2, part 2, 27; "Interview with Prince Johnson" and "Interview with Susan Snow," *Mississippi Narratives*, vol. 9, 82, 138; "Interview with Lou Griffin," *Missouri Narratives*, vol. 10, 144; and "Interview with George Snow," *South Carolina Narratives*, vol. 14, part 4, 250.

2. D. Wentworth and A Wide Awake, "Honest Old Abe" (Buffalo, NY: Blodgett and Bradford, 1860); D. W. C. Clarke, "Old Abe's Visit to the White House" in *Uncle Abe's Republican Songster* (San Francisco: Towne and Bacon, 1860), 3.

3. "Lincoln," in *Hutchinson's Republican Songster for 1860*, ed. John W. Hutchinson (New York: O Hutchinson, 1860), 65–66; "Shout for Our Prairie King" in *Wide-Awake Vocalist; or, Rail Splitters Song Book* (New York: E. A. Daggett, 1860), 12–13; "Hurrah for Lincoln," in *The Republican Campaign Songster for 1860*, ed. William H. Burleigh (New York: H. Dayton, 1860), 45–46.

4. Uncle Ned, "Then Put Away the Wedges and the Maul" and "The Taller Man Well Skilled," and G. W. B., "High Old Abe Shall Win," in *Wide-Awake Vocalist*, 14–15, 28–29, 41; B. G. W. and A. Cull, "Get Out De Way, You Little Giant," in *Wide Awake Vocalist*, 24–25.

5. For the three cited occurrences of "Abe of Illinois": Burleigh, *Republican Campaign Songster*, 19–20; Hutchinson, *Hutchinson's Republican Songster*, 19–20; *The Lincoln and Hamlin Songster* (Philadelphia: Fisher, 1860), 44.

6. "Lincoln, The Pride of the Nation," in Hutchinson, *Hutchinson's Republican Songster*, 46; Jesse Clement, "Old Abe, The Rail-Splitter," in Burleigh, *Republican Campaign Songster*, 54–55.

7. "Lincoln and Liberty" in Hutchinson, *Hutchinson's Republican Songster*, 71–72. The tune resurfaced in the 1864 election in *The Republican Campaign Songster for 1864* (Cincinnati: J. R. Hawley, 1864), 41.

8. James M. Stewart, "Good Old Father Abraham" (Providence, RI: John R. Cory, 1864); William Ross Wallace and J. R. Thomas, "Little Willie's Grave" (New York: William Hall and Son, 1862). Numerous presses published "We Are Coming Father Abra'am, 300,000 More," and several different songwriters set it to music (it was originally a poem), but the most popular setting was that of Luther O. Emerson. Christian McWhirter, *Battle Hymns: The Power and Popularity of Music in the Civil War* (Chapel Hill: University of North Carolina Press, 2012), 57.

9. George F. Root, "The Battle Cry of Freedom" (Chicago: Root and Cady, 1862); "Interview with Willie Williams," *Born in Slavery, Texas Narratives*, vol. 16, part 4, 172.

10. J. Smith Jr., and G. R. Lampard, "Uncle Abram, Bully for You!" (Chicago: H. M. Higgins, 1862); Abraham Lincoln to George W. Fawcett, January 26, 1863, in *The Collected Works of Abraham Lincoln*, 9 vols., ed. Roy P. Basler et al. (New Brunswick, NJ: Rutgers University Press, 1953–1955), 6:78. For more on the evolution of Howe's "Battle Hymn" during the war and its growing relationship to Lincoln see John Stauffer and Benjamin Soskis, *The Battle Hymn of the Republic: A Biography of the Song that Marches On* (New York: Oxford University Press, 2013), 73–105; McWhirter, *Battle Hymns*, 170–171.

11. Henry Clay Work, "Kingdom Coming" (Chicago: Root and Cady, 1862); Sambo, "The Year of Jubilee or Kingdom Has Come" (Chicago: Root and Cady, 1862); S. Fillmore Bennett and J. P. Webster, "The Negro Emancipation Song," in *The Patriotic Glee Book* (Chicago: H. M. Higgins, 1863), 45; J. K. Campbell and Fred Buckley, "We'll Fight for Uncle Abe" (Boston: Oliver Ditson, 1863).

12. William Wells Brown, *The Negro in the American Rebellion, His Heroism and His Fidelity* (Boston: Lee and Shepard, 1867), 116, 119.

13. Lawrence Van Alstyne, *Diary of an Enlisted Man* (New Haven, CT: Tuttle, Morehouse and Taylor, 1910), 241; Irwin Silber, *Songs of the Civil War* (New York: Dover, 1995), 293–295; entry for April 10, 1865, typescript copy of Civil War diary, 1862–1865, Walter H. Jackson Papers, Bentley Historical Library, University of Michigan; J. W. Muffly, *The Story of Our Regiment: A History of the 148th Pennsylvania Vols.* (Des Moines: Kenyon, 1904).

14. "Fight for the Nigger," in *Copperhead Minstrel* (New York: Feeks and Bancker, 1863), 34–35; Septimus Winner, "He's Gone to the Arms of Abraham" (Boston: Oliver Ditson, 1863).

15. *Copperhead Minstrel*, 13–15, 34–35.

16. "Where Are You Going, Abe Lincoln?" in *Allan's Lone Star Ballads: A Collection of Southern Patriotic Songs Made during Confederate Times*, ed. Francis D. Allan (Galveston, TX: J. D. Sawyer, 1872), 31–32; Ben Gray Lumpkin, "'The Happy Land of Canaan': An Unpublished Civil War Song," in *Civil War History* 11 (1995), 54–57; Katherine Helm, *The True Story of Mary, Wife of Lincoln* (New York: Harper, 1928), 174; William Miller Owen, *In Camp and Battle with the Washington Artillery of New Orleans* (Boston: Ticknor, 1885), 240.

17. James R. Randall, "Maryland, My Maryland" (Baltimore: Miller and Beacham, 1861).

18. "Abe's Doodle," in *The Little Mac Campaign Songster* (New York: T. R. Dawley. 1865), 31–32; Stephen C. Foster, "Little Mac! Little Mac! You're the Very Man" (Philadelphia: J. Marsh, 1864); "Five Hundred Thousand More," in *Democratic Presidential Campaign Songster* (New York: J. F. Feeks, 1864), 29–30; "Abraham the Nigger King," in *Little Mac Campaign Songster*, 22–23.

19. Patrick Casey, "Come Rouse Ye, Freemen," in *The Lincoln and Johnson Union Campaign Songster* (Philadelphia: A. Winch, 1864), 38; W. F. S., "Abraham, Our Abraham" (Albany, NY: W. F. Sherwin, 1864); John Adams and Mrs. Parkhurst, "Come Rally, Freemen Rally" (New York: Horace Waters, 1864).

20. J. W. Turner, "A Nation Weeps" (Boston: Oliver Ditson, 1865); "Live but One Moment" (Boston: Henry Tolman, 1865); "Little Tad" (Boston: Oliver Ditson, 1865); "The Assassin's Vision" (Boston: Henry Tolman, 1865); Louise S. Upham, "The Nation Is Weeping" (New York: Charles Magnus, 1865).

RIPPLING EFFECTS
Political and Military Conflicts

Battles are never isolated events and the rippling effects of Fredericksburg
respected few boundaries.
—**George C. Rable,** *Fredericksburg! Fredericksburg!* **(2002), 3**

George Rable's scholarship has always recognized the fluidity of violence, whether on or off the battlefield. The essays in this section examine the interconnectivity of war to larger social, cultural, and political forces. We see here the inner conflict within both the Union and the Confederacy over questions of law, race, environment, and gender.

Rachel K. Deale's "Acts of War: The Southern Seizure of Federal Forts and Arsenals, 1860–1861" focuses on constitutional debates over resupplying Fort Sumter at the highest level of Federal and Confederate governments. Deale's essay, which takes a well-worn event but offers a fresh perspective, reminds us to pay close attention to the divisions within both the Confederacy and the Union. As both sides grappled with how to wage—and how to respond to—secession, disagreement among Federals and secessionists foreshadowed disunity within their ranks that would only be compounded by the war. A. Wilson Greene's "United States Colored Troops and the Battle of the Crater" illuminates bitter disunity, too, within the Union army, even at levels of high command, as generals and officers debated how much to use—and whether or not to defend—African American soldiers. Greene describes white Federals passively allowing (or actively participating themselves in) the massacre of black troops. Racism prevented whites and blacks from unifying to defeat the same foe, often to the army's detriment.

Clashes within the Union army occurred off of the battlefield as well, particularly in camp and in interactions with southern women. Laura Mammina's "Domesticity in Conflict: Union Soldiers, Southern Women, and Gender Roles during the American Civil War" brings us to the southern home front, where Federal soldiers socialized, sometimes intimately, with white and black women. She notes important ties between the political and the private and the ways in which traditional gender roles were strained but not entirely broken by the conflict. Charity Rakestraw and Kristopher A. Teters's "An Elusive Freedom: Black Women, Labor, and Liberation during the Civil War" moves us beyond Union lines and into refugee camps, where black women took on conventional and not-so-conventional roles as cooks, nurses, and disguised soldiers. These women adapted and adjusted, as they had during enslavement, to survive and claim some autonomy in a world where they were still deemed powerless. Struggles within private domestic spaces and refugee camps were significant; they involved the very nature of freedom and national inclusion.

The natural environment, too, was a factor in affecting and being affected by the war. Lindsay Rae Privette's "Contaminated Water and Dehydration during the Vicksburg Campaign" focuses on Vicksburg, where Union and Confederate armies faced severe water shortages, and Adam H. Petty's "Fires at the Battles of Chancellorsville and the Wilderness" notes the impact forest conflagrations had on the Petersburg Campaign and the soldiers who fought there. Privette and Petty emphasize the misery and horror soldiers experienced, suffering exacerbated by the external conditions of active campaigning. It was not just battles that had "rippling effects"; the war's destructive force shook and disoriented nearly everything it touched.

Acts of War

The Southern Seizure of Federal Forts and Arsenals, 1860–1861

RACHEL K. DEALE

A little over a month after John Brown's execution on December 2, 1859, the House of Representatives engaged in a fierce debate over potential emancipation and jurisdiction over federal property throughout the country. Radical Republican Thaddeus Stevens defended "what [he] considered the principles of the Republican Party." Although the Constitution did not give the Republican Party the "power to interfere with any institution in the States," it did grant Congress "the power to regulate and the right to abolish slavery" in "the Territories, the District of Columbia, the navy-yards, and the arsenals [that] have no legislative bodies but Congress, or those granted by Congress."[1]

Furious over Stevens's bold assertions that Congress had the power to eliminate slavery on public property located in slave states, Virginia congressman Sherrard Clemens asked if the Republican Party's policy "was to encircle the slave States of this Union with free States as a cordon of fire, and that slavery, like a scorpion, would sting itself to death." Without hesitation Stevens retorted, "If I did, it is in the books." Frustrated with the taunts coming from the Republicans in the chamber, Clemens continued to press Stevens on his proposed desire to abolish slavery at federal forts, arsenals, and dockyards. "If his [Stevens's] policy is carried out, whether today, tomorrow, or fifty years hence; if not a single new slave State is admitted into the Union; if slavery is abolished in the District of Columbia, in the Territories, in the arsenals, dockyards, and forts; if, in addition to that, his party grasps the power of the Presidency, with the patronage attached to it, and with the prestige of the Army and Navy calling upon the people of the South to be tried under the laws of the United States for treason," Clemons asked if Stevens sought to destroy slavery from within. With laughter Stevens simply replied, "I do not know, not being a prophet."[2]

Some historians have argued that this debate revealed that the Republican Party's goal was to ensure that slavery was put on the course of ultimate extinction, but this discussion also shows that the South feared that the Republican Party planned to use control of public property to undermine slavery.[3] Even before Stevens suggested that Congress had the authority to abolish slavery on public property, Mississippi representative Otho Singleton argued that the South was "fully awake" and "preparing to meet" the North's desire to abolish "slavery in the District of Columbia; in the dockyards, the arsenals, and all public places."[4] North Carolina senator Thomas Clingman agreed that the Republican Party threatened the South by supporting repeal of the Fugitive Slave Law and the abolition of slavery in "the District of Columbia, the forts and arsenals, and wherever the United States has exclusive jurisdiction."[5] As a result, William Gwin, a Democratic senator from California, argued that the southern states should "take possession of all the public property within their limits, and prepare against any aggression from the non-slaveholding States, or any other power that may choose to infringe upon what they conceive to be their rights." As he saw it, the installations along the southern "harbors [were] so fortified, that if they [took] possession of them in advance, they [could] defend themselves against any enemy who may attack them."[6] Secessionists obviously agreed with Gwin because three months before Abraham Lincoln's inauguration, Deep South officials seized virtually all the federal property in their states.[7]

The Civil War began long before Edmund Ruffin fired his famous shot at Fort Sumter. Before seceding, southern states already committed acts of war by aggressively seizing the federal forts and arsenals within their borders.[8] Yet despite the importance of these events, historians have not properly examined the capture of federal property.[9] While scholars have argued that the Confederacy engaged in a "pre-emptive counterrevolution," they have primarily focused on secession, the creation of the Confederacy, and the failure of political compromise.[10] The South's most dramatic and threatening actions during the secession crisis have received scant attention. As a result, historians have not fully explained how the Confederacy launched their preemptive strike.

In late October 1860, General in Chief of the US Army Winfield Scott warned Secretary of War John B. Floyd that secessionists might try to take pre-emptive military action by capturing federal military property in Mississippi, Alabama, Florida, South Carolina, and Virginia. He feared that southern states could easily seize the federal forts along the Atlantic and Gulf coasts because they were not garrisoned at the recommended strength. Before the secessionists made "any attempt to take any one of them by surprise," Scott advised the War Department to reinforce all military installations immediately.[11]

The southerners in Buchanan's cabinet asserted that adopting General Scott's plan would create more problems for the administration. Floyd expressed deep concerns about reinforcing the forts and added that he could not consent to sending "a military power that would choke [the South] to the ground." Floyd told Buchanan that he could strengthen the forts but warned that "it [would] lead to the effusion of blood."[12] It was clear that Scott intended his "Views" to be public, as he sent a copy not only to the president but also to his political friends and newspaper editors. The *Charleston Courier* reported that the publication of General Scott's call for reinforcements "created the most intense excitement" throughout the city."[13] The *Charleston Mercury* warned that the forts would "be filled with enemies to enforce the authority of a Government as unscrupulous as it is tyrannical."[14] Eventually, Buchanan sided with the southern cabinet members because he worried that reinforcing the forts would lend credence to southern fears. But he later argued that Scott's plan "excited much indignation throughout the South, caused the violent and unsparing abuse of its author throughout the Southern States and afforded the pretext, if not the reason, for their rash and unjustifiable conduct in seizing the forts."[15]

The crisis showed that mid-nineteenth-century politicians did not understand federal authority. On November 6, 1860, the president warned Secretary of War John Floyd that if South Carolina forces captured the forts in Charleston Harbor because "of our neglect to put them in a defensible condition, it [would] be better for you and me both to be thrown into the Potomac with millstones tied about our necks."[16] When Buchanan told his cabinet that he intended to protect the federal property located in the South, some southern cabinet members claimed he had no authority to do so. Unsure of what authority he had to prevent secession and the seizure of public property, Buchanan asked Attorney General Jeremiah Black five questions concerning the legal authority of the executive office. Two of these dealt directly with the issue of the forts and arsenals. First, he inquired, "What right have I to defend the public property (for instance, a fort, arsenal, and navy yard), in case it should be assaulted?" Secondly, he asked, "Can a military force be used for any purpose whatever under the Acts of 1795 and 1807, within the limits of a State where there are no judges, marshal, or other civil officers?"[17]

A few days after receiving the president's questions, Black presented an opinion that helped Buchanan define a policy on secession. Unfortunately, Black's answer left a lot to be desired because he encouraged the president not to adopt any precautionary defensive measures and showed little desire to preserve the

Union. Rather than explicitly defining the legal parameters of presidential power, Black left a lot of room for Buchanan to interpret the law himself. In fact, Black's response suggests that even the attorney general did not understand presidential authority. Black thought that the Militia Act of 1795 "imposes upon the President the sole responsibility of deciding whether the exigency has arisen, which requires the use of military force." Similarly, the Insurrection Act of 1807 gave the president the authority to use land and naval forces "as [he] may judge necessary" to enforce the law in the face of insurrection and rebellion. This meant that the president had the authority to call on the militia as a defensive measure "to repel an assault on the public property." Yet, despite asserting that the president had the authority to protect federal property, Black recommended that Buchanan continue to "execute the laws to the extent of the defensive means placed in [his] hands." Black encouraged Buchanan to act as if southern states still belonged to the Union "until a new order" was "established by either law or force." Additionally, Black maintained that although Congress had the power to declare war against a foreign power, the founders did not grant Congress the authority to declare war against one or more states. As he saw it, "The Union must utterly perish at the moment when Congress shall arm one part of the people against another for any purpose beyond that of merely protecting the General Government in the exercise of its proper constitutional functions."[18]

Despite advising Buchanan not to take action, Black unequivocally argued that the president had the right to protect government property because the government "bought, built, and paid for" the forts and arsenals. Moreover, according to article 1, section 8, of the Constitution, the federal government had the authority to regulate and control the property. "If any one of an owner's rights is plainer than another," Black argued, "it is that of keeping exclusive possession and repelling intrusion." As Black saw it, "The right of defending the public property includes also the right of recapture after it has been unlawfully taken by another" as seen by the fact that "every one acknowledged the legal justice" of the government's response to John Brown's raid at Harpers Ferry.[19] But suggesting that John Brown's raid set a precedent for executive power protecting public property is problematic. Although Brown could have been prosecuted by the federal government, the Buchanan administration placated southern fears by allowing Virginia to try Brown. Even though Brown seized a federal arsenal, he was found guilty of treason against the commonwealth of Virginia, not the United States.[20] If anything, Buchanan's handling of the Harpers Ferry

fiasco established the precedent of placating the South to prevent potential violence and not using federal power to protect public property.

Armed with Black's legal guidance, Buchanan began writing his fourth annual message and interpreted the entire situation as a northern problem rather
than a national or southern problem. The president observed that the Union
was not "a mere voluntary association of States" that could be dissolved at any
instant. In his view, the founders "never intended to implant in its bosoms the
seeds of its own destruction" through dissolution. He pleaded for the South to
"wait for the overt act," by maintaining that Lincoln's election in itself did not
justify radical action. Yet, after firmly denying a constitutional right to secede,
Buchanan tempered his statement by announcing that he had no power to
prevent a state from leaving the Union. Nor did he believe that Congress possessed the power to "coerce a State into submission." Buchanan believed that
Congress could only preserve the Union through conciliation because the Constitution did not grant them the power "to preserve it by force." Just minutes
after declaring that he stood for the Union and the Constitution, the president
conceded that the Union "must one day perish."[21]

President Buchanan clearly interpreted the crisis through a partisan lens.
If war occurred, it would be a Republican war, not a Democratic war. Consequently, navigating the crisis would be the Republican Party's responsibility.
It was merely his job to hand over the Union intact to the incoming Lincoln
administration. Those closest to Buchanan thought that no matter what course
of action he pursued, the administration would face "bitter hostility."[22] Americans, especially in the North, were losing confidence in the administration.
On December 12, Secretary of State Lewis Cass resigned because the president
refused to reinforce the southern forts.[23] Ohio governor William Dennison
maintained that "the sacredness of private and public property is the life of republican forms of government, and one of the very highest duties of the legislator, is to surround it with all the necessary safe-guards of law."[24] The *New-York
Tribune* complained that "the President's Message insults reason, outrages humanity, falsifies history, and defies common sense."[25] A Connecticut editor proclaimed that "Mr. Buchanan [showed] weakness, imbecility and inconsistency
which proves him utterly unfit for the emergencies of the times, and that he
has no better remedy for preventing a dissolution of the Union, than a concession of all and everything asked by the disunionists." The paper ridiculed Buchanan's claim that the federal government had no power to enforce laws in the
states.[26] A friend of Illinois congressman John A. Logan suggested that if the

federal government had "no power to coerce a rebellious state to obedience to the law," then the founders "must have been fools."[27] Others simply questioned the federal government's purpose "if it had no resources in an emergency."[28]

Meanwhile President-elect Lincoln chose not to address southern concerns publicly. He did, however, respond to North Carolina congressman John Gilmer's fear that Lincoln supported congressional measures to eliminate slavery in the District of Columbia and on federal property in the slave states.[29] Although Lincoln was "greatly disinclined" to "even privately" respond to Gilmer's questions, he thought it necessary because he feared Gilmer would misinterpret his silence. He promised Gilmer that he had "no thought of recommending the abolition of slavery in the District of Columbia, nor the slave trade among the slave states . . . and if I were to make such recommendation, it is quite clear Congress would not follow it." Furthermore, he claimed that "freeing slaves in Arsenals and Dockyards" was "a thing I never thought of in my life."[30] Several days later, Lincoln wrote a similar letter to Alexander Stephens asking if "the people of the South really entertain fears that a Republican administration would, *directly*, or *indirectly*, interfere with their slaves, or with them, about their slaves?" Lincoln assured the Georgian that "there is no cause for such fears."[31]

Unlike Buchanan, Lincoln made it clear to those closest to him that he believed the president had the authority to maintain order in the states. Though he remained silent publicly, he confidently asserted that no state had the right to secede from the Union and that "it is the duty of the President, and other government functionaries to run the machine as it is."[32] As a result, Lincoln requested that his friend Elihu Washburne instruct General Winfield Scott "to be as prepared as he can to either *hold*, or *retake*, the forts, as the case may require, at, and after the inauguration."[33] When Lincoln heard rumors in late December that Buchanan had ordered Anderson to surrender Fort Moultrie if it was attacked, he angrily snapped, "If that is true they ought to hang him!"[34]

But during the interregnum the government's authority still rested in the weak hands of James Buchanan, and the events of late December and early January came too fast for the timid and indecisive Buchanan administration. On December 20, South Carolina became the first state to secede from the Union. Excitement and celebration filled the streets of Charleston. Shortly after seceding, the South Carolina secession convention appointed three commissioners to discuss with President Buchanan the "delivery" of the forts, arsenals, magazines, and other federal installations within the state's borders.[35] Negotiations were cut short, however, because on December 26, Major Robert Anderson felt that his position at Fort Moultrie on Sullivan's Island was vulnerable. As a result, Anderson decided to spike his guns and move to Fort Sumter, an unfinished fort in the middle of the Charleston Harbor. In retaliation, Governor Francis Pickens ordered the state militia to seize Fort Moultrie, Fort Johnson, Castle Pickney, the US arsenal, and the US Custom House under the "authority of the sovereign state of South Carolina."[36] In a letter to the president of the South Carolina secession convention, David Flavel Jamison, Governor Pickens declared that Major Anderson's move to Fort Sumter "brought on a state of war." He believed it was in the state's best interest to occupy, hold, and maintain all remaining federal property.[37]

To an extent Pickens was right. The seizure of federal property was clearly an act of war, but Anderson and the United States were not the guilty party. As Jeremiah Black had told Buchanan in late November, according to the Constitution the federal property scattered throughout the South belonged to the federal government, not the states. But Buchanan continued to stand by his claim that even though South Carolina did not have the right to secede, neither he nor Congress had the power to stop them. While the Buchanan administration stalled, by January 2, 1861, South Carolina forces facing no federal opposition successfully captured all the federal installations within its borders except Fort Sumter.

Although South Carolina only seized federal property after formally seceding, most Deep South states took action before their secession conventions even met. Throughout January 1861, government facilities in Alabama, Louisiana, Georgia, and Florida fell into the hands of state militias on an almost daily basis. After hearing a rumor that Buchanan intended to appoint Joseph Holt, a "bitter foe" of the South, as the next secretary of war, state political and military leaders feared that the president intended to reinforce the southern forts. On January 1, 1861, Georgia governor Joseph E. Brown met in Savannah with Colonel William J. Hardee and Colonel Alexander Lawton "to discuss the seizure of Fort Pulaski."[38] Located on Cockspur Island near the mouth of the Savannah River, the fort guarded Savannah, the state's most important commercial city. Although the fort was designed to protect the city from foreign attack, in January 1861 Secretary of War John Floyd had "scattered the army so that much of it could be capture[d] when hostilities" commenced.[39] At the time, there were only two federal soldiers stationed at Fort Pulaski. Confident that Georgia would secede, Brown wanted to take the fort before the federal government had time to send reinforcements that might prevent the state from holding a secession convention.

Rachel K. Deale

On January 2, 1861, more than two weeks before the state seceded from the Union, Governor Brown ordered Colonel Alexander Lawton to seize Fort Pulaski. Brown justified his decision by arguing that the federal government had "decided on the policy of coercing a seceded state back into the Union, and it is believed now has a movement on foot to occupy with Federal Troops, the Southern Forts, including Fort Pulaski." The next morning over one hundred armed Georgians demanded the fort's surrender.[40] Neither of the two US soldiers stationed there had received orders on how to respond, but seeing that they were vastly outnumbered, the two men agreed to surrender the fort.[41] Georgia troops immediately went to work strengthening the fort's defenses.[42] As one Georgia soldier told the *Savannah Republican*, "There is the best feeling imaginable between all the corps here, and a brotherly sympathy which is gratifying."[43]

In Georgia support for Brown's decision was overwhelming. The *Federal Union* proclaimed that Brown acted out "of peace and a desire to save bloodshed in case hostilities actually begin." As the paper saw it, "For his promptness and energy in this crisis, Gov. Brown deserved the gratitude of every citizen of Georgia."[44] When Brown returned to Milledgeville, he was greeted by "a large number of citizens with music and torches. The Alabama *Spirit of the South* lauded Brown, who "executes his plans with the nerve of a soldier and the skill of a statesman. He defies the threats of Federal power, and laughs his enemies to scorn. He is full of Jacksonian will and courage; possessing wisdom to devise and boldness and sagacity to execute." The *Augusta Democrat* maintained that Brown "exhibited an intelligence, firmness and comprehensive statesmanship, equaled by few and surpassed by none in the annals of the state."[45] When the state's secession convention met two weeks later, they celebrated the governor's "energetic and patriotic conduct" and promised to hold onto "Fort Pulaski, and all other Federal property within her borders."[46]

The reaction to Georgia's takeover indicates that secessionists did not believe that the federal government actually owned the federal installations. Many thought that the southern states had ceded the fortifications built on southern soil to the federal government for protection from foreign enemies, but now they believed that the government planned to use the fortifications "against her own people in an effort to subjugate them." As a result, they thought it was necessary to reclaim what they considered their property.[47] The *Albany Patriot* claimed that "there [was] no division of opinion in our community as to the wisdom of his policy." "Nothing [could] be more abhorrent to the hearts of our people, nothing more shocking to their sense of justice," the paper proclaimed, than for the federal government to turn fortifications built on Georgia soil "into instruments of police coercion."[48] The *Fayetteville Observer* suggested that Governor Brown had to order the seizure of the fort, or a mob would have taken matters into their own hands.[49]

Once South Carolina and Georgia officials seized the forts and arsenals in their states, they justified their actions by claiming the property belonged to the state and not the federal government. The Milledgeville *Federal Union* believed that handling federal property within the seceded states was "the most dangerous problem" of secession.[50] Following the capture of Fort Pulaski, one Georgia soldier proclaimed that "there [were] many opinions amongst the privates as to the propriety of the step we have taken in obtaining this fort."[51] The Georgia secession convention, however, made clear its belief that the state was the true owner of the public property. Before signing an ordinance of secession, the delegates declared that "the buildings, machinery, fortifications, or other improvements, erected on the land so heretofore ceded to the said United States, or other property found therein, shall be held by this State."[52] Jefferson Davis argued later that even though southern states ceded land to the federal government for military installations, "the ultimate ownership of the soil ... remains with the people of the State in which it lies, by virtue of their sovereignty." According to Davis, the forts "should be used solely and exclusively for the purposes for which they were granted" or the state could reclaim the property.[53]

Believing that the federal military installations really belonged to the state, Governor Brown also advised the governors of Alabama, Louisiana, and Florida to take preemptive action. Citing rumors of potential federal occupation, on January 5, Brown encouraged the Deep South governors to "cooperate and occupy the Forts." According to Brown, capturing the federal installations was the only way the states could ensure the federal government would not interfere with their secession conventions.[54] The governors readily agreed with Brown and almost immediately ordered the capture of the federal installations in their states.

On January 3, the same day that Georgia seized Fort Pulaski and eight days before Alabama seceded, Alabama Governor Andrew B. Moore ordered Colonel John Todd of the 1st Volunteer Regiment to occupy Forts Morgan and Gaines and "to take possession of the U.S. arsenal immediately and to hold them for the State of Alabama" until the state convention dictated otherwise. Moore repeatedly maintained that this was not an act of hostility toward the federal government and that "both the forts and the arsenal" should be taken "without bloodshed."[55] The next day four companies of Alabama volunteers took over the Mount Vernon arsenal in Mobile. As in South Carolina and Georgia, Federal troops did not resist the demand for surrender. Jesse L. Reno, commander of Federal troops stationed at Mount Vernon, reported the affair as an "unexpected catastrophe" because the Alabama volunteers caught him and his seventeen men completely off guard. Reno decided that there was no way eighteen men could have prevented the hundred plus Alabamans from seizing the arsenal.[56] The *New York Herald* reported that the arsenal was "probably the strongest and best built arsenal" in the United States as it sat almost five hundred feet "above the rest of the country." Additionally, the paper warned that the Mount Vernon Arsenal housed enough arms and ammunition to equip Alabama, Mississippi, Louisiana, and Florida troops.[57] That might have been an exaggeration, as the arsenal contained only 150,000 pounds of gunpowder and enough weapons to arm roughly 20,000 men.[58]

On January 5, Todd's forces of roughly five hundred men seized Fort Morgan and the unfinished Fort Gaines located at the mouth of Mobile Bay. The *Mobile Tribune* referred to the event as an "exciting little dash at Dauphin Island."[59] Together the two forts housed roughly 220 guns.[60] As with the previous takeovers, instead of resisting, US Lieutenant Chauncey Barnes Reese complied with the secessionists' demands. Upon learning of the capture of the two forts, the city of Montgomery celebrated with a one-hundred-gun salute. State troops paraded throughout the city with drum and fife.[61] Abraham Lincoln's private secretary John Nicolay later described the process well: "The ordinary process [of seizing property] was, the sudden appearance of a superior armed force, a demand for surrender in the name of the State, and the compliance under protest by the officer in charge—salutes to the flag, peaceable evacuation, and unmolested transit home being graciously permitted as a military courtesy."[62]

As Alabama troops seized federal property, on January 4 Governor Moore informed President Buchanan why he ordered the state militia to capture the forts and arsenals. Moore assured the president that "the purpose with which my order was given and had been executed was to avoid and not to provoke hostilities between the State and Federal government." Believing that Alabama was about to secede, Moore contended that seizing federal military installations was a "precautionary step to make the secession of the State peaceful, and prevent detriment to her people." Because he feared that the federal government would attempt to reinforce southern forts and arsenals, Moore argued that it would have been an "unwise policy" not to act. He therefore had acted in "self-defense." He assured Buchanan that if Alabama voted not to secede, he would peacefully return all forts, arsenals, and ammunition.[63]

On January 5, eighteen days before Louisiana's secession convention even assembled, General Elisha L. Tracy met with militia captains to discuss the seizure of the five federal forts and an arsenal located in the state.[64] Governor Thomas Moore maintained that "the safety of the state of Louisiana demands that I take possession of all Government property within her limits."[65] Although the Buchanan administration had yet to take any action to stop the seizures or recapture federal property, Moore believed that Congress's "hostile language" and the "tyrannical purposes" of the incoming administration were enough to merit preemptive action.[66] But Moore had been planning military action for well over a month. On December 12, 1860, the governor had established a military board designed to protect the state from federal coercion by raising a five-thousand-man army. One of the first people appointed to the board was Colonel Braxton Bragg, who still held a commission in the US Army. Despite being opposed to secession, Bragg agreed to serve his state, though before Bragg could raise any forces or resign his commission with the US Army, Governor Moore decided that the state needed to act.[67]

After receiving his orders to take the federal arsenal in Baton Rouge, Bragg told his wife, Elise, that he had reservations about Moore's decision to seize the property but admitted that he thought it was the "only course [Moore] could adopt to avoid bloodshed."[68] Despite his fears, on January 7, Bragg led six hundred men to take control of the arsenal and barracks at Baton Rouge. Under a flag of truce, Moore's aides-de-camp Richard Taylor and Braxton Bragg warned the Federal captain Joseph A. Haskin that "any attempt at defense on your part will be a rash sacrifice of life." Vastly outnumbered and not expecting reinforcements or additional support, Haskin surrendered.[69] Following this success, Bragg boasted that he had handled the negotiations with "prudence and conciliation" and exulted that Federal "officers left perfectly satisfied."[70]

The seizure of the Baton Rouge arsenal greatly strengthened the nascent Confederacy's military capability at the beginning of the Civil War. Before the capture, Louisiana had experienced a shortage in arms and ammunition. Seizing the arsenal provided the state over four thousand rifles, almost thirty thousand percussion muskets, and over eight thousand flintlock muskets. Governor Moore gave Mississippi enough weapons to arm its newly formed volunteer army. Yet capturing the Baton Rouge arsenal was only a temporary solution to the weapons shortage because the arsenal did not contain the machinery needed to produce more arms and ordnance.[71] Well-armed and with superior numbers, the Louisiana militia proceeded to seize Forts Jackson, St. Philip, Livingston, Pike, and Macomb without bloodshed.

Not everyone, however, celebrated Moore's decision. General William Tecumseh Sherman, who had recently retired from the military and taught at the Louisiana Seminary of Learning and Military Academy, later pointed out that "long before the North, or the Federal Government, dreamed of war the South seized the U.S. arsenals, forts, mints, and custom-houses."[72] He concluded that "war existed against the General Govt. from the date of the first seizure of property—I did resent it as an act of hostility and Treason." After watching what he thought to be acts of war, Sherman headed to Washington to help suppress the South's treasonous actions, but Buchanan told him that "military men were not needed."[73] In a letter to Robert Anderson's brother in 1863, Sherman recalled the circumstances in more detail:

> War existed before Sumter was fired on. The seizure of our Forts and arsenals by armed bodies led by Governors and Commissioned officers preceded the attack on Sumter. It was the seizure of the Forts and mails of Louisiana, more especially the arsenal at Baton Rouge with its small Garrison by a force of vols. led by Governor Moore and Col. (now Genl.) Bragg, then my most intimate friends, that made me declare it *"high Treason,"* and I quit the state, before as in your case malignant men had wrought up public feeling to a maddened State.[74]

Unionists and northerners were appalled by the South's capture of federal military installations. The pro-Lincoln *Daily Palladium* argued that the South struck the first blow by "seizing the property of the Union, garrison[ing] its forts against the officers of law, tak[ing] possession of its revenue-cutters, rifl[ing] its arsenals to arm their forces against its authority." "This is not secession; it is not dissolution; *it is rebellion and aggressive war!*" the paper boldly argued. According to the editors, the Gulf states' "deliberate purpose to seize the Government by force is at last unmasked, and they have swept the cotton states into open, armed, aggressive rebellion."[75] On January 12, a concerned Ohio citizen asked Congressman John Sherman, "Is it not the duty, and the true policy of its government to arm and keep all the forts, arsenals, and government property? Possess it and then wait arm and defend it until wiser council shall give forth the opinion of the South and cooler councilors shall be heard."[76] Another Ohioan believed that the "insecurity of government property at Washington . . . is a serious affair and should be forthwith guarded against . . . any possible degree of danger." He warned Congressman John Sherman that "if the federal property [fell] into the Rebel's hands it will double their numbers in 24 hours."[77]

Northerners also argued that the South had committed acts of war and treason by capturing federal military installations. Douglas Democrat and Illinois senator John A. Logan argued that "the recognition of the South as an independent sovereignty, the forts, the arsenals, all government property" will "embroil the sections in a war."[78] The Fifth Ward Republican Association argued that "the inhabitants of Louisiana are now in a state of insurrection" and have committed "treason to their country."[79] On January 14, US Circuit Court Judge Smalley termed the secessionists' aggressive seizure of forts, arsenals, and barracks "high treason by levying war. . . . There can be no doubt about it."[80] According to Smalley, "It is well known that war—civil war—exists in person of the Union." Judge Smalley repeatedly maintained that "the actual seizing of the Forts in Carolina, and in other States, is a levying of war against the United States."[81] Abraham Lincoln's private secretary John Nicolay also agreed that the South's actions were "nothing less than levying actual war against the United States, though as yet attended by no violence or bloodshed."[82]

Because the federal government did nothing to stop the southern militias, by February 1, South Carolina, Georgia, Alabama, Louisiana, and Florida had seized all of the federal installations within their borders except Fort Sumter in Charleston and Forts Pickens, Jefferson, and Taylor in Florida. As Lincoln traveled to Washington in February 1861, he stopped to speak from the balcony of Bates House in Indianapolis, Indiana. In exploring the meaning of "coercion" and "invasion," Lincoln argued that "the marching of an army into South Carolina . . . without the consent of her people, and in hostility against them" would constitute both coercion and invasion if Federal forces forced South Carolinians to submit to federal authority. He then asked the audience what if the government "simply insists upon holding its own forts, or retaking those forts which belong to it, or the enforcement of the laws of the United States in the collection of duties upon foreign importations, or even the withdrawal of the mails from those portions of the country where the mails themselves are habitually violated; would any or all of these things be coercion?" According to Lincoln, anyone who believed that reclaiming federal property to preserve the Union was coercion must be "of a thin and airy character." Comparing the

Union to a family, Lincoln suggested that Americans who did not wish to maintain a federal presence in the seceded states was similar to preferring a "free-love arrangement" to marriage.[83]

The *New-York Tribune*, however, cited Lincoln's Indianapolis speech as evidence of his intention to embrace coercion. The *New York Herald* warned that Lincoln's speech "was the signal for massacre and bloodshed by the incoming administration."[84] Similarly, a Washington correspondent for the *Tribune* reported that Lincoln was claiming "the right to use force against the seceding States to the extent of recovering United States property, collecting the revenues, and enforcing the laws generally."[85] These responses to Lincoln's Indianapolis address probably encouraged him to tone down his language as he made his way to Washington. Speaking to the New Jersey General Assembly in Trenton, Lincoln sounded more cautious, claiming to harbor "no malice toward any section." He would do all within his power to "promote a peaceful settlement of all our difficulties" but nevertheless thought "it may be necessary to put the foot down firmly ... and if I do my duty, and do right, you will sustain me will you not?"[86]

Lincoln fully understood what the seizure of federal property meant for the Union; that is why he was so adamant about maintaining possession of the property. He recognized that surrendering the property meant accepting disunion and possibly war. In the initial draft of his first inaugural address Lincoln directly discussed the seizure of property. He wanted to assure people that "there will be no invasion of any State" but promised to use his presidential authority to "reclaim the public property and places which have fallen" that belong to the federal government.[87] Unlike Buchanan, Lincoln believed the president had the power to maintain the Union and wanted to make his policy on secession clear.[88]

Nevertheless, those closest to Lincoln did have to encourage him to temper his strong stance against southern secession.[89] This is not to suggest that Lincoln did not understand southern attitudes toward federal authority but that Lincoln was not afraid to stand firm against southern aggression. After reading a draft of Lincoln's address, Orville Browning told him that "the declaration of the purpose of reclamation [of federal properties], [would] be construed into a threat, or menace, and [would] irritate even ... the border states." While Browning agreed that the property must be reclaimed, he asked, "Cannot that be accomplished as well, or even better without announcing the purpose in your inaugural?"[90] William Seward agreed and suggested some changes to "soothe the public mind." Most notably, Seward wanted Lincoln to replace the word "treasonable" with "revolutionary."[91]

Some of Seward's suggested edits, however, changed the meaning behind what Lincoln wanted to say. Originally Lincoln wrote, "A disruption of the Federal Union is menaced, and, so far as can be on paper, is already effected." Seward, however, encouraged Lincoln to say, "A disruption of the Federal Union heretofore only menaced is now formidably attempted."[92] Lincoln was trying to make the argument that the South was already in open rebellion. In other words, Lincoln was arguing that the war had already started. Seward's phrasing, on the other hand, sought to soften this point. In the end, Lincoln decided it was best to placate the South, but he did say that he intended to "hold, occupy, and possess the property, and places belonging to the government."[93]

Once Lincoln assumed office, northerners continued to comment on southern acts of war. Northern Democratic papers such as the *Pittsburgh Post* argued that the "forts were built to protect the States where located against foreign aggression, not to be used against the people of the States themselves. . . . There is no humiliation in the abandonment. The reason of it will be fully appreciated by the nation and by the world. It will be regarded as a willingly offered, a voluntary peace measure, magnanimously adopted to save the Union."[94] But other northerners had had their fill of secessionist aggression. On March 28, President Lincoln received a letter that begged, "In the name of reason and consistency don't subject our country to another burning disgrace and shame in the shape of evacuating any of the Forts and defenses without an effort to save them from that lawless rattlesnake crew that are not only wrenching State after State from our Union but are cutting up States and establishing Capitals to suit their own purposes and designs."[95]

If southerners really thought that seizing public property would prevent potential conflict, they were sorely mistaken. As state and local authorities seized federal installations, northerners concluded that the South had committed acts of war. In Lincoln's call for seventy-five thousand militia volunteers after the Confederate firing on Fort Sumter he asserted that their first assignment would "be to repossess the forts, places, and property which have been seized from the Union."[96] The *New York Herald* insisted that an "appeal to arms" was necessary to regain control of federal "customs houses, forts, arsenals, navy yards, mints, marine hospitals, courts of justice, post offices and post roads." As the *Herald* saw it, all public property needed to be returned and "the utmost penalties due to treason" imposed upon the seceding states.[97] According to northerners, the Civil War began with the seizure of federal property.

Notes

1. *Congressional Globe*, 36th Cong., 1st Sess., 586.

2. Ibid.

3. James Oakes uses this same passage to argue that the Republican Party intended to abolish slavery before the Civil War began. Oakes, *The Scorpion's Sting: Antislavery and the Coming of the Civil War* (New York: W. W. Norton, 2014).

4. *Daily Mississippian* (Jackson), January 18, 1860.

5. *Daily Globe*, January 17, 1860, quoted in *New York Herald*, January 28, 1860.

6. Speech delivered on December 12, 1859, published in *Sacramento Daily Union*, January 12, 1860.

7. This challenges William Freehling's assertion that the seizure of federal property had nothing to do with slavery. See Freehling, *The Road to Disunion*, vol. 2, *Secessionist Triumphant, 1854–1861* (New York: Oxford University Press, 2008).

8. Silvana Siddali persuasively argues that many northerners focused their discussions on the seizure of property rather than political rhetoric and the Confederate capture of federal property brought "unexpectedly painful questions before the northern public." This implies that northerners had more concrete reasons to fight than James McPherson suggests. Siddali, *From Property to Person: Slavery and the Confiscation Acts, 1861–1862* (Baton Rouge: Louisiana State University Press, 2005), 49. See also James McPherson, *For Cause and Comrades: Why Men Fought in the Civil War* (New York: Oxford University Press, 1998); and Rachel K. Deale, "Acts of War: The Southern Seizure of Federal Property, 1860–1861" (PhD diss., University of Alabama, 2017).

9. Almost every book on the coming of the Civil War or early war mentions the seizure of federal property, but no full-length study exists on the topic. Kenneth Stampp's *And the War Came* spends little time examining the northern reactions to the South's aggressive captures outside of Charleston, South Carolina. Edwin Bearss examines the capture of federal forts, arsenals, and barracks in Louisiana, but his work provides no explanation of why Louisiana Governor Thomas Overton Moore ordered the state militia to seize the property or what the seizure meant for the coming of the Civil War. James McPherson's *Battle Cry of Freedom* briefly discusses that the South captured federal forts, but he does not explain who was responsible for the seizures, how they captured the forts, or why they decided to take the property. He also does not examine the North's response to the seizures. More recent works on the secession crisis, such as Russell McClintock's *Lincoln and the Decision for War* and William J. Cooper's *We Have the War upon Us* focus primarily on efforts of political compromise. See Stampp, *And the War Came: The North and the Secession Crisis, 1860–1861* (Baton Rouge: Louisiana State University Press, 1950); Edwin C. Bearss, "The Seizure of the Forts and Public Property in Louisiana," *Louisiana History* 2 (Autumn 1961): 401–409; James McPherson, *Battle Cry of Freedom: The Civil War Era* (New York: Oxford University Press, 1988); Russell McClintock, *Lincoln and the Decision for War: The Northern Response to Secession* (Chapel Hill:

University of North Carolina Press, 2008); William J. Cooper, *We Have the War upon Us: The Onset of the Civil War, November 1860–April 1861* (New York: Alfred A. Knopf, 2012).

10. This argument supports James McPherson's *Battle Cry of Freedom* and Arno Mayer's *The Dynamics of Counterrevolution in Europe*. According to Mayer, a "pre-emptive counterrevolution" occurs when a group is so fearful of a revolutionary movement that they "intentionally exaggerate the magnitude and imminence of the revolutionary threat" and rather than waiting for the revolutionary force to take power, they attack before the revolutionaries have time to defend themselves. See McPherson, *Battle Cry of Freedom*, 245; Mayer, *The Dynamics of Counterrevolution in Europe, 1870–1956: An Analytic Framework* (New York: Harper and Row, 1971), 86.

11. Winfield Scott, "Views," October 29, 1860, John J. Crittenden Papers, Manuscript Division, Library of Congress, Washington, DC.

12. *Southern Recorder* (Milledgeville, GA), January 22, 1861.

13. *Charleston Courier*, January 10, 1861.

14. *Charleston Mercury*, January 1, 1861.

15. James Buchanan to Edwin Stanton, April 8, 1861, in Philip Gerald Auchampaugh, *James Buchanan and His Cabinet on the Eve of Secession* (Duluth: privately printed, 1926), 63–64.

16. Horatio King, *Turning on the Light: A Dispassionate Survey of President Buchanan's Administration from 1860 to Its Close*, (Philadelphia: J. B. Lippincott, 1895), 120; interview with Judge Jeremiah Black published in *Chicago Daily Tribune*, August 7, 1881, quoted in Philip Shriver Klein, *President James Buchanan: A Biography* (University Park: Pennsylvania State University Press, 1962), 359; Roy F. Nichols, *Disruption of Democracy* (New York: Macmillan, 1948), 381.

17. James Buchanan to Jeremiah Black, November 17, 1860, James Buchanan Papers, Historical Society of Pennsylvania, Philadelphia, Pennsylvania.

18. Attorney General Jeremiah Black, "Power of the President in Executing the Laws," November 20, 1860, in *A Documentary History of the American Civil War Era*, ed. Thomas C. Mackey (Knoxville: University of Tennessee Press, 2013), 2:204–206.

19. Mackey, *A Documentary History*, 2:204.

20. William A. Blair, *With Malice toward Some: Treason and Loyalty in the Civil War Era* (Chapel Hill: University of North Carolina Press, 2014), 13.

21. James Buchanan, Fourth Annual Message, December 3, 1860, in *The Works of James Buchanan: Comprising His Speeches, State Papers, and Private Correspondence*, ed. John Bassett Moore (New York: Antiquarian, 1960), 11:7–40.

22. Jeremiah Black's Historic Notes no. 1, Jeremiah Black Papers, Library of Congress Manuscript Division, Washington, DC.

23. Edward McPherson, *Political History of the United States of America, during the Great Rebellion* (Washington, DC: Philip and Solomons, 1865), 28.

24. *Daily Cleveland Herald*, January 9, 1860.

25. *New-York Tribune*, December 5, 1860.

26. *Morning Journal and Courier* (New Haven, CT), December 6, 1860, in Howard Cecil Perkins, *Northern Editorials on Secession* (New York: D. Appleton-Century, 1942), 1:136.

27. J. H. Wilson to John Logan, January 9, 1861, Logan Family Papers, Library of Congress Manuscript Division, Washington, DC.

28. *Buffalo Daily Courier*, December 6, 1860, in Perkins, *Northern Editorials on Secession*, 1:139.

29. John A Gilmer to Abraham Lincoln, December 10, 1860, Abraham Lincoln Papers, Library of Congress Manuscript Division, Washington, DC.

30. Abraham Lincoln to John Gilmer, December 15, 1860, in *The Collected Works of Abraham Lincoln*, 9 vols., ed. Roy P. Basler et al., (New Brunswick, NJ: Rutgers University Press, 1953), 151–153.

31. Abraham Lincoln to Alexander Stephens, December 22, 1860, in *Collected Works of Abraham Lincoln*, 4:160.

32. Abraham Lincoln to Thurlow Weed, December 17, 1860, in *Collected Works of Abraham Lincoln*, 4:154.

33. Abraham Lincoln to Elihu B. Washburne, December 21, 1860, in *Collected Works of Abraham Lincoln*, 4:159.

34. Memorandum, Springfield, Illinois, December 22, 1860, John G. Nicolay Papers, Library of Congress Manuscript Division, Washington, DC.

35. McPherson, *Political History of the United States*, 29.

36. *The War of the Rebellion: A Compilation of the Official Records of the Union and Confederate Armies*, 127 vols. (Washington, DC: Government Printing Office, 1880–1901), ser.1, vol. 1, 112 (hereafter cited as *OR*). For more information about the seizure of federal property in South Carolina see Deale, "Acts of War."

37. *OR*, ser. 1, vol. 1, 252.

38. *Savannah Republican*, December 31, 1860; *OR*, ser. 1, vol. 53, 112–113; *Albany (GA) Patriot*, January 3, 1861.

39. Ulysses Simpson Grant, *Personal Memoirs of U. S. Grant* (New York: Century, 1903), 1:181.

40. At the time, Governor Brown believed that Buchanan had issued an order to reinforce all southern forts. This order was issued the last week of November but was almost immediately rescinded. See *New York Times*, January 18, 1861; Auchampaugh, *James Buchanan and His Cabinet*, 150; Joseph Brown, Executive Minutebook, January 2, 1861, Georgia Archives, Morrow, Georgia; *OR*, ser. 1, vol. 1, 318, 319; Allen D. Candler, *The Confederate Records of the State of Georgia: Compiled and Published under Authority of the Legislature* (Atlanta: Charles P. Byrd, 1910), 2:9–19. See also Freehling, *The Road to Disunion*, 2:482–483; Joseph Howard Parks, *Joseph E. Brown of Georgia* (Baton Rouge: Louisiana State University Press, 1999), 124–126.

41. *OR*, ser. 1, vol. 1, 319.

42. *Southern Watchman* (Athens, GA), January 9, 1861.

43. *Savannah Republican*, January 5, 1861, quoted in *New York Herald*, January 12, 1861.

44. *Federal Union* (Milledgeville, GA), January 8, 1861.

45. Papers quoted from I. W. Avery, *The History of the State of Georgia from 1850 to 1881, Embracing the Three Important Epochs: The Decade before the War of 1861–5; The War; The Period of Reconstruction, With Portraits of the Leading Public Men of This Era* (New York: Brown and Derby, 1881), 148.

46. *Journal of the Public and Secret Proceedings of the Convention of the People of Georgia Held in Milledgeville and Savannah in 1861* (Milledgeville, GA: Boughton, Nisbet and Barnes, 1861), 19, 26.

47. *Daily Morning News* (Savannah, GA), January 3, 1861.

48. *Albany (GA) Patriot*, January 10, 1861.

49. *Fayetteville (NC) Observer*, January 7, 1861.

50. *Federal Union* (Milledgeville, GA), January 15, 1861.

51. *New York Herald*, January 12, 1861.

52. *Journal of the Public and Secret Proceedings of the Convention of the People of Georgia Held in Milledgeville and Savannah in 1861*, 61.

53. Jefferson Davis, *The Rise and Fall of the Confederate Government* (New York: Sagamore, 1953), 1:209.

54. Joseph E. Brown to Governor Moore, January 5, 1861, Samuel Crawford Papers, Library of Congress Manuscript Division, Washington, DC.

55. Andrew B. Moore to John Todd, January 3, 1861, John B. Todd Correspondence, Alabama Department of Archives and History, Montgomery, Alabama.

56. *OR*, ser. 1, vol. 1, 327.

57. *New York Herald*, January 12, 1861.

58. *Confederate War Journal* 1, no. 1 (1893): 48.

59. *Mobile Tribune*, quoted in the *New York Herald*, January 14, 1861.

60. There were 132 guns at Fort Morgan and 89 guns stored at Fort Gaines. *New York Herald*, January 14, 1861; *Daily National Intelligencer* (Washington, DC), February 5, 1861.

61. Thomas J. McClellan to wife (Martha Fleming Beatie), January 6, 1861, Thomas J. McClellan Letters, 1861, Alabama Department of Archives and History.

62. John G. Nicolay, *The Outbreak of Rebellion* (New York: Charles Scribner's Sons, 1881), 16.

63. *OR*, ser. 1, vol.1, 327, 328; William Russell Smith, *The History and Debates of the Convention of the People of Alabama, Begun and Held in the City of Montgomery, on the Seventh Day of January, 1861; in Which is Preserved the Speeches of the Secret Sessions, and Many valuable State Papers* (Montgomery: White, Pfister, 1861), 40–41.

64. Bearss, "The Seizure of the Forts," 401.

65. *OR*, ser. 1, vol. 1, 490.

66. *OR*, ser. 1, vol. 1, 495.

67. For more information about Braxton Bragg during the secession crisis see Grady McWhiney, *Braxton Bragg and Confederate Defeat*, vol. 1 (New York: Columbia University Press, 1969); and Earl J. Hess, *Braxton Bragg: The Most Hated Man of the Confederacy* (Chapel Hill: University of North Carolina Press, 2016).

68. Braxton Bragg to Elise Bragg, January 11, 1861, William K. Bixby Collection of Braxton Bragg Papers, Missouri Historical Society, St. Louis, Missouri; McWhiney, *Braxton Bragg*, 150–151.

69. *OR*, ser. 1, vol. 1, p. 490.

70. Braxton Bragg to Elise Bragg, January 11, 1861, William K. Bixby Collection of Braxton Bragg Papers, Missouri Historical Society, St. Louis, Missouri.

71. *OR*, ser. 1, vol. 1, 495. For more information about the problems of southern arms shortages and Major Josiah Gorgas, chief of Confederate ordnance, see Frank E. Vandiver, *Ploughshares into Swords: Josiah Gorgas and Confederate Ordnance* (Austin: University of Texas Press, 1952); and Bearss, "The Seizure of the Forts," 404.

72. William T. Sherman to James Guthrie, August 14, 1864, in *Sherman's Civil War: Selected Correspondence of William T. Sherman, 1860–1865*, ed. Brooks D. Simpson and Jean V. Berlin (Chapel Hill: University of North Carolina Press, 1999), 693.

73. William T. Sherman to Thomas Ewing Jr., April 26, 1861, in Simpson and Berlin, *Sherman's Civil War*, 75.

74. William T. Sherman to Charles Anderson, ca. August 1863, in Simpson and Berlin, *Sherman's Civil War*, 510.

75. *Daily Palladium* (New Haven, CT), January 11, 1861, in Perkins, *Northern Editorials on Secession*, 1:210.

76. Peleg Bunker to John Sherman, January 12, 1861, John Sherman Papers, Library of Congress Manuscript Division, Washington, DC.

77. Jake L. Smith to John Sherman, January 15, 1861, John Sherman Papers, Library of Congress Manuscript Division, Washington, DC.

78. John A. Logan to I. N. Haynie, January 1, 1861, John A. Logan Correspondence, Library of Congress Manuscript Division, Washington, DC.

79. Copy of the Resolutions Adopted by the Fifth Ward Republican Association, January 14, 1861, John Sherman Papers, Library of Congress Manuscript Division, Washington, DC.

80. *New York Times*, January 15, 1861.

81. Ibid.; *Daily Picayune* (New Orleans), January 24, 1861.

82. Nicolay, *The Outbreak of Rebellion*, 16.

83. *Collected Works of Abraham Lincoln*, 4:194–196.

84. *New York Herald*, February 13, 1861.

85. *New-York Tribune*, February 18, 1861.

86. Address to the New Jersey General Assembly at Trenton, New Jersey; *Collected Works of Abraham Lincoln*, 4:236–237.

87. *Collected Works of Abraham Lincoln*, 4:254.

88. David Donald refers to Lincoln's first draft as a "no-nonsense document." Donald, *Lincoln* (New York: Simon and Schuster, 1996), 283.

89. For more analysis of Lincoln's first inaugural address see Douglas L. Wilson, *Lincoln's Sword: The Presidency and the Power of Words* (New York: Alfred A. Knopf, 2006).

90. Orville Browning to Abraham Lincoln, February 17, 1861, Abraham Lincoln Papers, Springfield, Illinois.

91. Douglas Wilson also argues that most of Seward's changes were designed to "placate the South and play down the seriousness of the crisis." William H. Seward to Abraham Lincoln, February 24, 1861, in John G. Nicolay and John Hay, *Abraham Lincoln: A History*, 10 vols. (New York: Century, 1890), 3:319; Wilson, *Lincoln's Sword*, 61.

92. For the first edition and revisions to Lincoln's first inaugural address see *Collected Works of Abraham Lincoln*, 4:249–262.

93. *Collected Works of Abraham Lincoln*, 4:266.

94. *Pittsburgh Post*, March 18, 1861, in Perkins, *Northern Editorials on Secession*, 2:649.

95. Joseph Blanchard to Abraham Lincoln, March 28, 1861, Abraham Lincoln Papers, Library of Congress Manuscript Division, Washington, DC.

96. *Collected Works of Abraham Lincoln*, 4:159.

97. *New York Herald*, April 24, 1861.

Contaminated Water and Dehydration during the Vicksburg Campaign

LINDSAY RAE PRIVETTE

On July 6, 1863, Confederate troops under the command of General Joseph E. Johnston evacuated their camp at Birdsong's Ferry along the Big Black River. In light of Vicksburg's recent surrender, Johnston was certain that Major General Ulysses S. Grant would send a detachment to destroy the last remnants of the Confederate army in the region. He was right. Pursued by forces under the command of Major General William T. Sherman, Johnston made a hasty retreat to Jackson, Mississippi. The march was long and hard, exacerbated by scorching heat and lack of rain. "We had a terrible march today," wrote Robert Patrick of the 4th Louisiana. "Dust, dust, dust. My God it is awful." Patrick's misery was aggravated by his inability to find fresh water. "The citizens all along the route take the buckets off the well ropes to prevent our getting water—and we are suffering for the want of it."[1] Captain William Edwards regarded the march as the "severest ordeal" his regiment had yet endured. "More than half the men gave out, completely exhausted."[2] The Confederates moved fast, covering twenty miles in just two days. And though they suffered for water, they retained an advantage. They had primary access to whatever water sources the land did have, and the opportunity to destroy those sources in their wake. On Johnston's orders, Confederate soldiers slaughtered nearby livestock, dumping the remains into ponds and lagoons where they rotted in the Mississippi sun. Years after the war, Sherman still remembered how his men hauled the "dead and stinking carcasses" out of the ponds so that they could use the water.[3] "It was the means of great annoyance," recalled Thad Smith, "and in many instances may have operated disastrously on the health of the command."[4]

For better or worse, Civil War soldiers' lives were defined by their proximity to water. Campaigning armies were routinely exposed to chilling rains. Soldiers fished from the same murky waters where they washed their clothes. Countless men suffered from water-borne illnesses. Yet studies examining the contentious relationship between soldiers and nature's most valuable resource remain limited. Traditionally, scholars examined how water influenced an army's effectiveness in combat. Rivers, swamps, mud, and rain created points of resistance that hindered troop movements and undermined military strategy.[5] While these works establish a valuable connection between water and the conduct of war, they do not consider how water shaped soldiers' individual experience. More recent scholarship has rectified this oversight, emphasizing how soldiers interpreted water-dominated landscapes as potential health threats.[6] In response, wary soldiers scrutinized the smell, taste, color, and location of their water in an effort to ensure their well-being. By focusing on soldiers' efforts to preserve their health, these works often overlook the consequences of their failure. Environmental factors as well as military strategy often required soldiers to abandon the traditional methods of water collection they knew to be safe. Instead, they were forced to acquire water by whatever means necessary. The inability to access clean drinking water was not only devastating to soldiers' individual health. It weakened the strength of the entire army.

The siege of Vicksburg offers a unique opportunity to examine how water influenced an army's success in the field.[7] By the spring of 1863, Vicksburg was the last Confederate stronghold on the Mississippi River. Towering nearly two hundred feet above the river's murky waters, Confederate batteries posted a formidable threat against Union naval forces. After two failed assaults, the Army of the Tennessee crossed the Mississippi River on April 29. Once within enemy territory, Union forces conducted a twenty-day campaign that ended on the outskirts of the city. Unable to gain control of the Confederate fortifications, Federal troops besieged the town for forty-seven days. From the start, Union and Confederate soldiers suffered for water. By May, the heat was already unbearable, and thick clouds of dust hung over the unshaded trenches. Soldiers yearned for water to ward off sunstroke and ease their thirst, but they were keenly aware that bad water was just as dangerous as the heat—perhaps more. Most attempted to differentiate between good and bad water. Unfortunately, as the siege wore on, water became a scarce commodity, and soldiers were forced to drink what was available. In the end, the health of both armies suffered, but not to the same extent. Union soldiers' mobility increased the commands' longevity while the Confederate garrison, suffering from dehydration, malnutrition, and heat exhaustion, collapsed.

Despite their differences, the Union and Confederate troops who fought at Vicksburg shared a common adversary. They were surrounded by a hostile environment that undermined their survival. Traditional medical thought held that a healthy body depended upon the proper balance of the four humors: blood, phlegm, yellow bile, and black bile. While humoral theory had mostly fallen out of favor by the middle of the nineteenth century, the idea that a healthy body was a balanced body remained. As a result, soldiers scrutinized their bodies for potential signs of imbalance. Congestion, chills, fever, and sweat were all indicators that the body's natural forces were inhibited. Because the body existed in tandem with its natural surroundings, the environment was scrutinized in the same way. Extreme fluctuations in temperature, water, and air indicated potential health threats. As a result, soldiers were suspicious of environments deemed "unnatural" or "unbalanced," and the land around Vicksburg seemed to be anything but natural.[8]

The unrelenting sun posed the greatest threat to soldiers' sense of balance. To Robert Edwin Jameson, it was as if the very earth withered in the sun. He complained that "the country . . . seems to be destitute of everything," including water.[9] The result was deadly. Philip Roesche of the 25th Wisconsin wrote that after landing on Haynes Bluff, a combination of hot weather and marching through the cornfields caused several soldiers to overheat and die. "The rest of us got through but were so over heated that it made many of us sick and even the colonel's horse died from the effects of the heat."[10] Sunstroke became a severe issue as soldiers converged on the beleaguered city. George C. Burmeister lost several of his men to the "intolerable heat."[11] Surgeon James Whitehill recorded a similar occurrence as he accompanied Kimball's division to the Vicksburg fortifications: "The day was very warm . . . quite a number of the men had succumbed to the heat and were lying by the roadside." Unable to slow the army's progress to accommodate the sick men, Whitehill arranged for an ambulance to "follow each regiment and pick up the men as they fell out." By the end of the day Whitehill himself had fallen victim to the extreme temperature: "I was so overdone with the heat, and suffered to such extent from a violent headache, was so exhausted they had to lift me from my horse."[12]

Sunstroke results from the body's swing toward a dangerous extreme. As the body loses fluids, water moves from cells into the bloodstream. Cells begin to shrink, blood becomes more concentrated, and the brain starts to swell. As a result, victims in the early stages of dehydration suffer from severe headaches, a parched mouth, and a swollen tongue. If left unchecked, symptoms progress to include muscle fatigue, dizziness, and possible seizures. For nineteenth-century Americans, many of these symptoms indicated a blockage within the body.[13] Aware of the dangers, soldiers anxiously noted any unusual pain or fatigue. Jameson developed a severe headache after an eight-mile march but was relieved to discover that he did not suffer sunstroke. He had another close call a week later: "We were marching rapidly for what cause, I can't imagine. Several men were sunstroke. I came very near." Jameson believed that better water would have eased the regiment's suffering. "Water was scarce," he lamented, "and what we did get was not fit to drink."[14] Chauncey Cooke also suffered from sunstroke. Cooke's regiment was sent to the rear in search of Johnston when the seventeen-year-old began to feel weak. He immediately began divesting himself of excess weight: "I had thrown away a woolen shirt, and torn my blanket in two and left a part of that to lighten my load. My cartridge box was the heaviest thing we had. Every man was loaded with all the bullets he could carry." Still, Cooke nearly fainted. "One of the Indiana boys said, 'my boy you better lay down, your face is awful red.' We were on the bank of a muddy creek, I walked away from the road up among the trees and after taking a drink from the creek I lay down in the shade of a tree with no one in sight and fell asleep."[15]

For many soldiers, the thirst was almost unbearable. Stranded on the battlefield after charging the Confederate fortifications on May 19, George Crooke was in agony. "It was a boiling hot day [and] the earth which we hugged so closely was like the floor of an oven," he recalled. As he lay on the battlefield "covered with dust and perspiration," Crooke became fixated on a single plum, hanging from a nearby tree: "As my lips became hot and parched with thirst and my throat struggled to relieve itself, this green plum hung temptingly before me and bade me risk my life for it." Crooke resisted the temptation for a while but eventually gave in. "The few drops of juice more than repaid me for the risk and the sweetest morsel of fruit ever tasted by man will live in my memory forever."[16] Crooke's experience was by no means unique. Confederate surgeon Edward Cade considered scarce water among soldiers' greatest hardships. If only the civilian population could understand what it was like to endure such thirst, Cade believed they would be more grateful for his sacrifices:

> Could they see men marching all day through the broiling sun with the thermometer over a hundred, carrying a load of forty pounds and suffering the intense thirst that is caused by heat, dust, and perspiration and no water to drink for hours at a time and when night comes camp upon some stream with water thick with insects and warm as water can be made by sun and eat their supper of cornbread and beef, they then would show more sympathy

for their condition and appreciate what they do without damning them for what they do not accomplish.[17]

For Cade, it was not just the physical distress that made these marches excruciating. "I could stand all of this readily," he wrote, "but it is the mental suffering" that made him want to give up.[18] Chauncey Cooke perhaps explained it simplest: "If the water were good, we would be happy."[19]

Overheated soldiers yearned for water, but surgeons often discouraged them from drinking their fill. Extreme thirst, they believed, was just as dangerous as extreme heat, and surgeons feared that water might cool the body too rapidly, resulting in death.[20] "The excessive thirst which follows violent exertion or loss of blood is unnatural, and is not quenched by large and repeated draughts," explained Surgeon General William Hammond. For this reason, Hammond encouraged soldiers to deny their thirst. "Experience teaches the old soldiers that the less he drinks when on the march the better and that he suffers less in the end by controlling the desire to drink, however urgent."[21] Exceptions were made on the battlefield where wounded men lost precious fluids through blood and sweat. Douglas Bushnell recalled how pleas for water filled the air after the Battle of Chickasaw Bayou. "Poor fellows were crawling about the field which was in possession of the enemy, calling for help and water, almost within our hearing and within sight of our camp."[22] In the helplessness of battle, thirst was a tangible need that could be met. Soldiers did what they could for the fallen. While walking the front lines at Vicksburg, George Burmeister was overcome by the way the dead and wounded lay in piles. "They presented an awful sight," he wrote. Yet Burmeister did not linger on this image. Instead, he wrote of a wounded soldier who asked him for a drink of water. "I gave it to him," he admitted, adding optimistically that "it appeared to do him a great deal of good."[23]

If the heat tormented the soldiers stationed around Vicksburg, their suffering was exacerbated by an inability to identify and obtain clean water. It was ironic, really, that a shortage of clean water defined soldiers' experience of the siege. Water dominated the geography of the lower Mississippi River valley, its terrain etched by seasonal floods. Oxbow lakes appeared when the river overflowed its boundaries. Abandoned river channels created a series of interconnected waterways. On the east bank of the river, Vicksburg sat proudly atop rolling hills of loess soil, where runoff water carved the land into an intricate system of deep ravines and high, flat-topped ridges. Yet the same soil that was so vulnerable to water's carving force was also impermeable. Most locals drew their water from cisterns, large underground containers designed to collect rainwater.[24] These cisterns became the dominant water source for both Confederate and Union troops.

For soldiers in a foreign land, unfamiliar with nearby creeks, streams, and eddies, the easiest way to identify clean water was to drink what the locals drank. As Grant's army snaked through the Mississippi countryside, it moved from plantation to plantation, using household stores to supplement meager rations. Soldiers took more than food and blankets. They took water. Shortly after the Battle of Champion Hill, exhausted troops flocked to a local farmstead in search of rest. The men gathered around the property's well, taking turns quenching their thirst.[25] Plantations and farms were often the only place soldiers were guaranteed potable water. Upon receiving orders to pursue Johnston's army to Jackson, the men in William Eddington's regiment made sure to fill their canteens before they left the city. "They held three pints each," Eddington wrote. "We had to make it twenty miles before we could get any more." With cisterns and wells no longer ensured, Eddington's comrades had to forage. They could guess where there might be water, but there was no certainty. One night, the regiment camped near a creek with hopes of replenishing their canteens. Unfortunately, when they arrived, they found "a few little holes covered with green scum about an inch thick . . . you could smell it long before you got to it."[26]

Soldiers were often anxious about drinking standing water. Frequently cloudy, smelly, or bad tasting, stagnant water—even from wells and cisterns—was synonymous with bad water. Having drunk from the Vicksburg cisterns for several months, Matthew Rawley Banner was surprised at his continued health. "The water is quite good so far," he declared in a letter to his family, adding that "I like it very well since I got used to it."[27] Many soldiers, however, did not want to risk their health at the cisterns. Instead, they preferred clear, running spring water. But even these waters were dangerous. Chauncey Cooke of the 25th Wisconsin marveled at the presence of a "pretty" nearby spring. It was marked with a sign that read, "Don't drink this water, poison." "It is as big as the spring at the head of our coulee and as pure looking," he explained to his mother. "It seems strange that we cannot drink out of the springs here that look just as they do in Wisconsin." Many of Cooke's comrades felt the same and ignored the sign to devastating consequences. "Some that are burning up with fever and thirst manage to stagger down here and fill up with water," Cooke wrote. Then they "go back to their tents and die."[28]

Because appearances could be misleading, soldiers depended on word of mouth to distinguish good water from bad. Surgeon Charles Johnson was directed by locals to obtain his hospital's water from the Mississippi River. Despite the recommendation, Johnson remained dubious. "There was so much sediment that a bucket dipped in the current would be filled with water which, after a time, would have more than an inch of 'settling' in the bottom. But the natives insisted Mississippi River water was healthy, and after sedimentation it was certainly pleasant to drink."[29] The soldiers in Reuben Scott's regiment, though, were warned not to drink the water from the Yazoo. Scott found this challenging. The water "was [so] dark blue and very pretty compared to that of the Mississippi" it was a "temptation to the boys to fill their canteens with this pretty clear water."[30] While most of the men in Scott's regiment heeded the warning, many in the 96th Ohio did not. "We soon learned the value of the advice we had scouted," recalled Joseph Thatcher Woods. "In the hundreds of men [that] became suddenly and very seriously ill was demonstrated that insidious poison may lurk in sparkling sweets."[31] Indeed, the Yazoo was so characterized by sickness that soldiers called it the "River of Death."[32]

Even when soldiers successfully identified sources of clean water, the supply was often limited. Cisterns, wells, and springs depended on rainfall to replenish their reservoir. Unfortunately, rain was erratic during the hottest months. Creeks that ran full during the winter faded into a sporadic chain of puddles during the summer. Even in an ordinary year local cisterns were depleted by the end of the dry season.[33] Fearing a siege, Vicksburg residents grew concerned that a water system built to sustain five thousand residents could not withstand the burden of a hundred thousand additional lives. In March, the Warren County Board of Police had recommended a series of repairs aimed at increasing the town's supply. These recommendations were never heeded.[34] In some cases cistern water lasted mere days before soldiers were forced to find another source.[35] Inside the city, residents and soldiers carefully rationed the remaining supply. One fortunate woman who owned two cisterns allowed soldiers to draw water from one while reserving the other for herself.[36] Where rationing did not work, soldiers confiscated what they needed. So many people accessed the spring on Aquila Bowie's property that it was nearly dry when the army stationed a guard over it with strict orders that only soldiers drink from the spring. Eventually, the water returned, but Bowie and his family had to find another source.[37]

Some sources were more abundant than others, but accessing them could be dangerous. The closest spring to Thomas Barton's regiment was situated directly between the contending armies, forcing thirsty soldiers to expose themselves to enemy fire. "It was like running a blockade to get a drink of water," wrote Barton. "I frequently made the dangerous journey and about the time I reached the spring would hear the sharp report of the enemy's guns. Sometimes I would remain half an hour to throw them off their guard, and then double quick back with a small supply of water."[38] Soldiers collecting water from the Mississippi River experienced similar dangers. The regularity of their visits made them an easy target for enemy fire. On May 23, Sherman complained to Admiral David Dixon Porter of his men's vulnerability. "Men get water out of the Mississippi at the cattle pens. The enemy have a 32 parrot which sometimes reaches that point."[39] Inside the city, Confederates regularly hauled muddy water to the trenches in barrels. As the siege wore on, the trips became more perilous. On June 18, Samuel Swan reported that enemy fire was "beginning to interfere with the water haulers and are making the lower part of the town rather warm."[40]

Because of its scarcity, soldiers and surgeons were often forced to abandon the standard practices of water collection. With no access to fresh, cool, running water, soldiers began to dig.[41] Illinois private Job Yaggy was one of thirty men from his regiment sent over the next hill to dig a well. Yaggy and his comrades labored for two hours before Yaggy was sent to fetch them something to eat. He was shot returning to camp.[42] William T. Rigby's regiment also dug a well, but Rigby found the water unsavory. "It is seep water," he announced, "and all of it is more or less affected by the clay soil of the country."[43] Like Rigby, most nineteenth-century Americans believed that sickness was conveyed through decaying organic material. Whether spread through the air (miasma) or through the water, this material poisoned the body.[44] Surgeons were especially wary of groundwater. When the cisterns supplying Union field hospitals gave out, medical inspector John Summers was dissatisfied with the alternative sources. "It is hard water, containing lime and magnesia, with a large quantity of vegetable matter in solution." Upon questioning locals, Summers determined that groundwater was used exclusively for cooking and washing, "cistern water having been substituted even in the large fields for the Negroes." Nevertheless, soldiers had no choice. The cisterns were dry. As a result, Summers reported that nearly half the command was "suffering from a very relaxed condition of the bowels."[45]

Even if soldiers and surgeons believed their water was contaminated, they could do little about it. They had to drink. "Our worst hardship here was lack of good water," wrote Charles Willison; "frequently all we could get was out of rank looking, scum-covered puddles, and much sickness resulted."[46] Camped amid the Louisiana swamps, Edward Cade declared his water "not fit for a horse." "I have been busy sending the sick of our Brigade to a hospital," he added. "The men are getting sick very rapidly in these close bottoms, drinking the water we are compelled to drink."[47] Some soldiers attempted to minimize their suffering in letters home. At the end of June, John Wesley Largent wrote a detailed letter describing a nearby watering hole. "[It's] composed of snakes, frogs, lizards, tad-poles, leeches, turtles, aligators, and numerous other birds. . . . It feels kinder slimy to get in an squirm around among them, but it's better than nothing. . . . When we want a drink, it is but little trouble." Unsurprisingly, Largent's health was suffering. "I have been having a little individual battle of my own, with the bilious diarrhea and fever for the last 3 days," he admitted. "The health of the regiment is giving way under so much duty."[48]

While diarrhea and dysentery were common ailments throughout the war, siege operations increased soldiers' chances of consuming contaminated water. Union regimental returns indicate that cases of unspecified diarrhea rose from 9,291 in May to 14,589 in June, a 57 percent increase.[49] During the campaign, Federal troops were not stationary long enough to contaminate their immediate surroundings. However, the siege forced soldiers into overcrowded camps where sanitation gradually deteriorated. Surgeons struggled to ensure that water was not contaminated by feces. To this end, several manuals offered guidelines regarding the construction of camp latrines. John Ordronaux, for example, recommended that regimental sinks should be "encircled by bushes, and every evening a portion of the earth dug out of them should be thrown in." Ordronaux was especially concerned about the proper disposal of waste produced by hospital patients. He recommended that sick soldiers have their own privy that was to be disinfected daily.[50] Unfortunately, these measures were not always observed. Summers was appalled by the deplorable conditions of the camps surrounding Vicksburg:

> I regret to say I found some brigades that had been in camp ten days or more and were without sinks or any convenience for the command or even the officers, and a general indifference exhibited by them on this subject. . . .

> Where sinks had been made, they were seldom found attractive of the men; without arbors over them as a general thing, and not unfrequently without a pole to sit on.[51]

Instead, men relieved their bowels in nearby bushes, not thirty or forty feet from their camp. The result was that "human excrement has been promiscuously deposited in every direction, until the atmosphere, as the dampness of evening and night approaches, is so heavily loaded with the effluvia that it is sickening."[52]

Sanitation inside Confederate lines was not any better. Union soldiers frequently commented on the deplorable conditions they encountered upon entering the city after the siege. "The debris of a large army cooped up within its limits for 47 days had rendered [Vicksburg] almost uninhabitable," reported Thad Smith.[53] Sylvester Strong declared the Confederate camps "awful" places, filled with the decaying carcasses of horses and mules. "They make a very disagreeable smell," he observed. However, it was not just the environment. Confederates themselves were filthy. "They looked more like a lot of pigs a coming out of their pen than men," Strong wrote, adding that most Confederates had not left the entrenchments since the siege began. "They had to cook, eat, sleep, and drink in the ditches."[54] James West Smith spent forty-three days lying in a crowded trench measuring approximately four feet deep and six feet wide. He did not have a clean change of clothes, never had a proper bath, and when it rained one afternoon, he found himself sitting in mud. "It is now two to five inches ... all over the trenches" he griped; "the like of mud I may have seen before, but am satisfied was never so completely engulfed in it."[55] No doubt such conditions undermined any regulations regarding sinks and the proper disposal of human waste, making it difficult to ensure that nearby water sources remained uncontaminated.

Although siege operations exposed both Union and Confederate soldiers to dangerous waters, the Union army's health benefited from several factors that offset the threat of extreme heat and water shortage. One of these factors was the landscape that surrounded Union camps. Charles Dana recalled that the army was "in an incomparable position for a siege as regarded the health and comfort of our men. The high wooded hills afforded pure air and shade, and the deep ravines abounded in springs of excellent water, and if they failed, it was easy to bring it from the Mississippi River."[56] Additionally, soldiers were surrounded by fresh fruits and vegetables ripe for picking. "We go out foraging every day," James Forbis wrote to his family. "I went out yesterday and got a mess of green beans and strawberries and raspberries and plums."[57] While trees sheltered soldiers from the sun's rays and fresh fruits and vegetables helped to supplement their diet with vital nutrients, these resources would have been useless without soldiers' ability to access them. As a result, Union soldiers' greatest asset was their mobility. This is not to say that life in the trenches was easy. Indeed, Federal soldiers endured the same trials as their Confederate counterparts. The Union position, however, meant that northern soldiers were not exposed to these hardships the entire forty-seven days. "We had not been many days in the rear," explained Dana, "before we settled into regular habits. The men were detailed in reliefs for work in the trenches and being relieved at fixed hours, everybody seemed to lead a systematic life."[58]

Confederate soldiers were not so fortunate. For most, there was no escape from the ravages of the sun, deteriorating rations, and inadequate water. Traditional studies emphasize starvation as the primary reason for the army's defeat. And soldiers did starve. Two days before the garrison's surrender, James West Smith drew his rations. "We get four ounce of flour, twelve of coarse, sour, dirty, weevil-eaten unsifted cornmeal, one and a third of rice, four of pickled pork, eight of fresh beef, and eighteen of sugar, which is to do us three days." This, however, was not the worst of it. "It is an undisputed fact that mules are being killed for the subsistence of the Army," he added.[59] Soldiers went hungry. They and their surgeon reported widespread cases of dizziness, lethargy, fever, and a lack of energy. But malnutrition was not the only factor that weakened their bodies; these symptoms also indicate dehydration. Confederate soldiers spent weeks lying in trenches, exposed to the blistering sun without suitable water. Gabriel Killgore described how he and his men entered the trenches one day before noon. There, they were "exposed fully to the Sun which was very hot. It seemed that I could hardly stand the heat but did."[60] Edward Cade reported that many of his patients were nearly "suffocated by heat," while Joseph Allison blamed the deterioration of his regiment on the "men having lain in the trenches for three weeks with no protection from the sun."[61] Indeed, Allison is one of several Confederates who suggest that soldiers' muscles atrophied due to lack of exercise. "They can't stand up without having a dozen bullets whistling around their heads," he complained. "To attempt to walk around is certain death."[62]

The combination of high temperatures, poor water, and low rations caused Confederate bodies to deteriorate quicker than their northern counterparts.

By July, disease was ubiquitous throughout the Confederate army. Nearly one-third of the garrison was hospitalized and the remaining two-thirds were in questionable health. Realizing that his army was near the end of its endurance, Pemberton sent a dispatch to his generals, inquiring if their soldiers were strong enough to fight their way out of the city. Colonel Alexander Reynolds was doubtful: "Owing to the reduced quantity and quality of the rations on which they have subsisted for six weeks past, to their close confinement in the trenches, constant exposure to the intense heat of the sun and frequent rains, and to impure water they are obliged to drink, my men are . . . in many instances entirely prostrated." Reynolds estimated that they would not make it ten miles. His assessment was echoed throughout the command. The soldiers are "debilitated from the long exposure and inaction of the trenches," reported Brigadier General Seth Barton. Brigadier General Alfred Cumming estimated that 50 percent of the troops along the front lines were not fit for duty.[63] Unable to break the siege, Lieutenant General John C. Pemberton surrendered his army on July 4.

Water is essential for survival, even more than food. But while many historians acknowledge the relationship between water and soldiers' health, fewer studies examine soldiers' struggle to obtain clean, fresh water while in the field.[64] Unlike food, clothing, and munitions, water was not provided by the army. Instead, soldiers lived off of the land. They collected water from nearby springs and dipped their canteens into barren cisterns. As a result, acquiring water was unpredictable, determined by a number of environmental variables. For soldiers stationed around Vicksburg, these variables were in constant flux. Some sources that existed in May had vanished by June. Others remained but were contaminated. All the while soldiers, dehydrated from the heat, diarrhea, or blood loss needed more water to replenish lost fluids. Consequently, soldiers adapted to the changing water supply. They dug their own wells or hauled water from afar. Many soldiers rationed what they had or confiscated what they needed. It was not just the environmental factors that made water scarce. Water was also vulnerable to military strategy. Union siege operations burdened the already limited resource while cannoneers interfered with water collection. Retreating Confederate forces tried to slow the Union advance by polluting local streams and ponds. Whether intentional or not, soldiers' health was broken by a contaminated and inadequate water supply.

Vicksburg's surrender was a bitter defeat for Confederates, but soldiers wrote optimistically about how their health might improve after the surrender.

With Union occupation came Union supplies. Federal quartermasters distributed food, medicine, and even water.[65] "I went into the lines of the enemy and told them I was nearly starved," wrote Eleazor Thornhill. "They gave me bacon, coffee, and bread. . . . We had plenty to eat while they retained us. I improved as does a pig that is placed in a pen and fed on rich slop."[66] Matthew Rawley Banner echoed the sentiment. Upon being paroled Banner and his regiment were marched out of the city. He was glad to see the town behind him. "I am not well but better than I have been as I seem to improve by a change of water." Indeed, soon Banner would be quite recovered. After all, he was going home.[67]

Notes

1. Jay F. Taylor, ed., *The Reluctant Rebel: The Secret Diary of Robert Patrick, 1861–1865* (Baton Rouge: Louisiana State University Press, 1987), 119–120.

2. William Henry Edwards, *A Condensed History of the Seventeenth Regiment S.C.V. C.S.A.: From Its Organization to the Close of the War* (Columbia, SC: R. L. Bryan, 1908), 35.

3. William Tecumseh Sherman, *Memoirs of General W. T. Sherman* (New York: Library of America, 1990), 356.

4. Thad L. Smith, "The Twenty-Fourth Iowa Volunteers: From Muscatine to Winchester, after the Siege of Vicksburg," *Annals of Iowa* 1, no. 3 (October 1893): 181.

5. One of the earliest works examining the relationship between water and combat is Harold Winters et al., *Battling the Elements: Weather and Terrain in the Conduct of War* (Baltimore: Johns Hopkins University Press, 1998). Winter's book is a collection of essays written by geographers and military experts who demonstrate that weather and climate affect battlefield conditions regardless of time or place. Lisa M. Brady's "Nature as Friction: Integrating Clausewitz into Environmental Histories of the Civil War," in *The Blue, the Gray, and the Green: Toward an Environmental History of the Civil War*, ed. Brian Allen Drake (Athens: University of Georgia Press, 2015), 144–162, examines how nature can function as friction in war. While Brady uses the phenomenon of acoustic shadows to demonstrate her point, Adam H. Petty's "Wilderness, Weathers, and Waging War in the Mine Run Campaign," *Civil War History* 63, no. 1 (March 2017): 7–35, applies the theory to the Battle of Mine Run, demonstrating how rain, mud, and local rivers affected army maneuvers. Additionally, Warren Grabau's *Ninety-Eight Days: A Geographer's View of the Vicksburg Campaign* (Knoxville: University of Tennessee Press, 2000) is an excellent book, detailing how the geographical features of the lower Mississippi River valley shaped Grant's campaign strategy.

6. The introduction to Lisa M. Brady's *War upon the Land: Military Strategy and the Transformation of Southern Landscapes during the American Civil War* (Athens: University of Georgia Press, 2012) is useful to understanding how Union soldiers interpreted the untamed landscapes of the Mississippi swamps and bayous. Similarly, both Conevery Bolton Valenčius, *The Health of the Country: How American Settlers Understood Themselves and Their Land* (New York: Basic Books, 2002), and Andrew McIlwaine Bell, *Mosquito Soldiers: Malaria, Yellow Fever, and the Course of the American Civil War* (Baton Rouge: Louisiana State University Press, 2010), offer insight regarding the perceived relationship between the land, the body, and an individual's health. Finally, Kathryn

Shively Meier, *Nature's Civil War: Common Soldiers and the Environment in 1862 Virginia* (Chapel Hill: University of North Carolina Press, 2013) is another beneficial study, examining how these cultural interpretations affected soldiers' behavior as they made decisions regarding what water to drink, what food to eat, and where to rest.

7. There are a number of excellent studies that examine the military strategy employed by Grant's army as well as the personal experiences of soldiers and civilians. Of particular note are Edwin Cole Bearss's *The Campaign for Vicksburg*, 3 vols. (Dayton, OH: Morningside, 1989); William L. Shea and Terrence J. Winschel's *Vicksburg Is the Key: The Struggle for the Mississippi River* (Lincoln: University of Nebraska Press, 2003); Terrence J. Winschel's *Triumph and Defeat: The Vicksburg Campaign* (Mason City, IA: Savas, 1999); and Michael Ballard's *Vicksburg: The Campaign That Opened the Mississippi* (Chapel Hill: University of North Carolina Press, 2004). Each of these works acknowledges that Union and Confederate soldiers experienced a shortage of clean water during the campaign and siege. This fact, however, is often mentioned as an example of the harsh conditions in which soldiers lived. The consequences of this shortage and the steps soldiers took to mitigate the situation have yet to be fully explored.

8. Valenčius, *The Health of the Country*, 58–60; Brady, *War upon the Land*, 11–12.

9. Robert Edwin Jameson Diary, June 30, 1863, Robert Edwin Jameson Papers, Library of Congress, Washington, DC.

10. Philip Roesch Memoirs, 7, Folder 21, Box 99, United States Heritage and Education Center, Carlisle, Pennsylvania.

11. George C. Burmeister Diary, May 2, 1863, Folder 19, Box 18, United States Army Heritage and Education Center, Carlisle, Pennsylvania.

12. James C. Whitehill Memoirs, 2, Folder 10, Box 233, United States Army Heritage and Education Center, Carlisle, Pennsylvania.

13. Megan Kate Nelson, "The Difficulties and Seduction of the Desert: Landscapes of War in 1861 New Mexico," in *The Blue, the Gray, and the Green: Toward an Environmental History of the Civil War*, ed. Brian Allen Drake (Athens: University of Georgia Press, 2015), 44; Albert J. Bellows, *How Not to Be Sick: A Sequel to "Philosophy of Eating"*(New York: Hurd and Houghton, 1868), 335, Reynolds Finley Historical Library, University of Alabama at Birmingham, Birmingham, Alabama.

14. Robert Edwin Jameson Diary, July 7, 1863, Robert Edwin Jameson Papers, Library of Congress, Washington, DC.

15. Chauncey H. Cooke, *A Badger Boy in Blue: The Civil War Letters of Chauncey H. Cooke* (Detroit: Wayne State University Press, 2007), 63.

16. George Crooke, *The Twenty-First Regiment of Iowa Volunteer Infantry: A Narrative of Its Experiences in Active Service Including a Military Record of Each Officer, Non-commissioned Officer, and Private Soldier in the Organization* (Milwaukee: King, Fowle, 1891), 84–85.

17. John Q. Anderson, *A Texas Surgeon in the CSA* (Tuscaloosa: Confederate, 1957), 67–68.

18. Ibid.

19. Cooke, *A Badger Boy in Blue*, 67.

20. Bellows, *How Not to Be Sick*, 335.

21. William A. Hammond, MD, *Military Medical and Surgical Essays: Prepared for the United States Sanitary Commission* (Philadelphia: J. B. Lippincott, 1864), 4–5.

22. Douglas Ritchie Bushnell to Dear Wife, January 26, 1863, Douglas Ritchie Bushnell Letters, Folder 10, Box 19, United States Army Heritage and Education Center, Carlisle, Pennsylvania.

23. George C. Burmeister Diary, May 19, 1863, Folder 19, Box 18, United States Army Heritage and Education Center, Carlisle Pennsylvania.

24. Grabau, *Ninety-Eight Days*, 18–27.

25. Sherman, *Memoirs of General W. T. Sherman*, 348.

26. W. R. Eddington, "My Civil War Memoirs and Other Reminiscences as Written by My Father," W. R. Eddington Papers, Abraham Lincoln Presidential Library, Springfield, Illinois.

27. Charles S. Tripler and George C. Blackmon, *Hand-book for the Military Surgeon* (Cincinnati: Robert Clark, 1862), 16; Matthew Rawley Banner to Addie, March 27, 1863, Matthew Rawley Banner Letters, Old Courthouse Museum, Vicksburg, Mississippi. Even the Medical Department stressed the superiority of running water, emphasizing that the quality of local water was of extreme importance when selecting a campsite. For more information on popular conceptions of stagnant water, see Valenčius, *The Health of the Country*, 139.

28. Cooke, *A Badger Boy in Blue*, 79.

29. Charles Beneulyn Johnson, *Muskets and Medicine, or, Army Life in the Sixties* (Philadelphia: F A. Davis, 1917), 69.

30. Reuben Scott, *The History of the 67th Regiment Indiana Volunteers* (Bedford, IN: Herald Book and Job Print, 1892), 15.

31. Joseph Thatcher Woods, *Services of the Ninety-Sixth Ohio Volunteers* (Toledo: Blade Print and Paper, 1874), 20.

32. This nickname is pervasive and appears in a number of sources. See Samuel Black, *A Soldier's Recollections of the Civil War with Supplemental Chapters by Comrades* (Minco, OK: Minco Minstral, 1911), 30; Cooke, *A Badger Boy in Blue*, 76; Scott, *The History of the 67th Regiment Indiana Volunteers*, 15; and Woods, *Services of the Ninety-Sixth Ohio Volunteers*, 20.

33. This "dry season" lasted approximately from June to the middle of October. See Grabau, *Ninety-Eight Days*, 18–27.

34. Minutes of the Board of Police of Warren County, March 21, 1863, reprinted in the *Vicksburg Daily Whig*, March 24, 1863.

35. Surgeon General's Office, *The Medical and Surgical History of the War of the Rebellion: Prepared in Accordance with the Acts of Congress, under the Direction of Surgeon General Joseph K. Barnes* (Washington, DC: Government Printing Office, 1870–1879), 4:95.

36. "A Woman's Diary," *Century Magazine* 30 (May–October 1885): 772.

37. Aquila Bowie Memoirs, 3, Old Courthouse Museum, Vicksburg, Mississippi.

38. T. H. Barton, *Autobiography of Dr. Thomas Barton, The Self-Made Physician of Syracuse, Ohio* (Charleston: West Virginia Print, 1890), 155.

39. David Dixon Porter to William T. Sherman, May 23, 1863, James McClintock Signal Corps Messages, Library of Congress, Washington, DC.

40. George C. Osborn, "A Tennessean at the Siege of Vicksburg: The Diary of Samuel Alexander Ramsey Swan, May–July, 1863," *Tennessee Historical Quarterly* 14, no. 4 (December 1955): 367.

41. John Ordronaux, *Hints on Health in Armies for the Use of Volunteer Officers*, 2nd ed. (New York: D. Van Nostrand, 1863), 46–47, 52, 54, Reynolds Finley Historical Library, University of Alabama at Birmingham, Birmingham, Alabama.

42. Job H. Yaggy Diary, June 28, 1863, Abraham Lincoln Presidential Museum, Springfield, Illinois.

43. William T. Rigby to Brother, July 1, 1863, William T. Rigby Series, Folder 18, Box 1, Vicksburg National Military Park, Vicksburg, Mississippi.

44. William A. Hammond, "Miasmatic Fevers," in *Military Medical and Surgical Essays Prepared for the United States Sanitary Commission* (Philadelphia: J. B. Lippincott, 1864), 207–208; Valenčius, *The Health of the Country*, 125.

45. Surgeon General's Office, *The Medical and Surgical History of the War of the Rebellion*, 4:95.

46. Charles A. Willison, *Reminiscences of a Boy's Service with the 76th Ohio: In the Fifteenth Army Corps, under General Sherman, during the Civil War by that "Boy" at Three Scores* (Huntington, WV: Blue Acorn, 1995), 64.

47. Anderson, *A Texas Surgeon*, 61.

48. John Wesley Largent to Sister and Family, June 25, 1863, John Wesley Largent Letters, Wisconsin Historical Society, Madison, Wisconsin.

49. Surgeon General's Office, *The Medical and Surgical History of the War of the Rebellion*, 1:241. For a comparative analysis of the soldiers' health see Frank R. Freemon, "Medical Care at the Siege of Vicksburg, 1863," *Bulletin of the New York Academy of Medicine* 67 (Sept–Oct. 1991): 429–438; and Frank R. Freemon, "The Medical Challenge of Military Operations in the Mississippi Valley during the American Civil War," *Military Medicine* 157 (September 1992): 494–497.

50. Ordronaux, *Hints on Health in Armies*, 58.

51. Surgeon General's Office, *The Medical and Surgical History of the War of the Rebellion*, 4:95.

52. Ibid.

53. Tad Smith, "The Twenty-Fourth Iowa," 182.

54. Sylvester Strong to Parents, July 6, 1863, Sylvester and Albert Strong Civil War Letters, Wisconsin Historical Society, Madison, Wisconsin.

55. James West Smith, "A Confederate Soldier's Diary: Vicksburg in 1863," *Southwest Review* 28, no. 3 (Spring 1943): 303, 312–313.

56. Charles A. Dana, *Recollections of the Civil War: With the Leaders at Washington and in the Field in the Sixties* (New York: D. Appleton, 1902), 78.

57. James Forbis to Companion and Children, June 1, 1863, Folder 18, Box 40, United States Army Heritage and Education Center, Carlisle, Pennsylvania.

58. Dana, *Recollections of the Civil War*, 78.

59. James West Smith, "A Confederate Soldier's Diary," 321.

60. Douglas Maynard, "Vicksburg Diary, the Journal of Gabriel Killgore," *Civil War History* 10 (1964): 48.

61. Anderson, *A Texas Surgeon*, 61.

62. Joseph Dill Allison Diary, June 10, 1863, Old Courthouse Museum, Vicksburg, Mississippi.

63. *The War of the Rebellion: A Compilation of the Official Records of the Union and Confederate Armies*, 127 vols. (Washington, DC: Government Printing Office, 1880–1901), ser. 1, vol. 24, pt. 2, 347–349 (hereafter cited as *OR*).

64. The relationship between poor sanitation, contaminated water, and soldiers' deteriorating health, for example, is a dominant theme in literature on Civil War prison camps. See William Best Hesseltine, *Civil War Prisons: A Study in War Psychology* (Kent, OH: Kent State University Press, 1962); Lonnie R. Speer, *Portals to Hell: Military Prisons of the Civil War* (Mechanicsburg, PA: Stackpole Books, 1997); and J. Michael Martinez, *Life and Death in Civil War Prisons: The Parallel*

Torments of Corporal John Wesley Minnich, CSA and Sergeant Warren Lee Goss, USA (Nashville: Rutledge Hill, 2004).

65. *OR*, ser. 1, vol. 24, pt. 3, 489.

66. Eleazor W. Thornhill Memoirs, 14, Old Courthouse Museum, Vicksburg, Mississippi.

67. Matthew Rawley Banner to Addie, July 15, 1863, Matthew Rawley Banner Letters, Old Courthouse Museum, Vicksburg, Mississippi.

Fires at the Battles of Chancellorsville and the Wilderness

ADAM H. PETTY

H istorians are no strangers to the fires that swept the Wilderness—a forested region in Virginia—during the Battles of Chancellorsville (1863) and the Wilderness (1864). Most if not all histories of these engagements mention the forest fires, and the hellish scenes of combat amid the flames with wounded men burning to death are as well known as they are haunting. Yet no historian has systematically analyzed these fires. Instead, the fires serve as an alluring detail or perhaps a source of drama during the battle.[1] This essay seeks to remedy this by providing a careful look at four aspects of the Wilderness fires. First, what caused them? Second, how did they affect combat? Third, how did the soldiers react to them? Finally, were these forest fires unique to the battles in the Wilderness?

In answering these questions, certain conclusions quickly become apparent. First, the Wilderness fires were accidental, even though some contemporary accounts betrayed a suspicion that the enemy had intentionally started these fires for their own ends. Second, while it is unclear to what degree the fires altered the course of battle, they certainly created uncomfortable and dangerous combat conditions and often proved deadly to the wounded, although it is impossible to determine how many soldiers actually perished because of the flames. Third, regardless of how many soldiers burned to death, both contemporary and postwar accounts confirm that the soldiers had a deep fear of dying in the flames and were horrified at the thought of others suffering this fate. They found the burning of the wounded profoundly disturbing as they experienced it through thought, sight, smell, and hearing. For them, these experiences and the desperate struggle amid the flames were the culmination of the horrors of battle, a vision of hell itself. The terror felt by those in peril of burning as well as the suffering of those who actually burned to death also left a deep impression on soldiers' minds. Curiously, some veterans used these fiery trials as a vehicle to promote reconciliation, reminiscing about Union and Confederate soldiers coming together to save their comrades from the flames. These narratives stand in stark contrast to the accusations often leveled at their opponents in contemporary accounts. Finally, these fires and their attendant terrors were not unique to the Wilderness but could be found in other engagements, like Chickamauga and Kennesaw Mountain.

* * * *

Traditionally, historians have explained the Wilderness fires as accidents, and most contemporary accounts do suggest accidental causes. At the Battle of Chancellorsville, many witnesses pointed to artillery fire and dry weather conditions as the primary culprits.[2] During the Battle of the Wilderness, dry conditions again prevailed, and it should come as no surprise that fires broke out during a battle marked for heavy and incessant musketry.[3]

A minority of soldiers, however, argued that their opponents had intentionally set the forest ablaze to gain tactical advantages. At Chancellorsville, a few Confederates, like John Piney Oden, a captain in the 10th Alabama, argued that the Federals had set the fires to cover their retreat, while David R. Winn of the 4th Georgia accused the Federals of burning the woods to destroy ammunition they had left behind.[4] In a similar fashion, a number of Union soldiers at the Battle of the Wilderness pointed their fingers at the Confederates, arguing that they had intentionally set fires. Some thought it was to prevent a Union advance at one time or another. North of the Orange Turnpike, for instance, Emory Upton, a general in the Federal VI Corps, thought "the woods in front and around our position had been set on fire by the enemy to prevent our advance."[5] Other Union soldiers thought the Confederates burned the woods to create a smoke screen for their attacks. Josiah F. Murphey, a sergeant in the 20th Massachusetts thought either "the enemy set the underbrush on fire or it caught fire," but was sure that "under cover of the smoke they charged on us."[6] A soldier in the 5th New Jersey similarly noted how the Confederates located the unprotected Union flank along the Orange Plank Road and then proceeded to "set fire to the woods, advancing under cover of the smoke upon our flank." The Federals soon became aware of the fact when they received "a volley . . . from about 300 yards in our rear."[7] Likewise, James Freeman of the 11th New Jersey concluded that the Confederates had "got upon our left flank . . . by setting the leaves on fire in front of us, and drove us entirely out of the woods."[8] Others thought the Confederates used fire to smoke them out. Robert Robertson, a member of the

93rd New York, claimed "the Rebels set the woods on fire to drive us out of our position."[9]

Despite these assertions, however, there is no evidence that the Federals at Chancellorsville or the Confederates at the Battle of the Wilderness intentionally started any fires. Moreover, neither side ever claimed to have started fires intentionally. Nevertheless, these assertions tell us something about the soldiers who made them. It is interesting to note that the Confederates thought the Union forces had set fires for defensive reasons, while the Federals usually assumed the rebels had done so for offensive purposes. These reactions demonstrate how assumptions about an opponent's intentions could influence how a soldier interpreted certain events on a battlefield, such as the fires in the Wilderness. Some rebels at Chancellorsville saw the Federals retreating and assumed that they were using the fires to aid their efforts. In a similar manner, some Federals at the Battle of the Wilderness observed the problems the fires caused their army and assumed the Confederates were employing the flames and smoke to enhance their attacks. Union soldiers in particular often demonstrated a conspiratorial mind-set when it came to Lee and the Army of Northern Virginia, and their reaction to the fires at the Battle of the Wilderness is a prime example of this tendency.[10]

* * * *

Regardless of how they started, many historians have pointed to the fires' ability to alter the course of battle, even if only temporarily. The most notorious example of this was at the Battle of the Wilderness during the Confederate attack on the Union Brock Road entrenchments on the afternoon of May 6, 1864.[11] Francis Galwey painted the scene graphically. "Some of the brush had taken fire and the flames, smoke, and heat had driven many of the men out of the works," he wrote, and during this weak moment the Confederates pressed their attack "in heavy masses" and "some of them got in through the burnt-out sections of the log parapets and were subjecting our first lines to attacks simultaneously in front and flank." The Confederates soon had control of a portion of the Union breastworks and "their little red flags" flew about them.[12] Despite this stroke of luck, the Union forces were able to expel the Confederates from the burning entrenchments through a one-two punch of close-range canister fire and an infantry charge.[13] In short, historians have relied on the fires to explain a momentary Confederate success in an otherwise fruitless assault.

These fires, however, may have received too much credit. Winfield S. Hancock, whose soldiers manned these entrenchments, hinted that the fiery breastworks may have merely aggravated an already deteriorating situation. He reported that the Confederate musketry "was very heavy" although not very effective. "Some of the troops began to waver," though, after about half an hour, and some of the soldiers stationed at the breastworks "gave way, retiring in disorder toward Chancellorsville." Hancock claimed that the "confusion and disorganization among a portion of the troops . . . on this occasion was greatly increased, if not originated, by the front line of breast-works having taken fire a short time before the enemy made his attack." The soldiers stationed there faced "the intense heat and the smoke, which was driven by the wind directly into" them, which "prevented them on portions of the line from firing over the parapet, and at some points compelled them to abandon the line."[14] Hancock's account, then, suggests that, in one way or another, the blazing entrenchments influenced the Federal soldiers' actions. Whether the fires acted as a catalyst, speeding a process already under way, or were chiefly responsible for the Union soldiers' retreat is unclear.

Most contemporary witnesses and historians have concluded that the fires were the primary cause of the Union withdrawal and thus the Confederates' fleeting success. But some have questioned this interpretation. Although William Swan, a Union V Corps veteran, acknowledged that the blazing entrenchments were usually blamed for "the temporary loss of the works," he argued "that too much importance has been given to this fire."[15] While he did not explain his reasoning, there were other circumstances besides the fires that might have influenced the Federals' behavior. For instance, Francis Walker, in his history of the II Corps, judged that "some of Mott's troops in the second line gave way [during the Confederate assault], without the slightest cause other than excitement and the strain, the labors and the losses of the morning."[16] These same types of strains no doubt affected the troops in the front line as well. Perhaps the fires just pushed the soldiers—already exhausted and demoralized to some degree—too far. How they would have reacted to the fires had they been fresh is unclear, but it is unquestionably an issue worth considering. Then again, perhaps the flaming entrenchments simply served as a convenient excuse to explain away the actions of unsteady troops.

While the role the fires played on May 6, 1864, might have been exaggerated, combat amid a flaming forest was still a perilous business. During the Battle of the Wilderness, George A. Bowen of the 12th New Jersey found fighting among the flames taxing, as "the heat and smoke [were] almost suffocating," and a Union signal officer in the II Corps opined that "the living were no light sufferers from the intense heat and smoke."[17] There was also the danger of explosions when the fires ignited the black powder the men carried. At Chancellorsville, Warren B. Persons of the 64th New York found that "everywhere we could hear guns going off which had been thrown away loaded, and shells bursting which had not exploded before."[18] Edwin Dow of the 6th Maine battery gave a good example of this danger at the Battle of the Wilderness. He complained that his unit's entrenchments, which were "composed of dry logs, caught fire," and some of his green men brought up cartridges to a gun near the fiery works. "The cartridges took fire . . . and exploded, burning 5 of the cannoneers severely."[19] Dealing with flaming entrenchments was a delicate matter as well. Josiah Murphey, a sergeant in the 20th Massachusetts, explained how the Union entrenchments "were built of dead trees and earth hastily thrown up," and when they caught fire, the soldiers were obliged to let the breastworks burn until the battle was concluded. Once the shooting had stopped, they felt at liberty to tear down the entrenchments near the burning portion and simply "built around it letting the fire burn itself out."[20]

Although the presence of forest fires certainly complicated combat in the Wilderness, these blazes also posed a distinct danger to the men who lay in the woods, crippled by ball, shot, and shell. It is no wonder soldiers reported that many were burned to death in the fires. At Chancellorsville, "Many wounded who could not be got away were burnt to death or suffocated by the smoke," reported J. W. McFarland, a Union chaplain. He recalled that while the Union soldiers "saw comparatively little of that burnt and bloody battle ground where friend and foe perished together," he considered what they saw to be "enough . . . to know something of its unspeakable horrors."[21] At the Battle of the Wilderness, similar reports circulated. Andrew J. McBride, a soldier in the 10th Georgia, wrote that "the woods took fire during the forenoon" on May 6, 1864, and "many of the poor fellows burned to death."[22] Emory Upton likewise observed that "the ground had been fought over and was strewn with wounded of both sides, many of whom must have perished in the flames, as corpses were found partly consumed."[23] In a similar vein, Jacob Raymer, a Confederate soldier in the 4th North Carolina, recorded that "many of the enemy's wounded were lying on the field uncared for, as well as all of their dead unburied," and "some of them partially burned to cinders by the fearful woods-fire which followed in the wake of our column."[24]

Even though efforts were made to save the wounded from their hellish fate, the soldiers' ability to fight the fires was limited at best. Some tried to remove any fuel that might allow the flames to reach the wounded. George Hugunin, a soldier with the 147th New York, described how, during the Battle of the Wilderness, he and some comrades "stopped and scraped the leaves away from 2 men, one a Fed. & one a reb. & gave them some water for the woods were on fire and they would burn otherwise."[25] Others tried to fight the fires once they were already burning. John R. Adams, a Union chaplain, "was putting out one of the fires, when General [John] Sedgwick passed, and said, 'That is right, chaplain, and get all the men to help you.'"[26] While these efforts might save fortunate individuals, they were not enough to extinguish the blazes, much less prevent them from spreading.

Despite the abundance of witnesses who testified that men burned to death, it is impossible to determine how many actually perished by fire. There are several problems to consider. First, not all witnesses actually saw men burn to death. Some only heard or assumed that men had burned to death. Others might have found ashen corpses and accepted this as proof. It is difficult, however, to know what killed a soldier who was caught in the flames. It can be assumed that they were either severely wounded or already dead, but how can it be determined whether they were dead before the fire arrived or died because of the fire's effects? It is not even clear whether the flames did the killing or whether smoke suffocated the soldiers. Frank Wilkeson, for one, pointed to the smoke that "rolled heavily and slowly before the fire" as the primary killer. This smoke, he explained, "enveloped the wounded, and I think that by far the larger portions of the men who were roasted were suffocated before the flames curled round them."[27] Moreover, most witnesses did not distinguish between those who were already dead and those who burned to death. Some, like John R. Adams, who recorded that "one of the men saw two Rebels, previously dead, crisped by the flames," did so on occasion, but this was exceptional.[28] Even here, though, the good chaplain was relying on hearsay. There is also the issue of finding the remains. The very nature of the Wilderness, covered with thick vegetation, made it hard to find the wounded and dead, and even years after the fact people were finding unburied bones in the Wilderness.[29]

Although there is no official estimate of how many men died from the flames at Chancellorsville, some individuals did venture guesses. John Tiffany of the 27th Virginia claimed four hundred Yankees had met a fiery end in the Chancellor house, while David R. Winn of the 4th Georgia alleged that "thousands of

Yankee wounded and hundreds of Confederates were burned."[30] The only thing approaching an official estimate of the number that perished in the blazes at the Battle of the Wilderness is provided by Thomas McParlin, a Union medical official, who freely admitted that "the number who thus perished is unknown, but it is supposed to have been about 200." Despite this, whenever an author wants to provide a rough figure of those who lost their lives because of the fires, they lean on McParlin's estimate.[31]

* * * *

No matter how many men actually burned in the woods, the soldiers who wrote about these events found them profoundly disturbing. Taken as a whole, their reactions to the Wilderness fires suggest four things: first, the horror they felt at men burning to death; second, their own fears of suffering that fate; third, the impression that the suffering of the wounded made upon them; and fourth, their desire to reconcile with their old enemies. These reactions tell us a great deal about the soldiers. In particular they demonstrated an instinctive fear of fire. No one needed to tell them that fire was terrifying or deadly. They knew the flames were a terrible foe. Not surprisingly, postwar writers portrayed the Blue and the Gray finding common cause in battling this mutual adversary and saving their fellow men from its destructive power.

The horror that soldiers felt at the idea of men burning to death was overwhelming. Just the thought of this happening troubled a number of soldiers on both sides. Robert McAllister speculated that during the Battle of Chancellorsville "some of the wounded were burnt" in the Chancellor house and "no doubt many shared the same sad fate" in the fiery woods. He confessed, "It is horrible to think of it," but he suspected that "some will no doubt survive to tell the particulars of these sad and painful stories," particulars that McAllister simply did not know.[32] Alexander Boteler, a member of Jeb Stuart's staff, also found it "horrible to think of hundreds of wounded men [being] in danger of being roasted alive."[33] Charles Wainwright, a Union artillery officer, shared a similar sentiment at the prospect of soldiers suffering a fiery death, and his only comfort was the hope "that many of them crawled, or were got off before the fire reached them, and that it made quick work with the others."[34]

There were soldiers, however, who actually experienced the fires at work in one capacity or another. Some saw the burnt corpses. A soldier from the 11th

Massachusetts recalled that at Chancellorsville "the fire ran so fast a number were taken out stripped naked and burned so badly that death would soon close their eyes."[35] At the Battle of the Wilderness, William W. Williamson, an officer in the 8th Georgia, saw that the "dead and wounded were burned and scorched until they looked as black as negroes."[36] Likewise, William D. Landon, a soldier in the 14th Indiana argued that "the ground in front of the position so hotly contested for on the 5th and 6th of May [1864] presented all the horrors of a battlefield, including the charred and blackened remains of those who were burned and smothered in the blazing leaves and underbrush."[37] Sight, however, was only one way to experience the fires. At the Battle of the Wilderness, Williamson agreed that "it was a most horrible sight" but also found "the smell that the burnt corpses emitted extremely shocking and sickening to the senses."[38] The cries of the wounded could be awful as well. During the fighting at Chancellorsville, J. W. McFarland, a Union chaplain, found it "sad to hear their piteous cries when no help could be given."[39] These cries were sometimes accompanied by the sound that burning bodies made. Jacob Raymer of the 4th North Carolina discovered at the Battle of the Wilderness that "bodies burned with a crackling noise" and "the screams, the unearthly shrieks made the night hideous."[40]

Given the intense ways that soldiers experienced the burning of the wounded, it is not surprising that for many it was the culmination of the horrors they experienced during combat in the Wilderness. John Tiffany of the 27th Virginia called the burning of the wounded "one of the most horrible sights I ever witnessed in my life," observing that when his unit got to the Chancellor house, "the bodies were singeing and frying among the burning fragments of the house."[41] Francis S. Johnson, a soldier in the 45th Georgia, similarly expressed the strong reaction that witnessing such scenes could elicit. "One of the most horrible and heart rending things," explained Johnson, occurred on May 3, 1863, at Chancellorsville when the wood fires caught the wounded. "The poor fellows tried to get out of the way but could not do it," Johnson said and concluded, "It was the worst thing I ever saw in my life and I have seen many bad sights."[42] While describing the Battle of Chancellorsville, Charles Wainwright likewise judged that "the most horrible thing of the day," was the burning of the wounded.[43] In a similar vein, Jacob Raymer of the 4th North Carolina emphasized that the forest fires at the Battle of the Wilderness infused "untold horrors to the scene of carnage." He observed that "many dead bodies . . . and not a few wounded," which "could not be brought out, . . . were left to their horrible fate." While "the greater portion of the dead and living who were thus burned in one awful funeral pile were our enemies," observed Raymer, "that signified nothing."[44]

Veterans writing after the war compared fighting in the flames to a battle in hell. The historian of the 106th Pennsylvania depicted the Confederates, who attacked the fiery Brock Road entrenchments on May 6, 1864, as pressing forward "like so many devils through the flames, charging over the burning works upon our retreating lines."[45] Others compared the burning of the wounded to some terrible vision of hell. "To add to the horrors of the scene," recalled Channing M. Smith, a Confederate, "the woods caught fire, and many of the wounded of Grant's army were burned alive." Smith doubted whether "the scenes depicted in 'Dante's inferno,'" could top what he saw in the Wilderness.[46] Of all the memoirists, perhaps Horace Porter, a Union veteran, best captured the spirit of how the Wilderness fires came to be remembered. "All circumstances seemed to combine to make the scene one of unutterable horror," explained Porter, as "forest fires raged; ammunition-trains exploded; the dead were roasted in the conflagration; the wounded, roused by its hot breath, dragged themselves along, with their torn and mangled limbs, in the mad energy of despair, to escape the ravages of the flames; and every bush seemed hung with shreds of blood-stained clothing. It was as though Christian men had turned to fiends, and hell itself had usurped the place of earth."[47]

Some soldiers' memoirs also captured the terror felt by those in peril of being consumed by the merciless flames. Warren Lee Goss, a Union veteran, repeated the story he had heard from a wounded man at Chancellorsville, in which the soldier "watched the flames and counted the moments when it would strike him, when the progress of the flames were arrested by a little stagnant pool of water."[48] Frank Wilkeson, another Federal veteran, emphasized the fear the soldiers reportedly felt during the Battle of the Wilderness at the thought of burning to death. The night before the engagement, a veteran of Chancellorsville sat with a group of soldiers around a campfire on the old battleground warning them of what lay before them. He concluded: "'This region,' indicating the woods beyond us with a wave of his arm, 'is an awful place to fight in. . . . The wounded are liable to be burned to death. I am willing to take my chances of getting killed, but I dread to have a leg broken and then to be burned slowly; and these woods will surely be burned if we fight here. I hope we will get through this chaparral without fighting.'" Once the battle had commenced, "the wounded were haunted with the dread of fire." Wilkeson recalled that "they conjured the scenes of the previous year, when some wounded men were burned to death, and their hearts well-nigh ceased to beat when they thought they detected the smell of burning wood in the air." Once wounded, "the bare prospect of fire running through the woods where they lay helpless, unnerved the most courageous of men, and made them call aloud for help," and "many wounded soldiers in the Wilderness . . . hung on to their rifles," with their "intention . . . clearly stamped on their pallid faces." One instance in particular stuck with Wilkeson, when he saw a wounded soldier who "meant to kill himself in case of fire—knew it as surely as though [he] could read [the man's] thoughts."[49]

Other writers dwelt at length on the suffering of the wounded. Warren Lee Goss told a story of one young Confederate that several men were trying to extricate from the fire at Chancellorsville. "The fire was all around him," wrote Goss, and his rescuers failed to save him from the merciless flames. One of the men trying to retrieve the Confederate remembered that "the last I saw of that fellow was his face. It was a handsome face. His eyes were big and blue, and his hair like raw silk surrounded by a wreath of fire, and then I heard him scream 'O mother! O God!'" The witness confessed, "It left [him] trembling all over like a leaf."[50] At the Battle of the Wilderness, the historian of the 146th New York recorded how "as the fire advanced it ignited the powder in the cartridge-boxes of the men and blew great holes in their sides. The almost cheerful sounding 'Pop! Pop!' of the cartridges gave no hint of the dreadful horror their noise bespoke." Meanwhile, "the wounded tried desperately to crawl to the road or the bare gully, but many were overtaken by the flames and perished miserably, some when safety seemed almost within their reach."[51] In contrast to these accounts, Frank Wilkeson questioned how much those caught in the fires really suffered. The prospect of men burning to death, he admitted "was courage-sapping and pitiful, and it appealed strongly to the imagination of the spectator," but he for one did "not believe that the wounded soldiers, who were being burned, suffered greatly, if they suffered at all."[52]

Oddly enough, some postwar accounts of the Wilderness fires reflected the theme of reconciliation: recognizing both sides for their bravery and stressing their common values rather than the divisive issues that caused the war. Usually these accounts involved soldiers halting the fight to save the wounded and even fighting the fire together to do so, which demonstrated their common humanity as well as their valor. Warren Lee Goss, a Union veteran, recounted the experience of one Federal soldier at Chancellorsville, who though wounded "couldn't see the poor devils burn up in that way" and, rousing himself, "began to pull away the burning brushwood, and got some of them out." As he was working, a wounded rebel came up to lend him a hand as he "wa'n't goin' to have a d—d Yank beat him at anything." Soon another Confederate joined them and they "fought the fire all together." The firefighting left the Union soldier's hands "blistered and burned so [he] could not open or shut them, but [he] and [the] rebs tried to shake hands." In the end, the Federal concluded that "them two fellers wer'n't so bad," noting that one of them went out of his way to help him to the river crossing and to procure a guide to get him to the other side.[53] Another instance of this coming together to save the wounded was at the Battle of the Wilderness in the Orange Turnpike sector. When fires sparked and spread across the field and woods in that area, "Friend and foe joined in fighting the common enemy, for the dead and wounded of both sides lay upon the ground between the lines."[54] Other times, there is the added detail of the men halting to fight to save the wounded only to go back to shooting at each other once they completed rescuing their comrades. A postwar newspaper article on the Battle of the Wilderness recorded how "on one part of the lines both Federal and Confederate momentarily laid aside their rifles and rushed into the flames to save the wretched wounded, and when this was completed and the fire controlled they seized anew their rifles, [and] renewed the conflict."[55] These remembrances stand in curious juxtaposition to the contemporary accounts of soldiers who accused their opponents of intentionally starting fires.

* * * *

It is important to recognize, however, that despite their close association with forest fires, Chancellorsville and the Wilderness were far from the only engagements where blazes raged and flames threatened to engulf the wounded. At Chickamauga (September 18–20, 1863), N. J. Hampton saw how "the woods caught fire, burning our wounded men before we could take them up." As at the Battle of the Wilderness and Chancellorsville, men would try to save themselves but to no avail. Hampton recalled seeing "numbers of wounded soldiers who in some way would get a stick or dead limb, and in an attempt to save their lives would rake the ground around them perfectly clean so that the fire could not reach them." Despite "their hard struggles, many of them were scorched to death with the sticks in their hands." As did many of the witnesses of such scenes at the battles in the Wilderness, Hampton concluded that "this was one of the most terrible sights man ever witnessed."[56] Other similarities are also apparent. As at the Battle of the Wilderness, the Union breastworks at Chickamauga sometimes caught fire. The historian of the 38th Indiana remembered such a scene, noting how the men "who had only a few drops of water in their canteens, passed them up until the fire was extinguished."[57]

Reminiscent of the postwar accounts from the Wilderness battles, Kennesaw Mountain provides an excellent example of Federals and Confederates coming together to save their wounded from the flames. At Kennesaw Mountain (June 27, 1864), "the dry leaves and undergrowth in the forest before Cleburne's Division were set on fire by . . . shells and gun wadding." Soon they "began burning rapidly around the Federal wounded and dead, exposing them to a horrible death."[58] Seeing the situation, the colonel of the 1st Arkansas called for a cease-fire to rescue the wounded men. One veteran recalled that "our men, scaling the head logs as though for a counter charge, were soon mixed with Yankees, carrying out dead and wounded Feds," and "together, the Rebs and Yanks soon had the fire beat out and the dead and wounded removed."[59] A contemporary account, however, reveals that others were not so fortunate. J. L. Bostick, a soldier in the 20th Tennessee, recalled that similar fires broke out on his part of the front. "Our men proposed to cease firing" explained Bostick, "but it was not agreed to, and consequently some of the enemy who were too badly hurt to move out of the way of the fire, were burned to death."[60]

* * * *

While forest fires were hardly unique to the Wilderness, the fires became part of the forest's image, part of its romance and horror, part of why we like to read about the battles that took place there. The attraction is only human. It comes from our primordial fear of fire, our love of drama, and our appetite for the macabre. Here amid the Wilderness fires we see ourselves reflected. Yet these same fires tell us something about the people who witnessed them. We see their fears and their feeling for their fellow man. We see the trials of combat and how assumptions about the enemy can taint how soldiers interpreted a battle. We can also see the postwar need for reconciliation. Despite the passage of time, as one veteran put it, "The agonizing shrieks of helpless men, who perished in the flames in that Wilderness of woe, are not forgotten. They never will be forgotten this side of eternity."[61] And he was right.

Adam H. Petty

1. For examples see Gordon C. Rhea, *The Battle of the Wilderness: May 5–6, 1864* (Baton Rouge: Louisiana State University Press, 1994); and Stephen W. Sears, *Chancellorsville* (Boston: Houghton Mifflin, 1996). John Hennessey has provided the closest thing to a focused analysis in a blog post. John Hennessey, "Capturing the Wilderness's Signature Horror: Fire," https://npsfrsp.wordpress .com/2014/05/03/capturing-the-wildernesss-signature-horror-fire/. Also see Stephen Cushman, *Bloody Promenade: Reflections on a Civil War Battle* (Charlottesville: University Press of Virginia, 1999).

2. "From Berry's Fighting Division," *Salem (MA) Register*, May 14, 1863; Charles S. Wainwright, *A Diary of Battle: The Personal Journals of Colonel Charles S. Wainwright, 1861–1865*, ed. Allan Nevins (New York: Harcourt, Brace and World, 1962), 197; May 9, 1863, published letter from Rev. J. W. McFarland in Joseph S. Graham to Ellen Lee, May 29, 1863, in *A Compilation of Graham Family Letters*, ed. Janice B. McFadden, 87, bound volume 121, Fredericksburg and Spotsylvania County Battlefields Memorial National Military Park and Cemetery, Fredericksburg, VA (hereafter FSNMP); John Piney Oden, "The End of Oden's War: A Confederate Captain's Diary," ed. Michael Barton, *Alabama Historical Quarterly* 43, no. 2 (Summer 1981): 84; Alpheus S. Williams, *From the Cannon's Mouth: The Civil War Letters of General Alpheus S. Williams*, ed. Milo M. Quaife (Detroit: Wayne State University Press, 1959), 199.

3. See "Letter from Chaplain Perkins," *Boston Recorder*, May 27, 1864; "From the 140th Regiment," *Washington (PA) Reporter*, June 1, 1864; Edward Perkins Preble Diary, May 6, 1864, bound volume 34,. FSNMP.

4. Oden, "The End of Oden's War," 84; David Read Evans Winn to Fannie, May 9, 1863, David Read Evans Winn Papers, Stuart A. Rose Manuscript, Archives, and Rare Book Library, Emory University, Atlanta.

5. *The War of the Rebellion: A Compilation of the Official Records of the Union and Confederate Armies*, 127 vols. (Washington, DC: Government Printing Office, 1880–1901), ser. 1, vol. 36, pt. 1, 665–666 (hereafter cited as *OR*).

6. Josiah F. Murphey Reminiscences, Ms. "20th" Cab. 6.5, Boston Public Library, Boston.

7. "The 5th Regiment—One Month's Record," *Newark (NJ) Daily Advertiser*, June 17, 1864.

8. James W. Freeman Diary, May 6, 1864, bound volume 480, FSNMP.

9. Robert S. Robertson to his parents, May 14, 1864, bound volume 219, FSNMP.

10. For more on the Federal inferiority complex in the Virginia theater of the war, see Michael C. C. Adams, *Our Masters the Rebels: A Speculation on Union Military Failure in the East, 1861–1865* (Cambridge, MA: Harvard University Press, 1978).

11. For examples, see Rhea, *Battle of the Wilderness*, 394; and William Swinton, *Campaigns of the Army of the Potomac* (New York: Charles B. Richardson, 1866), 436–437.

12. Thomas F. Galwey, *The Valiant Hours: An Irishman in the Civil War*, ed. W. S. Nye (Harrisburg, PA: Stackpole, 1961), 200–201.

13. Francis B. Harris Diary, May 6, 1864, bound volume 352, FSNMP; "Grant's Virginia Campaign," *Columbia Democrat* (Bloomsburg, PA), June 18, 1864.

14. *OR*, ser. 1, vol. 36, pt. 1, 324.

15. William W. Swan, "Battle of the Wilderness," in *Papers of the Military Historical Society of Massachusetts* (Boston: Military Historical Society of Massachusetts, 1881–1918), 4:161.

16. Francis A. Walker, *History of the Second Army Corps in the Army of the Potomac* (New York: Charles Scribner's Sons, 1887), 432.

17. George A. Bowen Diary, May 10, 1864, bound volume 228, FSNMP; "From the Army," *Brockport (NY) Republic*, June 16, 1864.

18. Warren B. Persons to Daniel Dodge Persons, May 30, 1863, bound volume 147, FSNMP.

19. *OR*, ser. 1, vol. 36, pt. 1, 514.

20. Josiah F. Murphey Reminiscences, Ms. "20th" Cab. 6.5, Boston Public Library.

21. May 9, 1863 published letter from Rev. J. W. McFarland in Joseph S. Graham to Ellen Lee, May 29, 1863, in *A Compilation of Graham Family Letters*, ed. Janice B. McFadden, 87, bound volume 121, FSNMP.

22. Andrew J. McBride to Mary Frances Johnson, May 6, 1864, Andrew J. McBride Papers, Rubenstein Rare Book and Manuscript Library, Perkins Library, Duke University, Durham, North Carolina.

23. *OR*, ser. 1, vol. 36, pt.1, 665–666.

24. Jacob Nathaniel Raymer, *Confederate Correspondent: The Civil War Reports of Jacob Nathaniel Raymer, Fourth North Carolina*, ed. E. B. Munson (Jefferson, NC: McFarland, 2008), 127.

25. George Hugunin Diary/Memoir, May 5, 1864, bound volume 358, FSNMP.

26. John R. Adams, *Memorial and Letters of Rev. John R. Adams, D.D., Chaplain of the Fifth Maine and One Hundred and Twenty-First New York Regiments during the War of the Rebellion, Serving from the Beginning to Its Close* (Cambridge, MA: University Press, 1890), 153.

27. Frank Wilkeson, *Recollections of a Private* (New York: G. P. Putnam's Sons, 1887), 201.

28. Adams, *Memorial and Letters of Rev. John R. Adams*, 153.

29. "An Ex-Campaigner in Virginia," in *Rifle Shots and Bugle Notes; or, the National Military Album of Sketches of the Principal Battles, Marches, Picket Duty, Camp Fires, Love Adventures, and Poems Connected with the Late War*, ed. Joseph A. Joel and Lewis R. Stegman (New York: Grand Army Gazette, 1884), 428.

30. John Tiffany to his parents, May 8, 1863, bound volume 207, FSNMP; David Read Evans Winn to Fannie, May 9, 1863, David Read Evans Winn Papers, Stuart A. Rose Manuscript, Archives, and Rare Book Library, Emory University, Atlanta.

31. For examples see Warren Lee Goss, *Recollections of a Private: A Story of the Army of the Potomac* (New York: Thomas Y. Cromwell, 1890), 277; and Andrew A. Humphreys, *The Virginia Campaign of '64 and '65* (New York: Charles Scribner's Sons, 1885), 54.

32. Robert McAllister, *The Civil War Letters of General Robert McAllister*, ed. James I. Robertson Jr. (New Brunswick, NJ: Rutgers University Press, 1965), 307.

33. Alexander Boteler Diary, May 4, 1864, William Elizabeth Brooks Collection, Library of Congress, Washington, DC.

34. Wainwright, *A Diary of Battle*, 197.

35. "From Berry's Fighting Division," *Salem (MA) Register*, May 14, 1863.

36. *Confederate Union* (Milledgeville, GA), June 7, 1864.

37. William D. Landon, "Fourteenth Indiana Regiment, Letters to the Vicennes Western Sun," *Indiana Magazine of History* 34 (March 1938): 93.

38. *Confederate Union* (Milledgeville, GA), June 7, 1864.

39. May 9, 1863, published letter from Rev. J. W. McFarland in Joseph S. Graham to Ellen Lee,

Adam H. Petty

May 29, 1863 in *A Compilation of Graham Family Letters*, ed. Janice B. McFadden, 87, bound volume 121, FSNMP.

40. Raymer, *Confederate Correspondent*, 67.

41. John Tiffany to his parents, May 8, 1863, bound volume 207, FSNMP.

42. Francis Solomon Johnson Jr. to Emily Hutchings, May 9, 1863, Ms. 243, Special Collections, University of Georgia, Athens, Georgia.

43. Wainwright, *A Diary of Battle*, 197.

44. Raymer, *Confederate Correspondent*, 67.

45. Joseph R. C. Ward, *History of the 106th Regiment Pennsylvania Volunteers, 2d Brigade, 2d Division, 2d Corps, 1861–1865* (Philadelphia, F. McManus Jr, 1906), 242.

46. Channing M. Smith, "In the Wilderness," *Confederate Veteran* 29, no. 6 (June 1921): 212.

47. Horace Porter, *Campaigning with Grant* (New York: Century, 1897), 72–73.

48. Goss, *Recollections of a Private*, 163.

49. Wilkeson, *Recollections of a Private*, 50, 66–67.

50. Goss, *Recollections of a Private*, 164–165.

51. Mary Genevie Green Brainard, *Campaigns of the One Hundred and Forty-Sixth Regiment New York State Volunteers, Also Known as Halleck's Infantry, the Fifth Oneida, and Garrard's Tigers* (New York: G. P. Putnam's Sons, 1915), 195.

52. Wilkeson, *Recollections of a Private*, 201.

53. Goss, *Recollections of a Private*, 163–165.

54. Brainard, *Campaigns of the One Hundred and Forty-Sixth Regiment*, 195.

55. "Three Heroes of the Civil War: Further Recollections of the Featherston-Posey-Harris Brigade," *New Orleans Times Picayune*, September 8, 1902.

56. N. J. Hampton, *An Eyewitness to the Dark Days of 1861–65* (Nashville, 1898), 34.

57. Henry Fales, *History of the Thirty-Eighth Regiment Indiana Volunteer Infantry* (Palo Alto, CA: F. A. Stuart, 1906), 93.

58. William E. Bevens, *Reminiscences of a Private: William E. Bevens of the First Arkansas Infantry, C.S.A.*, ed. Daniel E. Sutherland (Fayetteville: University of Arkansas Press, 1992), 175.

59. W. T. Barnes, "An Incident of Kennesaw," *Confederate Veteran* 30, no. 2 (February 1922): 49. For another account of this ceasefire incident see Samuel G. French, *Two Wars: An Autobiography of Gen. Samuel G. French* (Nashville: Confederate Veteran, 1901), 211.

60. J. L. Bostick to his mother, June 28, 1864, in *Old Enough to Die*, ed. Ridley Wills (Franklin, TN: Hillsboro, 1996), 127.

61. "Down in Dixie: Personal Recollections of the War of the Rebellion," *Troy (NY) Daily Times*, April 19, 1888.

United States Colored Troops and the Battle of the Crater

A. WILSON GREENE

At 6:00 p.m. on July 28, 1864, Lieutenant Colonel Henry Pleasants, commander of the 48th Pennsylvania Infantry, stood outside the entrance to his mine. Pleasants had just completed overseeing the placement of short stretches of fuse leading to eight thousand pounds of black powder carefully lodged underneath a prominent Confederate fort barely more than a mile southeast of Petersburg, Virginia. In a mere thirty-four days, Pleasants and the men of his regiment—many experienced miners in civilian life—had excavated a shaft 510.8 feet long and then prepared twin galleries in which the explosives had been silently placed. The specifics of how the Union army would use Pleasants's engineering marvel, however, had yet to be determined.[1]

The contending armies had been at Petersburg six weeks. Beginning on June 12, Lieutenant General Ulysses S. Grant had brilliantly transferred the Army of the Potomac under Major General George G. Meade from the northeastern outskirts of Richmond across the James River. Three days later he launched his first attempt to capture the logistically critical city on the right bank of the Appomattox River, two dozen miles south of Richmond. Joined by Major General Benjamin F. Butler's Army of the James, Meade's forces hammered at a thin Confederate line east and south of Petersburg, forcing the rebels to retreat—twice—before they stiffened on their last possible defensible terrain. Once General Robert E. Lee's Army of Northern Virginia shifted south from the Richmond earthworks, the Federal offensive at Petersburg stalled.

Disenchanted with frontal attacks, Grant tried a major flanking movement a few days later, designed to encircle Lee's defenders and cut Confederate communications. This gambit failed in spectacular fashion, signaling the first of what would be many interregnums between Union initiatives at Petersburg. It was during this interlude that Major General Ambrose E. Burnside's 9th Corps authorized construction of the mine targeting a strong point along Lee's perimeter known as Pegram's or Elliott's Salient. Grant and Meade tolerated Burnside's experiment but considered the mine a tactical afterthought until the final days of July, when their offensive north of the James River—styled First Deep Bottom—failed. The Union high command now turned to the mine to salvage their third attempt to capture Petersburg.[2]

Burnside's corps had participated in Grant's relentless campaign since early May, including prominent assaults on June 17 and 18. The corps's three white divisions had suffered severe casualties and, in their commanders' minds, teetered on the edge of demoralization. Thus Burnside turned to his 4th Division, consisting of two brigades of US Colored Troops, to exploit the opportunity promised by his mine's explosion.[3]

Burnside recalled that Brigadier General Edward Ferrero, commander of the 4th Division, and his brigade commanders, Colonel Henry Thomas and Lieutenant Colonel Joshua K. Sigfried, "expressed to me their utmost confidence" in their troops' "ability to make a charge." Such confidence found its origin in faith rather than experience, as few of Ferrero's forty-three hundred enlisted men had ever fired a shot in anger. Still, the black soldiers were fresh and eager for the chance to prove themselves in battle.[4]

Attitudes of white Union soldiers varied toward these untested African American troops. Grant's other black division, members of the 18th Corps in Butler's army, had acquitted themselves well during the first Petersburg offensive and earned the grudging respect of many whites. "The colored boys are brave and loyal soldiers and they look as fat and sleek as Henry Clay's slaves," wrote a Wisconsin private. Colonel William Wirt Henry of the 10th Vermont agreed. "In these fights around Petersburg, they have fought nobly and if there was prejudice among some before it is all gone now in this army," but Henry clearly overstated the case. "No amount of money could hire me to serve with niggers," wrote Private Andrew Jackson Crossley of the engineers. Captain Josiah Jones of the 6th New Hampshire concluded that "the negroes do us no good." Private Elon G. Mills of the 17th Michigan in Burnside's 3rd Division took a middle ground, typical of many of Grant's men at this stage of the war. "We have the 4 div. colored for our support but have not given them any chance to show their grit as yet," wrote Mills. "A great many of them are anxious to have a chance at the Johnnys & stated they will never take them as a prisoner."[5]

No such ambivalence muddied Confederate perceptions. Wherever black soldiers had appeared along the lines, gray-clad marksmen opened a particularly intense fire. "The rebels would never allow the negroes, or the troops immediately associated with them, to rest in peace, and on the front held by the

9th Corps there was a constant, distressing, deadly dropping of musketry and artillery kept up," reported a Massachusetts soldier. General Henry A. Wise, Confederate commander of the Post of Petersburg, recognized that "the negro soldiers are no doubt incited to give no quarter from the fury with which they are excited by the enemy's accounts of Fort Pillow. We certainly will show them & their white officers no quarter." Events would confirm the accuracy of Wise's prediction.[6]

Ferrero proposed that once the mine exploded, his men would charge immediately, hitting the enemy line just south of the resulting crater, using the debris as flank protection for his right. The leading regiments would then move behind the Confederate works and peel off to the left and right, widening the breach, while the rest of the division dashed forward toward the commanding ground on Cemetery Hill, 533 yards to the northwest. The corps's white divisions would follow, securing this key terrain and controlling with artillery the rear of Lee's lines, placing Petersburg itself at the mercy of Federal cannons. Burnside readily approved this scheme, and Ferrero provided his two brigade commanders with a rough map of the ground, instructing them to study the details of their assault.[7]

The degree to which Ferrero's men prepared for their dangerous mission remains cloaked in controversy. Abundant testimony avers that the black soldiers trained extensively. Captain William H. Harris of Burnside's staff recorded in his journal that the 4th Division had been learning "their duty by constant application . . . for the previous month." Sergeant Major Leander O. Merriam of the 31st Maine, a unit in the 9th Corps's 2nd Division, remembered watching "the niggers drill . . . for many an hour . . . day after day." Captain Ervin T. Case of the 9th New Hampshire wrote that "the colored division . . . were kept in reserve and in constant drill."[8]

However, the bulk of the evidence suggests that little if any preparation occurred more than ten days before the mine's eventual explosion. Ferrero complained that most of his men were either on picket or engaged in building fortifications prior to July 30. His own official report mentioned nothing of any special training provided for his troops. Lieutenant Freeman Bowley of the 30th US Colored Troops (USCT), one of the regiments designated to lead the attack, stated that he had no knowledge of the mine until the day before it ignited. Robert K. Beecham, an officer in the 23rd USCT, provided an unambiguous assessment of the training received by his regiment. "I was on duty with my company and regiment every day from the 22nd of June until after the battle of the Mine on the 30th day of July. . . . I am prepared to say from actual knowledge derived from personal experience with the Fourth Division that the only duty assigned to the said division for more than a month before the battle . . . was work upon our trenches and fortifications." While it may not be possible to reconcile such conflicting accounts, it seems likely that few of Ferrero's men received extensive training and many received none at all in preparation for leading the attack.[9]

As it turned out, the black soldiers' training—or lack thereof—would be irrelevant. Although the Union offensive at Deep Bottom gained little traction, it did draw all but three of Lee's infantry divisions north of the James River. Now, with Confederate manpower so weakened around Petersburg, Burnside's mine assumed centrality in Grant's operational thinking. The Federal general in chief laid aside whatever reservations he harbored regarding the mine's offensive potential and ordered its detonation for the morning of July 30. Meade, however, believed Burnside's plan required tweaking. On July 28 he calmly informed the 9th Corps commander that the US Colored Troops could not spearhead the assault. A shocked Burnside protested vigorously, so Meade agreed to place the matter before Grant that afternoon, promising to abide by his decision.[10]

The rest of the day and most of the following morning passed at 9th Corps headquarters with no word from Meade. Burnside reached the conclusion, unjustifiably as it developed, that no news was good news and that Grant had sustained his plan. But about 11:00 a.m. Meade informed Burnside that, on the contrary, Grant had agreed that the 4th Division should not lead the attack. Up until that point, Burnside had done everything right, but now his indulgent personality prompted him to make a terrible mistake. Instead of assigning the division of either Brigadier General Robert Potter or Brigadier General Orlando Willcox—both competent commanders—to assume the lead role, Burnside left the decision to chance—and lady luck deserted him. Brigadier General James Ledlie drew the short straw and his 1st Division would now make the initial charge. Ledlie had a justifiably flawed reputation, an officer at Meade's headquarters considering him "a wretched, incapable drunkard, not fit to command a company, and was the ruin of his division." Meade's lack of confidence in the black troops (and his fear that if the attack failed, the army would be accused of callously sacrificing African American men) and Burnside's unwillingness to compel the reluctant Potter or Willcox to undertake the dangerous assignment resulted in entrusting the fate of the offensive to the least competent division commander in Grant's army group.[11]

Ledlie made hasty preparations for his critical assignment, including issuing orders that conflicted with the approved tactics. The 1st Division and the rest of 9th Corps quietly shuffled into position after dark on July 29. Ferrero's men were the last to deploy after midnight, Sigfried's brigade in the lead, with Thomas's in support. The men enjoyed a "soldiers' hasty breakfast" of hardtack and salt pork, stacked their knapsacks, and listened as their officers explained their new and diminished role in the assault.[12]

The mine exploded at 4:44 a.m., and with sad predictability, Ledlie's soldiers went forward absent their leader, who sought cowardly refuge in a rear-area aid station. Their attack faltered, impeded by the sheer chaos of the situation at the front and the lack of a guiding hand. When Potter's and Willcox's men followed the 1st Division, the situation grew hopelessly confused. The Federals milled about the ruins of the Confederate fortifications or sought shelter within the jagged crater created by the blast, as the rebels gradually recovered from their initial shock and began to pour artillery and infantry fire into the packed mass of humanity.[13]

For more than an hour, the black troops waited expectantly in the covered ways leading to the front, occasionally making room for rebel prisoners heading to the rear who, upon seeing Ferrero's men, beseeched their guards "not to let the niggers bayonet them." Burnside sent Ferrero multiple instructions to join the offensive, but each time the 4th Division commander demurred from the comfort of the same bombproof that sheltered Ledlie, citing with some justification the overcrowded conditions around the Crater. Meade berated Burnside to employ all of his men, so at 7:30 a.m. the corps commander ordered Ferrero to advance his division, irrespective of conditions at the front.[14]

Although some disagreement remains as to whether the 30th USCT or 43rd USCT led the way, every witness agreed that as soon as the black troops crested the rise between the front Union lines and the Crater, they encountered vicious canister and small-arms fire. Sergeant Harry Reese, who had superintended the day-to-day excavation of the mine, felt "furious to see a division of colored soldiers rush[ing] into the jaws of death with no prospect of success; but they went in cheering as though they didn't mind it." Captain Charles F. Stinson of the 19th USCT in Thomas's brigade considered "the slaughter . . . fearful" and remembered that "the bullets came in amongst us like hailstones." Many white soldiers, some no admirers of the African American units, praised the fortitude they showed as they pushed their way to the front.[15]

The stubborn Confederate defenders who had formed along the margins of the Federal penetration heard the shouts of Ferrero's men: "No quarter!" and "Remember Fort Pillow!" "Oh but they looked black and ugly" thought Private William Day of the 49th North Carolina, who claimed to have seen the blacks bayonet some of the wounded rebels still alive around the Crater and firmly believed that being captured by the USCTs meant certain death. "We had no cowards," wrote Day. "Every man stood square to his post and fought with the heroism of men reduced to desperation." Colonel Delavan Bates of the 30th USCT echoed Day's grim assessment of the nature of the struggle: "It is the only battle I was ever in where it appeared to be just pure enjoyment to kill an opponent."[16]

The combat now became intensely personal. Some Confederates were "ruthlessly bayoneted" as they begged for mercy. Many of the outnumbered graycoats remained defiant, rallying their comrades by reminding them that "they are nothing but niggers." Eventually Ferrero's soldiers secured between 100 and 250 rebel prisoners along with at least one Confederate battle flag. Yet the surviving southerners maintained such a hot fire that Colonel Thomas reported that "half the few who came out of the works were shot."[17]

Twenty minutes of relative calm transpired before an officer from Ferrero's staff appeared with a message for his brigade commanders: "Colonels Sigfried and Thomas, if you have not already done so, you will immediately proceed to take the crest in your front." These orders may have made sense if issued during the first assaults, but now any attempt to cross the open ground west of the captured Confederate works would amount to suicide. Nevertheless, by 8:45 a.m. Thomas, along with Colonel Bates, had organized about five hundred of their men to execute the patently pointless attack. "The surroundings were such that a line of battle could not be formed and all that I could do was to order an advance to the front," admitted Colonel Bates. "We reached the open plain beyond the line of breast-works in which we were partially protected. . . . How far we went I do not know, for a volley from our front and right disabled about one-half of our officers and one-third of the privates."[18]

"Never in all my experience did I see artillery do such awful execution as was done that morning in the ranks of those black men," testified an officer in a USCT regiment. "It looked as if one side of hell had been opened, and fire and brimstone were belching forth." Lieutenant Colonel John A. Bross, commanding the 29th USCT, was among the most prominent of Ferrero's casualties. Wearing his full dress uniform and endowed with a distinguished civilian career in Chicago and an army reputation to match, Bross sprang over the works holding his regimental banner aloft. "Boys, I want you to follow this flag," he shouted to his men. "We'll show the world today that the colored troops are soldiers. Forward, my brave boys." At that moment a ball struck the left side of Bross's head, killing him almost instantly.[19]

By this time, the first Confederate reinforcements had arrived on the field. Brigadier General William Mahone's division started the day on the far right of the rebel line, well west of the Crater. When orders arrived to respond to the crisis to the east, Mahone quickly designated two of his brigades—Georgians under Lieutenant Colonel Matthew R. Hall and his old Virginia troops, now under Colonel David A. Weisiger—to secretly disengage from their positions on the line and move quickly to the scene of action. Many of Weisiger's men hailed from the Petersburg area and when informed that blacks were among the Federals threatening the city, they found special motivation. "The Petersburg boys knew that they were the only line between their homes and the thousands of drunken negroes making that cry and they must be stopped or life would not be worth living," explained one southerner. The Virginians deployed about 9:00 a.m. in a shallow ravine some two hundred yards west of the Crater. "The sight of the Negro troops inflamed them," according to a Confederate artillerist, "& without waiting for the Georgians who were coming up, the whole line charged."[20]

Although Confederate veterans engaged in a bitter postwar debate regarding who ordered the Virginians forward, many would testify that a conspicuous Union officer appeared to be readying a charge, signaling the need to initiate the counterattack. That officer was, apparently, Colonel Bross. Weisiger's brigade, some eight hundred men, rose accordingly and advanced across the gently rising ground toward numberless but disorganized Federals. "Mahone's men, like Putnam's at Bunker Hill, reserved their fire until they saw the whites of their adversary's eyes—not a difficult matter since many of the combatants were contraband of a sooty hue," reported a Richmond newspaper. Once the Virginians reached the captured works, they unleashed a massive volley that, according to an officer in the 61st Virginia, crashed "into a mass of humanity, for the ditches and parapets were so crowded with men that they were in each other's way." A private in that regiment remembered that "it was not necessary to take aim, because they were so crowded that we could not miss." Some Virginians, in mock imitation of the African Americans' war cry, shouted "Remember Beast Butler."[21]

Now with empty rifles, the southerners leapt into the works, initiating a period of unspeakable brutality. "For many minutes, which seemed like hours, amid the roar of artillery and musketry, the groans of the wounded, the prayers of the dying, and the imprecations of the living, men pierced each other's hearts and crushed each other's skulls until the place seemed a veritable hell," recalled one witness. Although the Union defenders included blacks and whites, Confederates focused most of their attention on the African American soldiers. "We slaughtered hundreds of whites and blacks with decided preference to the Ethiopians," boasted one gray-clad officer. Colonel Stephen M. Weld of the 56th Massachusetts remembered a black soldier falling by his side as a Confederate shouted, "Shoot the nigger, but don't kill the white man."[22]

Both sides, including the USCTs, fought "like tigers" or "devils." Black soldiers found particular incentive to defend themselves, as surrendering likely meant death. "How the negroes' skulls cracked under the blows," boasted one bloodthirsty rebel. "You may rest assured 'no quarter' was shown," recalled another. "An indiscriminate butchery commenced and hardly a negro remained to tell the story. . . . Not a single negro ought to have been captured." The bodies stacked up, making it difficult to maneuver, and two of Weisiger's regimental commanders detailed soldiers to move the corpses out of the way. "The blood was running nearly shoe sole deep in the trenches," explained one of the officers. "Men fell dead in heaps, and human gore ran in streams that made the very earth mire beneath the tread of victorious soldiers."[23]

For some beleaguered black soldiers, the combat reached a breaking point. "A panic seized the colored troops, and they went pouring through and over our men," reported the 2nd Division's Brigadier General Simon G. Griffin. A Michigan soldier believed that "abject terror had infused itself into every one of them." Some witnesses blamed their panic on the tremendous casualties sustained by their officers, leaving them leaderless, while others chalked it up to a perceived innate inability of African American men to endure battle.[24]

Retreating black soldiers swept many white Federals along with them. "I saw more Yankee soldiers than I had ever seen before—as far as the eyes could reach . . . one fleeing & retreating mass which I will remember caused a sense of pleasure to observe the direction," beamed Virginia Lieutenant William Fielding Baugh. Some of Ferrero's men declined to run the gauntlet to the rear and jumped into the trenches still occupied by white troops, or into the Crater it-self, creating a new kind of mayhem. A few exasperated and equally frightened whites attempted to embolden their black comrades by shooting at them. "Give the black devils a dose, and then take the bayonet to the rebels," screamed one New Hampshire soldier. "I think that many of the colored troops were killed by our men purposely on account of the darks rushing back into the trenches occupied by the whites," explained Private Warren S. Gurney of the 56th Mas-sachusetts. "One of our Regt told me that he fired twenty rounds at them and thinks he killed a nigger every time."[25]

The Federals retained enough organized determination to repel a feeble attack by Hall's Georgians. The situation around the Crater then degenerated into an exchange of fire from sheltered locations, both sides debilitated by the midday heat and almost superhuman exertion expended during the battle. The survivors in and around the Crater endured conditions unprecedented in their horror. "At the hour of 1 p.m. the bottom, sides, and nearly all parts of the Crater were strewn with dead, dying, and wounded soldiers, causing pools of blood to be formed at the bottom," wrote Captain Theodore Gregg of the 45th Pennsyl-vania. "It seemed impossible to maintain life from the heat of the sun." Another participant remembered that "blood was everywhere, trickling down the sides of the Crater in streamlets, and in many places ponds of it as large as an ordi-nary wash basin." An officer in the 57th Massachusetts considered the Crater "one seething cauldron of struggling, dying men."[26]

By this time, Grant and Meade had given up on the offensive and ordered Burnside to suspend his attacks and return to the main Union lines. Burnside preferred to hold the ground he had captured, but neither risking a retreat across the open ground subject to blanketing Confederate fire or remaining in the hellish environment around the Crater offered an attractive option. Some soldiers attempted to dig trenches leading back to the Federal works, while others stacked corpses into a macabre breastwork to shield themselves from rebel bullets and shells. For the Union soldiers remaining around the Crater, the question ceased to be one of victory or defeat: it was now a matter of sur-vival. Brigadier General John C. C. Sanders, commander of Mahone's Alabama Brigade, would put that question to the test.[27]

Shortly after Mahone had arrived near the Crater, he realized that two bri-gades would not be enough to remedy the situation, so he sent orders to Sanders to join Weisiger and Hall. By about 1:00 p.m. Sanders had arrayed his 632 men in the same ravine from which Weisiger and Hall had launched their attacks. Joined by perhaps 250 additional Confederates from a variety of units west of the Crater, the Alabamians prepared to "die or retake that salient."[28]

At the appointed hour, Sanders's regiments executed a disciplined advance, sufficiently impressive that the demoralized and exhausted Federals occupying the works on either side of the Crater fled, surrendered, or sought shelter in the Crater itself. This left perhaps one thousand bluecoats—blacks and whites—to meet the Alabamians in what would prove to be a sanguinary and uneven contest. Mahone had informed the Alabamians that the black troops had cried "No quarter" during their attacks. "He did not say, 'show no quarter,'" remembered Lieutenant Phillip M. Vance of the 11th Alabama, "but Sanders's men decided that point." The Confederates reached the rim of the Crater "and poured volley after volley into this heaped-up mass of terrified negroes and their brave officers," wrote Captain William L. Fagan of the 8th Alabama. "Shattering volleys were fired into the seething abyss," shuddered another witness, "till it became a perfect hell of blood."[29]

The struggle proved short-lived. Some terrified Federals bolted and others surrendered, absent the command and control required to halt combat that had become more butchery than battle. As during the earlier Confederate counterattack, Sanders's men vented particular rage on the African American soldiers. "Our men . . . clubbed their guns and knocked them in the head like killing hogs," reported Private Aaron T. Fleming of the 10th Alabama. South Carolina quartermaster Hall T. McGee wrote in his diary that "the negro troops were slaughtered without mercy, we were not allowing them to surrender, they huddled together in the pit formed by the explosion and our men deliberately capped down on them and beat out their brains and bayonetted them until worn out with exhaustion." One eager Alabamian continued his murderous spree even after an officer ordered him to stop. "Well gen let me kill one more," he replied, whereupon "he deliberately took out his pocket knife and cut one's throat."[30]

Some watched the horrifying spectacle of white Union soldiers shooting their black comrades in order to curry favor with their Confederate captors. Lieutenant George Emery of the 9th New Hampshire explained that "the men was bound not to be taken prisoner among the niggers," and Private George Kilmer of the 14th New York Heavy Artillery wrote that white soldiers "bayonetted blacks who fell into the Crater. This was in order to preserve the whites from Confederate vengeance. Men boasted in my presence that blacks had thus been disposed of, particularly when the Confederates came up." Meanwhile, the southerners continued their deadly work. "Every bomb proof I saw had one or two dead negroes in them who had skulked out of the fight & had been found & killed by our men," reported Virginia artillerist Willie Pegram. "The slorter of Negroes was awful," added cannoneer Andrew S. Barksdale of a Virginia battery. They "were laying so thick here it was impossible to step without treading on the dead boddys." North Carolina Major Rufus A. Barrier told his father a few days after the battle that "the blood ran in streams" from the "worthless carcasses" of the black soldiers. "The poor nigger realized the awful meaning of the words 'no quarters,'" added Barrier.[31]

Why otherwise honorable Victorian-era soldiers would engage in such atrocities seems beyond modern explanation. In the context of the times, however, armed black men in the South were considered slaves in rebellion, and such behavior demanded swift and certain capital punishment. A Union officer explained that "it seemed to add increased poison to the sting of death to be shot by a negro. The Confederates considered such an act as violating all rules of warfare and the sacred rights of humanity." Less articulately, Mississippi soldier David Holt wrote that "the sight of a nigger in a blue uniform with a gun was more than 'Johnnie Reb' could stand."[32]

The massacre of United States Colored Troops at the Crater may thus be explicable, but Billy Mahone, among others, did not consider it justifiable. "Our men fought until Brigadier General Mahone thought it too bad to see men slortered in that stile," explained Corporal Barksdale, "and at once sprang from his saddle rushed to his men and cryed out to them 'men for God's sake observe humanity, and don't be so destructive of life.'" Gradually the murders stopped and the surviving African Americans, along with their white comrades, became prisoners of war. This, however, gave the Confederates a second chance to execute black Yankees. "Most of the negroes were killed after they surrendered," confirmed one Confederate. Another admitted that "a number were shot or hung after being brought to the rear."[33]

There were no official repercussions from the Confederate authorities for this wholesale violation of the accepted rules of war. In fact, much opinion within the army and among southern civilians sustained the rectitude of the massacre. "I think it is right to kill every negro, formerly a slave, found in arms against us," wrote a Confederate surgeon. Willie Pegram agreed: "This was perfectly right as a matter of policy." The Richmond press expressed disappointment that the extermination of black soldiers proved incomplete. "Let every salient we are called upon to defend be a Fort Pillow, and butcher every negro that Grant hurls against our brave troops, and permit them not to soil their hands with the capture of one negro." The editor went on to criticize Mahone for stopping the killing: "We beg [Mahone] hereafter, when negroes are sent forward to murder the wounded, and come shouting 'no quarter,' shut your eyes, General, strengthen your stomach with a little brandy and water, and let the work which God has entrusted to you and your brave men, go forward to its full completion; that is until every negro has been slaughtered."[34]

Those African Americans who managed to survive both the battle and the short march to the rear employed several strategies to avoid their apparent fate. Some of the timorous black captives, informed by their officers that morning that they would be killed if taken alive and having witnessed actual atrocities, humbled themselves before their captors. "The poor darkies thought their last day had come," recalled Confederate Lieutenant Colonel William W. Blackford, and "many came marching to our men in underclothing alone, or stripping off their uniforms as they ran and calling out piteously 'Oh Lord, master, please don't shoot.'" Others cleverly implored the most likely looking Confederates to claim them as their slaves, preferring bondage to the distinct possibility of imminent execution. Several of the white officers in USCT regiments attempted to avoid what they feared would be special punishment by denying affiliation with the black troops or by attempting to blend in with the enlisted prisoners by removing their shoulder straps.[35]

Many of the prisoners fell victim to robbery, including white officers of black regiments. "We were taken to the city of Petersburg and it did not take them long to disrobe us," remembered Lieutenant William Baird of the 23rd USCT. "We were stripped of our hats, boots, socks, blouse, money, watches, swords. They left me with a shirt and a pair of pants." His colleague, Lieutenant Beecham, agreed that the officers were "systematically . . . robbed of nearly everything they possessed . . . and by the time they were done with us we were a sorry looking set."[36]

The Confederates had one more indignity in mind for the Union prisoners. After enduring a night with little or nothing to eat, the captives received instructions on the morning of July 31 to form a long line. Under the direction of Lieutenant General Ambrose Powell Hill, the POWs were forced to march through the streets of Petersburg for the benefit of the local population. Hill ensured they did so in a racially integrated fashion, which prompted shouts from the crowd such as "See the white and nigger equality soldiers." "We were assailed by a volley of abuse from men, women, and children which exceeded anything of the kind I ever heard," thought Lieutenant Bowley. Not only did this parade afford "a little innocent amusement to the good people of Petersburg," observed a sarcastic Union officer, but it served to disgrace many of the white Federal troops who resented marching side by side with African Americans. "It almost broke the hearts of very many of the officers of white divisions, a majority of whom, I honestly believe, would have been glad to see the officers of the Fourth Division hanged or shot, if thereby they could have been relieved from the terrible humiliation of marching through Petersburg with negro soldiers," wrote Beecham. The next day the prisoners boarded freight cars bound for Danville, Virginia, where the white enlisted men were incarcerated. The officers continued their journey to the Richland County jail in Columbia, South Carolina. Black prisoners remained in Petersburg, either to be reclaimed by their former owners or used as military laborers by the Confederates.[37]

Some of those captives participated in the final act of the Crater tragedy. The process of obtaining a formal cessation of hostilities in order to recover the wounded and bury the dead unfolded slowly—almost criminally so—as officers in both armies indulged pride and protocol, while wounded men lay dying between the lines. At last the commanders agreed to initiate a truce beginning at 5:00 a.m. on August 1. Each side established a line of sentries standing just six feet apart. Then a contingent of black prisoners emerged from the Confederate works carrying shovels and stretchers, and on the Federal side a Massachusetts regiment joined by one of the USCT units began to dig burial trenches. They were joined by other members of the 4th Division, assigned responsibility for bringing the dead to the pits.[38]

The prisoners brought the bodies lying on the Confederate side of the sentry line to the neutral ground, where they were then taken up by Ferrero's men and delivered to the burial trenches. Once at the grave sites, the corpses were rolled or dumped into the hole up to twelve inches from the top, "laid crosswise, side by side as closely as they could be laid, then quickly covered," men "occasionally stopping to flatten down with their foot or shovel an arm or leg that would otherwise protrude beyond its covering." The scene was nauseating. "I was on the field and Oh God! What a sight," wrote a Pennsylvania soldier. "Men cut into a thousand pieces and as black as your hat. You could not tell the white from the black only by their hair. The wounded were fly-blown and the dead were all maggot eaten, so we had to lift them on shovels."[39]

The cease-fire expired at 9:00 a.m., but the Confederates extended it long enough to complete the gruesome work. General Lee would report that seven hundred Federals had been interred, but Burnside informed Meade that morning that "about 220 dead were found between the lines and are now buried." Estimates of total Union casualties at the Battle of the Crater range from 3,500 to 4,400, although the official tally was 3,798. Similarly, Ferrero's official casualty report listed a total of 1,327, although credible revisions raise that number to 1,665. The black troops sustained one man killed for every 1.8 wounded, while the average ratio of killed to wounded in the Civil War was 1:4.8, a stark reminder of the merciless and mortal combat that engulfed the United States Colored Troops at the Crater.[40]

Inevitable recriminations quickly followed the disaster, and many in the Union army found it convenient to blame the calamity on the panicked retreat of Ferrero's men. A New York cavalryman, for example, informed a friend that the operation at the Crater "would have done something if it hadn't been for the nigger troops." A 9th Corps soldier declared that "I say put the niggers out of our corps as I do not want to be in the corps they are." Before the year was out this man would have his wish, as all the African American infantry in Grant's army group was placed in the segregated 25th Corps. Of the twenty-four medals of honor awarded for service at the Crater, only four men from the 4th Division received one, and of them, only Sergeant Decatur Dorsey of the 39th USCT was black. The African American troops in Butler's army would participate in an offensive north of the James in September and acquit themselves well, but the 9th Corps USCT would see only limited action for the duration of the campaign. Colonel Thomas remembered with pride that the night before the battle, his troops "formed circles in their company streets . . . and . . . began to sing 'We-e looks li-ike me-en a-marchin' on, We looks li-ike men-er-war.'" After their experience on July 30, 1864, wrote Thomas, they sang this song no more.[41]

Notes

1. The best description of the mine construction is Earl J. Hess, *Into the Crater: The Mine Attack at Petersburg* (Columbia: University of South Carolina Press, 2010), 11–17, 21–24.

2. Thomas J. Howe, *Wasted Valor: June 15–18, 1864* (Lynchburg, VA: H. E. Howard, 1988), addresses the first offensive. The second offensive is covered in Edwin C. Bearss, *The Petersburg Campaign*, vol. 1, *The Eastern Front Battles, June–August 1864* (El Dorado Hills, CA: Savas Beattie, 2012), 131–200. James S. Price, *The Battle of First Deep Bottom* (Charleston, SC: History Press, 2014) is the best source on this operation. The most useful overview of the Petersburg Campaign is Earl J. Hess, *In the Trenches at Petersburg: Field Fortifications and Confederate Defeat* (Chapel Hill: University of North Carolina Press, 2009).

3. Testimony of Lieutenant Colonel Charles G. Loring in *Report of the Joint Committee on the*

Conduct of the War, Army of the Potomac, Battle of Petersburg (Washington, DC: Government Printing Office, 1865), 91 (hereafter cited as *RJCCW*).

4. *The War of the Rebellion: A Compilation of the Official Records of the Union and Confederate Armies*, 127 vols. (Washington, DC: Government Printing Office, 1880–1901), ser. 1, vol. 40, pt. 1, 58 (hereafter cited as *OR*).

5. David Coon to "My dear wife," July 23, 1864, David Coon Civil War Letters, Library of Congress (hereafter cited as LC); William Wirt Henry to "My beloved wife," July 3, 1864, William Wirt Henry Family Papers, Vermont Historical Society, Barre, Vermont; Andrew Jackson Crossley to "Friend Sam," July 17, 1864, Samuel Bradbury Papers, Perkins Library, Duke University, Durham, NC; Josiah N. Jones Diary, July 11, 1864, New Hampshire Historical Society, Concord, New Hampshire; Elon G. Mills to "Dear Folks," June 22, 1864, Elon G. Mills Diary and Letters, Bentley Historical Library, University of Michigan, Ann Arbor, Michigan (hereafter cited as BLUM).

6. Charles F. Walcott, *History of the Twenty-First Regiment Massachusetts Volunteers* (Boston: Houghton, Mifflin, 1882), 341; Henry Wise to "My beloved wife," June 27, 1864, Wise Family Papers, 1816–1898, Virginia Historical Society, Richmond, Virginia (hereafter cited as VHS). Confederates were widely accused of massacring the garrison of US Colored Troops and white Union Tennessee soldiers at Fort Pillow, Tennessee, in April 1864. The echoes of Fort Pillow's alleged atrocities resounded in North Carolina at Plymouth and in Mississippi at Brice's Cross Roads in the subsequent weeks and engendered an almost universal determination by black troops and their white officers to respond in kind. See William A. Dobak, *Freedom by the Sword: The U.S. Colored Troops, 1862–1867* (Washington, DC: Center of Military History, 2011), 333–334; and Andrew Ward, *River Run Red: The Fort Pillow Massacre in the American Civil War* (New York: Viking, 2005), 335. The brutal legacy of Fort Pillow and the Crater is ably addressed in George S. Burkhardt, *Confederate Rage, Yankee Wrath: No Quarter in the Civil War* (Carbondale: Southern Illinois University Press, 2007); Gregory J. W. Urwin, *Black Flag over Dixie: Racial Atrocities and Reprisals in the Civil War* (Carbondale: Southern Illinois University Press, 2004); and Joseph T. Wilson, *The Black Phalanx: History of the Negro Soldiers of the United States* (New York: Arno, 1968).

7. *OR*, ser 1, vol., 40, pt. 1, 59; testimony of Brevet Major General Edward Ferrero, *RJCCW*, 106; Henry Goddard Thomas, "The Colored Troops at Petersburg," in *Battles and Leaders of the Civil War*, ed. Robert Underwood Johnson and Clarence Clough Buel, 4 vols. (New York: Castle Books, 1956), 4:563; Noah Andre Trudeau, *Like Men of War: Black Troops in the Civil War, 1862–1865* (Boston: Little, Brown, 1998), 231.

8. William Hamilton Harris Journal and Papers, July 29, 1864, New York Public Library, New York; Leander O. Merriam, "Personal Recollections of the War for the Union," bound volume 190, Fredericksburg and Spotsylvania County Battlefields Memorial National Military Park and Cemetery; Ervin T. Case, "Battle of the Mine," in *Personal Narratives of Events in the War of the Rebellion, Being Papers Read before the Rhode Island Soldiers and Sailors Historical Society* (hereafter cited as *RISSHS*), 100 vols. (Providence: The Society, 1878–1915), 1:5–37.

9. *OR*, ser 1, vol. 40, pt. 3, 240, 304, 320–321; Keith Wilson, ed., *Honor in Command: Lt. Freeman S. Bowley's Civil War Service in the 30th United States Colored Infantry* (Gainesville: University Press of Florida, 2006), 121; Michael E. Stevens, ed., *As If It Were Glory: Robert Beecham's Civil War from the Iron Brigade to the Black Regiments* (Madison, WI: Madison House, 1998), 178; Capt. R. K. Beecham, "Adventures of an Iron Brigade Man," *National Tribune* (hereafter cited as *NT*), November 20, 1902.

10. *OR*, ser. 1, vol. 40, pt. 3, 552; pt. 1, 16; *RJCCW*, 17, 38.

11. *OR*, ser. 1, vol.,40, pt.1, 46–47, 61, 137; pt. 3, 608; testimony of Major General Ambrose E. Burnside, *RJCCW*, 18; testimony of Major General George G. Meade, *RJCCW*, 50–51; testimony of Brevet Major General Robert B. Potter, *RJCCW*, 85; William Marvel, *Burnside* (Chapel Hill: University of North Carolina Press, 1991), 394–395; David W. Lowe, ed., *Meade's Army: The Private Notebooks of Lt. Col. Theodore Lyman* (Kent, OH: Kent State University Press, 2007), 241.

12. Wilson, *Honor in Command*, 122; Thomas, "Colored Troops at Petersburg," 564; David Edwin Proctor to "Friend Harvey," August 1, 1864, Petersburg National Battlefield; Edwin S. Redkey, ed., *A Grand Army of Black Men: Letters from African-American Soldiers in the Union Army, 1861–1865* (Cambridge: Cambridge University Press, 1992), 113–114; *OR*, ser.1, vol. 40, pt. 1, 595.

13. For the springing of the mine and the initial Union assaults, see Hess, *Into the Crater*, 77–123.

14. *OR*, ser.1, vol. 40, pt. 1, 596, 598; Freeman S. Bowley, "The Petersburg Mine," in *Civil War Papers of the California Commandery of the Military Order of the Loyal Legion of the United States* (Wilmington, NC: Broadfoot, 1995), 31; H. Seymour Hall, "Mine Run to Petersburg," in *War Talks in Kansas: A Series of Papers Read before the Kansas Commandery of the Military Order of the Loyal Legion of the United States* (Wilmington, NC: Broadfoot, 1992), 222; Thomas, "Colored Troops at Petersburg," 564; Warren H. Hurd Diary, July 30, 1864, Historical Society of Schuylkill County, Pottsville, Pennsylvania (hereafter cited as HSSC).

15. Hall, "Mine Run to Petersburg," 234–236; Captain David E. Proctor, "The Massacre in the Crater," *NT*, October 17, 1907; Edward A. Miller Jr., *The Black Civil War Soldiers of Illinois: The Story of the Twenty-Ninth U.S. Colored Infantry* (Columbia: University of South Carolina Press, 1998), 69; Charles F. Stinson to "Dear Ones at Home," August 1, 1864, Charles F. Stinson Papers, Lewis Leigh Collection, Army Heritage and Education Center, Carlisle, Pennsylvania; James H. Clark, *The Iron Hearted Regiment: Being an Account of the Battles, Marches, and Gallant Deeds Performed by the 115th Regiment N.Y. Vols.* (Albany, NY: J. Munsell, 1865), 148–149.

16. William A. Day, *A True History of Co. I, 49th Regiment North Carolina Troops* (Newton, NC: Enterprise Job Office, 1893), 83; Delevan Bates, "A Day with the Colored Troops," *NT*, January 30, 1908.

17. Bowley, "The Petersburg Mine," 32; Wilson, *Honor in Command*, 132; Hall, "Mine Run to Petersburg," 222, 233, 236; *OR*, ser. 1, vol. 40, pt. 1, 598.

18. *OR*, ser. 1, vol. 40, pt 1, 598; Thomas, "Colored Troops at Petersburg," 565; George S. Bernard, ed., *War Talks of Confederate Veterans* (Petersburg, VA: Fenn and Owen, 1892), 183.

19. John McMurray, *Recollections of a Colored Troop* (Brookville, PA: McMurray, 1994), 44; Wilson, *The Black Phalanx*, 417; Arthur Swazey, *Memorial of Colonel John A. Bross, 29th USCT Who Fell Leading the Assault on Petersburg, July 30, 1864* (Chicago: Tribune Book and Job Office, 1865), 17–18; Thomas, "Colored Troops at Petersburg," 565; Miller, *Black Soldiers of Illinois*, 71, 100; Carl G. Hodges and Helene H. Levene, eds., *Illinois Negro History Makers* (Chicago: Emancipation Centennial Commission, 1964), 25–26; Stevens, *As If It Were Glory*, 184.

20. Carter R. Bishop to "Dear Madam" [Miss Laura Lee Richardson], February 13, 1932, Richmond, Virginia, Petersburg National Battlefield; Gary W. Gallagher, ed., *Fighting for the Confederacy: The Personal Recollections of General Edward Porter Alexander* (Chapel Hill: University of North Carolina Press, 1989), 465. Mahone's march to the battlefield and his deployment is covered in Hess, *Into the Crater*, 142–149.

21. Bernard, *War Talks*, 217–222, 187; William H. Stewart, Statement No. 6, July 3, 1903, William H. Etheredge, Statement No. 30, July 27, 1903, John T. West, Statement No. 47, September 8, 1903, Amnon Peek, Statement No. 48, September 15, 1903, and Robert F. Norfleet, Statement No. 50, September 15, 1903, Crater Collection, Museum of the Confederacy (hereafter cited as MOC); William H. Stewart, *The Spirit of the South: Orations, Essays, and Lectures by Colonel William H. Stewart* (New York: Neale, 1908), 134; *Richmond Daily Dispatch*, August 1, 1864.

22. West, Crater Collection, MOC; Miller, *Black Soldiers of Illinois*, 72; Stephen M. Weld, "The Petersburg Mine," in *Papers of the Military Historical Society of Massachusetts*, 15 vols. (Wilmington, NC: Broadfoot, 1989) 5:211.

23. Warren Wilkinson, *Mother, May You Never See the Sights I Have Seen: The Fifty-Seventh Massachusetts Veteran Volunteers in the Last Year of the Civil War* (New York: Harper and Row, 1990), 255; Harris, Journal and Papers, July 30, 1864; Day, *A True History*, 83; Clyde G. Wiggins III, ed., *My Dear Friend: The Civil War Letters of Alva Benjamin Spencer, 3rd Georgia Regiment, Company C* (Macon, GA: Mercer University Press, 2007), 137–138; William H. Etheredge, "Another Story of the Crater Battle," *Southern Historical Society Papers*, 52 vols. (Richmond, VA: Southern Historical Society, 1876–1959), 37:205; Etheredge, Crater Collection, MOC; William H. Stewart, *Description of the Battle of the Crater* (Norfolk, VA: Landmark Book and Job Office, 1876), 10; Stewart, *Spirit of the South*, 135.

24. *OR*, ser. 1, vol. 40, pt 1, 567; William A. Childs to "Dear Friend Spalding," August 1, 1864, Spalding Family Papers, BLUM; Henry F. Young to "Dear Delia," August 4, 1864, Henry Falls Young Papers, Wisconsin Historical Society; William Hamilton to "Dear Boyd," August 3, 1864, William Hamilton Letters, 1864–1865, LC.

25. *OR*, ser. 1, vol., 40, pt. 1, 103, 567, 599; William Fielding Baugh, Statement No. 72, December 4, 1905, Crater Collection, MOC; Edward Lord, ed., *History of the Ninth New Hampshire Volunteers in the War of the Rebellion* (Concord, NH: Republican Press Association, 1895), 502; William Marvel, *Race of the Soil: The Ninth New Hampshire Regiment in the Civil War* (Wilmington, NC: Broadfoot, 1988), 269; Warren S. Gurney to "Dear Folks at Home," August 2, 1864, Warren S. Gurney Papers, John Hay Library, Brown University.

26. *OR*, ser. 1, vol., 40, pt. 1, 555–556; Howard Aston, *History and Roster of the Fourth and Fifth Independent Battalions and Thirteenth Regiment, Ohio Cavalry Volunteers* (Columbus, OH: Fred J. Heer, 1902), 104; John Anderson, *The Fifty-Seventh Regiment of Massachusetts Volunteers, in the War of the Rebellion, Army of the Potomac* (Boston: E. B. Stillings, 1896), 181.

27. Allen D. Albert, *History of the Forty-Fifth Regiment Pennsylvania Veteran Volunteer Infantry, 1861–1865* (Williamsport, PA: Grit, 1912), 155; Freeman S. Bowley, "The Crater," in *Battles and Leaders of the Civil War*, ed. Peter Cozzens (Urbana: University of Illinois Press, 2004), 6:427; Aston, *History and Roster*, 104; Hess, *Into the Crater*, 175.

28. William L. Fagan, "The Petersburg Crater: A Participant's Description of the Fierce Struggle for the Recapture of the Salient," *Philadelphia Weekly Times*, January 6, 1883; George A. Clark, *A Glance Backward: Or, Some Events in the Past History of My Life* (Houston: Rein and Sons, 1914), 59.

29. P. M. Vance, "Incidents of the Crater Battle," *Confederate Veteran* 14, no. 4 (April 1906): 178; Clark, *Glance Backward*, 60; Fagan, "The Petersburg Crater"; David MacRae, *The Americans at Home: Pen-and-Ink Sketches of American Men, Manners and Institutions*, 2 vols. (Edinburgh: Edmonston and Douglas, 1870), 1:175–176.

30. A. T. Fleming to "My dear and affectionate wife," August 3, 1864, HSSC; Hall T. McGee Diary, July 30, 1864, South Carolina Historical Society; "Well gen let me kill one more," quoted in Bell Irvin Wiley, *The Life of Johnny Reb: The Common Soldier of the Confederacy* (Indianapolis: Bobbs-Merrill, 1943), 315.

31. Frank Kenfield, "Captured by the Rebels: A Vermonter at Petersburg, 1864," *Vermont History* 36, no. 4 (Autumn 1968): 230–235; Miller, *Black Soldiers of Illinois*, 77; Marvel, *Race of the Soil*, 270; George L. Kilmer, "The Dash into the Crater," *Century Magazine* 34 (September 1887): 774–776; Willie Pegram to "My dear Jennie," August 1, 1864, Pegram-Johnston-McIntosh Family Papers, VHS; Andrew S. Barksdale to "Dear Sister Omis," August 1, 1864, Barksdale Letters, MOC; Beverly Barrier Troxler and Billy Dawn Barrier, eds., *Dear Father: Confederate Letters Never Before Published* (Margate, FL: Auciello, 1989), 60–61.

32. Anderson, *Fifty-Seventh Massachusetts*, 193; Thomas D. Cockrell and Michael B. Ballard, eds., *A Mississippi Rebel in the Army of Northern Virginia: The Civil War Memoirs of Private David Holt* (Baton Rouge: Louisiana State University Press, 1995), 287. For a persuasive argument linking the Confederate atrocities to perceiving the black soldiers as slaves in rebellion, see Kevin M. Levin, *Remembering the Battle of the Crater: War as Murder* (Lexington: University Press of Kentucky, 2012).

33. Andrew S. Barksdale to "Dear Sister Omis," August 1, 1864, Barksdale Letters, MOC; Robert G. Evans, ed., *The 16th Mississippi Infantry: Civil War Letters and Reminiscences* (Jackson: University Press of Mississippi, 2002), 281; McGee Diary, July 30, 1864, South Carolina Historical Society.

34. Henry Augustine Minor to "My dear Sister," August 1, 1864, Minor Papers, Special Collections Library, University of Virginia; Willie Pegram to "My dear Jennie," August 1, 1864, Pegram-Johnston-McIntosh Family Papers, VHS; *Richmond Enquirer*, August 1–2, 1864.

35. Alfred Lewis Scott Memoirs, 1910, VHS; W. W. Blackford, "Memoirs: First and Last, or Battles in Virginia," 462, Library of Virginia, Richmond; William H. Stewart, *A Pair of Blankets: War-Time History in Letters to the Young People of the South* (New York: Broadway, 1911), 161; Kenneth Wiley, ed., *Norfolk Blues: The Civil War Diary of the Norfolk Light Artillery Blues* (Shippensburg, PA: Burd Street, 1997), 138; Lieutenant George H. Wing to "Dear Captain," July 18, 1865, Wiley Sword Collection, Pamplin Historical Park, Petersburg, Virginia; William Miller Owen, *In Camp and Battle with the Washington Artillery of New Orleans* (Boston: Ticknor, 1885), 345; James H. Rickard, "Services with Colored Troops in Burnside's Corps," *RISSHS* (1894), 8:31.

36. Lieutenant William Baird, Memoir, Baird Family Papers, BLUM; Beecham, "Adventures of an Iron Brigade Man."

37. Beecham, "Adventures of an Iron Brigade Man"; Bowley, "The Crater," 430; Kenfield, "Captured by Rebels," 234.

38. Susan P. Lee, ed., *Memoirs of William Nelson Pendleton, D.D.* (Philadelphia: J. B. Lippincott, 1893), 359; *Richmond Daily Dispatch*, August 3, 1864; *New York Times*, August 4, 1864; Josiah N. Jones Diary, August 1, 1864; Stephen S. Chandler, "Petersburg: The 24th NY Cav at the Mine Explosion," *NT*, August 16, 1888; William P. Hopkins, *The Seventh Rhode Island Volunteers in the Civil War, 1862–1865* (Providence: Snow and Farnham, 1903), 209–210; Lowe, *Meade's Army*, 244; Sumner Carruth et al., *History of the Thirty-Fifth Regiment Massachusetts Volunteers, 1862–1865* (Boston: Mills, Knight), 279; Hess, *Into the Crater*, 207–212.

39. Chandler, "Petersburg"; Etheredge, Crater Collection; Lowe, *Meade's Army*, 244; Owen, *Washington Artillery*, 346–347; Warren S. Gurney to "Dear Folks at Home," August 2, 1864, Gurney Papers; Wiley, *Norfolk Blues*, 140; William Gilfillan Gavin, *Campaigning with the Roundheads: The History of the Hundredth Pennsylvania Veteran Volunteer Infantry Regiment in the American Civil War, 1861–1865* (Dayton, OH: Morningside House, 1989), 526–527.

40. *OR*, ser. 1, vol. 40, pt. 1, 17–18, 167, 246–249, 753; pt. 3, 707; 42; pt. 2, 10; Bowley, "The Crater," 430; Beecham, "Adventures of an Iron Brigade Man"; Bryce A. Suderow, "The Battle of the Crater: The Civil War's Worst Massacre," *Civil War History* 43, no. 3 (September 1997): 219–225.

41. Trudeau, *Like Men of War*, 249–251; Thomas, "Colored Troops at Petersburg," 563–564.

Domesticity in Conflict

Union Soldiers, Southern Women, and Gender Roles
during the American Civil War

LAURA MAMMINA

After a year and a half in the Union army, Kentuckian Alfred Pirtle had reason to find fault with military service. While Pirtle had no complaints with his rank, his company, his commanding officers, the amount of marching, or the quality of food or accommodations, he bemoaned that he was "losing a good deal of [his] small share of refinement." He was not the only one who felt this way. The night before, he and his comrades sadly reflected that they were not "as good men as when we joined the service." The cause of Pirtle's problem, the reason that army life chipped away at civilized behavior and turned men into savages and animals, was this: he and his friends were deprived of the "pleasure of ladies society."[1]

By the time of the American Civil War, many middle- and upper-class white Americans—a group of which Pirtle was a part—had espoused strict and complementary notions of gender. Trumpeted in sermons, periodicals, novels, and even textbooks, these ideas insisted that men, formed for daring deeds and yet prone to vice, required the civilizing and moralizing influence of women in order to be made fit for society and fit for heaven.[2] Although the cult of domesticity was formed in northeastern urban areas and applied specifically to the burgeoning middle class, its influence was felt across the country. White middle- and upper-class southerners ascribed to notions of domesticity, and white yeomen and free and enslaved black women at least felt the influence of these ideas, if they did not embrace certain elements themselves.[3] Even white women moving west on overland trails carried these aspirations with them, for, as one historian observes, women hoped that "th[e] domestic sphere would provide . . . social and cultural stability in a changing world."[4] War proved the persistence of these ideas. As Pirtle and his friends demonstrate, to be without the society of women was to return to an animal-like state. These attitudes explain why, in the midst of the American Civil War, white and black Union soldiers and southern women not only interacted but also actively sought each other out in social settings. Complementary gender roles, pervasive throughout the United States and ingrained in many since their youth, discouraged men and women from forgoing each other's company even during a time of war.

In spite of the volume of interactions between Union soldiers and southern women, scholars have not yet examined these exchanges. Instead, they tend to study soldiers and women independently of each other.[5] When scholars do study their interactions, they focus almost exclusively on military policy.[6] But as this essay argues, Federal soldiers and southern women's social interactions— as they assessed each other's appearances, observed each other's character, formed acquaintances, lodged together, and even formed romantic and sexual attachments—are essential to understanding their exchanges over military policy. It was in these initial encounters that soldiers and women formed opinions about each other and built (or refused to build) relationships. Social interactions, then, are not peripheral to interactions over military policy. Instead, they are integral exchanges between soldiers and noncombatants in the midst of a war that destabilized American politics and yet did not significantly alter seemingly ironclad gender roles. While these gender roles did not dictate the behavior of Union soldiers and southern women—both men and women chose to what degree they ascribed to domesticity—they did continue to powerfully influence behavior because they were closely tied to political power. Even those men and women who purposefully transgressed parts of the idea still clung to certain aspects, as domesticity, with its language of independence and dependence, men's physical superiority and women's moral superiority, complemented ideas that defined who had access to political power and why. Domesticity, then, carried enormous political ramifications, which in turn explains its resonance with Americans regardless of gender, race, class, or region.[7]

This essay focuses on four soldiers and four women in order to demonstrate the powerful resonance of domesticity. Some, like Susie King Taylor and Sarah Morgan, are familiar to historians; others are more obscure.[8] Taken together, they attempt to replicate the diversity of the Union army and southern society.[9]

Born in Massachusetts in 1832 to a wealthy merchant family, Wilder Dwight attended West Point and then Cambridge Law School. After traveling western Europe, he practiced law in Boston. An ardent Republican, Dwight campaigned for Abraham Lincoln before organizing a regiment of Massachusetts volunteers. He took a commission as a major, serving until his death at the Battle of

Antietam.[10] As a wealthy white abolitionist northeasterner, Dwight exemplified his region's strong antislavery ties and genteel attitudes.

African American George E. Stephens, born in Philadelphia in 1832 to Virginian parents, worked as a cabinetmaker while advocating abolition. Stephens enlisted as a sergeant in the 54th Massachusetts and also served as war correspondent for the prominent African American–owned and –edited New York *Weekly Anglo-African*, widely read by black enlisted men.[11] Married in 1857, Stephens exemplifies the few northern-born African American soldiers who escaped slavery, received an education, and worked for emancipation.

Alfred Pirtle of Louisville, Kentucky, was born in 1837 to a well-connected slave-owning family. Before joining the Louisville Home Guards in the fall of 1861, he pursued studies in civil engineering. In February 1862 he enlisted in the 10th Ohio Volunteer Infantry, where he served as an ordnance officer and then as an aide-de-camp.[12] As an upper-middle-class southerner with Union sympathies, Pirtle exemplifies whites from border states who fought to preserve the Union.

Charles O. Musser came from much more humble beginnings. The son of poor white farmers, Charles and his siblings lived for years in Ohio before his family settled in Iowa. In 1860, he and his family farmed just twenty improved acres. Nineteen years old in 1861, Musser joined the 29th Iowa Volunteer Infantry, where he served as a private, working his way up to the rank of sergeant by the end of the war.[13] Musser's letters reflect the opinions of a single, working-class young man with decidedly Union sentiments in the violent western theater.

Katherine Couse, born in New Jersey, immigrated with her family to a fourteen-hundred-acre Spotsylvania County, Virginia, farm in 1840. Here her parents, William and Elizabeth, raised their seven children, worked 420 improved acres, operated a sawmill, and purchased three slaves. After William's death in the late 1850s, the family either sold or divided up the farm and no longer owned slaves. Katherine, twenty-six and single at the time of the conflict, exemplifies northern attitudes with her Unionist principles, middle-class values, and nonslaveholding status in a wealthy agricultural region.[14]

A resident of Baton Rouge and New Orleans, Louisiana, Sarah Morgan was the seventh child and youngest daughter of Thomas Gibbes Morgan and Sarah Hunt Fowler Morgan. Thomas, a judge with a successful law practice, and Sarah, a northerner and orphan raised by wealthy plantation-owning relatives, lived a comfortable if not wealthy existence, owning eight slaves and a spacious house. Sarah, nineteen at the beginning of the war, was a firm yet not uncritical Confederate supporter, and her family moved in the highest circles of Louisiana society, as evidenced by her genteel values and concern with propriety.[15]

Little is known about Nancy Jett (née Evins), the wife of yeoman farmer and miller Richard Burch Jett. Born in 1821, Jett was Richard's second wife and settled with her new husband and several stepchildren in North Fulton County, Georgia. Richard, a private in the Confederate army in 1863 (most likely, at such a late date, due to conscription), left Nancy and the children to work the farm. Jett demonstrates the concerns of an older, married yeoman farmer's wife struggling to provide for her family and her farm.[16]

Susie King Taylor was born into slavery in Liberty County, Georgia, in 1848. At age seven, Taylor went to Savannah to live with her grandmother and attended six years of school. In 1862, Taylor headed to Union lines, where, for the remainder of the war, she served as a teacher, laundress, cook, and nurse to the 33rd US Colored Troops. She also met and married African American noncommissioned officer Edward King.[17] As a young, literate enslaved woman raised in an urban environment, Taylor demonstrates a southern black woman's observations of black southern soldiers and white northern officers.

While these eight people came from very different backgrounds, they did share a few common assumptions. One of the most important in terms of soldiers' and women's social interactions was the belief that a person's character could be read in their physical appearance. In fact, nineteenth-century Americans firmly believed in the necessity of assessing the appearance of newcomers, and this process took on new significance during a time of war. Societal upheaval due to industrial, agricultural, and westward expansion created considerable flux in population, and the ability to "read" strangers' countenance for indications of their character was tantamount. This exercise found new application during the war when Union soldiers and civilian women used it as a way to determine exactly what type of people they encountered. In New Orleans, Sarah Morgan observed with distaste Federal officers who were "contemplating" her from a balcony. This seemingly inconsequential incident influenced Morgan's opinion of Federal soldiers—her comment about the men "staring" was pointed, because men of good breeding did not stare at female strangers. Morgan held herself up as an example—she "never look[ed] at . . . people after the first glance."[18] Later on, two of the officers passed by her friend's house as she sat on the steps and "examined each one of us as though they meant to know us again, never pretending to turn their heads the other way." Morgan's mother reinforced this thought by insisting that the men "thought [Morgan] was dressed to attract their attention, and [they] wished to gratify me [with their stares]." As a southern elite lady, and a Confederate one at that, Morgan found the idea of "dress[ing] to please the Yankees" to be "a little too much."[19] Not only did Morgan not want to attract the attention of strange men, but she certainly did not want to invite the attention of Federals.[20]

Other southern women displayed little concern that Federal soldiers might stare at them—instead, they emphasized the need to see Union soldiers for themselves in order to determine what type of men they were. Susie King Taylor had to wait a year after the outbreak of the war to finally get a glimpse of Union soldiers, and during that time she wondered what they would be like. From slave owners she heard warnings that Federal soldiers would "harness [African Americans] to carts and make them pull the carts around, in place of horses," while from her parents she learned that the "Yankee" was going to "set all the slaves free." From these conflicting messages of continued servitude or imminent liberation, Taylor concluded that she needed to see Federal soldiers for herself. As a young enslaved black woman, Taylor did not have the luxury of avoiding public attention. Her skin color and her status as a woman who worked for a living disqualified her from being a lady, so the fact that seeing Union soldiers would also mean being seen by them did not hold the same perils as it did for upper-class white southern women. Instead, Taylor prioritized two concerns: first, that white slave owners could not be trusted to tell her the truth and, second, that her family, having never seen Union soldiers, did not know exactly what type of people they were. What Taylor had appropriated from the cult of domesticity was the importance of her assessing the appearance of Union soldiers herself—as she stated in her memoirs, she was "very anxious to see them." Indeed, in her journey from Liberty County to Union protection on St. Catherine's Island and finally within Union lines on St. Simon's Island, what was significant for Taylor was that "at last, to [her] unbounded joy, [she] saw the 'Yankee.'" Finally, Taylor could make up her own mind about what type of men Union soldiers truly were by observing their appearance.[21]

As a citizen and a northern-born woman, Katherine Couse did not have to wonder about what clues Union soldiers' appearance might contain about their character. Even before she met them, Couse regarded Federals as "knights in Blue" who would rescue her and her family from "robbery and rogiushness." Couse's first encounter with Federal soldiers seemed to bode well for the restoration of law and order. When three Federal soldiers came galloping up, Couse and her sisters "went out to see them." As nonslaveholders, the women had no slaves to send out to greet the soldiers, and as white middle-class Union women, they felt they had nothing to fear from the men. Indeed, Couse recounts how she "shook hands with the officer" and "told him we were glad to see them." In return, the soldier "smiled and said he was glad they had some friends here." This man's status as an officer made this first meeting a smooth one—Couse would later find these officers "very handsome intelligent agreeable men," denoting them as middle class. But what was most important for both the officers and the women were political sympathies. During a time of war, what took precedence was not equal social standing but political loyalties.[22] Couse seemed willing to accept, on the basis of appearance and political sympathies, that Federal soldiers really were the "knights in Blue" she had looked for.

Political sympathies also colored Union soldiers' assessments of southern women. While southerners prized amiability, piety, and beauty in white ladies, decades of sectional conflict brought these ideals into question—did amiability and piety mean staying out of sectional concerns? Or did ladies' involvement in political affairs give politics a nobler purpose? While one contingent of northerners and southerners insisted that women serve as sectional peacemakers, some northerners insisted that true ladies, in keeping with Republican motherhood, adhered to the Union, and some southerners insisted that women's espousal of the South and eventually the Confederacy sanctified the cause.[23] Alfred Pirtle demonstrated the effect of sectional conflict on ladylike behavior when he observed the "frowns and clouded brows" on the faces of Middle Tennessee women, telling his family that "the ladies are—well I can't say much, except they are secesh and very Southern." Pirtle's comments demonstrate how sectional conflict and war colored the way nineteenth-century southern men viewed nineteenth-century southern ladies.[24] Instead of labeling Middle Tennessee women virtuous or beautiful, Pirtle asserted that their primary identity was that of their political sympathies. Rather than finding this behavior to be in conflict with ladylike ideals, Pirtle believed it made these women "more honorable" than ladies in border states who tried to hide their political leanings. Thus Pirtle articulated that outspoken Confederate women were more ladylike than those who dissembled—a sentiment that his northern-born comrades did not share. In effect, southern-born Union soldiers found no contradiction between ladylike behavior and Confederate sentiments.

Even as sectional conflict expanded ideas of ladylike behavior, war stripped away some of the trappings of femininity. Native westerner Charles O. Musser was particularly attuned to these changes. He observed not only the "want . . . sufferings and misery" of the war but also the way in which women were drawn outside of the home because of it. The need for income drove Little Rock women to be "glad to even get washing and Sewing to do." While nineteenth-century middle-class domesticity insisted that women remain at home while men worked, families—particularly those in the West—recognized that occasionally the family's survival depended on women taking on other work. But many saw this as a temporary arrangement.[25] War destabilized these ideas. With male relatives away or deceased, women were forced to support families. And women's outward appearance, a key aspect of their femininity, also suffered as a result of war. Instead of buying soft, light cotton or calico, Arkansas women reverted to spinning their own course cloth for garments. As Musser so well understood, wartime women shared similarities to frontier women by taking on traditionally male labor and by forgoing the outward markings of femininity. But instead of a temporary solution with an end in sight, the Civil War raised concerns, particularly as it dragged on, that a return to normal might not be possible.[26]

While sectional conflict and war reframed middle-class definitions of ladylike behavior, middle-class contempt for poor white and black southern women remained consistent with prewar ideas. George E. Stephens discovered Virginians to be either "dirty, ragged, dreamy-eyed" African Americans or "seedy looking, stupid whites." Stephens interpreted their appearance as evidence of "sloth and thriftlessness, the twin sisters . . . of unrequited toil." As a black man and an abolitionist, Stephens believed that slavery degraded both enslaved blacks and working-class whites. In this way, he revealed his commitment both to emancipation and free labor: slavery was wrong not only because it deprived African Americans of liberty but also because depriving others of liberty inevitably caused moral decay. Unlike northern workers motivated by wages, enslaved men and women had no such incentive to work efficiently. Unable to compete with wealthy plantation owners, southern whites took no pride in their labor and worked only enough to get by. To Stephens, then, the appearance of southerners was not filtered primarily through war's effects or through adherence to ideas of gender but through the way its system of labor degraded society and morality. Southern blacks and whites could not truly conform to domesticity until they instituted a system of free labor.[27]

Abolitionist Wilder Dwight focused on the political questions raised by the presence of southern blacks in Union lines. Instead of describing them himself,

Dwight wanted to "photograph" the "large wagon full of negro men, women, and children" that arrived in the Union army camp. Rather than looking for signs of their character in the appearance of the enslaved men and women, Dwight described them in dependent, childlike terms: "helpless and deserted," their uncertain status serving as an "embarrassment and a question" to the Union army. To Dwight, these men and women were in need of a protector; whether the Union army would step in to resolve their status by granting them citizenship remained to be seen. Here Dwight asserted that "embarrassment," the chief vice of nineteenth-century Americans, had political connotations. In the family metaphor he created, the "status" of supposedly childlike enslaved southerners raised uncomfortable questions for their guardians, the Union army. The formerly enslaved needed a protector; how the North would respond to that need remained to be seen.[28]

After decoding each other's outward appearances, Union soldiers and southern women, recognizing that unprincipled people sometimes hid behind finery, looked for confirmation of character in a person's behavior.[29] Katherine Couse found much to recommend in the character of Federal soldiers. After observing them for a week, Couse declared that they were "ingenuous and frank" and "talk[ed] in a more liberal way." "There is more humanity about them," Couse stated simply. Couse drew on the language of nineteenth-century etiquette manuals in describing Federal soldiers—these men lacked duplicity and were sincere and truthful. Indeed, they embodied the ideal of sincerity, of there being "a perfect outward revelation of all inward truth" in their "frank" manner. Couse linked all of these characteristics together when describing a Captain Cooly, who was "a very refined handsome young man."[30] Cooly represented the correspondence between appearance and character: he possessed the appearance of a gentleman and his manners proved him to be one.[31]

Susie King Taylor emphasized the expression of character in deeds. To her, the men of the 33rd US Colored Infantry possessed good character because of their acts of bravery performed in Charleston in February 1865. Finding that Confederate soldiers had set fire to the city, Taylor noted that the regiment "went to work assisting the citizens in subduing the flames" in order to save residents' property. White Charlestonians, rather than feeling grateful to the black soldiers—"many of them [who] had formerly been their slaves"—instead "sneer[ed at] and molest[ed them]." To Taylor, the African American regiment proved their manliness by protecting women and children, a key aspect of domesticity—and by this time, the laws of war—due to women's supposed delicate nature. More poignantly, the soldiers extended protection to the families of their former owners because the Confederate army put women and children in harm's way. Rather than exacting revenge after hundreds of years of forced labor, African American soldiers respected their commanders, observed military discipline, and extended protection to enemy civilians. Taylor drew out the contradictions and racial biases inherent in domesticity by emphasizing the mistreatment black soldiers received for respecting the laws of war and the tenets of domesticity. Drawing on abolitionist ideas that "the struggle against slavery [was] 'a question of manhood,'" Taylor posited that southern black men fully embodied what it meant to be a man, while white southern men shirked their domestic and wartime responsibilities. For Taylor, being a gentleman entailed rejecting racial and class biases, as demonstrated in her comment that white Union army Captain C. T. Trowbridge was "a thorough gentleman and a staunch friend to my race."[32]

Sincerity and bravery were two hallmarks of the ideal nineteenth-century middle- and upper-class white man.[33] Sarah Morgan found the third quality— self-control—also present in Federal soldiers. Upon closer inspection of the Federals in Baton Rouge, Morgan admitted that the men were "evidently gentlemen" because of the way that they "c[a]me as victors, without either pretensions to superiority, or the insolence of conquerors" but instead "walk[ed] quietly their way, offering no annoyance to the citizens." Refusing to boast, brag, or hold sway over noncombatants, Union soldiers demonstrated self-control. The way in which a man treated his dependents was the best measure of his character; in a time of war, the way in which soldiers treated noncombatants also revealed something essential about them. Even though she was a Confederate, Morgan believed it was imperative to recognize virtues even in her enemies, and she refused to call Federal officers "liars, thieves, murderers, scoundrels, the scum of the earth, etc." because "such epithets are unworthy of ladies." Morgan disagreed with many of her contemporaries that ladies could get angry and hurl insults and still be ladies as long as they espoused the Confederate cause. Instead, she believed that it was even more imperative during a time of war to cling to the manners that held society together. For Morgan and the officers in Baton Rouge, it was important to hold onto gender roles and manners—in effect, to civilization—when war threatened to tear these very things apart.[34]

Self-control could just as easily escape ladies and gentlemen. While Alfred Pirtle was stationed in Huntsville, Alabama, the behavior of ladies dramatically influenced his own behavior. In keeping with rules of etiquette that a woman must first acknowledge a man before he could attempt to make her acquaintance, Pirtle explained to his sister that he did not know any "Secesh belles" because they were "too devoted to the South, to more than glance at a National Officer." Instead, he and his fellow soldiers were reduced to "return[ing]" the "contemptuous glance[s]" of the citizens. In response to being treated as an enemy, Pirtle returned rudeness for rudeness. The women set the tone—in giving vent to their tempers, they not only transgressed standards of ladylike behavior but also provided a rationale for men to do the same. Instead of encouraging kindness and good behavior, the rudeness of Huntsville ladies spread throughout the community.[35]

Soldiers' and women's observations of each other's character paved the way for them to interact socially. The class status of Union soldiers and southern women greatly influenced who interacted with whom. According to George Stephens, many of the men in his company, drawn from the "cesspools of society . . . intemperate, brutal, and ignorant" were also "strangers to . . . honor or justice." Instead of learning the "effects of slavery upon a community" while stationed in the South, the men, "pregnant with negro hate," descended upon the home of a free African American family and "insulted [the] wife and daughters." In Stephens's estimation, these working-class men could not move past their prejudices so that they could truly understand enslaved African Americans. Unable to control their passions, they resorted to what they knew: stereotypes and brute force. Stephens contrasted their behavior with African Americans' commitment to family and community stability, thus creating a bond between his two very different audiences—freeborn middle-class black New Yorkers and recently enslaved, southern-born black enlisted men. In stark contrast to the behavior of his white fellow soldiers, Stephens recounted the travails of the "noble and heroic wife" of an enslaved man who, once her husband was within Union lines, risked her life to bring her family to freedom, and, when all seemed lost, "prayed to the good Lord." The piety and bravery of African American women stood in opposition to the vicious racism of white Union troops.[36] For Stephens, black women more closely modeled middle-class values than white working-class Union soldiers.

The violence of some working-class Union soldiers was also directed toward yeomen white women. Nancy Jett found this to be the case when she finally had the occasion to meet Federal soldiers in the summer of 1864. When Union soldiers stopped by Jett's house during the Atlanta campaign, she protested them entering, only to be met with the threat that if she tried to stop them, the soldier would "shoot [her] brains out." Jett called the soldier's bluff, telling him to shoot her if he must, but that she would keep talking "long as breth in me." But she showed a quickness to resort to violence with black soldiers. When two African American soldiers asked her for water, Jett responded that if she "still had A gun I blow them threw," later informing her husband that it "made [her] mad they talk so big." Instead of the self-controlled responses of the middle class, Jett and the working-class soldiers showed no qualms about expressing their anger. Rather than treating enemies with kindness and courtesy, Jett and the soldiers inhabited a world where one's place was never secure, and authority was often determined by violent means. Jett's quickness to resort to threats with African American soldiers demonstrates this to be true. Knocked from her place of relative privilege as a white woman and the wife of a yeoman farmer, Jett responded threateningly to freedpeople in order to assert her position in the social hierarchy.[37]

The ideal of congenial relationships between enemies, then, worked best when both parties spoke the "language" of gentility.[38] Compare the experience of Sarah Morgan and her family, who, although Confederates, approached Union officials in order to secure a guard for their property. Explaining that their "brothers were away, father dead" and that "we three [women] were alone and unprotected," the general's aide "insisted on a sentinel" for "there were many bad characters among the soldiers." Morgan remarked at the "singular situation": "our brothers off fighting them, while these Federal soldiers ... st[ood] on our steps to protect us." Morgan's ordeal illustrates that for middle-class women, the absence of male relatives created a void that required the assistance of Union soldiers. And Federal officers recognized their need for protection, given their status as upper-middle-class ladies. The very presence of men in the army who did not subscribe to genteel behavior necessitated this protection. Union soldiers' recognition of and respect for the Morgan family's status allowed Sarah to get to know Federal soldiers better.[39]

It was upper-class officer Wilder Dwight who demonstrated the most expansive and egalitarian vision of protecting southern women. Indeed, he took for granted that women wanted protection. Dwight preferred to use his privilege as an officer to secure comfortable accommodations in the homes of southern women. After intruding "upon an elderly lady"—a Unionist yeoman farmer—Dwight explained that there was no need to pay for the use of her house because she was "repaid by our protection." Unlike other Union officers, Dwight did not discriminate in choosing his accommodations. He also roomed with "an old negro woman" and a "good lady" who was a strong secessionist—she agreed to rent him rooms after declaring that she "hop[ed] you'll be beaten in your next battle." Dwight's behavior demonstrates a nuanced understanding of genteel values coupled with abolitionist sentiments and a firm commitment to the army's policy of conciliation. To Dwight, neither race nor class nor political sympathies were prerequisites for receiving the army's protection. Regardless of women's class status or political loyalties, the Union army was instructed to protect noncombatants. And as an abolitionist, Dwight included African American women in this estimation.[40]

Occupation brought soldiers and women in close contact, creating opportunities for more extended social interactions. Katherine Couse and her sisters regularly invited Union officers into their home. Couse indicated that these men had demonstrated themselves to be middle-class gentlemen in that she allowed them to call on her, remarking that they were all "such refined hansome looking men" and that she and her sisters had become "so attached to them" almost as if they were "near relative[s]." Couse responded as a hospitable middle-class woman by serving them "breakfast" and "tea" and even going so far for one officer as to "fi[x supper] nicely for him to eat." Shared political sympathies and middle-class values allowed Couse and the soldiers to find common ground (Couse did not invite Confederates into her home).[41] Because of the men's class status, Couse provided them with meals and company, even allowing herself to become so close to them that they almost felt as though they were related to her. By "barring" Confederates and working-class Union soldiers from her parlor but allowing Union officers, Couse signaled her privilege, as a white middle-class woman, to determine who was and was not a "social undesirable."

In contrast, Sarah Morgan did not allow Federal officers to visit her. In spite of what she viewed as all of the kindness they showed her family—including providing them with a guard and sending them food and other supplies when their storehouses were low—the women felt it necessary to "pass . . . over" Federal officers' willingness to call on them "in perfect silence." For Morgan, this raised difficult questions. "These gentlemen know us to be ladies," she felt certain, but given how she had behaved, she wondered, "Have [I] proved it?" Morgan's dilemma illustrates the uncertainty of exactly how to behave like an elite southern lady in a time of war. By Morgan's own admission, ladylike behavior was a performance requiring the approval of its audience—and this even included enemy soldiers. But during war, not receiving enemy soldiers—even if they were gentlemen—seemed to be the best course of action, although it directly contradicted standards of southern ladylike behavior, particularly the need to be "amiable" and "loved by all." Even so, Morgan did allow a few conversations with the men, describing one general's aide as "very entertaining" and "kind." These exchanges did not go unnoticed. Both "citizens" and "officers" gaped at this "unheard of occurrence," but Morgan paid them no mind. "I wont be rude to any one in my own house," she declared. As Morgan demonstrates, the dictates of ladylike behavior could be confusing and ultimately required community sanction. But such strictures proved impossible and even maddening. For Morgan, the priority was to avoid rudeness at all costs, and she accomplished this by drawing an arbitrary line between casual conversations and permitting Federal officers to call.[42]

Social calls between Union officers and elite Confederate women did take place. While stationed in Huntsville, Alfred Pirtle had frequent contact with his Confederate cousin Laura. Perhaps meaning to provoke him, Laura first visited him at his boarding house, bringing along "some rebel girls," leading the way in some "pretty sharp skirmishes" between Pirtle and the ladies. These visits soon dwindled as "Cousin Laura [grew] worse . . . than she ever was." Pirtle favored calling on a Mrs. Bunson, also a rebel, but one whose political sympathies "d[id] not prevent her receiving [Federal] officers politely." Pirtle eventually tired of calling on Confederate women altogether, instead spending his time with his commanding officer's northern-born daughters, ladies whom he "knew were with us heart and hand" and "in whose company we could feel no constraint, such as always is felt when with the Secesh ladies."[43] Although Pirtle did not deny that the Confederate women were ladies, his preference for Unionist women spoke volumes. In contrast to rebels, who doubted his character and forced him to be constantly on guard, northern-born Unionists were agreeable, as they recognized him as a gentleman and permitted those easy social interactions so prized by the genteel middle class. In this way, Pirtle demonstrates the unease and distrust that war injected into relations even between southerners— on opposite sides of the conflict, political sympathies divided rather than united the middle class.[44]

Working-class soldier Charles Musser well understood the pull of secessionist women. In fact, Musser found the young women of Arkansas to be so delightful that he even contemplated marrying one of them. However, he felt it was important to marry "some loyal Arkansians fair daughter," even though at church on Sunday he felt sorely tempted by the "beautyfull Daughters of the 'Sunny South.'" But rather than being influenced by a beautiful face or genteel manners, farmer Musser had more practical concerns. He decided against marrying an Arkansas girl because he found northern women to be more "buxom" (i.e., sturdy and suited to farm life), more "intelligent," and more "edjucated." While political sympathies partly informed his choice, Musser's chosen occupation as an aspiring commercial farmer necessitated picking a wife who was hardy, smart, and capable. Although Musser admitted that Little Rock women were "clever and amiable—good company to pass time with," such qualities, however attractive, did not make them wife material.[45]

For single northerners and southerners, the culmination of social interactions was courtship and marriage. And while relationships between Union soldiers and southern women did form, it was most common for men and women to marry within their own communities, if they married at all. Katherine Couse remained unmarried, while Sarah Morgan delayed marriage until well into her thirties (and then married an English man who fought for the Confederacy). Both Musser and Pirtle returned home and married local women.[46] These relationships demonstrate the preference of many to marry within their community—and the middle-class preference to marry within their social class.

Susie King Taylor was the lone southern woman examined here to marry a Union soldier. Her husband, although also African American and also from coastal Georgia, did not reside in her community. More interesting was Taylor's choice to marry at fourteen, considered a young age within southern enslaved communities. Although Taylor did not disclose her reasons for marrying, she faced similar circumstances as other enslaved women who married young: romantic attachment, dislocation from family, and concerns about sexual vulnerability. Some of the white soldiers who shared camp with Taylor certainly assumed she was sexually available, as many white northerners, even abolitionists, widely regarded black women to be promiscuous. This was particularly true in one of the Federal camps where Taylor and her husband lived. Not a year after their marriage, the commander of Port Royal faced a congressional inquiry into reports of the serialized rape of black women by white Union soldiers. Taylor's marriage, then, secured her love and companionship as well as some protection against sexual assault.[47]

African American abolitionists well understood the perils that black women faced, particularly those who were enslaved. George Stephens's regiment aided a young enslaved woman, Mary Thomas, in finding freedom. Although the men were certainly committed to emancipation, Stephens asserted that they intervened both because Thomas had fallen in love with a member of their regiment and because her owner intended to "prostitute" Thomas by selling her to an "old lecherous scoundrel." Stephens found her story to be inspiring—seemingly destined by "the hard remorseless necessities of her position" to live "the life which her master had marked out for her," Thomas took matters into her own hands by initiating her escape and thus achieving "salvation, liberty, and love."[48] Stephens thus asserted that rather than willing participants in their sexual exploitation, black women were pious and virtuous women committed to freedom, bodily integrity, and families built on love and mutual consent.

That few relationships ended in marriage does not mean there was an absence of sexual intercourse between Union soldiers and southern women. Such contact occurred disproportionately among working-class soldiers and women, with even married white yeoman women facing assumptions about their sexual behavior. Nancy Jett recounted an exchange with two Union soldiers, who, after asking how she was "getting long for soming to eat," told her that if she "wod comidate them" she "never shold suffr for nothing they wod fet[ch] me Any thing to eat I wanted." In response to such aspersions on her character, Jett told the men she hoped to see them "burnt Alive." The Union soldiers who propositioned Jett assumed, as did many Americans, that yeoman southern women, because of their poverty, might trade sexual favors for money. And in contrast to middle-class men, raised to protect women's supposed innate purity, working-class men regarded women not as pure and virtuous but as passionate, manipulative creatures. Jett's refusal of their advances—and the fact that she recounted it to her husband—signified her belief that she and her husband, and not enemy soldiers, would provide for their family.[49]

Not all yeoman women demonstrated Jett's disdain for infidelity. Within her own community, two married friends, Nance and Ann, took up with Union soldiers in exchange for "all they cud get," most likely supplies. Describing the women as "bace hoers [base whores]," Jett was astounded that one of them even behaved "as if she had never bin married" by "lay[ing] with" Federals. Although the relationships at first seemed to be merely an exchange of sex for food, both women, when "the fellows . . . time was out to go home" returned north with them "as bold goin with them A bout as they did with their [husbands]."[50] With the community in a state of disarray due to the war, the normal consequences for adultery proved impossible to enforce. But Jett's commentary demonstrates that even though courts and churches could not intervene, neighbors loudly voiced their opinions. Most troubling for Jett was not so much that the women had sinned or taken up with the enemy but that the women's behavior threatened community stability.

Social interactions between Union soldiers and southern women during the war demonstrate the pervasiveness of nineteenth-century gender roles. Although relationships between them were always inherently unstable, war called into question how, exactly, middle- and upper-class whites could behave as ladies and gentlemen during the conflict. And while working-class northerners and yeoman southern women deviated the most from these ideas, they could do so because, as white Americans (or, in the case of Irish Americans, not black), their place in the body politic secured their political rights and respect for their households. Abolitionists and enslaved African American women also demonstrated a preference for domesticity, recognizing that freedom—particularly the status conferred on free domestic spaces—gave them important rights and privileges. This adherence to domesticity even in the turbulence of war reveals that this idea—with its emphasis on the patriarchal control of male heads of household, the duty of a husband to support and protect his family, the woman's control over household matters, and the obedience and service that a wife owed to her husband—was intimately linked to ideas of political power. The most salient evidence of this is the way in which free and enslaved African Americans stressed their own adherence to a modified, racially egalitarian domesticity. Black Americans who used the language of domesticity were not merely copying white middle-class values; by doing so, they sought to gain access to political power, acquire respect for independent households, and bring fundamental change to the racial exclusion inherent in nineteenth-century domesticity.

Notes

1. Alfred Pirtle to "Sis," July 12, 1863, Alfred Pirtle Letters, Filson Historical Society, Louisville, Kentucky (hereafter FHS).

2. For the cult of domesticity, see Nancy F. Cott, *The Bonds of Womanhood: "Woman's Sphere" in New England, 1780–1835* (New Haven, CT: Yale University Press, 1977), 68, 95–99; Julie Roy Jeffrey, *Frontier Women: "Civilizing" the West? 1840–1880*, rev. ed. (Hill and Wang, 1998), 12–14; Linda K. Kerber, *No Constitutional Right to Be Ladies: Women and the Obligations of Citizenship* (New York: Hill and Wang, 1999), xxiii, 10, 11; Christine Stansell, *City of Women: Sex and Class in New York, 1789–1860* (Urbana: University of Illinois Press, 1986), 153, 155, 168, 211, 219.

3. For middle- and upper-class southern women and domesticity, see Anne Firor Scott, *The Southern Lady: From Pedestal to Politics, 1830–1930*, rev. ed. (Charlottesville: University Press of

Virginia, 1995), 4–21; Elizabeth Fox-Genovese, *Within the Plantation Household: Black and White Women of the Old South* (Chapel Hill: University of North Carolina Press, 1988), 64–65; Anya Jabour, *Scarlett's Sisters: Young Women in the Old South* (Chapel Hill: University of North Carolina Press, 2007), 35–45; Jonathan Daniel Wells, *The Origins of the Southern Middle Class, 1800–1861* (Chapel Hill: University of North Carolina Press, 2003), 76–80; Jeffrey, *Frontier Women*, 15–17; for yeoman women, see Stephanie McCurry, *Masters of Small Worlds: Yeoman Households, Gender Relations, and the Political Culture of the Antebellum South Carolina Low Country* (Oxford: Oxford University Press, 1995), 73–76; for black women and domesticity, see Thavolia Glymph, *Out of the House of Bondage: The Transformation of the Plantation Household* (Cambridge: Cambridge University Press, 2008), 64–65, 95; for western women and domesticity, see Jeffrey, *Frontier Women*, 17–32.

4. Jeffrey, *Frontier Women*, 15.

5. For Union soldiers, see Bell Irvin Wiley, *The Life of Billy Yank: The Common Soldier of the Union* (Baton Rouge: Louisiana State University Press, 1952); Reid Mitchell, *The Vacant Chair: The Northern Soldier Leaves Home* (New York: Oxford University Press, 1993); and Mitchell, *Civil War Soldiers* (New York: Penguin Books, 1997). For southern women, see Catherine Clinton, ed., *Southern Families at War: Loyalty and Conflict in the Civil War South* (Oxford: Oxford University Press, 2000); Catherine Clinton and Nina Silber, eds., *Battle Scars: Gender and Sexuality in the American Civil War* (Oxford: Oxford University Press, 2006); Laura Edwards, *Scarlett Doesn't Live Here Anymore: Southern Women in the Civil War Era* (Urbana: University of Illinois Press, 2000); Drew Gilpin Faust, *Mothers of Invention: Women of the Slaveholding South in the American Civil War* (Chapel Hill: University of North Carolina Press, 1996); George C. Rable, *Civil Wars: Women and the Crisis of Southern Nationalism* (Urbana: University of Illinois Press, 1989); LeeAnn Whites, *Gender Matters: Civil War, Reconstruction, and the Making of the New South* (New York: Palgrave Macmillan, 2005); LeeAnn Whites and Alecia P. Long, eds., *Occupied Women: Gender, Military Occupation, and the American Civil War* (Baton Rouge: Louisiana State University Press, 2009).

6. See Jacqueline Glass Campbell, *When Sherman Marched North from the Sea: Resistance on the Confederate Home Front* (Chapel Hill: University of North Carolina Press, 2003); Lisa Tendrich Frank, *The Civilian War: Confederate Women and Union Soldiers during Sherman's March* (Baton Rouge: Louisiana State University Press, 2015).

7. For the ways in which behavior differs from social and cultural norms, see Jeffrey, *Frontier Women*, 18.

8. Wilder Dwight, Charles O. Musser, and Nancy Jett wrote letters to family that capture wartime experience as they happened (but they might have censored some experiences or thoughts). Sarah Morgan and Katherine Couse kept diaries, and their records are a bit more complete, as they might have assumed their thoughts were private. Alfred Pirtle kept a diary and wrote letters, and they provide interesting contrast between the way he related experiences to family and the way he recorded them for himself. George E. Stephens's missives, published in an African American New York newspaper with an educated, middle-class black audience, were also a favorite among black enlisted men and highlighted issues of emancipation and equality. Susie King Taylor's account is the most challenging since she self-published her memoirs thirty-seven years after the end of the war. Her reminiscences raise issues about the problems of memory.

9. Considerations of race, ethnicity, class, gender, age, state of origin, marital status, and politi-

cal sympathies all influenced the selection of these eight historical actors. As each historical actor needed to have left a significant historical record, none of them were illiterate.

10. Wilder Dwight, *Life and Letters of Wilder Dwight, Lieut.-Col. Second Mass. Inf. Vols.* (Boston: Ticknor and Fields, 1868), 1, 3, 8, 10, 11, 14–23, 32–34, 44, 289; see also entry for William Dwight in Schedule of Free Inhabitants for Brookline, Norfolk County, Massachusetts, 1860 Federal Census, MS 653_514, National Archives and Records Administration, Washington, DC (hereafter NARA).

11. Donald Yacovone, ed., *A Voice of Thunder: The Civil War Letters of George E. Stephens* (Urbana: University of Illinois Press, 1997), 3–5, 63; see entry for George Stephens in New York, State Census, 1875; for the publication history of the *Weekly Anglo-African*, see Penelope L. Bullock, *The Afro-American Periodical Press, 1838–1909* (Baton Rouge: Louisiana State University Press, 1981); and Frankie Hutton, *The Early Black Press in America, 1827 to 1860* (New York: Praeger, 1992); for its relationship to the New York African American community, see Debra Jackson, "'A Cultural Stronghold': The 'Anglo-African' Newspaper and the Black Community in New York," *New York History* 4 (2004): 331–357; for readership information, see Erica Ball, *To Live an Antislavery Life: Personal Politics and the Antebellum Black Middle Class* (Athens: University of Georgia Press, 2012).

12. See biography of Alfred Pirtle in Alfred Pirtle Papers, FHS; see also entry for Henry Pirtle in Schedule of Free Inhabitants for Louisville, Jefferson County, Kentucky, 1860 Federal Census, MS 653_376, NARA, and entry for Henry Pirtle in 1860 Federal Census—Slave Schedules, NARA.

13. Charles O. Musser, *Soldier Boy: The Civil War Letters of Charles O. Musser, 29th Iowa*, ed. Bobby Popchock (Iowa City: University of Iowa Press, 2008), 2; John Musser in Production of Agriculture for Kane, Pottawattamie County, Iowa, 1860 Federal Census Non-Population Schedules, 1850–1880, T1156, roll 5, page 3, line 2, NARA.

14. Elizabeth A. Getz, "Between the Lines: The Diary of a Unionist Woman at the Battle of Spotsylvania Court House," *Fredericksburg History and Biography* 1 (2002): 57–58; see also entry for William Couse in 1850 Federal Census—Slave Schedule, NARA, and entry for Elizabeth Cause [Elisabeth Couse] in Production of Agriculture for Saint George, Spotsylvania County, Virginia, 1860 Federal Census Non-Population Schedules, 1850–1880, T1132, roll 8, page 464, line 18, NARA.

15. Sarah Morgan, *The Civil War Diary of a Southern Woman*, ed. Charles East (New York: Touchstone, 1991), xvii–xix.

16. Biographical Note, Richard Burch Jett Papers, Manuscript, Archives, and Rare Book Library Division, Emory University, Atlanta, Georgia (hereafter Emory); as of 1880, Richard owned 246 acres of land, only 26 of which were improved. See Richard B. Jett in Production of Agriculture for Buckhead, Fulton County, Georgia, 1880 Federal Census Non-Population Schedules, 1850–1880, T1137, roll 14, page 8, line 10, NARA.

17. Susie King Taylor, *Reminiscences of My Life in Camp: An African American Woman's Civil War Memoir* (Athens: University of Georgia Press, 2006), 2–9; Ronald E. Butchart, "Susie King Taylor (1848–1912)," *New Georgia Encyclopedia*, 2013, http://www.georgiaencyclopedia.org/articles/history-archaeology/susie-king-taylor-1848-1912.

18. For appearance in the nineteenth century, see John F. Kasson, *Rudeness and Civility: Manners in Nineteenth-Century Urban America* (New York: Hill and Wang, 1990), 92–111; for avoiding attention in public, see 117–118. In the South, these ideas expressed themselves in terms of honor, the individual's "understanding of who he is and where he belongs in the ordered ranks of society." Bertram Wyatt-Brown, *Southern Honor: Ethics and Behavior in the Old South* (New York: Oxford

University Press, 1982), 14, 20; for southern young ladies and bodily comportment, see Jabour, *Scarlett's Sisters*, 31–34.

19. By the term "lady" or "ladies," I refer to the nineteenth-century term for wealthy white women from families whose wealth allowed them to display, through their clothing, accoutrements, and good manners, their membership in the upper class. For being a "lady" in the northern United States, see Jeanie Attie, *Patriotic Toil: Northern Women and the American Civil War* (Ithaca, NY: Cornell University Press, 1998), 9–13; Karen Halttunen, *Confidence Men and Painted Women: A Study of Middle-Class Culture in America, 1830–1870*, (New Haven, CT: Yale University Press), 57–58, 79–80; and Kasson, *Rudeness and Civility*, 57, 67; for the southern version of a lady, see Jabour, *Scarlett's Sisters*, 19–45; and Scott, *The Southern Lady*, 3–21. Thavolia Glymph makes the important point that, for southern slave-owning women, being a lady entailed a certain socioeconomic status, because for these women, work outside the home was a "disqualifying act." See Glymph, *Out of the House of Bondage*, 4.

20. Morgan, *Civil War Diary*, 169–170.

21. Taylor, *Reminiscences of My Life in Camp*, 7–8; for black women's visibility as laborers, see Noralee Frankel, *Freedom's Women: Black Women and Families in Civil War Era Mississippi* (Bloomington: Indiana University Press, 1999), 29; and Victoria Bynum, *Unruly Women: The Politics of Social and Sexual Control in the Old South* (Chapel Hill: University of North Carolina Press, 1992), 57. For labor as a "disqualifying act," see Glymph, *Out of the House of Bondage*, 4. For black women's roles in making domesticity possible, see Glymph, *Out of the House of Bondage*, 64–65, 95; and compare this to the relationship between northern white women and domestics in Stansell, *City of Women*, 155–168.

22. Getz, "Between the Lines," 61, 63, 65, 67.

23. Alfred Pirtle to "Ma," March 1, 1862; Alfred Pirtle Diary, March 22, 1862, FHS; Elizabeth R. Varon, *We Mean to Be Counted: White Women and Politics in Antebellum Virginia* (Chapel Hill: University of North Carolina Press, 1998), 96, 102, 103, 137; for women and the Union, see Mitchell, *Vacant Chair*, 72–74, 90, 91–96. See also the ways in which the Civil War heightened and challenged gender relations in the North and South in Jean Bethke Elshtain, *Women and War* (New York: Basic Books, 1987), 94–106; and in the South in Leeann Whites, *The Civil War as a Crisis in Gender: Augusta, Georgia, 1860–1890* (Athens: University of Georgia Press, 1995), 15–63.

24. Alfred Pirtle to "Ma," March 1, 1862; Alfred Pirtle Diary, March 22, 1862, both FHS; Jabour, *Scarlett's Sisters*, 38–39.

25. Musser, *Soldier Boy*, 91; Jeffrey, *Frontier Women*, 91–92.

26. Compare this to western women's changing appearance in Jeffrey, *Frontier Women*, 55–56; Joan Cashin discusses elite white women's changing clothing throughout the war in "Torn Bonnets and Stolen Skirts: Fashion, Gender, Race, and Danger in the Wartime South," *Civil War History* 4 (2015): 349–350, 353.

27. Yacovone, *Voice of Thunder*, 138; see also Frederick Law Olmstead, *The Cotton Kingdom: A Traveller's Observations on Cotton and Slavery in the American Slave States, 1853–1861*, ed. Arthur M. Schlesinger (New York: Da Capo, 1996), 8, 11–12, 18, 19, 67, 75, 90, 103, 339, 402–403; Ronald G. Walters, *American Reformers, 1815–1860* (New York: Hill and Wang, 1978), 82–83; Lacy K. Ford, *Deliver Us from Evil: The Slavery Question in the Old South* (Oxford: Oxford University Press, 2009), 506; Mitchell, *Civil War Soldiers*, 109; Deborah Gray White, *Ar'n't I a Woman? Female Slaves*

in the Plantation South (New York: W. W. Norton, 1999); 38; for the link between slavery and sin, see Howard R. Floan, *The South through Northern Eyes, 1831–1861* (New York: McGraw Hill, 1958), 8–9.

28. Dwight, *Life and Letters*, 205; for embarrassment in the nineteenth-century, see Kasson, *Rudeness and Civility*, 114–115.

29. Halttunen, *Confidence Men and Painted Women*, xvi, xvii, 25, 39, 40, 51–52, 93; Kasson, *Rudeness and Civility*, 34–111.

30. Getz, "Between the Lines," 66, 71; Halttunen, *Confidence Men and Painted Women*, 50–52.

31. The idea of the nineteenth-century US gentleman varied by region. Similar to the label of "lady," it described a man's social and class status in addition to his manners, comportment, education, profession, and leisure activities. For gentlemen in the northern United States, see Halttunen, *Confidence Men and Painted Women*, 42, 46, 50–52; Michael Kimmel, *Manhood in America: A Cultural History* (New York: Free Press, 1996), 22–23, 45–50; for gentlemen in the South, see Kenneth S. Greenberg, *Honor and Slavery: Lies, Duels, Noses, Masks, Dressing as a Woman, Gifts, Strangers, Humanitarianism, Death, Slave Rebellions, the Proslavery Argument, Baseball, Hunting, and Gambling in the Old South* (Princeton, NJ: Princeton University Press, 1996), 3, 11, 25, 50, 145; Joan E. Cashin, *A Family Venture: Men and Women on the Southern Frontier* (Baltimore: Johns Hopkins University Press, 1991), 102–108; Stephen Berry, *All That Makes a Man: Love and Ambition in the Civil War South* (New York: Oxford University Press, 2002); similar to northern working-class men, southern yeomen distinguished themselves from southern gentlemen while insisting on many of their privileges; see McCurry, *Masters of Small Worlds*, 72, 75–80, 85, 206, 225, 276. Enslaved and free African Americans developed substantially different definitions of what it meant to be a man and a woman. See White, *Ar'n't I a Woman?*, 105–119; Glymph, *Out of the House of Bondage*, 90–91; Leslie M. Harris, *In the Shadow of Slavery: African Americans in New York City, 1626–1863* (Chicago: University of Chicago Press, 2004), 98–169; Erica L. Ball, *To Live an Antislavery Life: Personal Politics and the Antebellum Black Middle Class* (Athens: University of Georgia Press, 2012).

32. Taylor, *Reminiscences of My Life in Camp*, 15, 42; Kimmel, *Manhood in America*, 73–74; see also Christian G. Samito, *Becoming American under Fire: Irish Americans, African Americans, and the Politics of Citizenship during the Civil War Era* (Ithaca, NY: Cornell University Press, 2009), 5–6. Here I reference the "laws of war" rather than the Articles of War because the latter deals with civilians only in passing. The laws of war, as articulated by military theoreticians—most importantly in the United States by Henry W. Halleck—embraced ideas of domesticity by articulating boundaries between home front and battlefront and mandating respect for women and children. See Mark Grimsley, *The Hard Hand of War: Union Military Policy toward Southern Civilians, 1861–1865* (New York: Cambridge University Press, 1995), 15–17. Making "war against women and children" was a serious charge leveled by both sides. See Musser, *Soldier Boy*, 85; *The War of the Rebellion: A Compilation of the Official Records of the Union and Confederate Armies*, 127 vols. (Washington, DC: Government Printing Office, 1880–1901), ser. 1, vol. 51 pt. 1, 425–426; ser. 1, vol. 6, 670–671, ser. 1, vol.6, 488, 491, 493.

33. Those white middle- and upper-class Americans who embraced domesticity only expected sincerity, bravery, and self-control of prosperous white Anglo-Saxon Protestant men. Other men, particularly (but not limited to) working-class white men and men of color subscribed to alternative ideas of masculinity; see Lorien Foote, *The Gentlemen and the Roughs: Manhood, Honor, and Violence in the Union Army* (New York: New York University Press, 2010). Amy Greenberg agrees

Laura Mammina

that there was no hegemonic masculinity, but instead that ideas of gentility and domesticity resonated powerfully with many Americans. See Greenberg, *Manifest Manhood and the Antebellum American Empire* (Cambridge: Cambridge University Press, 2005), 9–13, 50–52, 177.

34. Morgan, *Civil War Diary*, 68, 73; for self-control and masculinity, see Kimmel, *Manhood in America*, 44–45, 50; Halttunen, *Confidence Men and Painted Women*, 25; and Kasson, *Rudeness and Civility*, 117.

35. Alfred Pirtle to Ashley, June 21, 1862; Alfred Pirtle to "Ma," May 4, 1862, both FHS; for elite women controlling their tempers, see Jabour, *Scarlett's Sisters*, 38–39; for women inculcating morality, see Jeffrey, *Frontier Women*, 14; and Kimmel, *Manhood in America*, 54–55; for women acknowledging men first, see Kasson, *Rudeness and Civility*, 143.

36. Yacovone, *Voice of Thunder*, 138, 139, 205, 208–209, 276; for the importance of family and community stability, see Stephanie McCurry, *Confederate Reckoning: Power and Politics in the Civil War South* (Cambridge, MA: Harvard University Press, 2010), 249–250; Leslie A. Schwalm, "Between Slavery and Freedom: African American Women and Occupation in the Slave South," in Whites and Long, *Occupied Women*, 139; for women and the destruction of slavery, see McCurry, *Confederate Reckoning*, 246; for the political implications of free black homes, see Glymph, *Out of the House of Bondage*, 145–146.

37. Nancy Jett to Richard Burch Jett, September 2, 1864, Richard Burch Jett Papers, Emory; for the tenuous position of yeoman households, see McCurry, *Masters of Small Worlds*, 70, 72–73, 75. While yeoman and working class households subscribed to some elements of domestic ideology, they placed more emphasis on patriarchal authority and did not consider women to be morally and spiritually superior. See McCurry, *Masters of Small Worlds*, 85, 87, 89–90; Stansell, *City of Women*, 77–82; Kimmel, *Manhood in America*, 56–57; for etiquette manuals and protection, see Kasson, *Rudeness and Civility*, 132–133.

38. By "genteel behavior" and "gentility," I refer to a nineteenth-century US social standing defined by adherence to particular manners, purchase and display of fashionable goods, and conformity to etiquette in the home and out in public. Kasson notes that middle- and upper-class white Americans hoped to use it as a way to exclude working-class whites and blacks from their ranks. See Kasson, *Rudeness and Civility*, 35–37, 40, 43, 59–60, 62, 64–65; see also Halttunen, *Confidence Men and Painted Women*, 118.

39. Morgan, *Civil War Diary*, 105–107; for differing values among middle- and working-class Federals, see Foote, *The Gentlemen and the Roughs*, 70–72.

40. Dwight, *Life and Letters*, 158, 199, 201; Kimmel, *Manhood in America*, 23, 26, 43, 44, 54–55; for conciliation, see Grimsley, *The Hard Hand of War*, 19.

41. Getz, "Between the Lines," 65, 67, 68; for not visiting with Confederates, see 72; for middle-class women's duty to serve, see Cott, *Bonds of Womanhood*, 71–74; Jabour, *Scarlett's Sisters*, 35–36; Jeffrey, *Frontier Women*, 90–92, 104, 129–130; for the politics of the parlor, see Halttunen, *Confidence Men and Painted Women*, 111–112.

42. Morgan, *Civil War Diary*, 108, 115; for southern women and avoiding rudeness, see Jabour, *Scarlett's Sisters*, 44–45; for receiving callers, see Kasson, *Rudeness and Civility*, 172–176; and Halttunen, *Confidence Men and Painted Women*, 59–60, 92–95, 102–103, 112–113.

43. Alfred Pirtle to "Ma," June 8, 1862; Alfred Pirtle to "Ma," August 22, 1862; Alfred Pirtle Diary, April 24 and June 10, 1862, all FHS; for ladies being agreeable, see Jabour, *Scarlett's Sisters*,

45; for the importance of sincerity, see Halttunen, *Confidence Men and Painted Women*, 51–52; for ease in social interactions, see ibid., 93.

44. Young men and women in the Early Republic also preferred partners from the same political party. See Rosemarie Zagarri, *Revolutionary Backlash: Women and Politics in the Early American Republic* (Philadelphia: University of Pennsylvania Press, 2007), 90–91.

45. Musser, *Soldier Boy*, 90; for qualities prized among western women, see Jeffery, *Frontier Women*, 55–56, 78–80, 85; for southerners prizing cleverness and amiability, see Jabour, *Scarlett's Sisters*, 38–39; for the prevalence of public education in the West, see Jeffrey, *Frontier Women*, 99, 109–110, 112; for the sparseness of public education in the South, see Christie Anne Farnham, *The Education of the Southern Belle: Higher Education and Student Socialization in the Antebellum South* (New York: New York University Press, 1994); and Sarah L. Hyde, *Schooling in the Antebellum South: The Rise of Public and Private Education in Louisiana, Mississippi, and Alabama* (Baton Rouge: Louisiana State University Press, 2016), 117, 125, 128.

46. Testimony of Katherine Couse, Claim of Peter Couse, Spotsylvania County, Virginia, Records of the Accounting Officers of the Department of the Treasury, Southern Claims Commission, Record Group 217, NARA; Morgan, *Civil War Diary*, xxxv; Musser, *Soldier Boy*, 4; biography of Alfred Pirtle in Pirtle Papers, FHS; Taylor, *Reminiscences of My Life in Camp*, 9.

47. Taylor, *Reminiscences of My Life in Camp*, 9; Leslie Schwalm, *A Hard Fight for We: Women's Transition from Slavery to Freedom in South Carolina* (Urbana: University of Illinois Press, 1997), 100, 102–103; Walters, *American Reformers*, 82–83; Ford, *Deliver Us from Evil*, 506; Mitchell, *Civil War Soldiers*, 109; White, *Ar'n't I a Woman*, 38; Clare A. Lyons, *Sex among the Rabble: An Intimate History of Gender and Power in the Age of Revolution, Philadelphia, 1730–1830* (Chapel Hill: University of North Carolina Press, 2006), 4; Sharon Block, *Rape and Sexual Power in Early America* (Chapel Hill: University of North Carolina Press, 2006), 53; most enslaved men and women married in their late teens or early twenties. See Marie Jenkins Schwartz, *Born in Bondage: Growing Up Enslaved in the Antebellum South* (Cambridge, MA: Harvard University Press, 2000), 174, 179.

48. Yacovone, *Voice of Thunder*, 187.

49. Nancy Jett to Richard Burch Jett, September 2, 1864, Emory; Bynum, *Unruly Women*, 46; Diane Miller Sommerville, *Rape and Race in the Nineteenth-Century South* (Chapel Hill: University of North Carolina Press, 2004), 5–7, 11, 22, 27; Stansell, *City of Women*, 25–27, 98–99; Block, *Rape and Sexual Power in Early America*, 12; McCurry, *Masters of Small Worlds*, 183.

50. Nancy Jett to Richard Burch Jett, September 2, 1864, Emory; Bynum, *Unruly Women*, 90; McCurry, *Masters of Small Worlds*, 182–183.

An Elusive Freedom

Black Women, Labor, and Liberation during the Civil War

CHARITY RAKESTRAW AND KRISTOPHER A. TETERS

Aunt" Lucy Higgs Nichols experienced the Civil War like many thousands of other women who fled slavery for Union lines. She escaped, she served, and she survived. Nichols's life after the war, however, followed anything but a common trajectory. When news of an approaching Union regiment wound its way to the Higgs plantation in Tennessee in 1862, Lucy scooped up her infant daughter and fled to join the Yankee troops. Her owner tracked her to Bolivar and demanded that the soldiers return his property to him. Ignoring his commands, the 23rd Indiana provided Lucy with sanctuary, and for the remainder of the conflict she followed them, acting as their nurse and servant for about three years. She traveled with them from Tennessee to Mississippi to Georgia, tending to wounds, administering medicine, and performing domestic chores. After the Confederates surrendered, Lucy decided to stay near the men of the regiment and made her home in Indiana, marrying a black veteran of the 8th Colored Heavy Artillery named John Nichols. The only female servant of the 23rd Indiana, the troops gave her the (albeit problematic) nickname of "Aunt" and petitioned Congress in 1893 to grant her a pension.[1] Because of their letters of support and her proven contributions to the war effort, in 1898, Lucy Higgs Nichols became the first black woman to gain entry into the Grand Army of the Republic (GAR).

The extraordinary position that Lucy Higgs Nichols held (in the regiment and the GAR) attracted national attention. The *New York Times*, for instance, praised her as a "woman warrior"; the Janesville, Wisconsin, *Daily Gazette* described her as the "daughter of the regiment"; and the Denver *Sunday Post* compared her to Joan of Arc.[2] Newspapers across the United States detailed her story because Nichols stood out among black women. Her admittance into the GAR, the dedication of her regiment to her well-being, and the mythos surrounding her wartime heroism all drew notice. Other bondwomen who escaped to Union lines, however, often did not find the same care and courtesy, they did not witness a celebration of their contributions, and their stories remain largely undocumented.[3] This essay focuses on these women, whose voices and actions are often lost in the narrative, and argues that they sought to control their own fates in an unpredictable environment and with very little (if any) leverage.

Despite the lack of recognition that other women received in the aftermath of the war, Nichols's service during the conflict did not differ greatly from other black women who aided the Union. She performed similar tasks in the army and proved that she was very useful to the soldiers. Nichols's story exemplifies the agency that so many other black women demonstrated on the difficult road to freedom.[4] This essay examines the experiences and strategies of female refugees in Union camps during the Civil War. As bondwomen navigated the treacherous terrain between slavery and freedom, thousands of them sought refuge from white Union soldiers and officers. Women used great resourcefulness by caregiving, offering their domestic skills, providing information, and even performing hard labor. These tactics drew upon the skills and the social acumen that they developed while living in slavery. Black women also traversed gender roles, some presenting themselves as men to be accepted into the camps. In addition to acknowledging the activities of black women, this study also presents the attitudes of white Union soldiers toward the enslaved and formerly enslaved as many of the northern troops encountered black southerners for the first time. Soldiers relayed their sentiments to loved ones at home, exposing racial prejudices along with some sympathy for "contraband" women.[5]

In the absence of primary sources written by the women behind Union lines, historians have relied on the voices of Union soldiers, as well as the accounts of Confederate men and women, to trace and contextualize the activities of runaway women during the Civil War. In her article on the particular disadvantages bondwomen faced during the conflict, Thavolia Glymph argues that women developed their own methods of resistance during the conflict.[6] "Black women in refugee camps," she posits, "fought mightily against ideas that rendered them undeserving claimants to the nation's attention or freedom and citizenship. Despite the obstacles, they refused to turn back from the path of freedom and marked in concrete ways the moments that signaled that they were no longer slaves."[7] Gleaning from other studies and the statements of some officers, Glymph provides a window into the lives of "contraband" women in this period.

While Gylmph isolates her study to the Civil War period, other scholars integrate their analysis into a broader periodization, treating their discussion of Civil War activities as extensions of the resistance apparent in the antebellum period. In her seminal work on enslaved women in the plantation South, historian Stephanie Camp weaves examples from southern diary entries, Confederate and Union letters, and testimonies from the Reconstruction period to connect wartime activities with prewar challenges to bondage. "The Civil War's runaways had a history," Camp concludes. "During their enslavement, women, in ways shared with and distinct from those bondmen, had created secret forms of knowledge about and uses of southern space."[8] Even if not directly recognized by Union troops who encountered enslaved women, this unique knowledge of the southern landscape is apparent in soldiers' letters and officers' orders. More than the landscape, however, these writings indicate that women used every skill acquired in slavery to seek a new existence outside of the institution.[9]

At first, however, most black women did not find the Union army to be a liberating force. During the war's early stages, some Union officers prohibited slaves from entering Union lines, and some officers even returned slaves to their masters. Eventually, many officers allowed limited numbers of slaves into army camps. This gradual admittance grew out of adherence to the First Confiscation Act, which permitted the army to seize slaves that were being used by the Confederacy. The act applied less to female slaves, who were not as frequently utilized by the Confederacy for labor and other military purposes. For the most part, during the war's first fifteen months, the Union army had not yet assumed an emancipationist purpose. All of this changed in July 1862 when the Second Confiscation Act became law. This act enabled the Union to seize any slaves belonging to rebels, causing Union commanders to confiscate huge numbers of slaves in the field. The process of liberation accelerated and expanded after President Abraham Lincoln issued the final Emancipation Proclamation in January 1863. From then on, the Union army became a powerful force of emancipation, wrecking slavery wherever it went. Thousands and thousands of former female slaves had their first taste of freedom in Union lines, courageously striving to carve out an independent existence in the crucible of war.[10]

The promise of that new existence remained extremely tenuous as women made their way to Union camps, seeking sanctuary but unaware of what challenges and conditions they would find. The troops themselves often had similar concerns about runaways' futures. Lieutenant Alfred Trego, an officer in the 102nd Illinois marching with Major General William T. Sherman in 1864, noted the mass exodus of women and children and could not predict what would befall them. "One woman had her child fastened on her back like the Indian custom," he reported. "Another wore Pantaloons with a short dress to her knees. . . . What will become of them—is the question asked by all—yet answered by none."[11] The volume of formerly enslaved pouring out of plantations and seeking asylum distressed many Union officers, like Charles Dana Miller of the 76th Ohio, who witnessed "about three hundred negroes, men, women and children, follow[ing] the army loaded with bundles of all descriptions." "These poor people," he opined, "had run away from their masters and stepped forth into the unknown world of freedom. It was especially hard for the women who knew not what would become of them but were unwilling to part with their husbands; and the government could not give them employment as it could the men."[12] As these refugees arrived at camps in droves, Union forces did not have provisions to care for them and, at times, bemoaned having to consider their plight at all.

In fact, they often deemed women and children worthless in the war effort and burdensome to officers who could barely feed and shelter their troops. Writing from Memphis in 1863, Major General Stephen A. Hurlbut complained to President Lincoln about the burden of "contraband." "There are within the limits of my command about 5,000 negroes, male and female, of all ages, supported by the Government," Hurlbut grumbled. "Most of these, say, from two-thirds to three-fourths, are women and children, incapable of army labor—a weight and incumbrance."[13] Brigadier General James Garfield witnessed a similar situation in Murfreesboro, Tennessee, where he wrote to Secretary of the Treasury Salmon P. Chase about the dire situation facing black southerners and the camps that could not support them. While the Union army employed able-bodied men as teamsters and laborers, they did not use women in these roles and struggled with what to do with them. "The trouble arises with the swarms of Negro women and children that flock to our lines for protection and support," Garfield indicated, describing the devastation and starvation that befell many former slaves he encountered. "Thousands have been abandoned by their masters," he observed, "who have lost all hope of gain by keeping them and now cruelly turn them out to perish or to become a burden which this army cannot safely assume."[14] Women and the children in their care had no guarantee that camps would provide them with the minimum of necessities, and many camps were simply unequipped to do so.

The conditions in the camps were oftentimes inhospitable and interactions with troops sometimes dangerous and abusive. Medical historian Jim Downs explains that, during the deadliest war in the nation's history, freepeople suffered from illness and disease at higher rates than even soldiers, "since ex-slaves often lacked the basic necessities to survive."[15] Even if Union officers took them in, these refugees did not always have shelter from the elements or receive sufficient sustenance, clothing, or medical care, and thousands perished as a result. A northern white woman who volunteered in one of the Union camps revealed that "whether or not they found work at the camps, runaway women frequently encountered official neglect, received 'rude shelter' or none at all, and generally suffered 'from overcrowding, privation, neglect, and sickness.'"[16] Writing to his aunt in February 1864, Captain William Ferry of the 14th Michigan expressed concern over the continued plight of many black southerners in camps, explaining how in Jackson, Tennessee, conditions were so dire that officers requested that planters allow women and children back onto their plantations to care for them because the Union could not.[17] In this environment, it became imperative for "contraband" women to set themselves apart by laboring and assisting troops whenever possible as a matter of survival.

Former slaves not only faced neglect; they also sometimes encountered violence and cruelty at the hands of Union soldiers.[18] Troops plundered slave quarters, stole money in addition to supplies, beat men, and raped women, according to some accounts. Some soldiers took what little money slaves had been able to acquire, confiscated livestock and food by force, and set fire to homes.[19] In particular, women frequently found themselves defenseless in poorly supplied "contraband" camps, where at least some became victims of violence akin to what they experienced in slavery. "The negro women were debauched by our soldiers," a distressed Captain William Ferry wrote from Memphis. "A 'contraband camp' became by the allowance + practice of *officers* + men a scene of prostitution," he reported. "They were herded together like cattle, + the soldiers went among them picking out as they might fancy here + there one to satiate lust brutal lust."[20] Some officers punished such behavior, and others used their positions of power to abuse women themselves, making it difficult for women to discern who would protect and who would violate them.[21]

Thus, freedom sometimes proved elusive to the runaway women who made it to Union strongholds, where, if admitted, they often had few supplies, little if no shelter, were exposed to rampant disease, and at times encountered troops who were unwelcoming or even violent and abusive. To combat prejudices and the notion that they would impede Union efforts, women learned to present themselves as valuable laborers and grateful freedpeople. Like Lucy Higgs

Nichols, some offered medical expertise to aid Union efforts. Others provided domestic work, provisions, and information on Confederate troop movements and local geography.[22] Whatever skills they had acquired in their slave communities and on plantations they brought with them to Union lines and "contraband" camps to leverage their labor for freedom.[23] Although some Union officers and soldiers sympathized with the plight of black southerners, women had no guarantees that white men in blue uniforms would treat them with any more respect or humanity than their former masters.

Within this volatile atmosphere, some women used more unconventional approaches to try to protect themselves and find some sort of safety in the Union ranks. Colonel Hans Christian Heg of the 15th Wisconsin reported that one refugee presented himself as a "big fine looking Negro boy" when seeking admittance to the camp.[24] Suspecting that the young man was hiding his true identity, the colonel pressed him for his name, to which he "modestly replied 'Mary Ann.'" This "contraband" woman reached Union lines by donning male clothes and following one of the batteries, traveling safely with a group of men to the Union camp. Mary Ann expected her deception to cause the colonel to turn her away but, instead, Heg overlooked the misrepresentation and allowed Mary Ann to remain in camp as a washerwoman for the hospital under the condition that she wear the petticoats he provided to her.[25] As refugee women entered into an uncertain and unsafe environment, relying on white men who proved unpredictable, and with the future unclear, they developed diverse methods to try to control their own fates. In spite of these extreme variables, the demonstrated expertise, ingenuity, and resilience of black women remained constant in the accounts of the men who would be their liberators.

Some of that expertise stemmed from the ways that women had subsisted during their enslavement as they learned to adapt and stretch meager resources to care for themselves and their communities. Enslaved women often produced and prepared extravagant meals for their masters and mistresses as they hosted dinner parties to display their prestige and as a "symbol of elegance, distinction, and performance."[26] Their own diets (and the diets of their children) relied on what little their masters distributed to them, what male slaves contributed by hunting and fishing, and what they could grow themselves. With the permission of their masters, men were allowed some degree of mobility across plantations and used that relative flexibility to hunt and fish, which gave them a "mastery over [the] local environment."[27] Women often did not have even this limited mobility. Although women's "relative spatial illiteracy" proved challenging during the war as they traversed new terrain, once they arrived at Union camps, women combined their abilities to provide and perform as they had in their masters' homes with the resourcefulness they acquired in slave quarters.[28] Their knowledge of local vegetation and how to make the most out of limited supplies proved invaluable to Union officers and soldiers, many of whom relied on "contraband" women to cook for them during the war.

In the absence of their wives, Union troops in a foreign southern environment depended on formerly enslaved women to work in camp kitchens and to serve officers. Even if they had not arranged for a regular cook or servant, some recognized the important contributions black women made to the Union cause through their knowledge of the area and their ingenuity in difficult circumstances. Many soldiers, for instance, described the generosity of women as they offered food, water, and shelter during long travels. An adjutant in the 76th Ohio, Charles Dana Miller, wrote from Tennessee in 1862 that bondwomen had rescued him and his compatriots from thirst and starvation on several occasions. One such woman ladled out water to troops as they passed by her quarters, indicating to Miller that "the negroes seemed to take a secret delight in administering to the wants of Union soldiers." As he rode on, he "felt the pangs of hunger . . . not having eaten a morsel for twenty-four hours" and finally encountered another woman who used the only food she had, corn meal, to make a cake for him in a fire. "Although but partly baked and without salt," he recollected, "it was one of the sweetest morsels I ever partook of."[29] Soldiers often benefited from the knowledge of black women, at times accepting fairly lavish foodstuffs (not just corn cakes) that they found, grew, or made and donated to the troops. Lieutenant George W. Landrum of the 2nd Ohio proved especially fortunate as one bondwoman courted his favor by gifting "green peas, new potatoes, beats, lettuce, radishes, etc., raspberries and cherry tarts."[30] Reassuring his sister in a letter home that he had plenty to eat, he noted that the woman is "always sending me something nice."[31]

By willingly donating provisions to troops, black women emphasized to these soldiers their contributions to the war effort. When women arrived in Union camps, many used their culinary expertise and domestic abilities to reinforce their value to those who may have doubted their usefulness or considered them burdensome. Some Yankee men, however, like Major William G. Thompson of the 20th Iowa, remained skeptical of "contraband" women, illustrating the trials many women faced in finding employment and a modicum of security in the camps. Thompson noticed the appeals made by women to serve as laborers, noting in a letter home that "many of the females, or as they call them here nigger wenches, are importuning us every day to go as washerwomen, cooks, or at any work to be done."[32] He "refused to invest," insisting that he would "prefer a white person, although I wish the negro to have his freedom."[33] The major's racist rhetoric echoes that of other Union men and reinforces the barriers to that very freedom to which Thompson alluded.

Regardless of their racial attitudes, Union troops needed the help of bondwomen, who in turn needed refuge. A surgeon in the 18th Ohio, William Parker Johnson, recognized a shift in the army's attitudes toward taking in "contrabands" in September 1862, as "each regiment keeps all they can use to any advantage." Johnson remarked that he had "a first rate [female] Contraband" to cook for him.[34] Other soldiers offered similar, albeit problematic, sentiments regarding "contraband" women, noting that they "do the washing for the officers, and do it quite well" and that they mended pants "as neatly as any tailor would."[35] Captain John Corden of the 6th Michigan wrote to his wife from New Orleans in 1862 describing how one runaway woman "begged so hard to be allowed to do something for her living" that Corden had her work as a cook and a laundress in camp.[36] He described this refugee in racialized terms, indicating that she was "neat and clean" and "smart as a whip . . . only has no education."[37] The cook toiled tirelessly, essentially laboring her way to freedom. The officer also expressed interest in her continuing to serve him after the war, arguing to his wife that she is "worth a dozen of white girls to have in the house."[38] Troops needed black women to keep camps functioning and relied on them for fundamental needs.

Like Corden, some Union soldiers were so impressed with the work of the black women in their camps that they sought to send them back home. During the evacuation of Atlanta in November 1864, Brigadier General Alpheus S. Williams wrote that the "scramble at the depot" to flee the city left "thousands of Negroes . . . striving to get transportation." Because of the service they had provided him and his men, Williams recommended that two women be sent to Detroit to become house servants. "They are the best and steadiest Negroes I have ever seen," he insisted. "One of the women washed and sewed for our mess and cooked part of the time. She cooks, sews, and washes splendidly, and withal is a steady home body and a most excellent character."[39] Phibby, as this particular woman was called, determined to prove her value during the war and to survive it by serving Union men. Williams spoke of her often and described her as "the leading spirit" of the black workers in camp.[40] Although she worked diligently for the general, she also referred to him as "Pap." He perceived this as "a respectful and affectionate expression of her gratitude and love."[41] Thus Phibby ingratiated herself to Williams by using strategies similar to those learned in the plantation household: constant labor and personal deference.[42]

These strategies of service and submission are present in accounts of close relationships between Union men and black women. One account in particular reveals the bonds that Union men formed with the women who helped them through the war and the new power structures those women navigated in freedom. When Oscar Jackson became severely injured while serving as a captain in the 63rd Ohio, Jane, a former slave, tended to his wounds and nursed him to health. Throughout the winter of 1862, Jane "faithfully and devotedly" stayed by Jackson's side in the hospital until he recovered enough to travel back home to his wife in Ohio. Because of the kindness the freedwoman bestowed upon him, the recuperated officer asked his colonel, J. W. Sprague, to make a space for her in his own household. Jane made her way to Huron in December and the colonel's wife was "much pleased with her" service.[43] As a result of her actions and the relationship she formed with the officer, Jane escaped to the North and left her life of slavery behind. In most instances like Jane's, however, black women were not incorporated into the household or cared for as equals. Northern families, like the Spragues, expected servitude in exchange for sanctuary.

Although Mrs. Sprague seemingly welcomed the freedwoman into her home as a new domestic worker, some formerly enslaved women experienced a more difficult transition in the North due to racial attitudes. They used their skills to escape slavery only to encounter suspicion and denigration within a new subjugation. When Captain Edward S. Redington of the 28th Wisconsin wrote to his wife, Mary, in January of 1863, he provided some reassurances as well as instructions on how to manage the black woman he sent home as a family servant. "You say you do not know whether you will like your new girl or not," he remarked. "Colored people are not any of them as quick to get around as others but they are faithful and will accomplish as much as any if they are treated kindly."[44] He went further, encouraging his wife to allow the children to teach the new member of their household to read, which she would not have had the opportunity to learn as a bondwoman. This directive smacked more of paternalism than genuine care, however, as he added that his wife "must not make an equal of [blacks]; they will not bear it, not as well as an Irishman. We treat them fairly but keep them at arms length."[45] By teaching the servant to read, he posited, "you will have accomplished much in making her faithful and useful to you."[46] Many former slaves endured similar treatment as they navigated a new racial landscape in the North but with familiar prejudices.[47]

In a similar way that black women had diverse experiences in slavery, depending on region, form of labor, the treatment of their masters and mistresses, and their own communities and networks, they also encountered a range of challenges and conditions on the path to freedom. The hope of liberation and an existence in the free northern states caused thousands of women to flee plantations and make the harrowing journey to Union camps, where they did not know if soldiers would protect them, abuse them, or (prior to July 1862) turn them away. Perhaps the communication networks established in slavery between plantations provided some limited information about what they would encounter, but still they had no way to predict their treatment in the camps or what would happen to them after the war.[48] Adapting to this unfamiliar and often dangerous environment and controlling their situation within the given parameters, black women often turned to the familiar to establish relationships with soldiers and to demonstrate their value during the war and to seek a place in society after. In cooking for, washing for, and nursing soldiers, many refugee women used the skills they developed to survive slavery and secured their positions in Union camps and, then, in Union households.

Nurse Lucy Higgs Nichols not only secured her position in the 23rd Indiana; she became their compatriot. She nursed wounded soldiers, mended and washed clothes, foraged, and brought water during battle. Her dedication and contributions created a sense of indebtedness and familial fondness from the soldiers, who later petitioned for her pension and admittance into the GAR. After serving the regiment from June of 1862 to July 1865, "Aunt Lucy," like many other former slaves, served officers' families. The officers' wives and children, too, became close to the 23rd's favorite, inviting her to a wedding as a guest and doting on her when she fell ill with smallpox. In many ways, Nichols's biography is similar to those of other women who escaped slavery, braved the dangerous and often long trek to Union lines (Lucy traveled thirty miles), worked for the Union war effort, and served northern families after the war.[49]

The 23rd Indiana's nurse, however, also defied the standard narrative for refugee women in the Civil War. Her biography is unique not only for the care she was afforded by former troops and their families after the war or for the pension she earned from the US government. Nichols's story is distinctive because she is remembered and memorialized. Due to recent efforts of local historians in partnership with the Carnegie Center for Art and History in New Albany, where she settled after the war, "Aunt Lucy's" heroism has been honored with a permanent exhibition at the center. Indiana erected a historical marker for her in New Albany, and authors have penned a play and a novel about her life.[50] These dramatizations infuse a degree of romanticism into the narrative, but they also indicate a continued care and sentimental attachment many still have for "Aunt Lucy." The stories of other women who survived or perished during the Civil War as "contraband," aiding the Union efforts in meaningful and resourceful ways, have largely been lost in the historical narrative. These women warriors fought in their own ways not only for the Union and the men they served but for themselves, their families, and their communities, relying on the tools they used to survive slavery to forge a way to freedom.

Notes

1. There is only one known photograph of Lucy Higgs Nichols and a single source—her pension application—written in her name. The Carnegie Center for Art and History has collected the most relevant sources regarding Lucy Higgs Nichols, and they are on permanent exhibition. *Remembered: The Life of Lucy Higgs Nichols*, Carnegie Center for Art and History, New Albany, IN.

2. "Noted Woman Warrior from Ohio Receives Her Reward," *New York Times*, December 14, 1898; "Daughter of the Regiment," *Daily Gazette* (Janesville, WI), March 14, 1889; "Why Aunt Lucy Got a Pension," *Sunday Post* (Denver), December 18, 1898.

3. In *Embattled Freedom: Journeys through the Civil War's Slave Refugee Camps* (Chapel Hill: University of North Carolina Press, 2018), Amy Murrell Taylor has undertaken an "act of recovery" (7) of the history of contraband camps, which have largely been overlooked in Civil War histories and memorialization.

4. In her focused study of contraband camps, Chandra Manning explains the complications when considering agency and explores the "tension between structure and agency in the wartime destruction of slavery in the United States." "There is no question," she argues, "that the originating impulse toward emancipation came from the courage, determination, and resilience of slaves who wanted freedom, but no amount of human courage, determination, or resilience is invincible" See Manning, *Troubled Refuge: Struggling for Freedom in the Civil War* (New York: Vintage Books, 2017), 10. This essay recognizes the same tension and places the agency of former bondwomen within the larger context of the cultural, environmental, and political forces of the period.

5. The Union used the dehumanizing term "contraband" to describe enslaved peoples who sought refuge from troops, as they were still considered property by Confederates. Throughout this essay, the terms "contraband," refugee, enslaved, and formerly enslaved (post–Emancipation Proclamation) are used to describe this group of women who occupied the nebulous space between slavery and freedom during the conflict over slavery. "Contraband" is the historical term that highlights the difficulties refugees confronted during the war. The Union officially called the formerly enslaved "contraband" before the Emancipation Proclamation, but soldiers in the field continued to use the term in their diaries and correspondence after it went into effect. For more on the com-

plexity of this terminology, see Kate Masur, "'A Rare Phenomenon of Philological Vegetation': The Word 'Contraband' and the Meanings of Emancipation in the United States," *Journal of American History* 93, no. 4 (2007): 1050–1084.

6. Thavolia Glymph, "'Invisible Disabilities': Black Women in War and in Freedom," *Proceedings of the American Philosophical Society* 160, no. 3 (2016): 237–246.

7. Ibid., 241.

8. Stephanie M. H. Camp, *Closer to Freedom: Enslaved Women and Everyday Resistance in the Plantation South* (Chapel Hill: University of North Carolina Press, 2004), 138.

9. For more (and sometimes competing) narratives of black women's lives during slavery, see Elizabeth Fox-Genovese, *Within the Plantation Household: Black and White Women of the Old South* (Chapel Hill: University of North Carolina Press, 1988); Thavolia Glymph, *Out of the House of Bondage: The Transformation of the Plantation Household* (New York: Cambridge University Press, 2008); and Camp, *Closer to Freedom*.

10. See *The War of the Rebellion: Official Records of the Union and Confederate Armies*, 127 vols. (Washington, DC: Government Printing Office, 1881–1901), ser. 2, vol. 1, 778, 809; ser. 1, vol. 17, pt. 2, 15–16 (hereafter cited as *OR*); see John F. Marszalek, *Commander of All Lincoln's Armies: A Life of General Henry W. Halleck* (Cambridge, MA: Belknap Press of Harvard University Press, 2004), 104, for army policies that prohibited slaves from entering Union lines during the early part of the conflict. See Ulysses S. Grant, *The Papers of Ulysses S. Grant*, ed. John Y. Simon et al., 31 vols. (Carbondale: Southern Illinois University Press, 1967–2009), 5:273–274, 264, 311; *OR*, ser. 1, vol. 15, 162, for the importance of the Second Confiscation Act in pushing commanders to adopt more emancipationist policies.

11. Alfred H. Trego Diary, November 29, 1864, Chicago History Museum, Chicago.

12. Charles Dana Miller, *The Struggle for the Life of the Republic: A Civil War Narrative by Brevet Major Charles Dana Miller, 76th Ohio Volunteer Infantry*, ed. Stewart Bennett and Barbara Tillery (Kent, OH: Kent State University Press, 2004), 91. There are many examples of Union troops noting the numbers of slaves leaving plantations, marching toward freedom, and the lack of preparations the Union had made to support them. "These slaves desert their mistresses and come into the Union camps at night by hundreds," S. H. M. Byers remarked in December of 1862, "bearing their bundles on their heads and their pickaninnies under their arms." S. H. M. Byers, *With Fire and Sword* (New York: Neale, 1911), 45.

13. *OR*, ser. 1, vol. 24, pt. 3, 149–150.

14. James A. Garfield, *The Wild Life of the Army: Civil War Letters of James A. Garfield*, ed. Frederick D. Williams (East Lansing: Michigan State University Press, 1964), 257.

15. Jim Downs, *Sick from Freedom: African-American Illness and Suffering during the Civil War and Reconstruction* (New York: Oxford University Press, 2004), 4.

16. Stephanie M. H. Camp describes conditions in Union camps through the lens of a northern woman but does not describe the abuses some experienced. Camp, *Closer to Freedom*, 126.

17. Letter from William M. Ferry to his aunt, February 29, 1864, Ferry Family Papers, Bentley Historical Library, University of Michigan, Ann Arbor, Michigan (hereafter BHL).

18. Glymph provides an astute observation on the slave perspective when entering Union camps. "We can understand this best, perhaps," she argues, "by beginning with the recognition that enslaved people expected that they would have to fight for their freedom and understood that the brutality that had accompanied the making of slavery would also accompany its undoing. They

Charity Rakestraw and Kristopher A. Teters

knew many would suffer and die before any of them experienced freedom and that their families, despite their best efforts, would again be torn apart. As they gathered up their families to flee the plantations or fled alone to Union lines, they knew they were in 'for harder times' one Union officer wrote." See Glymph, "Invisible Disabilities," 239.

19. These instances were noted by officers who complained about the behavior of soldiers in their units. George C. Burmeister, for instance, described an incident where soldiers "threw a pound of powder" into the chimney of a slave's home, destroying the dwelling and killing the elderly woman inside. See unaddressed letter from George C. Burmeister to his wife, December 25, 1862, George C. Burmeister Diary, Civil War Miscellaneous Collection, US Army Military History Institute, Carlisle, Pennsylvania (hereafter CWMC). On another occasion, he witnessed troops plundering "negro shanties," stealing all of the money they could find, including $250 from an old man who had saved it over the course of his life, provisions from one woman, and gold earrings from another. See George C. Burmeister Diary, March 11, 1864, CWMC.

20. Letter from William M. Ferry to his aunt, February 29, 1864, Ferry Family Papers, BHL.

21. One such example was sent by Lieutenant A. F. Puffer to the editor of the New Orleans *Daily Picayune*, in which he reported that a young female slave was solicited for sex by a Union officer in violation of military codes. The slave determined to return to her mistress instead of remaining in the Union camp. See *OR*, ser. 1, vol. 15, 525. In 1862, Major General O. M. Mitchel investigated the rape of a young woman by soldiers that occurred in front of her mistress. See *OR*, ser. 1, vol. 10, pt. 2, 290–292.

22. Camp, *Closer to Freedom*,126–127.

23. After the Second Confiscation Act and the Emancipation Proclamation, many Union officers instituted more formal ways to use black women's labor in the army. Top-level Union commanders, like Generals Ulysses S. Grant, Benjamin F. Butler, and Nathaniel P. Banks, started labor programs that employed former slaves on plantations. Black women labored on plantations across the Mississippi valley and Louisiana and were compensated for their labor and provided with food and the basic necessities; see *OR*, ser. 1, vol. 15, 592–595, 610, 666–667; ser. 1, vol. 34, pt. 2, 227–231; Grant, *Papers of Ulysses S. Grant*, 6: 315–317, 329–330; Ulysses S. Grant, *Personal Memoirs of U. S. Grant*, 2 vols. (New York: C. L. Webster, 1885), 1: 424–426; Ira Berlin et al., *Freedom: A Documentary History of Emancipation, 1861–1867*, ser. 1, vol. 3, *The Wartime Genesis of Free Labor: The Lower South* (Cambridge: Cambridge University Press, 1990), 630–641, 699–702. Other Union officers, like Brigadier General Absalom Baird and Colonel William Utley, were known for their sympathy toward all runaway slaves; see James A. Connolly, *Three Years in the Army of the Cumberland: The Letters and Diary of Major James A. Connolly*, ed. Paul M. Angle (Bloomington: Indiana University Press, 1959), 339–340, 362–363; William M. Fliss, "Wisconsin's 'Abolition Regiment': The Twenty-Second Volunteer Infantry in Kentucky, 1862–1863," *Wisconsin Magazine of History* 86 (Winter 2002–2003): 3, 8, 9–12.

24. Hans Christian Heg, *The Civil War Letters of Colonel Hans Christian Heg*, ed. Theodore Christian Blegen (Northfield, MN: Norwegian-American Historical Association, 1936), 106.

25. Ibid., 106.

26. H. Z. Veit, *Food in the Civil War Era: The South* (East Lansing, MI: Michigan State University Press, 2015), 13.

27. Sergio A. Lussana, *My Brother Slaves: Friendship, Masculinity, and Resistance in the Antebellum South* (Lexington: University Press of Kentucky, 2016), 72–75.

28. Camp, *Closer to Freedom*, 126.

29. Miller, *Struggle for the Life of the Republic*, 47.

30. Letter from George W. Landrum to Amanda, June 16, 1863, George W. Landrum Letters, Ohio Historical Society, Columbus, OH.

31. Ibid.

32. William G. Thompson, *The Civil War Letters of Major William G. Thompson of the 20th Iowa Infantry Regiment*, ed. Edwin C. Bearss (Fayetteville, AR: Washington County Historical Society, 1966), 26–27.

33. Ibid.

34. Letter from William Parker Johnson to Julia, September 9, 1862, in *Ohio's War: The Civil War in Documents*, ed. Christine Dee (Athens: Ohio University Press, 2006), 101–102.

35. James Madison Bowler and Elizabeth Caleff Bowler, *Go If You Think It Your Duty: A Minnesota Couple's Civil War Letters*, ed. Andrea R. Foroughi (St. Paul: Minnesota Historical Society Press, 2008), 157; Charles Wright Wills, *Army Life of an Illinois Soldier Including a Day-by-Day Record of Sherman's March to the Sea: Letters and Diary of Charles W. Wills*, ed. Mary E. Kellogg (Washington, DC: Globe, 1906), 142.

36. Letter from John Corden to his wife, November 2, 1862, John Corden Papers, BHL.

37. Ibid.

38. Ibid.

39. Alpheus S. Williams, *From the Cannon's Mouth: The Civil War Letters of General Alpheus S. Williams*, ed. Milo M. Quaife (Lincoln: University of Nebraska Press, 1995), 351.

40. Ibid., 379.

41. Ibid.

42. On the plantation household, see Camp, *Closer to Freedom*; Fox-Genovese, *Within the Plantation Household*; Glymph, *Out of the House of Bondage*.

43. Oscar L. Jackson, *The Colonel's Diary; Journals Kept before and during the Civil War by the Late Colonel Oscar L. Jackson . . . Sometime Commander of the 63rd Regiment O.V.I.*, ed. David Prentice Jackson (privately published, 1922), 244–245.

44. Letter from Edward S. Redington to his wife, January 23, 1863, Edward S. Redington Papers, Wisconsin Historical Society, Madison, WI (hereafter WHS).

45. Ibid.

46. Ibid. For more on paternalism, see Eugene Genovese, *Roll, Jordan, Roll: The World the Slaves Made* (New York: Pantheon Books, 1974).

47. For additional examples of officers viewing the servants they sent home or wanted to as workers or laborers that were certainly not their equals, see Orville T. Chamberlain to his father, April 21, 1865, Joseph W. and Orville T. Chamberlain Papers, Indiana Historical Society, Indianapolis; Garfield, *The Wild Life of the Army*, 102, 243, 267; Albert J. Rockwell to Eva Rockwell, November 15, 1862, Rockwell Letters, WHS.

48. In her important work on black women's activities in the slave South, Camp describes the underground network that existed before the war, when enslaved peoples exchanged goods and information underground. Although the outbreak of war likely disrupted these networks, bondwomen continued to share information during the war with each other and often extended that knowledge to Union troops. Camp, *Closer to Freedom*, 109.

49. "Why Aunt Lucy Got a Pension," *Sunday Post* (Denver), December 18, 1898.

Charity Rakestraw and Kristopher A. Teters

50. Carnegie Center for Art and History, "Remembered: The Life of Lucy Higgs Nichols, Men and Women of the Underground Railroad"; Kathryn Grant, *Honorable: Purpose in Repose* (Mustang, OK: Tate, 2013); National Underground Railroad Freedom Center, "Lucy Higgs Nichols: If Not for Women," 2014; Kathryn Grant, *Honorable: Purpose in Repose* (Mustang, OK: Tate, 2013); Dani Pfaff, "Lucy Higgs Nichols Indiana State Historical Marker," March 25, 2011, http://www.in.gov/history /files/PRLucyHNichols_marker.pdf.

A THERMIDOREAN REACTION
Reconstruction and Counterrevolution

To expect the American people to have sustained the commitment necessary for a
radical transformation of the South is asking them to transcend their own humanity.
—George C. Rable, *But There Was No Peace,* 191

I n 1984, George Rable published *But There Was No Peace: The Role of Violence in the Politics of Reconstruction,* based on his doctoral dissertation.
Rable reacted against historians' penchant for treating Reconstruction "as a
morality play" in which Civil War–era Americans failed to remedy the nation's
besetting sins of chattel slavery and racial discrimination.[1] Conversely, Rable
argued that Reconstruction's agenda was profoundly radical in its potential,
and it prompted white southerners to resort to violent counterrevolution.

Rable's first monograph is his only one to date that focuses solely on Reconstruction. But it was prophetic in predicting trends in the field for the next
thirty-five years, as the essays in this section affirm. Daniel J. Burge's essay on
the fictional character Petroleum Vesuvius Nasby suggests that Republicans
hoped for a biracial society. White southerners recognized and reacted against
these transformative intentions. T. Robert Hart argues that former Confederates drew parallels between Reconstruction and revolutionary France, fearing
that "radical egalitarianism" would result in "monstrosities" similar to when
enslaved people of San Domingue "rose against the white population . . . as the
fiends of hell . . . were let loose on the earth."

It was this terror—this potential upending of white supremacy—that
prompted white southerners' turn to vigilante justice, a preemption that, Rable
attests, fits uncomfortably with the American political tradition.[2] Kevin L.
Hughes's examination of the 1876 Hamburg, South Carolina, massacre illustrates not only how white "Red Shirts" usurped the Republican-controlled justice system but also how white South Carolinians memorialized the saving of

their "Anglo-Saxon civilization." As T. Michael Parrish's essay on Texas Baptists makes clear, this violently enforced Anglo-Saxon civilization was divinely linked with the Manifest Destiny of the United States. The violence may have had its roots deep in American society, but it found its sanctity in American churches.

Republicans, including formerly enslaved southern blacks, looked to the federal government to enforce Reconstruction's transformations. Yet such a system was inherently imperfect. Although John F. Marszalek's comparative analysis of the memoirs of William T. Sherman and Ulysses S. Grant moves away from the Reconstruction South, he nevertheless reminds us that Grant and Sherman were men whose ambitions shaped their responses to the war and its aftermath. Other officers and politicians made similar individual calculations. By doing so, they altered the trajectory of Reconstruction.

These historians reach the somber conclusion that ordinary people faced a daunting task in the aftermath of a brutal civil war. As Rable noted, "a silent majority" of white southerners, uncomfortable with the reactionary violence, willingly chose to allow "more extreme elements [to] speak" for them.[3] In the end, indifference, pettiness, virulent racism, and violence undercut the potential to achieve the sublime.

Notes

1. George C. Rable, *But There Was No Peace: The Role of Violence in the Politics of Reconstruction* (Athens: University of Georgia Press, 1984), xvii.

2. Ibid., 96–98.

3. Ibid., 30.

Christian Paternalism and Racial Violence

White and Black Baptists in Texas during the Civil War Era

T. MICHAEL PARRISH

During the Civil War, indeed throughout the nineteenth century, most Protestant Americans believed strongly that the best soldier was the "Christian soldier." Morally upright and patriotic, Christian officers and enlisted volunteers offered effective leadership and served as sterling role models for their comrades. Devoted to their families and communities, Christian soldiers promised solemnly that they would fight and—if necessary—die, assured of salvation and glory in heaven, where all loved ones would be reunited in eternal bliss. Most importantly, Christian soldiers personified America as a chosen nation of Manifest Destiny, blessed by a providential Christian God to achieve global ascendency and millennial perfection. Union and Confederate soldiers and civilians thereby claimed holy public convictions and purposes—now termed "civil religion"—for themselves, their countries, and their civil war.[1]

In their quest for national independence, Confederates placed especially strong emphasis on their soldiers as supreme personifications of selfless white Christian males—pious, responsible, paternalistic servant-leaders and protectors of American democracy's greatest blessings: security, prosperity, social stability (family and community), and the rule of law. Among evangelical Protestants, Southern Baptists in particular gloried in their adherence to religious liberty, insisting that democracy's civil liberties derived their deepest meanings from a decidedly democratic devotion to religious liberty, congregational authority, and the Baptist "priesthood" of individual believers. In fact, Baptists typically took credit for the triumph of American democracy itself as the direct result of religious liberty. Civil liberties—free speech; freedom of the press, assembly, and voting; property rights; and others listed in the Bill of Rights—in turn preserved religious liberty (likewise enshrined in the Bill of Rights). Thus the two most precious liberties—civil and religious—were not only intertwined, reinforcing and proving one another, but they were also virtually interchangeable in the minds of Baptists. One form of liberty seemed impossible without the other. Even as the most zealous advocates for the separation of church and state, Southern Baptists, like most other Americans, had few serious qualms about mixing religion with politics (a dynamic distinct from an "established" religion supported by government), particularly when it came to the crucial politics of slavery. Clearly, a decidedly conservative brand of politics and government policies prevailed. Yet genuine civil and religious liberties contributed to a high degree of equality among white males, even in the slaveholding South, where an elite upper class, along with a strong upper middle class and a rising middle class, flourished in a booming cotton-rich economy and a rapidly modernizing commercial environment that compared favorably with the North.[2]

As the direct result of the volatile politics of slavery, Texas Baptists felt strongly compelled to secede from the Union and fight for Confederate independence. Throughout the Civil War, Baptist Christian soldiers—epitomizing virtuous manhood, male authority and responsibility, and southern honor— together with their families on the home front, derived comfort and strength from their faith, which in turn bolstered their political determination to continue struggling, suffering, and sacrificing on the battlefield and on the home front. Even with defeat looming and finally becoming reality, Baptists counted heavily among Confederates who showed defiance, acting as "diehard Rebels," refusing to accept Union authority, and resisting all perceived threats to their civil and religious liberties during Reconstruction.[3]

At the center of Texas Baptist life, Baylor University at Independence in Washington County was the most important institution of higher learning in antebellum Texas. With few other private schools available and no state schools created until well after the Civil War and Reconstruction, the people of Texas relied on Baylor to educate young men to become ministers, lawyers, judges, physicians, planters, and businessmen and young women to become schoolteachers, plantation mistresses, business partners, wives, and mothers. Situated in the heart of the Brazos River valley—one of the Deep South's richest cotton- and sugar-growing regions, running northwest from the Gulf coast nearly 250 miles to Waco in McLennan County—by 1860 Washington County ranked as one of the most populous, fastest-growing, and wealthiest counties in Texas and the entire South. Counties along the Brazos River saw slave populations double or even triple during the 1850s as a highly profitable slave trade and slave markets flourished from Galveston and Houston all the way to Waco. In 1860 Washington County's eight thousand slaves outnumbered whites, and slaves provided the lion's share of all labor, including labor for the construction of several substantial buildings on the Baylor campus at Independence.[4]

Nearly all of Baylor's faculty members, trustees, and benefactors came from the South, especially the Deep South, and nearly all were slaveholders. Naturally, they wielded enormous influence in the Texas Baptist Convention and in the Southern Baptist Convention. Easily mixing politics with religion along with other prominent Texas evangelical leaders, Baptists were among the most powerful politicians and public officials in Texas. Many if not most families who sent their sons and daughters to Baylor were slaveholders. Like other southern white evangelicals, Texas Baptists developed a keen counterattack against abolitionist propaganda, insisting (correctly) that the Bible justified slavery; that masters, true to paternalistic convictions, should Christianize their slaves; and that blacks actually benefited from slavery because of their inherent and permanent racial inferiority and latent savagery. "They have not the capacity to understand or appreciate the rights, duties and responsibilities of a free citizen," asserted George Washington Baines, who served as pastor of Independence Baptist Church, editor of the *Texas Baptist* newspaper, and president of Baylor during the Civil War. To believe otherwise, Baines contended, "is to declare what is positively absurd." Southern Baptists generally remained steadfast in their paternalistic proslavery convictions throughout the war and even long afterward, viewing virtually all African Americans as poorly suited for freedom and in need of constant supervision and guidance.[5]

Fears about slavery's security clearly compelled Texas Baptists along with the great majority of Texans to push for secession from the Union. With whites—slaveholders and nonslaveholders alike—still reeling from a massive slave insurrection panic, the so-called Texas Troubles during the summer of 1860, Judge Royal T. Wheeler, chief justice of the Texas Supreme Court and former Baylor law professor, reflected raw public opinion by responding to President-elect Abraham Lincoln's November victory in a series of emotional newspaper editorials. Lumping Lincoln and his Republican Party with radical abolitionists, in typically southern fashion, Wheeler accused them of "socialism, religious fanaticism, atheism, higher-law-ism, and all the isms concentrated into the one idea, the arch demon … abolitionism." He predicted "servile insurrection"—a nightmarish peril among southerners for generations—and ultimately the "political and social equality of the African race," unless the South seceded from the Union. Evoking divine favor, Wheeler equated the popular clamor for secession with "the voice of God" speaking to Moses from the burning bush.[6]

Texas Baptists were strongly represented in the state secession convention in early 1861. Dr. Jerome B. Robertson, a physician in Independence, benefactor of Baylor University, and future Confederate commander of Hood's Texas Brigade, and James E. Shepard, a future Confederate officer, judge, and Baylor law professor, were powerful delegates from Washington County. William P. Rogers, a former Baylor law professor, close friend of Sam Houston, and beloved cousin of Houston's wife, attained a particularly high profile as a delegate from Harris County, passionately calling for immediate secession and, if necessary, civil war. His friend Judge Royal T. Wheeler also participated as an unofficial advisor. Like the rest of the Deep South, disunion fever in Texas tended to be most vigorous in wealthy slaveholding plantation counties, particularly those with heavy concentrations of Baptists and other evangelical Protestants. That formula fit Independence and Washington County perfectly, where about 95 percent of voters cast their ballots for secession. The entire Brazos River valley followed suit, as did the Texas convention, which formally removed Texas from the Union.[7]

But not all Texas Baptists welcomed disunion and war. Although he owned a dozen slaves, Governor Sam Houston—the state's most famous Baptist and one of the South's most prominent Unionists—was removed from office by the secession convention after he refused to support the Confederacy. Houston knew Baylor and its leaders extremely well because for several years he and his family had a home in Independence. Before and even after his removal as governor, Houston delivered a series of public speeches explaining his opposition to secession and predicting disaster for the southern war effort. Standing before a hostile crowd in Brenham, the county seat of Washington County, Houston chastised Texans for joining the Deep South by seceding in reaction to Abraham Lincoln's election. He deliberately turned Judge Wheeler's religious rhetoric and imagery against him. "The Vox Populi is not always the voice of God," Houston declared, "for when demagogues and selfish political leaders succeed in arousing public prejudice . . . then on every hand can be heard the popular cry of 'Crucify him, crucify him.' The Vox Populi then becomes the voice of the devil." Expecting the worst from the coming conflict, Houston wailed, "The soil of our beloved South will drink deep the precious blood of our sons and brethren." Again, at Galveston, he employed biblical language, referring to the coming civil war as a "riotous adventure" that would cost "countless millions of treasure, and hundreds of thousands of precious lives." Houston foresaw "fire and rivers of blood."[8]

Even after Lincoln's election in late 1860, Baylor president Rev. Rufus C. Burleson agreed with his friend Sam Houston, whom he had baptized several years earlier, about the necessity to preserve the Union. But after Lincoln's call for volunteers to put down the rebellion in the wake of the Confederate seizure of Fort Sumter in April 1861, Burleson and most other Unionists in the Deep South switched allegiance to the new southern nation. The fiery Burleson had recently left Baylor for another Baptist school, Waco University, where he became president and brought with him the Baylor Male Department's faculty and its entire senior class of male students. Now a passionate Confederate, he urged all young men to volunteer for the army, and he joined them in the field, serving as chaplain of the 15th Texas Infantry. The regiment was led by Burleson's close friend Colonel Joseph W. Speight, a leading Baptist and founder of Waco University.[9]

In the summer of 1862, in a remarkable public letter featured on the front page of the most influential Texas newspaper (the Houston *Tri-Weekly Telegraph*, published by Burleson's friend E. H. Cushing, a prominent Presbyterian), Rev. Burleson vowed that he and his fellow Baptists would "fight on till the last Gothic invader is driven from our shores. . . . We must be free or perish. . . . Indeed it would be far cheaper to die than to live and work for Yankee tyrants." Echoing and then rejecting Sam Houston's specific warnings, Burleson proclaimed, "Our independence . . . may cost us rivers of blood and millions of treasure; if so . . . let it come. Liberty to a nation, like honor to a man, or virtue to a woman, is the gem of existence." Firmly linking Baptist religious liberty and civil liberty, he exhorted his readers to "arise as one man and swear by the Holy and Eternal One that the bones of 75,000 Texians shall whiten our prairies before Abolition despotism shall reign over this lovely land." A decisive majority of Texas Baptists agreed with Burleson, and like James W. Barnes, a Baylor trustee who became a brigadier general of Texas state troops, they emphasized the defense of their liberties. "The unholy and unnatural war now waged by the United States against our liberty, and disputing our right of self-government, was wicked in its conception," Barnes declared on behalf of Texas Baptists. "Our trust is in God, and our motto [is] . . . 'Give us Liberty or give us death.' Our lion-hearted soldiers go to battle with justice in their cause and God in their hearts. . . . If need be, we will burn our cotton . . . shed the last drop of blood, but be subjugated, never! never! never!"[10]

Responding to calls for volunteers, Texas Baptists, in concert with evangelical Christians across the South, served in disproportionate numbers as Christian soldiers. Many came from Washington County, which contributed young men to at least a dozen Confederate units. More than 250 current and former Baylor students volunteered, along with about 40 more from Rufus Burleson's Waco University. Dozens of faculty members, trustees, and benefactors from both schools joined in the fight. Most were from slaveholding families, undercutting claims by some historians that lower- and lower-middle-class nonslaveholders bore the brunt of a so-called rich man's war and poor man's fight. In fact, middle- and upper-middle-class and elite soldiers, especially officers, tended to be the most ardent proslavery Confederate patriots.[11]

For the female teachers and students at Baylor and Waco University, the Civil War was an ordeal that tested their faith in God. "I could not keep back the tears," wrote Sarah Jane Scott, a young Baylor teacher. "I pray every day for those whose lives are precious to me may be Christians and thus ready for either life or death." Baylor student Cary McNelly Wroe recalled that she and her classmates raised money, sang patriotic songs, and waved Confederate flags as "our boys in gray came marching by." But she also admitted, "Our school days were shadowed by terrible struggles" because all students had family members and friends defending their country. "Oftentimes came the death message that another one was bereft of a dear kinsman who had made the supreme sacrifice."[12]

Religious faith and Confederate nationalism—often described in tandem as the essence of "our liberties"—gave remarkable strength to families and their soldiers. A continual flow of letters between the battlefield and home front expressed deep mutual affection and fervent prayers. God usually received great praise, regardless the fears or traumas. A faithful Baptist matron, Margaret Lea Houston, Sam Houston's wife, described the capture of her son Sam Houston Jr. at the Battle of Shiloh in April 1862 as "the great trial of my life." Months later when she finally learned about his release from a Union prison camp, she wrote to him, "I almost tremble when I think of . . . the suffering through which the Good Lord has brought me safe." Two years later she continued praising God, exulting, "Oh how can I ever thank my Heavenly Father for sparing my boy . . . while so many of his youthful [friends] have fallen."[13]

In camp and on the battlefield, military chaplains also provided spiritual and patriotic strength to soldiers, sustaining their faith and persuading nonbelievers to convert. Chaplains' preaching, together with minsters' published sermons and tracts, emphasized the holiness of the Confederate cause, the need for constant reliance on God's power for strength, and the conquest of death through salvation in Christ. The best chaplains modeled the paternalistic role of a Christian soldier: ministering to the sick, wounded, and dying, and sharing soldiers' hardships, even to the extent of going into battle with them. Michael Moses Vanderhurst, one of Rufus Burleson's recent theology students, showed extraordinary courage in his role as chaplain of the 6th Texas Cavalry. Recalling the Battle of Corinth, Mississippi, in October 1862, a soldier in the unit wrote, "As we were about to assault the strong works of the enemy . . . [Vanderhurst] came to our company with a gun, went into the charge with us, and in the awful slaughter that followed was shot dead." Recent scholarship shows decisively that religious faith greatly eased soldiers' combat trauma and that chaplains made the largest impact on maintaining morale in the Confederate armies. Henry Renfro, a former pastor of the Independence Baptist Church and Rufus Burleson's successor as chaplain of the 15th Texas Infantry, wrote to his wife about his huge responsibilities: "I look for nothing else but trouble and sorrow until this war is over. . . . Let me ask you to pray for me that I may be preserved in the day of battle and shielded from harm."[14]

No ideal sustained a Christian soldier, his family, and his community more strongly than the assurance that his sacrificial death would result in eternal life and heroic martyrdom. Although the exact number of casualties among Baylor and Waco University students, alumni, and faculty remains uncertain, the tragedy of death proved inevitable and relentless. Some families reacted in grief and anger. When Absalom Renfro heard of his younger son Summerfield's death by disease in June 1863, he wrote, "Oh how I loved him, I loved him, I loved him. He died in defense of Southern Rights . . . in an unholy war brought on by Northern fanatics." Yet most family members and friends derived strength and comfort from their convictions of faith and salvation. In May 1864 young Hosea Garrett, nephew and namesake of Hosea Garrett, a Baylor founder and trustee, described his dear friend Private John Gary's death. "He wished me to tell his uncle John Walker that he died an honorable death," wrote Garrett. "He was shot near me while the battle was raging hottest. He is gone, I trust, to heaven. He was a member of the Baptist Church. He made one of the best soldiers. Let his uncle know this."[15]

According to Steven Woodworth (a leading expert on the religious lives of Civil War soldiers) the Christian soldier who proclaimed his faith as he approached the moment of death impressed everyone—especially other soldiers—

more deeply than any other spiritual act. A Baylor Law Department graduate and young attorney from Brenham, Private Virginius E. Pettey of the 5th Texas Infantry, Hood's Texas Brigade, was killed at Second Manassas, Virginia, in August 1862. A few months earlier he had written to his sister Mattie, "I like to feel myself a soldier in the field, a ready martyr any day upon the altar of my country's freedom." When news of his death reached home, his brother Tom comforted Mattie in a letter: "I know that [Virginius] died bravely, willingly and like a Christian, believing in God.... I feel certain that he is today in Heaven with our father and mother ... and all the dead of our family." Similarly, Pettey's fellow lawyers of the Washington County Bar paid tribute to him in a solemn courtroom ceremony. A resolution stated, "In the death of Mr. Pettey [we] have lost ... a soldier who prized his liberties more than the life he gave in defense of them. He died ... a martyr in defense of his country's liberties." Pettey's dying words resonated strongly: "Tell my sister that I have done my duty to my Country, and am at peace with my God." Overcome with emotion, the court's presiding judge, R. E. B. Baylor, whose namesake Baylor University he helped establish, referred to Pettey as "our young friend ... the gallant soldier and pious Christian." Judge Baylor concluded that Pettey was "an example of all that is worthy and brave in the Christian soldier." An expression of supreme faith, his willing sacrifice reinforced spiritual and patriotic strength among his family, friends, and fellow Confederates.[16]

The most well-known Baylor Confederate killed during the war was Colonel William P. Rogers, who fell while leading the 2nd Texas Infantry and other regiments at Corinth, Mississippi, in October 1862. A successful attorney and professor in the Baylor Law Department during the 1850s, Rogers was Margaret Lea Houston's favorite cousin and Governor Sam Houston's personal lawyer. Unlike Houston, however, Rogers vociferously supported secession. In frequent wartime letters to his wife, Martha, he repeatedly expressed love for his family members, asked for their prayers, and reassured them that he felt strength and protection from a "kind and merciful providence." In paternalistic fashion, Rogers also asked his wife to greet the family's slaves. A few weeks before the fatal battle, he wrote, "I still hope to be home with you by Christmas— Love and kisses for you and our children." When Martha Rogers learned of his death, she was crushed with agony. Writing later to a friend, she admitted, "All was black darkness.... Even the dearest consolation of religion did not, for a time, give comfort to our grief-stricken hearts.... But how kind and merciful is our Heavenly Father.... If I love, trust, and obey Him, these afflictions shall work out for me and mine." She also expressed gratitude that the family's finances were bolstered by the hiring out of several slaves.[17]

Late in the war, with the specter of defeat eroding public morale, Christian soldiers often took the lead in defiantly refusing to give up the struggle. In the depths of a cold Virginia winter in January 1865, the soldiers of Hood's Texas Brigade gathered to deliver patriotic speeches. On a motion by former Baylor student Private William Burges, a committee representing each regiment drafted a lengthy resolution that was soon published, distributed, and reprinted in newspapers across the South. The committee included Sergeant William M. Baines, who was the son of Rev. George W. Baines (recently Baylor's president) and whose brother had died of disease while serving in the brigade early in the war. Describing Union armies as "the Babel of modern times, in which is represented the African ... with his brother, the Yankee ... [and] the avaricious Hessian ... [from] the dungeons of Europe," the resolution bluntly accused the enemy of striving to "give pretended freedom to [four million] African negroes." These Baptist soldiers declared their "determination to maintain at all hazards, and to the last extremity, the rights and liberties which a merciful God has been pleased to bestow upon us." The resolution concluded, "Our final triumph is certain and inevitable, and our subjugation is an impossibility." Such defiance by religious diehard rebels carried over in countless ways after the Civil War, despite the Confederacy's decisive defeat and the abolition of slavery. Most white southerners expressed their passionate support for the Lost Cause through religious and patriotic commemorations. Their defiance fueled resistance to Union military occupation and the Republican Party's quest for freedmen's civil rights, inspiring Democrats to overthrow Reconstruction.[18]

While Confederate Christian soldiers fought a war for independence to preserve slavery, their slaves had long fought a war to gain freedom and genuine equality. Slaves and abolitionists (white and black) often described enslavement as a constant state of warfare. Responding to paternalistic efforts by their masters to convert them to Christianity, many slaves across the South had become believers, increasingly worshipping in and actually joining Baptist churches and other white churches at their masters' behest. But that was where paternalism's influence usually ended. Instead of absorbing white ministers' biblical appeals to "obey their masters," slaves gathered and listened secretly to their own preachers for inspiration, comparing themselves to the ancient Israelites in bondage and longing eagerly for a promised land of freedom and equality. In effect, they absorbed the Baptist devotion to religious and civil liberty and equality, gained spiritual and emotional strength and comfort from their faith, and when practical, showed resistance and defiance, including violence, in an effort to win a war against slavery and racism.

As Christian slaveholders, Texas Baptists believed or at least hoped that paternalistic ministry to their slaves was their responsibility and that paternalistic kindness helped justify slavery. Pastors of Independence Baptist Church, like other churches across Texas and the South, added scores of slaves to their membership rolls and often held worship services for them in order to reinforce a message of obedience. In addition, the Baptist State Convention of Texas and its regional associations of local churches repeatedly expressed regrets about limited efforts and mixed results in trying to minister to "the colored population." But in 1855 when a slave church with its own preacher in nearby Anderson, Texas, boldly applied for membership in the association of local churches—the Union Association, which included Independence Baptist Church—white leaders rejected the application "because the establishment of independent churches among our colored population would be inconsistent with their conditions as servants, and with the interests of their masters." Instead, the association stipulated "special [white] preaching for their benefit . . . and that they be encouraged to maintain a correct discipline . . . always to be aided in this work by the presence and counsel of some judicious white members." Thus did white Texas Baptists reject any hint of African American liberty, much less equality, while continuing to believe that paternalistic supervision was best for slaves.[19]

In fact, Texas Baptists categorized "the colored population," along with Germans, Tejanos, and Indians, as not so much *domestic* mission fields as *foreign* mission fields inside the boundaries of the state. Echoing the paternalism of white foreign missionaries by referring to slaves as "Africans," "Ethiopians," and "the sons of Ham," Texas Baptists at the state and local levels continually chastised one another for the spotty successes of evangelism toward slaves and the difficulties of controlling their worship services. "We should labor for the heathen abroad," argued Rev. Noah Hill, "but . . . let us not forget the heathen on our plantations—in our own families."[20]

Like other white evangelicals across the South, Baylor president Rufus Burleson insisted that if slaveholders had been more paternalistic in evangelizing their slaves, the Civil War never would have happened. As proof, he pointed to Albert C. Horton, a former Texas lieutenant governor, generous Baylor trustee, and owner of nearly 180 slaves. "Nothing impressed me more than his tender and deep interest for the comfort and religious welfare of his slaves," Burleson recalled. "He made a church house . . . and employed a preacher. . . . It was the most touching scene . . . to see Horton and his noble wife reading the Bible and praying for their servants." Burleson concluded, "If the South had been full of such Christian masters . . . God never would have allowed the abolition fanatics to set the slaves free." Clearly, like nearly all masters, Burleson felt little or no guilt and refused to see wrong in slavery itself. Slavery, he believed, was good and necessary for ignorant and uncivilized slaves. His only regret: slaveholders should have tried harder to bring their slaves closer to Christ, thereby proving slavery's alleged virtues.[21]

Rev. Rufus Burleson could not fathom what slaves knew quite well: no degree of Christian paternalism could ameliorate slavery. Yet, ironically, not only did Christian slaves gain their own brand of spiritual strength, enduring slavery by secretly believing, preaching, and praying for the day God and abolitionism would set them free, but they also rejected white paternalism outright by constantly resisting and sometimes refusing to obey their masters. Running away, a common method of resistance and defiance, increased dramatically during the 1850s. Slaves usually left for only a few days or sometimes more, visiting family at nearby plantations or hiding out in the woods. But some escaped permanently. Texas's version of the Underground Railroad to freedom led south to Mexico. Even the most paternalistic Baptist slaveholders lost slaves who ran away. The exceptional Albert Horton did manage to avoid a plague of runaways, yet Judge R. E. B. Baylor, another master who enjoyed a reputation for genuine kindness, counted at least six runaways among his thirty-three slaves in 1860. Likewise, several other Baylor faculty members, trustees, and benefactors lost scores of runaway slaves. During the Civil War a wholesale epidemic of runaways in Washington County compelled a committee of leading citizens to petition Governor Francis Lubbock to authorize a soldier named R. F. Harris to return home, because "his pack of negro dogs is of great service in keeping the negroes in subjection and without which the community would be subject to frequent disturbances and outbreaks among them." With Confederate conscription laws tying the governor's hands, Lubbock replied, "I am at a loss to know what I can do."[22]

Such extreme efforts by masters during the Civil War hardly surprised slaves. They knew that paternalism, even Christian paternalism, had limits, and that if necessary, masters would respond violently to slave resistance and defiance. Along with political leaders, newspaper editors, private citizens, and organizations throughout the Confederacy, in 1863 the Baptist State Convention of Texas veered into politics and public policy by condemning Lincoln's Emancipation Proclamation and hailing the draconian Confederate policy that condemned rebellious bondmen. Claiming that Lincoln and his armies meant to incite slave insurrections, the Texas Baptist Convention declared: "Found with our enemies, aiding them in their cruel war against us, [slaves] will be declared and treated as our enemies. . . . When they join the Federals, they absolve the master to protect and defend them, and they will be treated by the South as enemies of the Confederate Government."[23]

In lockstep with their fellow Confederates, Texas Baptists resorted to racial violence most mercilessly on the battlefield. Nothing infuriated Confederates more than the sight of black Union soldiers, most of whom were runaway slaves and many of whom were faithful Christians. While white Union and Confederate soldiers nearly always treated one another with respect and restraint, Christian masters—even the most genteel and paternalistic ones—often showed no mercy to black soldiers. Gideon J. Buck, the son of a Baptist preacher and a graduate of Union University, a Baptist institution in Tennessee, was a college administrator before and after the war, residing in Waco as a prominent lawyer and Baptist leader. In April 1864, as a member of the 30th Texas Cavalry, Buck fought in the notorious Battle of Poison Spring, Arkansas, where Confederates captured and deliberately killed 117 black soldiers. "We routed them completely," Buck wrote to his mother and sisters. "Somehow or other we couldn't manage to understand the Negroes when they wanted to surrender, and the ground was fairly strewn with the black rascals." As the war went on, many black soldiers retaliated in kind, showing no quarter to Confederates.[24]

Likewise, General Felix H. Robertson, son of General Jerome B. Robertson and a former Baylor student who had also attended West Point before the war, led Confederates to a victory and allowed a brutal massacre of black Union troops at Saltville, Virginia, in October 1864. Although Robertson did not order or participate personally in the atrocities, his soldiers—including the notorious guerrilla fighter Champ Ferguson—killed at least forty-five and wounded perhaps more than one hundred black soldiers. To Captain Edward Guerrant, a fellow officer, General Robertson admitted calmly that "he had killed nearly all the negroes." After the war Felix Robertson, Gideon Buck, and countless Southern Baptists and other veterans enjoyed status as Confederate heroes, their misdeeds—white Christian soldiers killing unarmed black Christian soldiers—ignored and forgotten.[25]

Along with his friends Robertson and Buck, Rufus Burleson (Waco University's president and again president of Baylor University after its Male Department moved to Waco in 1886 and combined with Waco University) contributed to the religiosity of the Lost Cause and participated energetically in Confederate veterans' reunions. At the same time, Burleson and most white Texans idealized the Old South and Confederacy and cultivated a romantic nostalgia for slavery as the best role for African Americans. Abolition proved a stupendous disaster because it turned "happy and contented slaves loose to become homeless vagabond[s]," making "the richest part of Texas little else than an African territory." The slaves, Burleson concluded, should have been "Christianized and prepared for citizenship, or to return home to Africa and colonize and Christianize 'the Dark Continent.' The African race thereby would have been a blessing to both continents." Emancipation seemed hard enough for whites to accept, but racial equality proved utterly unacceptable. Like the vast majority of southern white evangelicals, Burleson became active politically. He frequently declared, "I am a Democrat," and he actively defied and resisted Republicans, black and white alike, who sought equality for freedmen. Many Baptists and other white evangelicals either participated in the Ku Klux Klan–style violence against African Americans or simply ignored it and denied its existence. Regardless, Burleson despised Radical Republican governor Edmund J. Davis's "horrid reign of radical reconstruction" so much that he wrote more than two hundred letters to fellow Baptist leaders and other friends who opposed Davis's reelection in 1873.[26]

Like many other white Baptists, Burleson advocated not only paternalistic racial segregation but also outright removal of blacks from Texas. For several years after the Civil War he chaired the Committee on Colored Population for the Baptist State Convention and later the Baptist General Convention of Texas, which he also led as president. Burleson opined that "the race problem, or the destiny of the colored population, increases daily in importance" and that "the salvation of these people involves a responsibility of transcendent importance." He even secured a large gift on behalf of the Baptist Home Mission Society for founding a black Baptist college, Bishop College, at Marshall, Texas. "We are to educate the colored man. . . . But I will never ask him to sit down at my table or to come to see my daughter," Burleson admitted. Bishop College would "educate the colored man and get him wise enough and good enough to go back to Africa and civilize that country; for there won't be room enough for him in this country." Yet "Educators should always work together," Burleson affirmed. "For the glory of Texas and the uplifting of Texas and the colored man let us stand as a glorious unit."[27]

While Rufus Burleson longed for African Americans to "go back to Africa," black Baptists refused to cooperate during the postwar decades. Along with huge numbers of other southern freedmen and their families, in 1866 more than one hundred black members of Independence Baptist Church established their own congregation, Liberty Baptist Church. A clear effort to assert not only freedom from white control but also full equality, the rapid and prolific founding of black southern churches—most of them preferring to be Baptist—caused great anxiety for whites throughout the South. Black churches soon became the most important centers for African American social, educational, and political activities. First motivated to gain freedom and now compelled to gain equality, African American citizens responded religiously in prolific numbers to Baptist principles: liberty of conscience and equality before God; the autonomy of local congregations; the right of believers to read and interpret the Bible as the sole authority of God's truth; strength through fellowship, worship, and prayer; and faith in the transformative power of God's Holy Spirit.[28]

Ku Klux Klansmen and other white supremacists inflicted terror and sometimes murder against blacks, including black Christians, on behalf of the Democratic Party, and white Baptists largely remained silent. Washington County and the Brazos River valley was an especially violent region of Texas during Reconstruction. In one of many examples, in early 1867 an armed group of whites stormed into Liberty Baptist Church at Independence during a worship service. They deliberately pistol-whipped several congregants and expelled everyone from the church. Even in 1875, after Reconstruction had ended, whites assaulted blacks at a Republican meeting near Independence, pistol-whipping white and black leaders and threatening black women and children. When two black men, including David Graves, a Baptist preacher known as "an esteemed and outspoken Republican," brandished shotguns, the white attackers promptly shot and killed them. But such violence left black Baptists unfazed and, if anything, more determined to preach, pray, and press for equality. By the mid-1870s black Baptists formed their own statewide convention.[29]

The most defiant black Baptist leader in Texas during Reconstruction was Matthew Gaines. A huge inspiration to Liberty Baptist Church members and black congregations throughout the region, Matthew Gaines had been a rebellious slave in Louisiana and Texas. Taught to read and write by his Louisiana master's young son, Gaines secretly perfected his preaching skills by encouraging slaves to look toward a day of freedom. He attempted to escape from slavery at least twice, and after the war he quickly emerged as a popular minister and political activist. His congregation at Burton, about twenty miles from Independence in Washington County, became a center for black Republican political activity. During Radical Reconstruction, with African Americans voting in large numbers for the first time, the charismatic Gaines was easily elected to the Texas State Senate, serving as one of only two black senators. Outspoken and relentless, he lambasted efforts by Democrats to resist and undermine Reconstruction. He routinely shrugged off anonymous death threats from political enemies. He also demanded that white moderate and conservative Republicans should work more forcefully to protect African American civil rights. Gaines's main goals included racially integrated public schools (which failed to gain approval); the abolition of black convict leasing in the state prison system (which also failed); reform and regulation of tenant farming; and a state police force that included heavily armed black policemen to protect freedmen's rights to vote and gain election to public office. He even criticized Radical Republican governor Edmund J. Davis for rebuffing black leadership in the Republican Party. In a speech delivered on the steps of the Washington County courthouse, Gaines "denounced many leading white Republicans and advocated . . . a black man's party."[30]

In a legendary address to the Texas Senate in 1871 at the height of Radical Reconstruction, Matthew Gaines railed against an attempt by Democrats to authorize the state to replace black labor with white immigrants from Great Britain, Germany, and France. "Just as soon as foreign nations fill up this State, then the poor colored people will have to leave for some other one," Gaines argued. He lampooned white Texas Baptists like Rufus Burleson and other Democrats who claimed "that black men have no inherent rights . . . [and] that they ought to be back again in the ports of Africa." But "blacks have as much right here as the whites," Gaines protested. "Now if the Democrats . . . will agree with me that they will go back to Great Britain, and the Germans to Germany, and the French to France, then I am willing to go back to Africa—to my old home." Then the fiery Baptist preacher in Gaines erupted, scandalizing his listeners and condemning their sins. "Democrats think that it is hard for them to sit in the State Senate with colored men, and go to school with them, and live with them, yet they will not stop sleeping with colored women, and getting children by them," he shouted indignantly. "Let the Democrats remember that old times have played out, and new ones have taken their place. Look to the future and see what it will bring!"[31]

A short time after his incendiary speech, Democrats accused Gaines of bigamy, a felony. For years he had maintained that his first marriage was invalid because it was performed by an unauthorized lay preacher. Indicted in late 1871 and finally convicted in mid-1873, Gaines was forced to resign his Senate seat. After several months in jail, he prevailed in a formal legal appeal, then ran for reelection and won. But by early 1874 Democrats had regained control of the Senate and effectively overturned Reconstruction in Texas. In a bitter election, Democrats defeated Radical Republican Edmund J. Davis and installed a new governor, Waco judge and former Confederate officer Richard Coke—a man Rufus Burleson admired for "his undying courage and his immaculate honesty." The Senate summarily rejected Matthew Gaines's reelection and seated his Democratic opponent. Led by former slaveholders and ex-Confederates, Democrats likewise achieved "Redemption" throughout the South, severely weakening African American civil rights, if not their religious rights, and opening the door to further racial segregation, discrimination, persecution, and violence. In 1875 white authorities in Giddings, Texas, adjacent to Washington County, arrested Matthew Gaines for allegedly trying to organize a "secret society" for blacks to "make as much trouble as possible between them and the white people." Clearly, the "old times" had not played out.[32]

Regardless, Matthew Gaines, along with many other southern black religious and political leaders, remained active, organizing and holding black conventions, speaking at public meetings, preaching from church pulpits, and ensuring at least modest political influence for blacks and the survival of the Republican Party. Before he died in 1900, Gaines gave countless orations to crowds of African Americans, urging them to vote only for black political candidates and always proclaiming that "in the eyes of God, black men and women were as good and well loved as any white" and "exhorting them to hold up their heads with pride, even in troubled times." In effect, black ministers like Gaines and their supporters launched a long civil rights movement that continues.[33]

Historians often describe the shared Christian faith of masters and slaves as a tragic irony, especially since masters converted slaves to Christianity mainly as a way to control them, and paternalistic masters often used violence against rebellious slaves. Yet far more ironic, and far more remarkable, was the fact that Christian slaves and freedmen and their families adapted their masters' own spiritual and political values, goals, and methods—liberty, equality, strength, comfort, and defiance—to survive and resist slavery, segregation, discrimination, persecution, and violence.

Notes

1. George C. Rable, *God's Almost Chosen Peoples: A Religious History of the American Civil War* (Chapel Hill: University of North Carolina Press, 2010), 136–146; Ricardo A. Herrera, *For Liberty and the Republic: The American Citizen as Soldier, 1775–1861* (New York: New York University Press, 2015), especially chapter 4; Andrew S. Bledsoe, *Citizen-Officers: The Union and Confederate Volunteer Junior Officers in the American Civil War* (Baton Rouge: Louisiana State University Press, 2015), 112–115, 150–157, 180–181, 210–213.

2. Thomas S. Kidd, *God of Liberty: A Religious History of the American Revolution* (New York: Basic Books, 2010); George W. Truett, *Baptists and Religious Liberty* (Nashville: Sunday School Board, Southern Baptist Convention, 1920).

3. David T. Moon Jr., "Southern Baptists and Southern Men: Evangelical Perceptions of Manhood in Nineteenth-Century Georgia," *Journal of Southern History* 81 (August 2015): 563–606; Jason Phillips, *Diehard Rebels: The Confederate Culture of Invincibility* (Athens: University of Georgia Press, 2007).

4. The standard scholarly account of Baylor during the Civil War Era is Lois Smith Murray, *Baylor at Independence* (Waco, TX: Baylor University Press, 1972). On slavery in Texas, see Randolph B. Campbell, *An Empire for Slavery: The Peculiar Institution in Texas, 1821–1865* (Baton Rouge: Louisiana State University Press, 1989). On the Brazos River valley and slavery, see Sean M. Kelley, *Los Brazos de Dios: A Plantation Society in the Texas Borderlands, 1821–1865* (Baton Rouge: Louisiana State University Press, 2010). See also Calvin Schermerhorn, *The Business of Slavery and the Rise of American Capitalism, 1815–1860* (New Haven, CT: Yale University Press, 2015), chapter 7 and conclusion.

5. Joseph E. Early Jr., ed., *A Texas Baptist Sourcebook: A Companion to McBeth's Texas Baptists* (Denton: University of North Texas Press, 2004), 75. On Texas Baptists, see Richard Lee Elam, "Behold the Fields: Texas Baptists and the Problem of Slavery" (PhD diss., University of North Texas, 1993). On Southern Baptists, see Roger Charles Richards, "Actions and Attitudes of Southern Baptists toward Blacks, 1845–1895" (PhD. diss., Florida State University, 2008). On the persistence of proslavery doctrine, see Luke E. Harlow, "The Long Life of Proslavery Religion," in *The World the Civil War Made*, ed. Gregory P. Downs and Kate Masur (Chapel Hill: University of North Carolina Press), 132–158.

6. *Dallas Herald*, January 16, 1861; *San Antonio Ledger and Texan*, December 29, 1860. On the Texas Troubles, see Donald E. Reynolds, *Texas Terror: The Slave Insurrection Panic of 1860 and the Secession of the Lower South* (Baton Rouge: Louisiana State University Press, 2007).

7. Dale Baum, *The Shattering of Texas Unionism: Politics in the Lone Star State during the Civil War Era* (Baton Rouge: Louisiana State University Press, 1998), 48–57.

8. Amelia W. Williams and Eugene C. Barker, eds., *The Writings of Sam Houston, 1813–1863*, 8 vols. (Austin: University of Texas Press, 1938–1943), 8:295–299; Thomas North, *Five Years in Texas . . . from January 1861 to January 1866* (Cincinnati: Elm Street, 1871), 92–94.

9. Guy Nelson Jr., "Baylor University at Independence: The War Years: 1861–1865," *Texana* 2 (Summer 1964): 89–91; Murray, *Baylor at Independence*, 188–209.

10. *Tri-Weekly Telegraph* (Houston), June 27, 1862; Early, *A Texas Baptist History Sourcebook*, 107–108.

11. Stephen Chicoine, *The Confederates of Chappell Hill, Texas: Prosperity, Civil War and Decline* (Jefferson, NC: McFarland, 2005); Joseph H. Crute, *Units of the Confederate States Army* (Gaithersburg, MD: Olde Soldier Books, 1987); T. Michael Parrish, "Graves of Glory or Homes of Freedom," *Baylor Line* 73 (Summer 2011): 36–41; Colin Edward Woodward, *Marching Masters: Slavery, Race, and the Confederate Army during the Civil War* (Charlottesville: University of Virginia Press, 2014).

12. Sarah Jane Scott to George Scott, April 30, 1862, Sarah Jane Scott Papers, Texas Collection, Baylor University, Waco, Texas; Carey McNelly Wroe, "Baylor College in the Sixties," in *After Seventy-Five Years, By Student League and Alumnae Association of Baylor College, Belton, Texas*, ed. Elli Moore Townsend (Belton, TX: Baylor College, ca. 1920), 21–122.

13. Richard Lowe, "Warriors, Husbands, and Fathers: Confederate Soldiers and Their Families," in *The Fate of Texas: The Civil War in the Lone Star State*, ed. Charles D. Grear (Fayetteville: University of Arkansas Press, 2008), 25–36; Madge Thornall Roberts, ed., *The Personal Correspondence of Sam Houston*, 4 vols. (Denton: University of North Texas Press, 1996–2001), 4: 414.

14. Pamela Robinson-Durso, "Chaplains in the Confederate Army," *Journal of Church and State* 33 (Autumn 1991): 747–763; Levi Fowler, "Army Chaplains in Battle," *Confederate Veteran* 23 (May 1915): 205; Dillon J. Carroll, "'The God Who Shielded Me Before, Yet Watches over Us All': Confederate Soldiers, Mental Illness, and Religion," *Civil War History* 61 (September 2015): 252–280; William Clark Griggs, *Parson Henry Renfro: Free Thinking on the Texas Frontier* (Austin: University of Texas Press, 1994), 56.

15. Griggs, *Parson Henry Renfro*, 65; Chicoine, *Confederates of Chappell Hill, Texas*, 120.

16. Thomas S. Terrell, ed., *The Boys from Brenham: The Original Letters of Virginius E. Pettey, Co. E, 5th Texas Regiment, Hood's Brigade, Army of Northern Virginia* (Kerrville, TX: T. Terrell, 2006), 67–68, 223; Washington County, Texas, District Court, Civil and Criminal Minutes, 1861–1868, 1:90–92, Washington County Court House, Brenham, Texas.

17. Eleanor Damon Pace, ed., "The Diary and Letters of William P. Rogers, 1846–1862," *Southwestern Historical Quarterly* 32 (April 1929): 259–299; Langston James Goree V, ed., *The Thomas Jewett Goree Letters* (Bryan, TX: Family History Foundation, 1981), 221–224.

18. Benjamin S. Fitzgerald et al., *Resolutions of the Texas Brigade, Camp Texas Brigade, January 24th, 1865* (Richmond?, VA, 1865); Jason Phillips, "Against All Odds: Diehard Rebels Refused to Accept Defeat, Finding Strength in God," *Civil War Times* 46 (November–December 2007): 22–29.

19. Early, *A Texas Baptist History Sourcebook*, 73–74.

20. Ibid., 74–75.

21. Georgia J. Burleson, comp., *The Life and Writings of Rufus C. Burleson* ([Waco, TX], 1901), 710–711. On Horton, see Matthew Ellenberger, "Illuminating the Lesser Lights: Notes on the Life of Albert Clinton Horton," *Southwestern Historical Quarterly* 88 (April 1985): 363–386.

22. On R. E. B. Baylor, see Eugene C. Baker, *In His Traces: The Life and Times of R. E. B. Baylor* (Waco, TX: Baylor University Press, 1996). Dorman H. Winfrey and James M. Day, eds., *The Indian Papers of Texas and the Southwest, 1825–1916*, 5 vols. (Austin: Texas State Historical Association, 1995), 4:71–72.

23. Quoted in J. M. Carroll, *A History of Texas Baptists* (Dallas, TX: Baptist Standard, 1923).

24. Quoted in Heritage Auction Galleries, "Lot # 76252, Giddings Judson Buck Archive of Civil War Letters," *Texana Auction # 6003* (Dallas, TX: Heritage Auction Galleries, 2008), 132. On Poison Spring, see *"All Cut to Pieces and Gone to Hell": The Civil War, Race Relations, and the Battle of Poison Spring* (Little Rock: August House, 2003). Gregory J. W. Urwin, ed., *Black Flag over Dixie: Racial Atrocities and Reprisals in the Civil War* (Carbondale: Southern Illinois University Press, 2004).

25. Quoted in William C. Davis and Meredith Swentor, eds., *Bluegrass Confederate: The Headquarters Diary of Edward O. Guerrant* (Baton Rouge: Louisiana State University Press, 1999), 545. On Saltville, see Thomas D. Mays, *The Saltville Massacre* (Abilene, TX: McWhiney Foundation Press, 1998).

26. Burleson, *Life and Writings of Rufus C. Burleson*, 389, 557, 711, 743.

27. Michael R. Heintze, *Private Black Colleges in Texas, 1865–1954* (College Station: Texas A&M University Press, 1985), 28–31; Burleson, *Life and Writings of Rufus C. Burleson*, 387–388, 419–420.

28. On black churches in the South during Reconstruction, see William E. Montgomery, *Under Their Own Vine and Fig Tree: The African-American Church in the South, 1865–1900* (Baton Rouge: Louisiana State University Press, 1993), chapters 3 and 4.

29. On Reconstruction violence in Texas, see Kenneth W. Howell, ed., *Still the Arena of Civil War: Violence and Turmoil in Reconstruction Texas, 1865–1874* (Denton: University of North Texas Press, 2012). On violence in Washington County, including the incidents at Independence, see Donald G. Nieman, "African Americans and the Meaning of Freedom: Washington County, Texas, as a Case Study, 1865–1886, *Chicago-Kent Law Review* 70, no. 2 (1994): 541–582, available at http://scholarship.kentlaw.iit.edu/cklawreview/vol70/iss2/6.

30. Ann Patton Malone, "Matt Gaines: Reconstruction Politician," in *Black Leaders: Texans for Their Times*, ed. Alwyn Barr and Robert A. Calvert (Austin: Texas State Historical Association, 1981), 49–81; Merline Pitre, *Through Many Dangers, Toils, and Snares: Black Leadership in Texas* (Austin, TX: Eakin, 1997), 169–179, 271–272; Stephen Hahn, *A Nation under Our Feet: Black Political Struggles in the Rural South from Slavery to the Great Migration* (Cambridge, MA: Harvard University Press, 2003), 253.

31. Matthew Gaines, *Speech of Senator Mat. Gaines, on the Immigration Bill* ([Austin, TX], 1871).

32. Patsy McDonald Spaw, ed., *The Texas Senate*, vol. 2, *Civil War to the Eve of Reform, 1861–1889* (College Station: Texas A&M University Press, 1999), 102–105; Burleson, *Life and Writings of Rufus C. Burleson*, 593–595; Malone, "Matt Gaines," 68–70.

33. Lawrence D. Rice, *The Negro in Texas, 1874–1900* (Baton Rouge: Louisiana State University Press, 1971), 58; Malone, "Matt Gaines," 70–71.

Deriding the Democracy

The Partisan Humor of David Ross Locke

DANIEL J. BURGE

I n 1872, the Boston publishing firm of I. N. Richardson and Company asked Charles Sumner to pen an introduction to a soon-to-be published collection of letters and lectures. Sumner was one of the most influential political figures in the nation. Having survived the caning of Preston Brooks, Sumner had served in the US Senate for over twenty years, nearly a decade of which he spent as the chair of the Senate Foreign Relations Committee. Yet Sumner took time out of his busy schedule to write an introduction for the work that would be published under the title of *The Struggles (Social, Financial and Political) of Petroleum V. Nasby*.[1] A weighty volume that checked in at over seven hundred pages, this work contained the letters and lectures of Petroleum Vesuvius Nasby, a fictional character created by David Ross Locke. Charles Sumner did not hesitate to endorse this completely fictional work. In his introduction, Sumner recounted the hours that he had spent in the office of Abraham Lincoln listening to him praise the work of Nasby as he read the letters aloud. Speaking of the influence of Nasby's letters, Sumner noted: "It is impossible to measure their value ... each letter was like a speech, or one of those songs which stir the people. ... They belong to the political history of this critical period."[2]

Charles Sumner believed that Nasby's work transcended mere literature and that it played a significant role in shaping the political culture of the Civil War and Reconstruction periods. Posterity has been less appreciative.[3] Although the Nasby letters retained their popularity throughout the nineteenth century, Locke's reputation quickly dwindled. In 1882, Will M. Clemens published a collection of small biographies of humorists in a collection entitled *Famous Funny Fellows*, which included Mark Twain, Artemus Ward, Major Jack Downing, and Petroleum V. Nasby.[4] Clemens buried Locke in his list of humorists at number thirty, listing him alongside of authors who published sporadically in local newspapers. The first book-length study of American humor contained only a paragraph about Nasby.[5] Walter Blair and Hamlin Hill demonstrated the lasting influence of Clemens's volume when they lumped David Ross Locke into the chapter on "Phunny Phellows," a group of humorists that emerged during the Civil War most noted for "puns, malapropisms, assaults on grammar, weirdly shaped sentences, dialect distortions, parodies and burlesques of dramas and fictional works."[6] Following in the footsteps of Clemens and Blair, modern scholars typically classify Locke as a "literary comedian" or a "funny fellow," who used bizarre spelling and bad grammar to elicit mirth.[7] Most scholars do not even credit Locke for being very good at this. Walter Blair, an eminent scholar of American humor, noted: "Anyone reading this humor today has trouble even in imagining how such stuff could once have seemed so delicious. . . . Lovingood . . . and Nasby are generally dull and sometimes mildly nauseating."[8]

Whether or not one finds Locke to be "nauseating" today, literary critics and historians have done him a disservice by classifying him as little more than a literary comedian. While Locke's writings bear some similarities to his peers, his subject matter differed in one important regard: he made fun of Democrats.[9] A more fitting term for Locke is partisan humorist. Unlike political humor, which is aimed at vaguely defined politicians and demagogues, partisan humor denounces specific individuals within a specific party. Over the course of the nineteenth century, David Ross Locke excelled at this brand of humor.[10] Although partisan humor became unfashionable by the turn of the century, the career of David Ross Locke demonstrated that one could make a comfortable living in the nineteenth century by cleverly attacking those who voted the Democratic ticket.

David Ross Locke was not the first American to turn to partisan humor. Although he has most often been compared to midcentury comedians Charles Farrar Browne (Artemus Ward) and Henry Wheeler Shaw (Josh Billings), Locke's humorous style derived from a different source.[11] Nearly thirty years earlier Seba Smith originated partisan humor by creating a prototype of Petroleum V. Nasby. Seba Smith was a New Englander and graduate of Bowdoin.[12] In 1829 he began to publish the *Portland Courier* and a year later he hit upon an ingenious idea: he introduced an epistolary correspondent by the name of Jack Downing. The fictional Jack Downing was a young man who traveled to the city of Portland to sell a load of supplies. As the state legislature was meeting, Jack Downing found himself embroiled in the swirl of politics and ended up penning letters back to his family in the fictional city of Downingville. The letters of "Jack Downing" proved to be an immense hit, and Smith continued to sporadically publish them for over twenty years. By the end of his career, Smith had produced a fictional character who commented upon politics for almost two decades.

In creating the character of Major Jack Downing, Seba Smith became the first partisan humorist to explicitly mock the eccentricities and ideas of a prominent political party for an extended period of time.[13] Downing initially focused on local politics within the state of Maine. However, his eventual relocation to Washington, and his improbable friendship with Andrew Jackson, led him into a host of new topics. He became a stalwart Jacksonian who raised a militia troop to fight in the Aroostook War; he volunteered to put down the nullifiers in South Carolina and earned the titles of captain and then major; he intervened in the Eaton controversy and tried to replace Martin Van Buren as Jackson's right-hand man.[14] To those coming of age during the Jacksonian era, Downing personified an ardent Democrat. His mishaps and misunderstandings provided readers with a hearty chuckle at the expense of prominent Democratic politicians.

Major Jack Downing penned his last letter on January 21, 1856, as he took a final parting shot at James Buchanan.[15] Although there is no evidence that directly links David Ross Locke with Seba Smith, Locke had to be familiar with Smith's work. After all, Smith's letters appeared in prominent Whig papers for decades, and the letters of Jack Downing, over eighty of them, were collected and published in 1859 in *My Thirty Years Out of the Senate*. A mere two years later David Ross Locke published his first Nasby letter. For the next twenty years, Locke built upon the legacy of Smith and took partisan humor to new heights.

But what exactly were the central tenets and themes of partisan humor? What set Seba Smith and David Ross Locke apart from the countless other humorists who published their works under fictional names in newspapers? First, partisan humorists openly attacked prominent politicians. Petroleum V. Nasby was not an actual person, but he interacted within the bounds of historical time with historical figures. Second, and perhaps most importantly, partisan humor relied upon the creation of a caricature of the opposition party. Locke's work portrayed Democrats as venal spoilsmen, cowardly, illiterate, intemperate, and racist. Third, partisan humorists desired to effect political change and sway voters. While traditional humor seeks to evoke a laugh from the audience, partisan humor strives to evoke not just laughter but political action.

Partisan humorists believed that their humor could be effective if it portrayed a world that was fictional and yet realistic. Almost every letter that

Nasby penned included a date and location and was a reaction to a historical event.[16] By setting up his letters in this way, Locke enabled himself to comment upon the most pressing occurrences of the day.[17] More importantly, it allowed him to directly mock Democratic leaders, whom he called out by name. Had Locke merely created a fictional character in a fictional world, it would have been difficult to satirize those in positions of power. But Locke routinely had Nasby discuss current events and interact with contemporary figures.[18] During the Civil War, Nasby's favorite target was Clement Vallandigham, notorious Copperhead of Ohio. In 1863, for instance, Nasby grew tired of churches that preached against his democratic doctrines, and so he organized his own church, according to democratic principles. He began calling his congregation the "Church of St. Vallandigum."[19] In a subsequent letter, Nasby personally visited Vallandigham after his exile from Ohio.[20] In these letters, Vallandigham was the consummate Democratic villain, a hypocrite who fought the cause of the Union to advance his personal political career.[21] Using Vallandigham as a representative figure allowed Locke to satirize the policy of northern Democrats in the midst of the Civil War.[22]

As time passed Locke turned his acerbic wit on other prominent Democratic politicians. Vallandigham was a useful foil during the Civil War, but after the assassination of Abraham Lincoln, Locke turned his attention to another figure: Andrew Johnson. At first, Nasby expressed a somewhat ambivalent attitude toward Johnson, but as time progressed his satire sharpened. Johnson's veto of the Civil Rights Bill led Nasby to proclaim: "Blessed be Booth, who give us Androo."[23] From that point onward Johnson was a frequent target of Locke's satire.[24] Locke's willingness to use the names and characteristics of actual politicians in his fictional letters set his work apart from other Civil War–era humorists. Humorists such as Robert Henry Newell avoided singling out individuals by name, whereas others such as George Washington Harris and Charles Henry Smith only sporadically critiqued prominent figures such as Lincoln, Sumner, or Seward.[25] In contrast, Locke relentlessly targeted politicians by name and wrote the vast majority of his letters in direct response to ongoing political events.

Locke also created his own subject material. Realizing that he could not solely rely upon caricaturing prominent Democratic politicians, he created his own fictional Democratic world, replete with characters who could charitably be described as morally repugnant. Indeed, Locke's longest-running joke revolved around Nasby's pursuit of a political office for himself.[26] Nasby was unqualified for office, except for the fact that he had "voted ez often ez three times at one elekshun . . . .and hev spent the entire day a bringin in the agid and infirm, and in the patryotik biznis uv knockin down the opposition voters."[27] As time passed, Nasby refused to back down from his pursuit of the post office. It became the obsession of his life.[28] Finally, in August of 1866, after "five weary trips to Washington" to consult with President Johnson, Nasby secured his commission as Postmaster of Confedrit X Roads, Kentucky.[29] Unsurprisingly, Nasby used the office for his own personal gain and admitted, in subsequent letters, to opening the mail and removing money from the envelopes.[30]

Locke utilized Nasby's pursuit of the post office to illustrate an important point: Democrats lacked principles and were only interested in their own economic well-being. Of course, jokes about office seekers and corrupt politicians were common in the nineteenth century. Charles Heber Clark, who published the immensely popular comic novel *Out of the Hurly-Burly* in 1874, spoke for more than one humorist when he observed, "The average American legislator is both ignorant and dishonest."[31] Locke differed from his contemporary Clark, however, in that he labeled only one political party "ignorant and dishonest." Locke made it clear through his letters that Democrats, and not Republicans, were to blame for the spoils system. This view was perhaps best summarized by a toast given by the characters at a celebration of Jackson's victory at New Orleans: "The ancient Dimocrisy—troo to the country, ez long ez there is an office to be filled."[32] Nasby, Vallandigham, Fernando Wood, and the other Democratic politicians in these letters are uninterested in the well-being of the United States, even in the midst of Civil War and Reconstruction. Their goal, as evinced by Nasby, was to ensure the triumph of the Democratic Party so that they could gain notoriety and steady pay. Locke separated himself from his comedic contemporaries by specifically laying the blame for political corruption at the feet of the Democratic Party.

The pursuit of profit was hardly Nasby's only vice. Locke also characterized Democrats as cowards. This charge manifested itself in two ways. On the first level was personal cowardice. Locke portrayed Petroleum V. Nasby as an ardent supporter of the Confederacy who was nonetheless a craven. To avoid the war, Nasby attempted to use his poor health as an excuse, writing that "I hev lost, sence Stanton's order to draft, the use uv wun eye entirely, and hev kronic inflammashen in the other."[33] Over the course of the war, Nasby deserted from the Union army, joined the Confederacy, deserted from his unit, and returned to the North.[34] Even after the war, Nasby continually displayed his own cowardice.

Rejoicing at a recent Democratic victory at the polls, Nasby pondered whether or not he should go out and kill an African American to celebrate the occasion. "Nothin but the oncertainty ez to who wood be killed restrains me," he is forced to admit.[35] Shortly thereafter, while traveling to New York as a delegate to the Democratic national convention of 1868, Nasby confronted an African American and demanded that he remove himself from the car. The African American man refused to back down and ended up pummeling Nasby, who was only saved by a fellow passenger who noted, "Let him up. He's poor white trash, and not worth wastin yoor indignashen onto."[36]

Locke focused attention on Nasby's personal cowardice and also on the cowardice of northern Democrats. Locke routinely derided northern Democrats for truckling to the South and allowing wealthy planters—and later ex-planters—to run the party.[37] Locke vividly illustrated this point in a letter he wrote dealing with Reconstruction. In this letter, Nasby decides to meet up with General Boanerges Mosher, a stalwart Mississippian and Democrat who was in Washington to pick up his pardon. After exchanging pleasantries, Nasby suggests to Mosher that the South allow German and Irish immigrants to migrate into the region, to help bolster the Democratic ticket. General Mosher explodes in rage at this suggestion and as Nasby falls to his knees Mosher prepares to beat him with his cane. "'Why this violence?' Nasby asked; 'O, nothing,' replied the Ginral, relaxin his holt; 'I shall be elected to Congris, and ez I shel hev to mix with yoo Yankees, I wuz a practisin the old tactics, jist to git my hand in agin."[38] Locke was hardly the only humorist to mock southern planters for their gambling, love of whiskey, and sexual transgressions, but he adroitly used the trope of the unrepentant southern aristocrat to belittle northern Democrats. During the Civil War they hesitated to fight, continually defended the rights of the South, and harped on the "unconstitutional" actions of Lincoln. After the conflict they sought to prostrate themselves at the feet of the South to win elections.[39]

Locke was not content to simply caricature Democrats as cowardly men who openly supported the Confederate cause. He also mocked their ignorance. Time and time again, Locke utilized Nasby to poke fun at the general ignorance of Democratic voters. In 1864, for instance, Nasby helped to ordain a missionary for his democratic church and he gave him the following advice: "Learn to spell and pronounce Missenegenegenashun. It's a good word."[40] In this joke, Locke used dialect to emphasize the stupidity of Democrats. Nasby was smart enough to realize that racism could be used to bring voters to the polls, but he was not smart enough to learn how to write English correctly. Nasby lacked the rudiments of learning and saw education as the foe of his party. "Readin hez alluz bin agin us," he mused at one point. "Every schoolmaster is a engine uv Ablishnism. . . . General Wize, uv Virginia, when he thanked God there wuzn't a noosepaper in his deestrick, hed reason to; for do yoo spoze a readin consti-tooency wood hev ever kept sich a blatherskite ez him in Congress year after year?"[41] As seen in examples such as this, a key part of Locke's partisan humor derived from mocking the intelligence of the typical Democrat. Many literary critics have mistakenly argued that Locke employed dialect because that was the popular style of the day.[42] Even a cursory reading of Nasby shows that this was not the case, as Nasby's poor grammar and mangled spelling are repeatedly deployed to highlight the stupidity of the average Democratic voter.[43] As Nasby himself concludes, "The Dimekratik intellek is not hefty."[44]

Locke strategically deployed dialect in these letters to mock the intellect of Democratic voters. But dialect served other purposes as well. Locke often used it to puncture holes in the idea of white supremacy. Nasby and his coterie of Kentucky friends regularly launched into diatribes against African Americans, reciting pseudoscientific verbiage about the inferiority of African Americans. Yet they themselves lacked the ability to write or speak anything resembling grammatical English. In his letter of July 19, 1867, Locke managed to use this to great effect. In this letter Nasby gathers together his conclave of friends to discuss "the Negro question" and Nasby launches into one of his set speeches on the inferiority of the African American race.[45] Two audience members de-cide to test out Nasby's theories and so they measure one white member of the audience and then one African American and realized their measurements are nearly the same. The African American man then casually reads a news-paper handed to him "ez peert ez a Noo England skool marm," while the white member of the audience, "the gay desendant uv the sooperior race" is unable to read.[46] Locke, in examples such as this, used dialect to highlight the stupid-ity of Nasby and contrasted it with the intellectual attainments of newly freed African Americans.

Locke frequently played upon Nasby's venality, cowardly nature, and lack of education, but he resorted to one stereotype more than any other: intemper-ance. Democrats drank heartily and to the point of intoxication in letter after letter, setting up joke after joke. One such joke occurred when Nasby attempts to question a fellow attending a conference with him in New York: "'Sir,' sed he, 'are yoo a Johnson postmaster?' 'I am,' sed I, defiantly. 'How didst deter-

mine that pint?' 'By yoor breath,' sed he."[47] Democrats in these letters identified each other by the very redness of their noses. "We hev the patriotic cit-
izins whose noses blossom like the lobster," noted Nasby of the Democratic
Party.[48] Jokes about red noses and alcohol consumption were staples of mid-
nineteenth-century American humor and flourished during the Civil War, but
Locke applied these stereotypes exclusively to members of the Democratic
Party.[49] Locke's attribution of alcoholism to members of the Democratic Party
is a fitting example of how partisan humor functioned in nineteenth-century
America. By taking a common humorous trope, the red nose of the drunkard,
and applying it to Democrats, Locke managed to condemn intemperance while
also linking it to Democratic corruption.[50] If whiskey were outlawed, as Locke
hoped, then the fraudulent voting practices of the Democrats would be undermined and the Republican Party would triumph. Intemperance itself, in these
letters, morphed into a Democratic vice.[51]

The greatest vice of the democracy, however, was not intemperance; it was
racism. Nasby's political catechism directly stated that the chief end of man
was to "whale" African Americans and "vote the Dimekratik tickit forever."[52]
Being a political operator, Nasby sought to use racism to stir up his voting base.
"It's soothing to a ginooine, constooshnel, southern-rites Dimekrat," Nasby
mused, "to be constantly told that ther is a race uv men meaner than he is."[53]
Nasby thus saw racism as the key ingredient to the success of the Democratic
Party, the only factor that could rally men to the polls in order to save them
from the threat of amalgamation. "The Dimekratik party ariz for the purpus
uv keepin" the African American "down," he remarked at one point, "and that
deliteful biznis hez given them employment for more than 30 years."[54] Locke
believed that the Democratic Party was less interested in guaranteeing the
rights of ordinary citizens—and in protecting their constitutional liberties—
than it was in playing upon racial fears to win votes. Through the character of
Nasby he sought to show that alcohol and racism were the only things holding
together the base of the party.

Locke employed the blatant racism of the Democratic Party to achieve some
of his greatest humorous jibes. Locke frequently juxtaposed the illiterate and
ignorant white Democrat with the educated African American to illustrate
the absurdity of the Democratic position. He also commented on other racist
practices. In 1867, for instance, Nasby traveled to Ohio to investigate a local
school where African American children were allowed to learn with whites.
Nasby traveled with a group of concerned parents and entered the schoolhouse,

where he demanded that the teacher remove all the African American students. The teacher, a New Englander, refused and told Nasby to do it himself. Nasby then mistook three white children sitting in the back for the African American children. The white parents of the children then waylaid Nasby and beat him to a pulp.[55] Through stories such as these, Locke challenged segregated schools, segregated political parties, lynching, voter intimidation, literacy testing, and other practices of the Reconstruction era, all of which he blamed upon the Democratic Party.

Through his repeated attacks on the policies and personalities of the Democratic Party, Locke became one of the chief advocates of the Republican Party for three pivotal decades, stretching from the election of Lincoln through the presidency of Hayes. To call his style of humor merely political, however, does it a disservice. Political jokes abounded in the nineteenth century, and humorists often made light of office seekers, partisan rancor, and fraudulent voting practices. Locke's peers, however, fastidiously avoided partisanship in their political humor. Perhaps the most notable instance was Mark Twain and Charles Dudley Warner's novel *The Gilded Age*, wherein corruption within Washington is critiqued through the character of Senator Dilworthy.[56] A less coarse version of Nasby, Dilworthy sees his office as a way to enrich himself and tried to push a swindle through the US Senate.[57] Yet Dilworthy's political party is not named, nor are Republicans or Democrats faulted for corruption. Twain and Warner were clearly unhappy at the level of corruption within Washington during the Grant administration, but they refused to critique politicians by name and avoided mentioning party affiliations.

Newspaper humorists followed a similar path. Charles B. Lewis, who wrote under the name of M. Quad for the *Detroit Free Press*, told the story of a John Cain, "a quiet, unobtrusive citizen" who nonetheless "allowed the politicians to get after him."[58] Because of his innate honesty, Cain seemed to be the ideal candidate and so he ran for office: within a short space of time, he was deliberately lying in campaign speeches, handing out bribes, and buying votes with whiskey.[59] In this story, Lewis humorously depicts shady political characters who resemble Nasby, and yet neither party is mentioned by name. Robert J. Burdette, the Hawkeye Man, tells a humorous story of two neighbors who deplore the partisan nature of newspapers but then come to blows when they realize they belong to different parties and read the very paper the other decried.[60] Humor such as this condemns both Democrats and Republicans for their lack of toleration. Although many writers tried to write humor during the nineteenth century, with varying degrees of success, most fastidiously avoided immersing themselves in the muddy waters of partisanship.[61]

Clearly Locke believed his party's agenda could be advanced through humor. But how effective were his sketches? In terms of general merriment, many Americans found Nasby to be one of the greatest comic writers of his generation. The *Monthly Religious Magazine* wrote the following in a review of one collection of Nasby's letters: "We wish that there was less occasion on all sides for this broad satire. We cannot help laughing as we turn over these sketches."[62] A writer in *Harper's New Monthly Magazine* observed: "We have suffered considerably from side-ache at the hands both of Artemus Ward and of Petroleum V. Nasby. . . . The thought itself is funny, and the grotesque dress helps its humorous effect."[63] A good "hearty laugh" always seemed to accompany the reading of a Nasby sketch. As one magazine aptly observed, "Among the Americans who have been born to an affluence of laughter is Petroleum V. Nasby. . . . He is a man to whom the nation owes a large debt of gratitude."[64] Humor is not something that is easily transferable from generation to generation but countless of Locke's contemporaries found his humor to be quite humorous.

Many of his contemporaries also believed that Locke's writings were politically significant. Not surprisingly, Republicans and those who identified with Locke's cause heaped praise upon the letters and extolled their virtues. "Nast and Nasby," one magazine noted, "have together done as effective service to the Republican party as any dozen of its newspapers or any score of its popular orators. Their names have been in every mouth and their works quoted or described in every Republican newspaper in the land."[65] Praise such as this was somewhat common. Both Sumner and Lincoln, as noted previously, saw Nasby as an effective ally of the Republican Party, whose antics were able to reach the masses. Others agreed with this assessment and stressed the utilitarian value of Locke's style of humor. "D. R. Locke . . . is not only a humorist," Edwin P. Whipple concluded, "but he was a great force in carrying the reconstruction measures of the Republican party, after the war."[66] To those who agreed with his message, Locke was the warrior of the Republican Party, wielding Nasby as his weapon to battle the forces of disunion and bigotry. "Whatever weapon this rough soldier of the Lord wielded," one reviewer noted of his work, "he always used it in the defense of the right. . . . We are little disposed to criticise his style of slaughtering the Phillistines whom he made to bite the dust in the holy war."[67]

Not everyone agreed with this assessment. One of the drawbacks of writing partisan humor is that it targets a large segment of the American population and, quite naturally, draws forth a wide array of critics. Detractors, then and now, frequently lumped Locke together with Josh Billings and Artemus Ward and attributed his success to his unorthodox spelling. The Reverend Theo D. Cuyler waxed wroth at "those miserable literary buffoons—Doesticks, Artemus Ward, Nasby, Josh Bilings, and the rest" for inflicting upon the United States "the plague of slang."[68] Cuyler averred the humorists should imitate the refined style of Swift, Addison, Irving, Goldsmith, and Dickens.[69] One other critic fulminated: "Billings and Nasby did not rise to the rank of dialect writers. They were mere corruptors of language. . . . That their miserable effusions have for so long been tolerated is a disgrace to this country."[70] Whether they agreed or disagreed with him, Locke's writings evoked a visceral response. "To criticise 'Petroleum V. Nasby,'" one testy critic wrote, "is a waste of time. His last production is marked by all the stupidity and malice of the former works."[71]

During the nineteenth century Locke's work was appraised in widely divergent ways, and time has done little to clarify his legacy. Glancing through assessments of Petroleum V. Nasby it is difficult to tell if critics are writing about the same character. Some have written him off as a "buffoon" and charged Locke with being a mere funny fellow who amused his childish contemporaries with ludicrously bad spelling.[72] Conversely, one of his only biographers argued that Locke wrote "deadly serious" satire and that any humor was "incidental."[73] Two other writers have used the word "propagandist" to describe Locke's sketches.[74] More sympathetic readers, most of whom lived in the nineteenth century, revered Locke as the greatest humorist of his era, a scourge to the Democratic Party, and a champion of the rights of African Americans. While his admirers doubtlessly overstated his case, they recognized something that his detractors, and many literary critics, have subsequently overlooked: the uniqueness of Locke's humorous style.[75] Throughout the nineteenth century Locke worked in a genre of humor unlike any of his peers.

In contrast to other nineteenth-century humorists, Locke effectively managed to turn out partisan humor for over two decades. Like Major Jack Downing in the 1840s and 1850s, Petroleum V. Nasby relentlessly burlesqued the behavior and beliefs of Democrats, both fictional and real. By the time Locke laid down his pen in the 1880s, he had managed to construct a caricature of the Democratic politician that was as recognizable to a nineteenth-century American as Nast's drawings of Boss Tweed and his ring. Locke's Democrats were sordid office seekers, men who drank, swore, loved the Confederacy, and relied upon whiskey and racism to stir up the unwashed masses to vote early and often. At a time when most of his fellow humorists were resorting to mother-in-law jokes, ethnic humor, and laughing at the antics of bad boys, amorous widows, and hassled city dwellers, Locke wrote about miscegenation, lynching, and segregation. Locke's approach was one-sided, but his partisan style of humor provides a window into what was undeniably a violent, contentious, and partisan era.[76] More than most writers of the day, Nasby managed to capture the essence of Reconstruction, "a period uv gloom rarely ekalled, and never surpast, for the Democrisy."[77]

Notes

1. David Ross Locke, *The Struggles (Social, Financial and Political) of Petroleum V. Nasby* (Boston: I. N. Richardson, 1873).

2. Locke, *The Struggles (Social, Financial and Political) of Petroleum V. Nasby*, 13–14.

3. David Ross Locke (as a journalist) and Petroleum V. Nasby (as a fictional character) are missing from most studies on Reconstruction.

4. Will M. Clemens, *Famous Funny Fellows: Brief Biographical Sketches of American Humorists* (Cleveland: William W. Williams, 1882).

5. Constance Rourke, *American Humor: A Study of the National Character* (1931; reprint, New York: New York Review of Books, 2004), 174–175.

6. Walter Blair and Hamlin Hill, *America's Humor: From Poor Richard to Doonesbury* (New York: Oxford University Press, 1978), 276.

7. Blair and Hill, *America's Humor*, 289–290. In the footnote, Nasby is classified with over thirty other "Phunny Phellows," including Joseph C. Aby (Hoffenstein), Robert J. Burdette (the Hawkeye Man), Melville D. Landon (Eli Perkins), C. B. Lewis (M. Quad), Edgar Wilson Nye (Bill Nye), and Charles H. Webb (John Paul).

8. Walter Blair, *Horse Sense in American Humor: From Benjamin Franklin to Ogden Nash* (1942; reprint, New York: Russell and Russell, 1962), 170.

9. See Jon Grinspan, "'Sorrowfully Amusing': The Popular Comedy of the Civil War," *Journal of the Civil War Era* 1 (September 2011): 313–338. While Grinspan does call Nasby "the funniest character of the Civil War," he fails to see that Locke's satire was aimed at Democrats and how they behaved during the Civil War. Locke, unlike other Civil War comedians, rarely made light of the actual conflict. Perhaps that is why Nasby remained an important literary character, long after the last shots of the war had been fired.

10. For studies on the partisan nature of newspapers and the rise of the independent press in the Reconstruction era, see Paul S. Holbo, *Tarnished Expansion: The Alaska Scandal, the Press, and Congress, 1867–1871* (Knoxville: University of Tennessee Press, 1983); Thomas C. Leonard, *The Power of the Press: The Birth of American Political Reporting* (New York: Oxford University Press, 1986); James L. Crouthamel, *Bennett's New York Herald and the Rise of the Popular Press* (Syracuse, NY: Syracuse University Press, 1989); Donald A. Ritchie, *Press Gallery: Congress and the Washington Correspondents* (Cambridge, MA: Harvard University Press, 1991); Mark Wahlgren Summers, *The Press Gang: Newspapers and Politics, 1865–1878* (Chapel Hill: University of North Carolina

Daniel J. Burge

Press, 1994); Andrew L. Slap, *The Doom of Reconstruction: The Liberal Republicans in the Civil War Era* (New York: Fordham University Press, 2006).

11. Brian Kirk McManus, "Literary Comedy to Concert Comedy: The Achievements of Artemus Ward, Petroleum V. Nasby, and Josh Billings" (PhD diss., University of Texas at Austin, 1976).

12. Mary Alice Wyman, *Two American Pioneers: Seba Smith and Elizabeth Oakes Smith* (New York: Columbia University Press, 1927), 29–31.

13. Most writers have downplayed the partisan nature of Smith's humor. See Daniel Boorstin, *The Americans: The National Experience* (1965; reprint, New York: History Book Club, 2002), 322.

14. Seba Smith, *My Thirty Years Out of the Senate* (1859; reprint, New York: AMS Press, 1973), 229.

15. Smith, *My Thirty Years Out of the Senate*, 447.

16. Locke, *The Struggles (Social, Financial and Political) of Petroleum V. Nasby*, 41–42.

17. Locke, *The Struggles (Social, Financial and Political) of Petroleum V. Nasby*, 172.

18. John M. Harrison, *The Man Who Made Nasby, David Ross Locke* (Chapel Hill: University of North Carolina Press, 1969), 127–128.

19. Locke, *The Struggles (Social, Financial and Political) of Petroleum V. Nasby*, 71.

20. Ibid., 82.

21. Ibid., 124–125.

22. For an examination of how northerners perceived Vallandigham, see William A. Blair, *With Malice toward Some: Treason and Loyalty in the Civil War Era* (Chapel Hill: University of North Carolina Press, 2014), 176–180.

23. Locke, *The Struggles (Social, Financial and Political) of Petroleum V. Nasby*, 267.

24. David Ross Locke, *Swingin' Round the Cirkle* (Boston: Lee and Shephard, 1867), illustrated by Thomas Nast.

25. Robert Henry Newell, *A Complete Contemporaneous Military History of the Mackerel Brigade* (New York: G. W. Carleton, 1871). Only a handful of Newell's characters were meant to represent actual historical figures under a fictional name (Robert E. Lee in particular). Charles Henry Smith (Bill Arp) did have Arp interact with Lincoln (on occasion), but his fictional character never pursues a career in politics. See Charles Henry Smith, *Bill Arp's Peace Papers: Columns on War and Reconstructions, 1861–1873* (Columbia: University of South Carolina Press, 2009).

26. Locke, *The Struggles (Social, Financial and Political) of Petroleum V. Nasby*, 47.

27. Ibid.

28. Ibid., 249.

29. Ibid., 300.

30. Ibid., 382.

31. Charles Heber Clark, *Out of the Hurly-Burly; Or Life in an Odd Corner* (1874; reprint, New York: AMS, 1972), 364.

32. David Ross Locke, *Swingin' Round the Cirkle* (Boston: Lee and Shephard, 1867), 55.

33. Locke, *The Struggles (Social, Financial and Political) of Petroleum V. Nasby*, 50.

34. Ibid., 59–62.

35. Ibid., 490.

36. Ibid., 541.

37. Ibid., 185.

38. Ibid., 199.

39. For contemporary jokes about southern planters see the comic ballad "The South Carolina Gentleman" by Robert Henry Newell in *A Complete Contemporaneous Military History of the Mackerel Brigade*, 79. For a detailed analysis see Cameron C. Nickels, *Civil War Humor* (Jackson: University Press of Mississippi, 2010), 21–22.

40. Locke, *The Struggles (Social, Financial and Political) of Petroleum V. Nasby*, 117.

41. Ibid., 237.

42. Blair and Hill, *America's Humor*, 289–290.

43. Blair and Hill make the common mistake of relying too heavily upon Artemus Ward, Josh Billings, and Bill Arp as their exemplary "Phunny Phellows." While these three writers did write in dialect, a large portion of those listed (but not discussed) in Blair and Hill's chapter did not, including some of the most famous: Robert J. Burdette (the Hawkeye Man), Charles Heber Clark (Max Adeler), C. B. Lewis (M. Quad), Robert Henry Newell (Orpheus C. Kerr), and Marcus M. Pomeroy (Brick Pomeroy). The use of dialect always depended on the "guise" assumed by the author, hence the bombastic oratory of Orphaeus C. Kerr and the refined letters of the "editor" Max Adeler.

44. Locke, *The Struggles (Social, Financial and Political) of Petroleum V. Nasby*, 130.

45. Ibid., 456.

46. Ibid., 459.

47. Ibid., 534.

48. Ibid., 626.

49. The pervasive extent of alcohol jokes, especially in the North, can best be seen in Newell, *A Complete Contemporaneous Military History of the Mackerel Brigade*. "The God of Bottles be our aid / When rebels crack us / We'll bend the bottle-neck to him/And he will Bacchus" (50).

50. For an example of Nasby's famous red nose, see Charles H Brigham, "Take Care of Your Noses," *Herald of Health*, March 1870, 115.

51. James C. Austin, *Petroleum V. Nasby* (New York: Twayne, 1965), 60. As noted by Austin, Locke was an alcoholic who struggled with his addiction his entire life. His characterization of Democrats as compulsive drinkers is thus somewhat ironic.

52. Locke, *The Struggles (Social, Financial and Political) of Petroleum V. Nasby*, 70.

53. Ibid., 117.

54. Ibid., 189.

55. Ibid., 492–493.

56. Mark Twain and Charles Dudley Warner, *The Gilded Age: A Tale of Today* (1873), in Twain, *The Gilded Age and Later Novels* (New York: Library of America, 2002).

57. Twain and Warner, *The Gilded Age*, 152.

58. Charles Bertram Lewis, *Quad's Odds* (Detroit: R. D. S. Tyler, 1875), 212.

59. Ibid., 215.

60. See also Robert J. Burdette, *The Rise and Fall of the Mustache* (Upper Saddle River, NJ: Gregg, 1969), 139.

61. Summers, *The Press Gang*, 50–51. For an example, see Mark M. Pomeroy, *Nonsense, Or Hits and Criticisms on the Follies of the Day* (New York: G. W. Carleton, 1868), 14. Pomeroy was a prominent Democrat who, like Locke, also wrote humorous pieces. He avoided partisan humor. Most of his humor centered on his character Brick's amorous pursuit of New England women, whom he

Daniel J. Burge

relentlessly mocked for being prudish and for fawning upon African Americans. See also Pomeroy, *Brick-Dust: A Remedy for the Blues, and a Something for People to Talk About* (New York: G. W. Carleton, 1871).

62. "Review 1," *Monthly Magazine*, 39, no. 3 (March 1868): 251.

63. "Editor's Book Table," *Harper's New Monthly Magazine* 39, no. 233 (October 1869): 770; see also "Review 1," *Universalist Quarterly and General Review*, 4 (January 1867): 130.

64. Berwick, "The Americans Who Laugh: 'Rev. Petroleum V. Nasby, P.M.,'" *Independent*, July 11, 1872.

65. "Library Table," *The Round Table: A Saturday Review of Politics, Finance, Literature, Society and Arts*, March 9, 1867.

66. Edwin P. Whipple, "American Literature," *Harper's New Monthly Magazine* 52, no. 310 (March 1876): 526.

67. Berwick, "The Americans Who Laugh."

68. "American Speech and Manners," *Milwaukee Daily Sentinel*, May 20, 1867.

69. See also "American Humorists and Satirists," *Every Saturday: A Journal of Choice Reading*, January 2, 1869, 20.

70. "Humor of the Billings School," *Saturday Evening Post* (Philadelphia), December 15, 1877, 4.

71. "Review 1," *The Old Guard*, May 1868, 396.

72. Jennette Tandy, *Crackerbox Philosophers in American Humor and Satire* (New York: Kennikat, 1925), 131; Frank Luther Mott, *American Journalism: A History of Newspapers in the United States through 260 Years, 1690 to 1950*, rev. ed. (New York: MacMillan, 1953), 393; Brom Weber "The Misspellers," in *The Comic Imagination in American Literature*, ed. Louis D. Rubin, Jr. (New Brunswick, NJ: Rutgers University Press, 1973), 132.

73. Harrison, *The Man Who Made Nasby*, 4.

74. Austin, *Petroleum V. Nasby*, 97; Jack Clifford Ransome, "David Ross Locke: Civil War Propagandist," *Northwest Ohio Quarterly* 20, no. 1 (1948): 18.

75. Alice Fahs, *The Imagined Civil War: Popular Literature of the North & South, 1861–1865* (Chapel Hill: University of North Carolina Press, 2001), 202–218.

76. See George C. Rable, *But There Was No Peace: The Role of Violence in the Politics of Reconstruction* (Athens: University of Georgia Press, 1984), 190–191.

77. Locke, *The Struggles (Social, Financial and Political) of Petroleum V. Nasby*, 624.

Reconstruction and Historical Allusion

T. ROBERT HART

I came here this Winter with certain fixed opinions, drawn from the study of history and human nature, so far as I understand it, as to the inevitable result of the struggle which agitates the country. The fate of Greece, Rome, the Florentine Republics, and France before me, colored the facts of daily occurrence.
   —*Charleston Mercury*, January 30, 1867

When ROBESPIERRE the tiger, and MARAT the wolf, surrounded by the wild beasts of Paris were lapping the best blood of France, they little thought that their own was to follow.
   —*Charleston Mercury*, March 16, 1868

W hen the Civil War ended, white southerners who had supported the Confederacy found themselves thinking back to the French Revolution and comparing themselves frequently to the plight of loyalists, who either fled or faced imprisonment, and sometimes the guillotine. In 1865 Confederates looked around at a bleak landscape punctuated by burned homes and barren fields. In turn, some white southerners headed to Brazil, Mexico, or the western territories, but most of them remained on their land and pondered the future with much anxiety. Under President Andrew Johnson's lenient Reconstruction only 10 percent of white males had to take an oath of loyalty, and southern states had to ratify the Thirteenth Amendment; by the end of the year, the old Confederate states had new constitutions and elected former Democrats to state and national office and passed the infamous Black Codes, which relegated freedmen to near slave status. White southerners also engaged in a violent campaign to instill fear in the black community and extend the brutality of the antebellum slave system. Gloom soon set in for these former rebels, however, when Republicans in Congress made it clear that they did not intend to reconcile with them so quickly. After refusing to seat the newly elected congressmen, Republicans passed civil rights legislation, established a committee to investigate conditions in the South, and extended the life of the Freedmen's Bureau. These measures hardly solved the South's problems, as most landowners remained intransigent over sharecropping contracts, and in the summer of 1866 racial violence broke out in Memphis and spread across the region. In southern Tennessee former Confederate officers formed the Ku Klux Klan.

Things reached a fevered pitch in 1867 when congressional Republicans responded by passing the Military Reconstruction Acts, dividing the South into five military districts to ensure fair elections and protection for freedmen. A year later, with Federal troops occupying the region, former southern states held elections that resulted in a large percentage of Republicans winning office. These newly elected Republicans represented a coalition of white northerners and southerners and African Americans, some of whom had been slaves. African Americans only made up a majority of the legislative body in South Carolina, and their numbers in southern legislatures scarcely reflected the black population. Nonetheless, white southerners recoiled in horror at being ruled over by freedmen. Common exaggerations like "the world turned upside down" and "bottom rail on top" became ubiquitous in describing the political and social revolution that seemed to be taking place. Very quickly, though, historical allusions became a formidable part of the white southern rhetorical arsenal. Though these allusions recalled a number of historical tragedies, Reconstruction was most often compared to the horrors of the French Revolution, especially the Reign of Terror. In doing so, former Confederates sought to deny the legitimacy of the new Reconstruction legislatures by likening them to the tragically failed political experiment in France. Ex-Confederates also hoped to establish their own legitimacy by drawing analogies between the southern aristocracy and the nobility of Europe, the rightful rulers of society. In this way, they bound themselves together in the emotional experience of defeat and subsequent occupation but also linked themselves to an imagined community of sufferers throughout history.[1]

Defiant white southerners employed a variety of allusions to relate their perceived oppression to historical events that they saw as analogous to their own situation. The Spanish Duke of Alva held a special place in this repertoire. As a Missouri resident noted during the last days of the war, "The light of civilization fades into darkness; the noblest and freest institutions go down in hopeless barbarism. . . . We are living in the times of the Duke of Alva." White southerners did not have to stretch their imaginations to find this analogy germane. During the 1560s, Philip II strengthened his control over the Spanish

Netherlands by disregarding traditional privileges of the nobility, levying new taxes to support the interests of the Crown, and repressing Calvinism. When Dutch aristocrats attempted to secede from the Spanish Empire, Philip sent an army under the Duke of Alva to crush the rebellion. In short order, the duke invaded the provinces, suppressed the revolt, and established the Council of Troubles, a special tribunal that summarily executed many leading Dutch aristocrats. One teenaged Georgia girl described an occupying Union general as "a cold-blooded villain who keeps his counsel, just like Alva of Old, when he had a new piece of cruelty to perpetrate against the Hollanders."[2]

In the same way, some southerners focused on Oliver Cromwell, invoking his military-style reign, destruction of traditional institutions, and execution of Charles I. After destroying the monarchy, Cromwell's forces brutally crushed revolts in Ireland and Scotland. In 1655, Cromwell dismissed Parliament and established a military dictatorship, dividing the country into eleven districts, each ruled by a military governor. Not surprisingly, many southerners likened the Military Reconstruction Acts to Cromwellian tyranny. In 1866, George Fitzhugh explained that "Radicals in power always become the most cruel Conservatives, like Cromwell and the Puritan Fathers." Indeed, Fitzhugh contrasted the Cromwellian North and Cavalier South: "The antecedents of the New England people (who rule the North with an iron rod)" were "fanatics, radicals, and destructive by inheritance, just the same people now as in the days of Cromwell's Independents, and of the witch-burners and Quaker hangers two centuries ago."[3]

These southerners also compared the partitioning of Poland to their own perceived partitioning at the hands of North. In a diatribe against Reconstruction policies, Ryland Randolph asserted that Radicals led by Charles Sumner threatened "to make a Poland of the South." Erstwhile plantations owners identified with the eastern European nobility's failed attempts to resist centralization, yet Poland's inability to develop a strong monarchy and a large standing army had left it vulnerable to its most powerful neighbors; Prussia, Russia, and Austria conquered and partitioned Poland in 1772, 1793, and 1795. The third division came as a result of a failed independence movement led by Thaddeus Kosciuszko. For southerners, Poland's plight was their own: brutal military suppression of a noble independence movement.[4]

The most frequent allusions, however, referenced the French Revolution. Southern letters, newspapers, and speeches resounded with the words "reign of terror," "Jacobin," and "Robespierre." One editorial described Reconstruction as "the story of the French Revolution over again. . . . Blood stained the daily rule of men who mouthing noble phrases about universal liberty, excited the population to the darkest and most vindictive deeds." The French Revolution provided the most apt comparison because it connected political and social upheaval. Diarists, editors, and politicians found there the means of expressing their own trauma and despair.[5]

Though the French Revolution was a movement for liberty, white southern intellectuals abhorred its destruction of traditional institutions and its radical egalitarianism. Modern conservatism originated, in part, as a response to the Revolution. Edmund Burke's *Reflections on the Revolution in France* constituted both a critique of the French assault on aristocracy and a defense of traditional institutions, organic society, and hierarchical social relationships. Antebellum southerners drew much of their inspiration and guidance from Burkean principles. Southern conservatism rested on several philosophical premises. Conservatives emphasized community over the individual. John C. Calhoun, George Fitzhugh, James Henry Hammond, and other political thinkers advocated an organic society in which individuals recognized and accepted their places. Furthermore, they expressed hostility toward the impersonal relations of free-market society and attacked the ills of capitalism and industrialization in the North. These intellectuals feared democracy and radical egalitarianism, tracing the roots of these problems to the French Enlightenment and Revolution. They blamed Voltaire, Diderot, and other philosophes for introducing atheism and agnosticism into Western thought and culture. Southern intellectuals particularly hated the Revolution of 1789 because it rested upon abstract reason. Unlike the American Revolution, which was waged to preserve the tradition of the English constitution, the French Revolution was nothing more than a social experiment rooted in fanatical theories. Antebellum southerners' vitriol concentrated especially on the French notions of liberty and equality that imperiled the social order. The most conservative of these southerners even condemned Thomas Jefferson for imbibing French ideals. In one writer's words, "Jefferson's republicanism meant the republicanism . . . of numerical force, mob violence, popular frenzy, and democratic licentiousness." The author drew a direct connection from Jefferson to the Republican Party (in the United States), which espoused the "revolutionary *doctrinaire* philosophy that took its rise in the Jacobin clubs of Paris, [and] received the baptism of blood in the orgies of the French Revolution."[6]

With the weight of such a position in the antebellum era, it is not surprising that white southerners looked to historical allusions associated with the French Revolution as soon as the Union army occupied their territory. Rose Greenhow compared her imprisonment to that of "poor Marie Antoinette." Arrested during the northern occupation of Maryland in 1861, she railed against the repression of "freedom of opinion," which she thought indicative of a "reign of terror." During the occupation of New Orleans in 1862, residents also found allusions to the French Reign of Terror relevant. Belle Boyd described her capture and imprisonment to the "impenetrable recesses of the Bastille." In *Martyrdom in Missouri,* the Reverend W. M. Leftwich employed the same historical allusions to depict the treatment of civilians at the hands of Federal troops. During the early part of the war, his state had been devastated by guerrilla warfare. By 1864, Radicals had gained the upper hand, disfranchised their opponents through the requirement of loyalty oaths, and elected as Governor Thomas Fletcher. Following this victory, Fletcher extended his power by barring southern sympathizers from serving as lawyers, teachers, or ministers. Moreover, his forces confiscated secessionists' property, including former church lands. For the Reverend Leftwich, these last measures were intolerable. In his book, Leftwich made frequent allusions to the confiscation by the National Convention when it passed the Civil Constitution of the Clergy Act, and to the persecution and murder of Catholic priests by the Committee of Public Safety during the radical phase of the French Revolution. Leftwich's work was strikingly similar to chapter 8 of Edmund Burke's *Reflections*, particularly in his cataloging of the "trials and persecutions of ministers of the gospel" at the hands of irresponsible mobs. Leftwich insisted that the martyrs in his state would join the annals of religious persecution alongside the victims in France. Describing the suspension of religious and civil liberties, Leftwich wrote that the "fearful reign of terror was upon all."[7]

In a similar way, white southerners' historical allusions focused on the ruthless crushing of loyalists in La Vendée during the French Revolution. This western department had been a stronghold of devout Catholics and monarchists. Following the capture of Louis XVI, Vendée attempted to declare its independence from the new French Republic. Radical leaders, however, stamped out the rebellion by drowning a number of the loyalists on weighted rafts. Rejecting the term "traitors," former Confederates believed themselves as innocent as when "la Vendee was deemed to have 'rebelled' against Republican

France." References to Vendée resonated with those white southerners who continued to maintain that secession was morally and legally justified.[8]

As the federal government implemented Reconstruction throughout the southern states, historical allusions followed. White southerners detested the replacement of their courts with military commissions. One diarist wrote that the Yankees "have already begun their reign of terror in Richmond, by arresting many of the prominent citizens." The former Confederates perceived such outrages as comparable to their own experiences. As one editor asked, "What language can be too forcible as applicable to the fate of a people, without protection for their inherent liberty?" During the final weeks of the war Emma LeConte echoed these sentiments, asking, "How can the terror and excitement of today be described?" The daughter of scientist Joseph LeConte, then teaching chemistry at South Carolina College, Emma listened intently to conversations between her father and his colleagues, witnessed the burning of Columbia, and described it eloquently in her diary. "The burning of Columbia," she wrote, "was the most diabolical act of the barbarous war." Women also filled their diaries and letters with castigations of the invading troops. These mothers, wives, daughters, and sisters poured out their hatred for Yankees. Eliza Francis Andrews described Sherman's troops as "miserable oppressors" and also compared the occupation of Richmond to the "reign of terror" in France. Rose Greenhow viewed oppression in her home state of Maryland as "vulgar military despotism." She found "no precedent in a civilized land, unless we seek a parallel in the confinement of the children in the Temple, in the beginning of the French Revolution."[9]

Ex-Confederates also applied these analogies to the perceived violence and crime they deemed caused by military occupation and emancipation. Conflicts between Federal troops and white southerners as well as race riots plagued the southern states, and again, conservative writers and diarists found allusions to the French Revolution suitable to describe their trauma. Before her tragic death Greenhow described the contemporary milieu as "violence and intolerance never witnessed before, save in the National Assembly of France during the Reign of Terror." These allusions portrayed white southerners as the helpless victims of radical misrule and reflected the growing fear of social disorder. Language comparing Yankees to the "vile miscreants" of the French Revolution grew increasingly shrill as white southerners determined to rid their region of the occupying force, which had "ensanguined the earth with the blood of men, women, and children." Writers alluded to the French Revolution even more frequently when depicting the results of emancipation, as freedom for African Americans represented whites' worst nightmares. Black suffrage placed former masters on the level of political equality with their ex-slaves. The sight of freedmen roaming the city streets and county roads symbolized for whites the chaos of Reconstruction and deterioration of the social order to which they had clung so fervently in the year following Appomattox. Many white southerners blamed the rise of crime on freedmen and accused them of rape. Former slaves in Union military uniforms proved unbearable for the former Confederates. Eliza Andrews wrote that she "would rather be skinned alive and eaten by wild beasts than beholden to them for such protection."[10]

In regard to the freemen, the most often repeated allusions during 1865 and 1866 pertained to the San Domingo slave revolt in 1791, which white southerners believed had been sparked by the egalitarian, revolutionary spirit of the Parisians. Toussaint L'Ouverture had been inspired, they argued, by the mob spirit of the French Revolution. As one southerner wrote, "The demons of the Jacobin Club in France, Danton, Marat and Robespierre, had encouraged the Haytien revolt and wholesale murders on that hitherto, peaceful, faithful, and happy island." Another declared that emancipation meant nothing less than "monstrosities approachable to those perpetrated by the Negroes of San Domingo, when, under the encouragement of the frenzied humanitarians of France, they rose against the white population . . . as if the fiends of hell . . . were let loose on earth." John Townsend associated "Black Republicanism" with the "beastly horrors of . . . St. Domingo . . . [and] the ghastly massacres of the French Revolution." References to San Domingo were not new; they had been common in attacks on abolitionist schemes before the Civil War. As William H. Holcombe explained, the antislavery sentiment of the "era was partly derived from the radical influence of the French Revolution, the mad frenzies of which the Fearful convulsion, the fanatics of the North may yet repeat." The "character of the present philanthropists," wrote one observer, "is exactly that of the French reformers, whose childish notions of liberty, in connection with the other things, brought on the Reign of Terror."[11]

Convinced that Radical Republicans were inciting freedmen to insurrection, whites in Memphis attacked blacks preemptively. In 1866, Albert Pike, a Memphis editor, turned rhetoric into reality by convincing many white citizens that an uprising lay seething beneath the surface. On April 29, a riot occurred when white policemen battled with black civilians and soldiers in the streets. The violence lasted several days and claimed more than 150 casualties. Referring to this racial violence, Pike wrote: "The dark and bloody scenes of the French Revolution remind us . . . of the untold evils and dire calamities which fall upon a people through disregard and contempt of organic law." The organization of Union leagues across the South in 1866 and 1867 offered further proof of a conspiracy and the reign of "mob spirit" associated with the French Revolution. Observing the parades of armed freedmen, white southerners perceived themselves in a "condition of political and social anarchy, and kept so at bayonet's point." They drew a direct correlation between the "extravagant doctrines of liberty and equality" and black conspiracies. "It is easy for the Black Republican theorist, in his comfortable New England home," they thought, because "he need not fear the torch [and] then knife . . . [associated with] the experience of San Domingo." The threat of Radical Reconstruction and black suffrage thus intensified images of the northern Jacobins implementing a sinister plot to reenact in the southern states "the scenes of San Domingo."[12]

By granting social and political equality to freedmen, the northern "Jacobin" party was unleashing the forces that had swept through France from 1789 to 1795. In a letter to a Richmond editor, one citizen noted that the current *"reign of terror"* had "as in the case of the French Revolution," deposed the ruling class by mob tyranny. As in France, the Jacobins of the North sought to supplant conservatism with fanaticism: "Jacobinism has infected ten states with poison of despotic power." As a southern woman wrote, "The truth is, the Black 'Republican' party is revolutionary and agrarian." The North, she contended, followed France in its "saturnalia to the Goddess of Liberty." In a lengthy examination of the "True Origins of the Convention Plot," Kendall Holbrook compared Congress to the National Convention, and he argued that it employed "poor, deluded, unsophisticated freedmen" to accomplish "its own revolutionary and incendiary plot." Following the race riot in New Orleans, the *Picayune* editor held Jacobinical Republicans responsible for the "whole nefarious plot to overturn the Government of the State." Albert Pike proposed that his paper would "furnish our readers with some means of judging the progress of Jacobinism in the North." He accused the Radicals of "reproducing all the follies that led to crimes, of French Jacobinism." White southerners argued that freed slaves, like peasants in France, were ill-suited for suffrage and fated to become mere puppets of the Jacobins. As the editor of the *Picayune* put it, "The Radical interest in the negro is the interest for a serviceable tool." Albert Pike believed that the Reconstruction Revolution would devastate the region because "negro suffrage would be like a putrid poison in all the veins of the commonwealth . . . a deadly miasma, penetrating everywhere and diseasing the whole body of the state."[13]

Historical allusions were often effective in undermining the political legitimacy of Reconstruction governments. The *Charleston Mercury* declared that "there is nothing new in the caucus rule of the Radicals. It is exactly the Jacobin Club transferred to Washington." As Linton Stephens told an Augusta crowd, "The revolutionary usurpers have an impudent habit of calling themselves 'legitimists,' and Democrats 'revolutionaries.'" New Orleans editor Kendall Holbrook attempted to define the term "Reign" for his readers: "It expresses power and domination without respect to right. Kings and Emperors reign by acquisition or succession. There has been a Reign of Terror, as there have been times when, in this country, order and law, and with them peace reigned." He concluded, "The ideas which now reign throughout the United States are of the class which exist in supremacy by virtue of fraudulent use of authority." The vitriolic and unreconstructed Albert Pike capitalized on this sentiment when he drew a direct "Parallel" for his readers: "What France was during that transition period immediately preceding the fearful carnival of blood, known in history as the Reign of Terror, such is the United States of America to-day." Dwelling on the gory, Pike continued: "What France became when the streets of her capital were slippery with gore, and the walls of her prison and her palaces reeked with the best blood of her citizens; when the neck of her whole people awaited with trembling expectation the stroke of the relentless guillotine, such must be the condition" of the South "under the rule of the faction in power."[14]

Some former Confederates had maintained hope of restoring the old regime, but the Military Reconstruction Acts dealt them a severe psychological blow. Military rule under the new acts convinced white southerners that harsh invectives, sometimes accompanied by violence, were necessary to break the chains of oppression. Bristling with anger, Benjamin Hill of Georgia urged a LaGrange crowd to resist these "assassins of liberty" by any means necessary. In Albert Pike's view, marshal law recapitulated "the darkest days of the French Revolution, when France was reeling drunk with blood." Being governed by the "will of a Commanding General" conjured up images of the Committee of Public Safety. This Republican attack on their civil liberties represented the "excesses of the French Revolution." The *Charleston Mercury* offered South Carolinians some solace, suggesting that a Napoleon would overthrow the Radicals. Andrew Johnson's impeachment further demonstrated the "revolutionary" nature of Congress. Though southerners generally disliked the president's policy, they realized that it was a moderate alternative to the Radical plan. For them, the impeachment hearings completed the Radical Republicans' usurpation of executive power. Editors likened this "new stride of Jacobinism" to the National Convention's trial of Louis XVI. Pike proved the most ardent defender of Johnson, noting that "the Jacobin Chiefs are about to depose the President, and will then turn the rage of the Mountain against the Supreme Court. A Jacobin club legislates in the bosom of Congress."[15]

Certain Radical Republicans were subjected to attacks. Editors compared Benjamin Butler, Thaddeus Stevens, and Charles Sumner to Danton, Robespierre, and Couthon. The names were used interchangeably, and they evoked the same images of the Committee of Public Safety and the Reign of Terror. Southerners found remarkable similarity between speeches given by Republican leaders, which they thought must have been "borrowed from the Jacobins in France." Robert Barnwell Rhett of South Carolina proclaimed that "the STEVENSES—the SUMNERS—the BUTLERS" were "in France when it was drenched in gore." No single congressional figure incurred the wrath of the southern press more than Thaddeus Stevens. A leading abolitionist before the Civil War, he continuously waved the bloody shirt in the postwar era. In the minds of white southerners, the Republican House leader symbolized the radicalism of Reconstruction policy and the futility of reconciliation. Together with Wade and Sumner, Stevens created a blueprint for the Military Plan. A firm believer in the expansion of government power, he proposed a plan that would confiscate former Confederates' lands and redistribute them to freedmen. White southerners saw Stevens as Robespierre reincarnate, and they argued that he held a firm grip on "the reign of terror in Washington." One southern editorial argued that neither "a Conservative President nor an upright Supreme Bench of Magistrates . . . can stand for a moment in the way of the raging sea of popular opinion" manipulated by the "hateful exaggerations of MARAT, COUTHON, and THADDEUS STEVENS." "Such is the American Robespierre," an editor announced, "whose unhappy destiny it is to reproduce in this country the sanguinary horrors of the French Revolution." Some southerners found the comparison to Couthon, a leading figure on the Committee of Public Safety, more apt than to the incorruptible Robespierre. As another writer claimed, "We know of no base character in history whom he so much resembles, as COUTHON, the club-footed demagogue, whose voice was always for murder."[16]

This kind of language when focused on the local level tended to violence, exacerbating a preservative campaign of violence that began in the waning days of the Civil War. Ryland Randolph epitomized this process. Arriving in Tuscaloosa in 1867, this newspaper publisher made the destruction of Reconstruction his primary goal. Randolph soon became a leading figure in the Ku Klux Klan and an outspoken opponent of Jacobinism and "Negrophilia." In 1868, he was arrested by a "Revolutionary Tribunal" in Selma for assaulting a black man. After being tried and acquitted, he continued to advocate violence against freedmen, "carpetbaggers," "scalawags," and "miscegenators." When the Republican state legislature appointed new professors and trustees at the University of Alabama, Randolph charged that the action symbolized the vilest form of Jacobinism and would inaugurate a "Reign of Terror" in Tuscaloosa. Randolph exemplified the link between the political rhetoric of 1866 and 1867 and the counterrevolutionary violence in 1868 and afterward. In his paper, he called on the Ku Klux Klan to vindicate the South and kill the Jacobins in their midst. He printed a letter to the editor warning Radical Republicans that "like the leaders of the French Revolution, they have gone too far in advance of their party, and will fall victim to the returning tide of conservatism." As violence in Alabama swelled, Randolph exhorted white males to join the "war against Black Republicanism—which is more diabolical in its inception, and more radical and revolutionary in its results, than the Red-Republicanism of France." Moreover, Randolph argued that "white men of Tuskaloosa county [are] bound together as one family." Only by creating a sense of unity through rhetoric and violence could they "avert these evils, and save the South from becoming worse than Jamaica or San Domingo."[17]

The use of historical allusion by editors like Randolph enabled white southerners to make sense of their subjugation and deny the legitimacy of the politicians in power. As George Rable recently noted in *Damn Yankees!,* southerners had a rich history of demonizing their northern brethren as morally and culturally bankrupt infidels. During the war, "leading Confederates recognized the usefulness of trumpeting and exaggerating enemy savagery" because it "reassured wavering Confederates of their own rectitude." Defeat and subjugation only intensified white southern animosity. When they branded the Radical Republicans as "Revolutionary Jacobins," they created a language that adapted key words and phrases such as "Robespierre" and "Reign of Terror" to their own situation. Denying legitimacy was a necessary step for a successful counterrevolution if white southerners were to be successful in overthrowing Reconstruction governments, and by 1876 they had done just that, restoring white

T. Robert Hart

supremacy or "redeeming the South" from radicalism. Violence and infighting within the national Republican Party ultimately influenced the fall of Reconstruction. It would be hard to discount, however, the importance of language in stirring emotion. The focus on the French Revolution evoked passions and determined political responses, and though eventually white Democrats returned to power, the language of trauma expressed through historical allusion brought them solace. They also shared in the suffering of noble causes in the past and in so doing created a theme in the developing Lost Cause culture of the late nineteenth century, one of tragedy and victimhood.[18]

Notes

1. These historical allusions were used most commonly by the educated southern elite, a demographic steeped in history and the classics. This does not mean that these allusions had no impact on non-elites, as newspaper circulation (and the voice of editors) rebounded during Reconstruction. On newspapers, see E. Merton Coulter, *The South during Reconstruction, 1865–1877* (Baton Rouge: Louisiana State University Press, 1947), 284–290; Clement Eaton, *Freedom of Thought in the Old South* (New York: Harper Torchbooks, 1964); and Hodding Carter, *Their Words Were Bullets: The Southern Press in War, Reconstruction, and Peace* (Athens: University of Georgia Press, 1969). See also George C. Rable, "Bourbonism, Reconstruction, and the Persistence of Southern Distinctiveness," *Civil War History* 29, no. 2 (June 1983): 135–153.

2. William M. Leftwich, *Martyrdom in Missouri* (St. Louis: S. W. Book and Publishing, 1870), 349–350; Eliza Andrews, *The War-Time Diary of a Georgia Girl, 1864–1865*, ed. Spencer Bidwell King (Atlanta: Cherokee, 1976), 356; Geoffrey Parker, *The Army of Flanders and the Spanish Road, 1567–1659: The Logistics of Spanish Victory and Defeat in the Low Countries' Wars* (Cambridge: Cambridge University Press, 1995). For a similar allusion, see *Charleston Mercury*, February 8, 1866.

3. *Debow's Review*, December 1866.

4. *Tuscaloosa Independent Monitor*, November 17, 1868; Norman Davies, *Heart of Europe: The Past in Poland's Present* (Oxford: Oxford University Press, 2001); *Charleston Daily Courier*, February 11, 1867; *Memphis Daily Appeal*, March 28, 1868; Alexander H. Stephens, *The Reviewers Reviewed: A Supplement to the "War between the States"* (New York: D. Appleton, 1872), 232, 244.

5. *Memphis Daily Appeal*, February 1, 1867.

6. Edmund Burke, *Reflections on the Revolution in France* (London: Penguin Books, 1969); Eugene D. Genovese, *The Southern Tradition: The Achievement and Limitations of an American Conservatism* (Cambridge, MA: Harvard University Press, 1994), 10–40; Jeffrey L. Zvengrowski, "'They Stood Like the Old Guard of Napoleon': Jefferson Davis and the Pro-Bonaparte Democrats, 1815–1870" (PhD diss., University of Virginia, 2015); *Debow's Review*, February 1861. On Burke's influence in the postwar era see Richard Taylor, *Destruction and Reconstruction: Personal Experiences of the Late War* (New York: D. Appleton, 1883), 331; *Charleston Mercury*, March 27, 1868.

7. Rose O'Neal Greenhow, *My Imprisonment and the First Year of Abolition Rule at Washington* (London: Richard Bentley, 1863), 28–29, 119; Belle Boyd, *Belle Boyd in Camp and Prison*, ed. Cur-

234

tis Carroll Davis (New York: Thomas Yoseloff, 1968), 190; Leftwich, *Martyrdom in Missouri*, 280, 284, 139.

8. *Memphis Daily Appeal*, March 28, 1868.

9. *Memphis Daily Appeal*, November 15, 1865; Andrews, *War-Time Diary*, 188, 203; *Charleston Daily Courier*, February 21, 1867; Emma LeConte, *When the World Ended: The Wartime Diary of Emma LeConte*, ed. Earl Schenck Miers (New York: Oxford University Press, 1957), 32, 67, 91; Greenhow, *My Imprisonment*, 3, 244.

10. LeConte, *When the War Ended*, 6–24; George C. Rable, *But There Was No Peace: The Role of Violence in the Politics of Reconstruction* (Athens: University of Georgia Press, 1984), 1–15; Greenhow, *My Imprisonment*, 184; *Memphis Daily Appeal*, November 14, 1865; Andrews, *War-Time Diary*, 213; see also John Hammond Moore, ed., *The Juhl Letters to the Charleston Courier* (Athens: University of Georgia Press, 1974), 39–40; and James L. Roark, *Masters without Slaves: Southern Planters in the Civil War and Reconstruction* (New York: W. W. Norton, 1977), 111–209.

11. *Debow's Review*, November 1867; Rable, *But There Was No Peace*, 62; *Southern Literary Messenger*, February 1861; *Debow's Review*, July 1860; John Townshend, *The Doom of Slavery in the Union* (Charleston: Evans and Cogswell, 1860), 8; *Debow's Review*, July 1860.

12. *Memphis Daily Appeal*, November 8, 14, 22, 1865, May 3, 1866, June 1, 20, 1868; *New Orleans Picayune*, October 9, 1866; *Richmond Dispatch*, February 23, 1867.

13. *Richmond Dispatch*, February 5, 1867; *Memphis Daily Appeal*, February 2, 1867, March 21, 1867, June 1, 1868; Greenhow, *My Imprisonment*, 44, 336, 349; *New Orleans Picayune*, August 1, 1866, April 22, 1868.

14. *Charleston Mercury*, December 22, 1866; Stephens, *Reviewers Reviewed*, 250; *New Orleans Picayune*, March 26, 1868; *Memphis Daily Appeal*, January 13, 1867.

15. *Memphis Daily Appeal*, April 12, 1867, April 4, 1868, June 2, 1868; *Charleston Mercury*, January 29, 1867, and see March 29, April 1, and May 22, 1867, for good examples. For the role of violence see Rable, *But There Was No Peace*, 58–80; Allen W. Trelease, *White Terror: The Ku Klux Klan Conspiracy and Southern Reconstruction* (New York: Harper and Row, 1971) 3–27.

16. *New Orleans Picayune*, April 2, 12 1868; *Charleston Mercury*, December 22, 1866, March 14, 1868 (Rhett delivered a harsh invective against Wendell Phillips on January 10, 1867); Eric Foner, *Reconstruction: America's Unfinished Revolution, 1863–1877* (New York: Harper and Row, 1988), 228–281; *Memphis Daily Appeal*, February 1, 8, 13, 1867; *Richmond Enquirer*, February 20, 1867; *Charleston Mercury*, January 21, February 11, 1867. Also see Taylor, *Destruction and Reconstruction*, 319 and Alexander H. Stephens, *A Constitutional View of the Late War Between the States: Its Causes, Character, Conduct and Results* (Atlanta: National, 1868), 713.

17. Trelease, *White Terror*, 84–88, 252–260; *Tuscaloosa Independent Monitor*, October 6, November 10, 24, December 1, 1867. The *Charleston Mercury* defended Randolph—see April 22, 1868.

18. George C. Rable, *Damn Yankees! Demonization and Defiance in the Confederate South* (Baton Rouge: Louisiana State University Press, 2015), 61, 81.

Sherman and Grant

Different Men and Different Memoirs

JOHN F. MARSZALEK

During the Civil War, Ulysses S. Grant and William Tecumseh Sherman were as close as two men could be, each full of admiration for the other. Immediately after the war, this friendship continued, Grant serving as the commanding general of the US Army, and Sherman as head of the Military Division of the Missouri. During that time, Grant often complained to Sherman, one of his subordinates, about how the secretary of war was usurping authority from him. Yet when he became president and Sherman became the commanding general, Grant took the side of his secretary of war and did nothing to keep his friend from being ignored. Sherman was furious at what he considered to be a betrayal. He broke his relationship with the man he had admired for so long.[1]

Sherman then grew increasingly distant from Grant, and several secretaries of war made sure he understood that they had greater influence in the running of the army than he did. He grew so angry that he left Washington and moved to St. Louis in October of 1874. He was still officially commanding general, but he wanted to have nothing to do with the politicians in Washington, even Grant. So he left the capitol.

Living in St. Louis, Sherman realized that he had more time to himself than he had ever had since before the Civil War. At the same time, he worried about what the nation would remember about the meaning of that war and his role in it. He watched the increasing growth of what later would be called the "Lost Cause," and he worried that his significant place in the conflict would be forgotten. Former Confederate officers were writing essays about the war, and they were insisting that, while their side might have lost, they and their cause represented honor and virtue. The Union side, conversely, consisted of nothing more than the raw power of greater numbers. Increasingly, too, Sherman saw himself being viewed as the epitome of Yankee evil.[2]

Something had to be done. Earlier in the 1870s, when he had gone on his world tour, Sherman had met historian George Bancroft, then US minister to the new nation of Germany. Bancroft had urged the traveling general to write about the war, touching a particularly tender nerve in Sherman's psyche, when he warned him that, if he did not tell his story, others would, and they would publish untruths. The reputation of the real heroes would be lost; the traitors would receive unmerited remembrance.[3]

And so Sherman, who was already leaning in that literary direction, put pen to paper and began writing, emphasizing his central role in the war and reminding his readers that some other war participants were not as significant. By May 1875, the two-volume Sherman memoirs were on the market: blue book covers with gold lettering, 24 chapters, 814 pages in all. The last 17 chapters dealt exclusively with the Civil War.[4]

As he considered publication, Sherman tried to drive a hard financial bargain. He composed a three-year contract, which attempted to make sure that he owned the text. He bought the printing plates, so his publisher, D. Appleton and Company, could not print any books without his permission. The price for the two volumes was established at $5.50, with Sherman to earn a profit of forty cents per set, or 7 1/4 percent.[5]

The book was an immediate success, selling ten thousand sets within the first month. In 1885, about the time that Grant's memoirs appeared, Sherman printed a second edition, and in 1891, he had Mark Twain's Charles L. Webster Company, Grant's 1886 publisher, print another second edition. There is a belief that Sherman made $25,000 in all, but no one is sure if this is an accurate royalty figure. Sherman himself often said that he did not make much money on his writing, but his youngest son, P. Tecumseh Sherman, insisted that his father had turned a hefty profit. If he had, there is no record to sustain that premise.[6]

It is well known, however, that Sherman's publication, which was one of the first Civil War memoirs to be published, created an enormous stir when it first reached print. Reviews appeared in newspapers and magazines all over the nation, some written by individuals mentioned in the memoirs. *Galaxy* magazine in October 1875 concluded in an extended review "that his military deeds, while in the main highly beneficial to the country, have not been marked by the exhibition of the lofty attributes of a great captain." While the writing style was often "remarkably terse, clear, energetic, and flowing ... in many instances ... it is inexcusably profane, sometimes indelicate, and occasionally inapplicable or badly told," the unnamed reviewer said. Sherman was also guilty, the review insisted, of "unjust censure and criticism of man," but no contrary indications of "praise of successes and good qualities."[7]

This was the crux of the argument against Sherman's memoirs. He was accused of being overly critical of other generals, Union and Confederate, and of making little effort to say favorable things about those who deserved such praise. One of his generals, Alpheus S. Williams, who was already angry at Sherman for not giving him command of the 20th Corps during the Civil War, expressed a commonly held criticism about the memoirs. "There is one peculiarity that runs through Sherman's *Memoirs:* he did it all himself." In fact, Williams said, Sherman seemed to be saying that he believed that "not a division relieved its picket guard without a suggestion from the General-in-Chief."[8]

Yet there were also favorable comments in the popular magazines of that day and in the era's newspapers. Most significant was the fact that some favorable comments even came from the southern press. Traditionally, but not accurately, people have believed that the southern media universally condemned Sherman, remembering his destructive war. In fact, some members of the southern press exhibited solid support. For example, the *Louisiana State Register* on June 12, 1875, could not have been more approving: "We believe that Sherman has done a good thing by publishing the memoirs. He has raised a dust in many localities, but he has told the truth, for he is neither a liar, nor a coward, and if he has touched some people in a tender spot, they deserve it, and the row they are trying to raise about him, can have no effect on his record, or his fame." Yet at other times southerners were also merciless in their criticism. A Confederate veteran from Kentucky concluded, "He writes like a crazy man."[9]

A northern newspaper, in upstate New York, some three years after the publication of the memoirs, best expressed the attitude of those who supported Sherman's effort: "There is no notable discrepancy between the quality of General Sherman's writing and fighting. He is as dexterous and trenchant with the pen as with the sword."[10]

In fact, however, the general attitude toward Sherman's memoirs was one of dispute and disagreement, especially among those who found his prose insulting to so many people. Union generals Fighting Joe Hooker and John A. McClernand accused Sherman of bringing war disputes into the postwar period. Montgomery Blair thought Sherman was completely unfair to his brother, General Frank Blair. John A. Logan and his adoring wife found Sherman insulting to him, and they never forgave him for his wartime and memoirs treatment. Northern reporter Franc B. Wilke thought Sherman was too critical of the press, and others joined in the condemnation for a variety of other reasons. The general with whom Sherman battled the most was William "Sooy" Smith; Sherman castigated Smith mercilessly over his failure to reach Meridian in 1864.[11]

It was Henry Van Ness Boynton, an officer in the Union Army of the Cumberland, under George H. Thomas, and at that time a reporter for the *Cincinnati Gazette*, who most harshly condemned Sherman. Boynton believed that the general had not given adequate praise to the reporter's old army or its commander. To make sure that no one missed his criticism, Boynton named his 276-page, 20-chapter book *Sherman's Historical Raid: The Memoirs in the Light of the Record.*[12] He published it in 1875, the same year that Sherman's two volumes came out, and he made the cover blue with gold lettering, so that it looked just like the Sherman volumes. This way, he said, readers could put his accurate volume on their bookshelves right next to Sherman's error-filled memoirs.

Being both a reporter and an officer in the Army of the Cumberland, Boynton did not like Sherman to begin with. He pulled no punches throughout the book in criticizing Sherman's statements about the war or his evaluation of individuals in that conflict. In the introduction, for example, he said that his aim was "to furnish the future historian with facts which will guard him against perpetuating the error and the injustice which pervade both volumes of the work."[13]

As he wrote, Boynton intensified his criticism. He insisted that in his memoirs Sherman does "cruel injustice to whole armies" and "the harmless vanity of the successful general becomes the gigantic wrong of the false historian."[14] Repeatedly he insisted that he was only comparing Sherman's words to official documents in the War Department in order to present the truth about both the living and the dead.

Boynton at times could be brutal. The final chapter, containing five blistering pages, he entitled "Conclusion—The Case against the Memoirs Summed Up." Here he wrote that Sherman insisted that there was no surprise at Shiloh, but "the records prove it to have been complete, and due mainly to his own blindness and neglect." "While he contends that the failure to bring Johnston to battle at Resaca, was due to the timidity of General McPherson, the records show that this officer acted exactly in accordance with Sherman's own orders." Sherman was wrong, Boynton said, about Chattanooga, Kennesaw, Atlanta, and every other issue discussed in the memoirs. Finally, when it came to the negotiations with Joseph E. Johnston, at the end of the war, "he ended by surrendering to Johnston upon terms drawn up by a member of the rebel Cabinet," Boynton insisted.[15]

At first, Sherman did not react to Boynton's attack, but he simply could not allow a hated reporter, one of those individuals who had tried to bring him down during the war, to accomplish that feat ten years later. He mounted a strong rebuttal to Boynton. He had many of his military friends speak up for him in reviews, articles, and letters, but the major reaction went beyond that. Sherman got his brother-in-law, an experienced newsman, Charles W. Moulton, to work with him to write a rebuttal, and he provided funds for publication himself. Like Boynton, Moulton used a suggestive title: *The Review of General Sherman's Memoirs Examined, Chiefly in the Light of Its Own Evidence*.[16] Simultaneously, Sherman hired one of his former biographers, Samuel M. Bowman, to work with Henry Hitchcock, a former staff member, to prepare another edition of the memoirs. This never reached fruition, however, and over time, the war of words faded away.[17]

During all this rough-and-tumble debate, a key figure remained silent. The president of the United States and preeminent Civil War military hero Ulysses S. Grant said nothing about Sherman's memoirs. Sherman thus grew increasingly worried that Grant was keeping quiet because he agreed with the critics. Sherman and Grant were having little contact with each other at this time, and this also worried Sherman. Fortunately, however, he was able to talk to Grant at the 1875 annual meeting of the Army of the Cumberland. During their conversation and in a later letter, Grant told Sherman that he had read the memoirs and had no major criticisms. He only wished that Sherman had not been so hard on some of their fellow generals: "I do not believe a more correct 'Memoirs' can be given of the events recorded by you." With Grant on his side, Sherman did not have to fear Boynton or anyone else. He clearly felt relieved.[18]

This did not end the controversy, however. In 1880, the *Cleveland Leader* published an interview, and it was clear that Sherman had not gotten over his anger at Boynton. Sherman told the Ohio newspaper: "You could hire him to do anything for money. Why for a thousand dollars he would slander his own mother."[19] Boynton quickly wrote to Sherman and suggested that the general must have been misquoted. Sherman refused to budge. He meant every word he had ever said about Boynton, he insisted.

This exchange reopened the controversy. Boynton called on the War Department to court-martial Sherman for conduct unbecoming an officer, and Sherman responded that the department should institute civil action against Boynton. When the War Department insisted that it had no jurisdiction in civil matters, Boynton thought he was free. Instead, Sherman said that Boynton's refusal to proceed any further demonstrated he had always been wrong in the dispute. Even years later, in 1887, Sherman referred to Boynton as that "yellow cur."[20]

Satisfied that he had vanquished Boynton, Sherman decided to get Moulton to revise the 1875 edition of the memoirs. He added a new chapter on his early life and another on his later years. In two appendices, he included some of the critical letters he had received. In general, however, this new edition was not all that different from his first one. The fifty or so changes he made were minor, and he insisted: "Of omissions there are plenty, but of willful perversion of facts, none." Then he delayed going into print. He wanted Grant to publish his memoirs first.[21]

Despite all such controversy, all the heartache, and all the concern about how Grant would react, Sherman did not view his writings as the leading memoirs of those years. That honor, he said, belonged to Grant. "Grant's book will, of course, survive all time."[22] Sherman believed that just as was the case in the Civil War, when he was second to Grant among the most important figures of that conflict, so too were his memoirs secondary to Grant's. There could be no argument about that.

While Sherman wrote his volumes in the 1870s, Ulysses S. Grant wrote his memoirs during a different decade, under completely different circumstances. As a result, his volumes received a far different reception than did the writings of Sherman. The two men had always been different, both in their appearance and attitude, and thus their memoirs were clearly different, too.

Grant had experienced obvious success from the beginning of the war onward, so he saw no reason to do any writing. Unlike Sherman, he did not believe he should be the savior of the nation again. After all, he had saved the Union once already.

Throughout his life, Sherman seemed to need repeated affirmation, while Grant seemed to receive it regularly. His wife and children idolized him, while Sherman's wife never seemed happy with him, particularly with his lack of Catholicism.[23] All that Grant seemed to lack was money. Many of his friends were millionaires, and it sometimes bothered him that he was not.

People had been after Grant for many years to write his remembrances, but he had always ignored their interest and refused their offers. He did not believe he knew how to write and, besides, he had nothing to say about the Civil War that his friend Adam Badeau had not already said in his three-volume history.[24]

In the 1880s, *Century Magazine* began a Civil War series, "Battles and Leaders of the Civil War," and called on military leaders from both sides to tell their war stories. Some did so willingly, including Sherman, but Grant refused. He was living comfortably, and there was no reason to take on something he did not think he would enjoy.[25] He, his wife, and family were living a life of ease with his sons, Fred, Buck, and Jesse employed well, and his daughter, Nellie, married to the son of a British parliamentarian.

Buck Grant seemed particularly successful, partnering with Ferdinand Ward, considered one of the living financial experts on Wall Street. When Buck approached his father about joining Ward's firm, the senior Grant was intrigued with the idea. He had always wanted to be as wealthy as some of his friends were, and this might be his chance. He readily agreed to the offer, and soon he was making trips to the Grant and Ward offices to sign a paper here and there. It was not hard work at all, and the money just kept rolling in. Grant believed, as did so many others, that Ward was indeed the wizard of Wall Street.[26]

It turned out that Ward was no financial genius; he was a charlatan. He used a Ponzi scheme in which he paid his customers dividends based not on investment earnings but on recurring contributions. Even though Grant's name was in the company title, Ward cheated him too. Making matters even worse for the former president was the fact that he had been so pleased with the earnings on his investments that he had placed all his money into the company and encouraged family and friends to do the same. The firm came tumbling down on May 4, 1884, and with it fell Ulysses S. Grant, his family, and many friends. Having thought that he was financially secure, he suddenly owned only what was left in his wallet and in his wife's purse. Grant lost his money and his reputation. He looked like a financial babe in the woods who had allowed a charlatan to fleece him.

Grant's life now changed radically. Even though he had always refused to write any articles for *Century Magazine*'s Civil War series, he now had no choice. He agreed to write four articles at $500 per article: one each on Shiloh, Vicksburg, Chattanooga, and Appomattox (later on the Wilderness instead).[27] He needed the money to take care of the financial needs of his beloved wife, Julia.

At the same time that all this was happening and *Century* had also offered Grant a contract to write his memoirs, an individual who was already a friend arrived to influence Grant's thinking. Samuel L. Clemens, "Mark Twain," had heard rumors about Grant signing a contract with *Century*, so he rushed over to the Grant home. He learned, to his shock, that *Century* was offering Grant a royalty of only 10 percent. In his inimitable style, Clemens said that was outrageous. Why, he thundered, "They would have offered [that much] to any unknown Comanche Indian."[28]

While he was advising Grant, Clemens was also completing his monumental book *The Adventures of Huckleberry Finn*.[29] Not trusting publishers, he and his brother-in-law had founded their own publishing establishment, Charles L. Webster and Company. Clemens and Webster offered Grant a choice of a royalty of 20 percent of gross sales or 70 percent of the net. Grant thought he owed it to *Century* to publish with the magazine, but Clemens kept insisting that Grant would be better off if he published with his company. In the end, on February 27, 1885, Grant went with Clemens and took the 70 percent royalty in order to share the risk with his friend. Century Publishers were taken aback, but they could hardly attack a war hero like Grant, and, besides, he was prepared to complete the four contracted articles.[30]

Thus Grant committed himself to do something he thought he would never do: write his life story. He had to have considered the enormous problems he faced. First, on Christmas Eve 1883, he accidentally fell and damaged his left leg, an injury from which he never recovered. Then he learned that he was dying from cancer, which began with a sharp throat pain in May 1884. Consequently, he had to take narcotics to try to ease the pain, and this regimen made him feel groggy. Additionally he had to have several teeth removed because the medical science of his day worried that these teeth were diseased and were causing some of his problems. He also suffered from his long-recurring migraine headaches, he had practically no experience in writing, and his financial loss from the failure of Grant and Ward was devastating. However, he was determined to write. He had to leave his wife, Julia, with funds to live her life. Otherwise, once he died, she would be in poverty. The sick, financially destitute, literary neophyte had an enormous task before him, but he was determined to do it.

Besides all these difficulties, Grant's first *Century Magazine* writing experience had not gone well. When he had submitted the draft of his first article, in the spring of 1884, the magazine's editors were shocked at how bad it was. It read like a military battle report. One of the editors went to see Grant and explained his need to write the way he talked to friends. Grant took the advice, and his revision was much better.[31] Yet it was one thing to write an article, but how was anyone to know if Grant could write an entire book, especially since he had so many physical problems?

In truth, as he had functioned during the war, he would not turn back. Most individuals could not have carried on such work under the horrible health conditions Grant faced. He could. He made himself sit in his New York home office and dictate when he could, or write when his voice was gone. No matter how he felt, he wrote from five to seven hours a day. His oldest son, Fred, Adam Badeau, and others hovered around him to check facts or aid in any way they could. But it was mostly on his shoulders. He could taste death in his mouth, but he would not quit until the manuscript was complete.[32]

On June 16, 1885, as the weather grew increasingly hot and humid in New York City, he had himself moved to a friend's summer home on cooler Mount McGregor, near Saratoga, New York. This move brought him but little peace, however. He was the famous General Grant, and visitors kept coming to pay their respects, no matter the agony he was suffering in his throat and his determination to keep writing.[33]

His illness, and the cocaine doctors used to try to help him, resulted in the text becoming less literarily coherent the further along he went into the memoirs. But he kept writing. Sadly, in May 1885, he had to fire Adam Badeau, who erroneously and harshly insisted in public that he, not Grant, was the author of the memoirs and should get paid a great deal more than his salary.[34] In truth, Grant did the work himself. The memoirs were the result of his effort and battle against enormous odds.

Finally, on July 16, 1885, Grant decided that he had said all there was to say. He asked to be put to bed, so one was moved into the main room on the first floor of the house on Mount McGregor. There, surrounded by Julia, his children, grandchildren, several doctors, and his African American servant, Harrison Tyrell, he died at 8:08 a.m. on July 23, 1885. His son Fred stopped the mantel clock at the precise time his father breathed his last.[35]

The Personal Memoirs of U. S. Grant became an even greater success than Sherman's volumes. Clemens cleverly used former Union soldiers, many of whom had fought for Grant, as traveling agents to sell the two-volume set throughout the nation. The idea was that Grant's memoirs were to be placed in every Union-loving home, right next to the Bible. The memoirs were specifically made to be attractive. Most books, even today, are single-spaced; Grant's memoirs were double-spaced and thus easy on the eyes. There were maps throughout the text, but these were not as clear as was the written word. The cost of the memoirs to buyers was high. A two-volume set sold for seven dollars, while the leather edition cost an astounding twenty-five dollars.[36]

The volumes were eagerly purchased; over 300,000 of the two-volume set were sold. In February 1886, just half a year after Grant died, Charles L. Webster and Company sent Julia a check for $200,000, at that time the largest royalty check ever written. Over time, Julia received a total of between $420,000 and $450,000, today about $11 million.[37]

The reviews were generally favorable. The *Independence, Devoted to the Consideration of Politics, Social and Economic* insisted: "In its clearness, frank, and blunt honesty, to its command of military details, plans, and movements, it is a book to read with confidence and enthusiasm." While the *Spectator* found problems of style, it praised what these memoirs showed about Grant. "General Grant stands revealed here as a plain, unpretending, in all respects democratic and even plebian man . . . full of that unconscious stoicism of which the most lovable heroes are made." Former Confederates were not always as impressed, however. An issue of the *Southern Historical Society Papers* concluded its review of the memoirs by insisting on how "utterly unreliable and untrustworthy it is alike in its statement of events, and its expression of opinions whether about military or civil matters."[38]

As time went on, however, the Grant memoirs grew in stature and, even more importantly, in readership among Civil War scholars and buffs. Because he died before his memoirs appeared in print, Grant never had a chance to publish another edition, as Sherman did. His son Fred published a briefly annotated edition in 1895, and over the years, one after another reprint was published, each using Grant's writings and adding only new introductions.[39] But new editions never appeared.

The memoirs of William T. Sherman and Ulysses S. Grant were, like the two men, importantly different. Yet they were among the earliest such pieces of literature, and they have continued to influence Civil War scholarship ever since. Sherman admitted that Grant's writing was the best post–Civil War memoir, and a variety of literary figures, then and later, have recognized the superiority of Grant's work. They have noted his calm, evenhanded treatment, the determined drive to get it completed, despite the horror of his cancer, and the love for his wife that such determination demonstrated. Grant began writing his memoirs unwillingly, but once he began the task, he came to enjoy writing and recognized that he had important things to say about the Civil War.

Perhaps the best description of the difference between Sherman's and Grant's memoirs was expressed by W. F. G. Shanks, a reporter. Watching the two men smoking, he said that Grant enjoyed "tobacco as the Chinese do opium," while Sherman puffed away "as if it were a duty to finish in the shortest imaginable time."[40] Grant indeed displayed his personality and wrote calmly, while Sherman exhibited his personality through the feverish pace he set for his prose. Grant tried to persuade; Sherman insisted that his readers recognize his importance and agree with his insights. Grant could be critical, but he did it in an almost offhanded way. Sherman bluntly defended his actions and attacked those Civil War personalities he believed needed to be criticized. He carefully included long Civil War letters to buttress his arguments, while Grant only rarely cited correspondence. He did not feel as strongly as Sherman did that he had to prove anything.

Another major difference between the Sherman and Grant memoirs was that Sherman's were published first, and he willingly wrote them. On the other hand, Grant did not write his remembrances until some twenty years after the war. Then Grant only wrote because he needed the money to ward off bankruptcy. Sherman battled anyone and everyone who criticized his work and then published another edition eleven years later to try to mollify the many who were critical of his statements. He published his second edition with D. Appleton and Company in 1886 but then in 1891 he put out another second edition, this time with Samuel Clemens's Charles L. Webster and Company. He wanted his book to be linked with Grant's, as he had once been linked with him during the Civil War.[41] Considering the mostly favorable reception Grant's memoirs received, it seems doubtful that, had he lived, he would ever have issued a new edition like Sherman did.

Grant's publication was, by far, a bigger seller than Sherman's. It is known that Grant made a great deal of money on his memoirs, while Sherman almost certainly earned little. Grant's percentage was high, while Sherman's was low. Yet the two memoirs have both passed the test of time. Neither has ever been out of print, and both are routinely utilized in the study of the Civil War.

Despite the generally favorable reception both memoirs have enjoyed, neither man has escaped criticism for his efforts. In recent times, amateur historian Joseph A. Rose has self-published a massive 798-page book entitled *Grant under Fire: An Exposé of Generalship & Character in the American Civil War*. He concluded that "the *Memoirs* contained a welter of pretense, misrepresentation, bias, and error. . . . Grant rewrote the Civil War to suit his purposes," Rose said.[42]

As for Sherman's memoirs, historian Albert Castel wrote an article in *Civil War History*, whose very title indicated his view of at least one part of the memoirs: "Prevaricating through Georgia: Sherman's *Memoirs* as a Source on the Atlanta Campaign." In response, this author wrote a companion essay in the same issue and titled it to match his view: "Sherman Called It the Way He Saw It."[43]

And so it is fair to say that these memoirs continue to have an importance that either honors their authors or gives reasons for criticism. Neither is perfect, but each continues to contribute to the scholarly debate about America's Civil War. The memoirs are as different as the two men who wrote them, and their receptions have also demonstrated these differences. Grant and Sherman, the two exemplars of Union military victory, wrote major memoirs that provide important but different insights on the most significant event in American history. Both men would be pleased at the result of their efforts.

Notes

1. For the most in-depth study of the relationship between Grant and Sherman, see Charles Bracelen Flood, *Grant and Sherman: The Friendship That Won the Civil War* (New York: Harper Perennial, 2006). For an in-depth biography of William T. Sherman, see John F. Marszalek, *Sherman: A Soldier's Passion for Order* (New York: Free Press, 1992). Two excellent biographies of Grant are Ronald C. White, *American Ulysses: A Life of Ulysses S. Grant* (New York: Random House, 2016); and Ron Chernow, *Grant* (New York: Penguin, 2017).

2. The leading ex-Confederate spokesman for the Lost Cause was Jubal A. Early. See Benjamin Franklin Cooling III, *Jubal Early: Robert E. Lee's Old Man* (Lanham, MD: Rowan and Littlefield, 2014).

3. Stanley P. Hirshon, *The White Tecumseh: A Biography of William T. Sherman* (New York: John Wiley, 1997), 355.

4. William T. Sherman, *Memoirs of William T. Sherman (By Himself)* (New York: D. Appleton and Company, 1875).

5. Marszalek, *Sherman*, 462–464.

6. There is no source indicating the amount of royalty Sherman earned on his memoirs.

7. "Sherman's Memoirs," *Galaxy* 20 (October 1875): 462, 464.

8. Alpheus S. Williams to ?, 1875, HM 3730, Huntington Library, San Marino, California.

9. *Louisiana State Register*, June 12, 1875; *Confederate Veteran* 11 (1903): 458.

10. *Kingston (NY) Journal*, March 20, 1878.

11. Marszalek, *Sherman*, 466.

12. Henry Van Ness Boynton, *Sherman's Historical Raid: The Memoirs in the Light of the Record* (Cincinnati: Wilstach, Baldwin, 1875).

13. Ibid., 3.

14. Ibid., 8.

15. Ibid., 272, 276.

16. Charles W. Moulton, *The Review of General Sherman's Memoirs Examined Chiefly in the Light of Its Own Evidence* (Cincinnati: R. Clarke, 1875).

17. Marszalek, *Sherman*, 465.

18. Ibid., 466–467.

19. *Cleveland Leader*, January 15, 1880.

20. Marszalek, *Sherman*, 466.

21. Ibid., 467.

22. Ibid., 467.

23. See John Y. Simon, ed., *The Personal Memoirs of Julia Dent Grant* (Carbondale: Southern Illinois University Press, 1988); Candice Shy Hooper, *Lincoln's Generals' Wives* . . . (Kent, OH: Kent State University Press, 2016), "Part III: True Faith and Allegiance, Ellen Ewing Sherman."

24. Adam Badeau, *A Military History of Ulysses S. Grant: From April 1861 to April 1865*, 3 vols. (New York: D. Appleton, 1868–1881).

25. From November 1884 to November 1888, *Century Magazine*, edited by Robert Underwood Johnson and Clarence Clough Buell, and consisting of articles by leading Civil War figures on both the Union and Confederate sides, published the remembrances of some 230 participants in all.

26. Geoffrey C. Ward, *A Disposition to Be Rich* (New York: Alfred A. Knopf, 2012).

27. The four articles that Grant wrote for *Century Magazine*, which he also used in his memoirs were "The Battle of Shiloh," *Century*, new series, 7 (February 1885): 593–613; "The Siege of Vicksburg," *Century*, new series, 8 (September 1885): 752–773; "Chattanooga," *Century*, new series, 9 (November 1885), 129–145; "Preparing for the Campaign of 64," *Century*, new series, 9 (February 1886), 573–583.

28. *Autobiography of Mark Twain*, ed. Harriet Elinor Smith et al. (Berkeley: University of California Press, 2010), 278.

29. James M. McPherson, ed., *Personal Memoirs of Ulysses S. Grant* (New York: Penguin, 1999), xv.

30. *Autobiography of Mark Twain*, 81.

31. Robert Underwood Johnson, *Remembered Yesterdays* (Boston: Little, Brown, 1923), 213–216.

32. Philip Van Doren Stern, ed., *Personal Memoirs of Ulysses S. Grant, A Modern Abridgment* (Greenwich, CT: Fawcett, 1962), xiii.

33. www.grantscottage.net is the home page of the Friends of Grant's Cottage, the organization that is preserving this significant building.

34. Ulysses S. Grant to Charles L. Webster & Company, May 2, 1885, in *Papers of Ulysses S. Grant*, ed. John Y. Simon et al., 31 vols. (Carbondale: Southern Illinois University Press, 1967–2009), 31:347–348. See also 31:348–362.

35. Every newspaper in the nation and many overseas announced Grant's death, many with special editions.

36. *The Personal Memoirs of Ulysses S. Grant, Salesman's Prospectus* (New York: Charles L. Webster, 1885–1886). See also *How to Introduce the Personal Memoirs of U. S. Grant* (Chicago: R. S. Peale, 1885).

37. A copy of the check may be found in the Ulysses S. Grant Association Papers, Grant Presidential Library, Mississippi State University.

38. *The Independence, Devoted to the Consideration of Politics, Social and Economic*, June 24, 1886; *Southern Historical Society Papers* 14 (1886): 575.

39. Fredrick D. Grant, ed., *Personal Memoirs of Ulysses S. Grant* (New York: Century, 1895). The most recent edition of these memoirs is John F. Marszalek, with David Nolen and Louie Gallo, eds.,

Personal Memoirs of Ulysses S. Grant: A Completely Annotated Edition (Cambridge, MA: Belknap Press of the Harvard University Press, 2017).

40. Quoted in Earl Schenck Miers, ed., *Sherman's Civil War* (New York: Collier, 1962), 11–12.

41. Two second editions of Sherman volumes are *Memoirs of General William T. Sherman, Written by Himself* (New York: D. Appleton, 1886) and the same title published by Charles L. Webster and Company in 1891.

42. Joseph A. Rose, *Grant Under Fire: An Exposé of Generalship and Character in the American Civil War* (New York: Alderehanna, 2015), 596.

43. Albert Castel, "Prevaricating through Georgia: Sherman's *Memoirs* as a Source on the Atlanta Campaign," *Civil War History* 40 (March 1994): 48–71; John F. Marszalek, "Sherman Called It the Way He Saw It," *Civil War History* 40 (March 1994): 72–78.

The Evolution of the Public Memory
of the Hamburg Massacre

KEVIN L. HUGHES

I n the wake of two national tragedies—a white supremacist opening fire on black worshippers in a Charleston, South Carolina, church in 2015 and the death of a protestor of the "Unite the Right" rally in Charlottesville, Virginia, in 2017—debates over the twenty-first century relevance of Confederate memorials reached a fever pitch. In response around 115 memorials came down, some officially removed by local municipalities and others felled by impromptu protestors. Such support, however, has not been unanimous. In many areas of the country officials have chosen to ignore criticisms, and in some cases have gone so far as to pass legislation designed to protect Confederate monuments from removal.[1] In the midst of this controversy, one of the most blatantly racist memorials to white supremacy may provide a blueprint for how to productively settle this contentious debate.

Located in a small park in North Augusta, South Carolina's central thoroughfare, a single obelisk has cast a shadow on the city for over a century. Dedicated in 1916, the monument honors the sacrifice of Thomas McKie Meriwether, the one white man killed in what is now commonly known as the Hamburg Massacre. Its inscriptions are silent on the seven African Americans who lost their lives in the event—four of whom were executed in cold blood by Meriwether's compatriots—and instead celebrates Meriwether's sacrifice to "Anglo-Saxon civilization." Despite its unconcealed racism, the monument still stands.

Historical memory has of course been a popular area of inquiry for historians in recent decades, particularly for those studying the Civil War and its aftermath, but as cities across the country debate the removal of Confederate monuments and the rechristening of buildings, roads, and bridges named after famous Confederates, it seems as if the general public's interest in collective memory is growing as well. A cursory glance at the discourse surrounding these disputes, however, hints that the average American may not, as of yet, acknowledge a key principle of memory that most historians take for granted—that collective memory is both imagined and malleable. In light of this, a closer look at the evolution of the memory of the Hamburg Massacre and its subsequent commemorations could prove particularly useful.[2]

The German entrepreneur Henry Schultz built the town of Hamburg opposite the riverbank of Augusta, Georgia, in 1822, with the notion of directly competing with its more established neighbor for a stake of the cotton trade. Though marginally successful early on, the Savannah River's propensity for flooding and the steady improvements in Augusta's rail and water transportation sent Hamburg into a steady decline. In the wake of the Civil War, however, the town enjoyed a brief resurgence as many freedpeople from surrounding areas relocated there.[3]

The incident that would ingrain Hamburg in infamy began as a disagreement between a black militia company and two white men. On July 4, 1876, Thomas Butler and his cousin Henry Getzen were traveling home down Hamburg's Market Street when they came upon a local company of the South Carolina National Guard, made up mostly of freedmen.[4] According to Butler and Getzen, the parading militia, under the command of Captain D. L. "Doc" Adams, blocked the road and refused to allow the carriage to pass. On the other hand, the freedmen argued that Butler and Getzen charged toward the head of the column, provoking a confrontation. Words were exchanged, and though this incident ended without bloodshed, Butler and Getzen appealed to the court claiming to have been wrongfully detained by the militia.[5] The disagreement clearly delineated competing worldviews, with whites essentially claiming sole ownership of public spaces and thus deeming the black militia trespassers.[6]

Upon receiving the complaint, Justice Prince Rivers began an inquest to investigate the incident. Rivers, a former slave who had risen to prominence as a Republican, faced the difficult task of diffusing the growing animus between the two sides, which by now was nearing critical mass. The two white men procured prominent South Carolina lawyer and former Confederate General Matthew Calbraith Butler to represent them. At the initial hearing, Adams briefly appeared as a witness but was uncooperative. This forced Rivers to hold Adams in contempt and to order a delay until July 6 at 4:00 in the afternoon.[7]

By the time the case was to resume a large number of armed whites, estimated to be at least one hundred in number, had gathered on the scene and committed themselves to the command of Butler. Most were South Carolinians and members of the paramilitary white supremacist group the "Red Shirts," who were committed to controlling the election of 1876 through intimidation and violence. They were also joined by a number of Georgians from nearby Augusta, who crossed the river and added to the growing mob. Fearing for their lives, Doc Adams and the militiamen refused to return to the courthouse at the allotted time and instead prepared to defend themselves.[8]

With the situation spiraling toward violence, Butler erroneously assured Rivers that he could peaceably disarm Adams and the militia. Seeing no other recourse, Rivers conceded, and Butler set off to confront the militiamen. Not surprisingly, Adams and his men refused to disarm and instead sought refuge inside the Sibley building, their brick armory located near a railroad bridge that crossed the Savannah River into Georgia. Butler's men, by now numbering in the hundreds, prepared to lay siege to the structure. Accounts of who fired first vary, but soon a "miniature battle" broke out, and the first to fall was Thomas McKie Meriwether. Who fired the shot that struck him in the head remains unsettled, but Meriwether died within five minutes of receiving the wound.[9]

As the sun set and darkness led to a pause in the fighting, Adams surveyed his options. The militia men had defended their position well, but their opposition continued to grow in size. Even more concerning, word began to spread through the ranks that the whites had procured a small cannon from Augusta and were preparing to use it. Hopelessly outnumbered and fearing what would happen if he either surrendered or resumed fighting, Adams ordered his men to quietly slip away from the building and scatter into the countryside. The men complied, and all but one escaped. A volley from the white mob killed James Cook, who also served as Hamburg's sheriff, as he attempted to flee.[10]

When Butler and his men discovered their prey had fled, they began pursuit. The *Augusta Chronicle* described the feverish search, as an estimated 250 men combed Hamburg. The search yielded around two dozen African American men, some of whom were discovered hiding under steps or floorboards. By now it was 2:00 a.m., and the whites transported their black hostages near the river to debate their fate.[11]

General Butler had allegedly ordered the prisoners to be transported to the Aiken County jail and left the scene, but at some point those orders were abandoned. One by one the white militia identified black men they considered to be ring leaders and singled them out to be executed. For sport, some were allowed to run only to be shot in the back as they fled. At least four men, Allan Attaway, David Phillips, Hampton Stephens, and Albert Myniart, were executed in this manner, and several others were wounded when "as the remainder of the prisoners were turned loose, they were fired into."[12] Another, Moses Parks, died sometime during the night, though there is some degree of uncertainty as to when and where his death occurred.[13]

No one was ever punished for the bloodshed at Hamburg. Republican Governor Daniel H. Chamberlain immediately condemned the violence and wrote to Washington in hopes of federal intervention. He justified his request by arguing that if "large bodies of citizens can be coerced by force or fear into absenting themselves from the polls, or voting in a way contrary to their judgment or inclination, the foundation of every man's civil freedom is deeply if not fatally shaken." The president responded promptly, and while he agreed that the actions of the white militia were "cruel, bloodthirsty, wanton, unprovoked, and uncalled for," he lamented that such intimidation had become a common tactic throughout the South. With that in mind, Grant encouraged the governor to use the power at his disposal to pursue justice in the case but refused to intervene.[14] A coroner's jury indicted ninety-four white men for the murders at Hamburg, but none were ever prosecuted.[15]

How the events at Hamburg would be remembered was contentious from the start. Augusta's two daily newspapers covered the story extensively, even before the actual fighting took place. On July 8, the *Chronicle* had published an account of the standoff between Butler, Getzen, and the Hamburg militia. Not surprisingly, the paper came down solidly on the side of the whites, asserting that Judge Rivers was "making every effort in his power to preserve the supremacy of the civil law, which [the Hamburg militia] violate on every occasion." When Rivers was forced to hold Doc Adams in contempt and suspend the case, the paper declared it the "second time during the week that white citizens have been insulted by these marauders, and we are satisfied justice will be dealt out to them now that the matter is in the hands of a civil officer."[16]

When the sun rose the morning after the massacre, it still was not clear exactly what had occurred. Nonetheless, the *Chronicle* breathlessly reported what it called "a pitched battle in Hamburg," under the thick-lettered headline: "War of Races." As an addendum, the last paragraph of the story described the murder of the black prisoners. An editorial in the same issue called the event an "unfortunate affair" but also asserted "that for some time past" the Hamburg militia had "been a source of great annoyance, as well as a real danger to the people of Edgefield County." The editorial ended by reminding readers, "We cannot help but condemn lynch law in South Carolina as we have always condemned it in Georgia, but when we censure the deed, we must also remember the provocation."[17]

As it became clear that several unarmed men had been executed, the *Chronicle* softened its tone. Headlines calling the affair "The Hamburg Troubles" appeared less and less and were replaced instead with the moniker "The Hamburg Tragedy." A July 11 editorial explicitly condemned the killing of the prisoners, noting that at the time the paper first published the story, "We had not heard of the fate of the prisoners, or we should have condemned in fitting phrase their cruel and unnecessary murder." In this most stinging local critique, the *Chronicle* declared, "There is no extenuation of the butchery of unarmed and helpless captives. In real war such a deed would receive the execration of all civilized nations. How much more should it be reprobated when no state of war exists."[18] Such condemnation of the actions of the white militia was rare among southern papers, especially among those who supported the Democratic Party.

Conversely, most newspapers outside of the South condemned the bloodshed at Hamburg. The *San Francisco Chronicle* labeled the event an "outrage" carried out by a "late Rebel General."[19] Furthermore, the paper argued that "to speak" of the event as "a 'riot' or a 'disorder'" was "monstrous," as it was nothing less than "a deliberate, devilish, cold-blooded murder."[20] Likewise, the *Hartford Daily Courant* referred to the white militia as "the Hamburg murderers" and the event as the "Hamburg Massacre."[21] The *Christian Advocate* called it "the most barbarous and fiendish massacre in modern times."[22]

The *Chicago Daily Tribune* further highlighted the sectional nature of the coverage by labeling it "the Confederate defense of Hamburg." "Georgia Democrats," the paper contended, "went over to Hamburg, S.C., and murdered a half-score or so of Republicans, whose only offense consisted of having black skin and voting the Republican ticket," an outrage which several southern papers "openly and boldly" justified. Dumbfounded by such support, the *Tribune* rhetorically asked where else can "a mob . . . get together, seize upon citizens, imprison some of them, shoot others, and then pillage their residences, and not only escape punishment, but have their deeds justified because the victims do not vote to suit the mob?"[23] Echoing the *Tribune*'s coverage, the *New York Times* called the Hamburg killings a "slaughter" and branded the perpetrators as "white murderers." Even if the residents of Hamburg were guilty of the litany of offenses put forth by Butler and his compatriots, the paper declared there to be no justification "for the whites taking the law into their own hands and visiting such fearful and disproportionate punishment upon the alleged offenders."[24]

Harper's Weekly ran at least two cartoons decrying the murders of the black prisoners. In one, famed cartoonist Thomas Nast sketched a personification of justice, with her scales unbalanced by the multitude of black bodies on one side and only Meriwether's on the other. The foreground features the nation's founding documents, while in the background posters listed white terrorist groups responsible for tipping the scales of justice against African Americans in the South.[25]

Black southerners interpreted the event similarly. Charleston's African American community crafted a statement describing the actions of the white militia as "unmitigated and foul murder, premeditated and predetermined." It further argued that the violence was meant to intimidate black laborers and voters and to "'keep negroes in their place,' as they say." When the remaining portion of the address warned that African Americans may retaliate with their own violence, one newspaper dismissed the entire document as a fraud. For white southerners who refused to see African Americans as anything but docile, the address could only be "the product of some white incendiary intruder who would promote his own selfish ends at the expense of both races."[26]

As time passed and no one was held responsible for the deaths, several outlets continued to demand justice. The *Christian Advocate* lamented that "because of the political and social ostracism of the colored people of the South, the 'swift retribution' demanded is delayed." Particularly odious was the fact that "well known politicians, even in the halls of Congress, apologize for the perpetrators of the crime. Shame!"[27] Likewise, the *New York Witness* flatly declared that "Butler and his gang . . . deserved to be hung, but we hear no word of their being even tried."[28]

By now clear lines were drawn as to how each side would remember the events at Hamburg. The majority of southern whites chose to characterize it as a riot carried out by insolent and dangerous African Americans who had been justly put down by gallant white gentlemen. Others characterized the event differently. In their view, law-abiding members of a black militia had been ruthlessly murdered by a mob of whites who hoped to intimidate Republican voters and return political control of the state to the Democrats. More succinctly, most white southerners referred to the event as the Hamburg Riot. Most everyone else considered it the Hamburg Massacre.[29]

The election of Democrat Wade Hampton as governor in the fall of 1876, along with the end of federal intervention in the South, briefly extinguished national interest in the Hamburg Massacre. The story returned to the forefront just a year later, however, when South Carolina chose to send Butler to the US Senate. White South Carolinians certainly saw Butler as a heroic figure, but his provocative selection reignited the controversy over the Hamburg affair.

Several senators protested the appointment, citing Butler's leadership during the Hamburg Massacre. Perhaps the most hyperbolic objection came from Senator Roscoe Conkling of New York, who accused Butler of coming before the Senate "with his hands dripping with human gore." Butler's allies, on the other hand, rallied to his side, declaring him an upstanding citizen who was worthy of high office. Such a polarized political environment forced Butler to distance himself from the bloodshed at Hamburg. Instead he rehashed his old argument that the murders were the fault of a mob gone mad and that he had left the scene before the murders occurred. In the end, Butler assumed his Senate seat, though not without significant dissent.[30]

Ironically, Butler's attempts to distance himself from the Hamburg Massacre proved a detriment later in his career. In 1894 he found himself embroiled in a battle for his Senate seat against Benjamin Tillman, the fiery populist governor who proudly boasted of partaking in the violence at Hamburg. With the Reconstruction era now long passed and the shadow of Jim Crow stretching across the South, participation in the Hamburg Massacre became a badge of honor for conservative whites. Thus Tillman enthusiastically reminded South Carolinians that Butler had repeatedly downplayed his role at Hamburg. For his part, Butler denied that Tillman had even been present at Hamburg in the first place, declaring that when the shooting started Tillman was "not to be found." This struggle between Butler and Tillman demonstrated that the memory of what had occurred at Hamburg was malleable and still significant. In this case Tillman's superior political organization carried the day, and he ascended to the US Senate, where he served until his death in 1918.[31]

In this manner, the "Hamburg Riot" continued to be recycled by white supremacists to rally support for Democratic candidates. Tillman's own unrelenting reminders ensured that his followers never forgot that he was present at Hamburg. When speaking before a reunion of the Red Shirts in 1909, he chose to recount the struggle to "redeem" South Carolina. Never one to shy away from the subject, Tillman proudly stated that he had "nothing to conceal about the Hamburg Riot." Continuing to speak frankly, he affirmed, "I told the Republicans in the Senate that we had to shoot negroes to get relief from the galling tyranny to which we had been subjected; and while my words were used in the Republican campaign book for 1900, I think my very boldness and the frankness with which I explained conditions did more to enlighten and disarm the fanatics than anything else I could have said."[32]

Tillman's recollection left no doubt as to the original intent of the white militia, as he flatly stated, "It had been the settled purpose of leading men of Edgefield to seize the first opportunity . . . to provoke a riot." As to why they killed the seven African Americans, Tillman asserted, "It was generally believed that nothing but bloodshed and a good deal of it could answer the purpose of redeeming the state from negro and carpet bag rule." Tillman judged the violence effective, noting that "the purpose of our visit to Hamburg was to strike terror, and the next morning (Sunday) when" those "who had fled to the swamp returned to the town . . . the ghastly sight which met their gaze of seven dead negroes lying stark and stiff certainly had its effect."[33]

Tillman recalled the death of McKie Meriwether with particular sentiment in his reunion speech. The young man's death had become a key component in the white supremacist memory of Hamburg and would soon become the focus of a statewide memorial project. In the meantime, Tillman kept Meriwether's memory alive with a touching story of the man's final moments. According to Tillman, McKie's father, Joseph Meriwether, had joined the white mob carrying only a rifle. At that moment McKie, "a very handsome young man about twenty-five years of age came running towards" Joseph, "unbuckling his pistol belt." "As he ran, he handed the two pistols to his father and said, 'Here papa, take these and let me have the rifle.'" Tillman recalled that it was just a short time later when "we were all shocked and enraged by the news that young McKie Meriwether . . . had been killed."[34] Whether Tillman's story was true or not is difficult to determine, but its intended effect is not. Conservative whites were determined to ensure that Carolinians remembered Meriwether's death as a tragic sacrifice by a true hero of Hamburg.

Tillman's speech also featured another important component of the white supremacist memory of Hamburg, as he drew parallels between the struggle to "redeem" South Carolina and America's War for Independence. With particular flair Tillman declared, "The Spirit of 1776, which made Moultrie . . . man his palmetto fort and destroy Sir Peter Parker's Fleet, pulsated in the bosom of every brave Carolinian, when they learned a body of seventy-five poorly armed whites had dared to attack a legally organized militia company, capture its armory, and then put to death some of its members."[35] Without the Hamburg

Massacre, Tillman speculated, there would likely have been no "Redemption" for South Carolina in 1876. Thus the events at Hamburg became of mythical importance for the white supremacist narrative.

Southern newspapers also occasionally recounted the Hamburg story in historical columns meant to educate a new generation of readers on past events. In one such column, the author made sure to take the opportunity to denigrate the black militia and their leadership, remembering Doc Adams as "a smart fellow, but awfully unruly and self-willed." Offering further social commentary on the perils of emancipation, the paper lamented that "with freedom" Adams, "unrestrained, rejected the influences that had been thrown about him by his master." In contrast, Adams's mother was remembered as a "prized . . . good old negress," who "was greatly distressed by the part her son played in the rioting in 1876." In just a few short paragraphs, this column managed to reinforce both the white supremacist memory of Hamburg and the Lost Cause myth of plantations filled with docile slaves.[36]

In this manner, the memory of the Hamburg Massacre continued to live on, particularly for white southerners who glorified the actions of the white militia. As time passed, the white supremacist view of what happened at Hamburg slowly became the dominant memory of the event, as talk of the Hamburg Riot drowned out recollections of the Hamburg Massacre. As the nineteenth century gave way to the twentieth, aged veteran Red Shirts and their admirers turned their attention to creating more permanent memorials, designed to transmit the white supremacist memory of the events at Hamburg to future generations.

The first was a modest project to honor two unassuming citizens whose story was not well known. White South Carolinians pooled their resources and placed a monument on the otherwise unmarked graves of Reverend S. P. T. Field and his wife, Ann Dagnail Field, of Aiken. The Fields were otherwise "unostentatious, living in the ordinary channels of life, without title, or degree," who ran a small bakery. Yet many deemed them worthy of recognition because of the kindness they had shown nearly forty years earlier. D. S. Henderson, the last surviving lawyer who had represented the white militiamen indicted for the incidents at Hamburg, explained why the family deserved to be recognized. According to Henderson, in the wake of the events at Hamburg, a large number of whites facing charges for their actions gathered in Aiken "getting their bails prepared." Night fell leaving "many hungry, thirsty, men on the street." "As they passed . . . the Field's Bakery, the good old couple came to the door, and invited the hungry crowd to come in and eat up everything in the store, refusing to take a cent for it." Reporting on the monument's unveiling, the *Augusta Chronicle* revealed the efficacy of remembering not just the Fields but the now mythical tale of South Carolina's Redemption campaign, noting that "nineteen years after [the Fields's] death their memory is fresh and alive in the memory of not only those who intimately knew them, but the whole of Aiken County, and all over South Carolina."[37]

With this project complete, admirers shifted their energies toward erecting a monument to commemorate the death of McKie Meriwether. The prospect first gained steam in the South Carolina legislature, where J. P. DeLaughter of Edgefield sponsored a joint resolution to appropriate $400 toward the project. Though the measure passed unanimously, South Carolina's governor, Coleman Livingston Blease, vetoed the appropriation.[38] DeLaughter countered by giving a speech before the house to rally support to overturn the governor's veto. It was his first speech on the house floor in his two-year career, and according to the *Edgefield Advertiser*, it "yielded results." DeLaughter "painted a picture of the scene at the Hamburg riot . . . in which McKie Meriwether laid down his life to redeem South Carolina from Radical rule." In response to DeLaughter's "stirring maiden speech," the house overturned the veto by a vote of eighty to four, and "members crowded around [DeLaughter] to offer their congratulations."[39]

With this initial contribution secured, the search for private donations began in earnest. McKie Meriwether's cousin, James B. McKie, was one of the men chosen to oversee the monument's construction. In an appeal for contributions, McKie lamented that the appropriation of the legislature was "so small—about one fourth the value of an antebellum slave." "To this end," he wrote that he "would appreciate and duly acknowledge any contributions to the fund."[40] In response, McKie secured a small contribution from a famous donor, the aging Benjamin Tillman himself. In a personal letter to McKie, Tillman declared, "I am prompted to assist you in getting money for the purpose of erecting a monument to that brave and splendid boy—he was little else than a boy when he was killed." Tillman enclosed a check for twenty-five dollars and regretted that he could not afford to give more. He closed his letter by suggesting that McKie be sure to "get someone with good literary taste to write the inscription for the monument" and offered his sincere hope that enough money would be raised for the monument to build a "worthy one."[41]

The ladies of the North Augusta Civic League also worked tirelessly to see the Meriwether monument come to fruition. In the wake of the Civil War, women's auxiliary clubs took the lead in organizing Confederate memorial services and monuments and in fostering and preserving the Lost Cause myth. In December 1914, Mrs. A. M. Parker continued this tradition by delivering a paper titled "The Cause and Effects of the Hamburg Riot" before the Civic League. Parker filled her paper to the brim with the key elements of the white supremacist memory of the Hamburg Massacre and of the Reconstruction era in general. In setting up her story she described the "deplorable state of affairs" during the postwar era, a time when "law ... gave to every ignorant negro the right to vote and hold any office in South Carolina, taking such rights from white men connected with the Confederacy." Parker blamed black militia companies for terrorizing whites, opining that "drums could be heard all night. Smokehouses were robbed. Produce taken from wagons along roads, and any resistance meant you would be knocked on the head." As if this hyperbolic depiction was not enough, she added, "Houses were burned. Children's faces slapped. And on all sides, ignorant negro officers."[42]

Parker was particularly vicious in defaming Hamburg's black community. Hinting that the town's economic decline was due to emancipation and African American influence, she noted "Hamburg's streets now overrun with pickaninnies and washer women, were at that time [1876] very prosperous looking." Parker described the African American magistrate, Prince Rivers, "as black as a crow and as slick as a peeled onion, as shiny as a new mirror." She reveled in the fact that Rivers "had a very elaborate library," yet she alleged he "could neither read nor write, and signed his name in a kind of a scroll." Furthering the stereotypical depiction of emancipated slaves as incapable of fulfilling the serious duties of office, Parker noted that Rivers "used a typical low country dialect and as a magistrate was absurd in the extreme." In defense of the murder of the black prisoners, Parker ironically noted, "It is sometimes thought that [they] were shot at random, but this was not true, for only those who had committed some crime were shot, except in an instance or two."[43]

In a letter to the editor of the *Edgefield Advertiser* in May 1915, G. W. Medlock stressed that the proposed monument to Meriwether was to honor much more than just the sacrifice of one man. He reminded readers that Americans construct "towering monuments to the heroes of the past, not so much for perpetuating the deeds of some individual, as that of the cause for which they freely offered themselves." Thus the proposed memorial would not just honor Meriwether but would also serve as "a reminder of the times when the young men" of South Carolina "arose as one man and prompted alone by a high sense of patriotism, dared to risk life and personal liberty, in fact everything they held most dear in the effort to break up the degrading conditions, that existed as a result of the Civil War." The Hamburg Riot, Medlock reasoned, was the major turning point in this struggle and therefore deserved to be memorialized. "All we have to do is raise the money," he declared, "and that should be easy to do."[44] Easy or not, donors eventually responded to the many calls for aid, and sufficient funds were raised.

Organizers scheduled the long-awaited unveiling of the Meriwether monument for February 16, 1916. They secured D. S. Henderson, still active in the Hamburg memorial efforts, as keynote speaker, and the South Carolina legislature offered to send a delegation of three senators and three representatives to attend. An *Augusta Chronicle* article urged Georgians to cross the river and attend the ceremony as well, calling it "but proper that men and women of this city be present," because white Georgians had so prominently participated in the event.[45]

When the day of the event finally arrived, the crowds did not disappoint. People from all over South Carolina and Georgia gathered at North Augusta's high school, just across from the monument. Henderson's keynote speech held the attention of the audience, estimated at over one thousand, for nearly an hour. In it, he emphasized the active nature of memory, affirming that the purpose of the monument was not just to honor Meriwether's sacrifice but to "perpetuate the memory and the cause which he represented." Henderson avowed that the unveiling of the monument was not to be the end of the story, declaring that "McKie Meriwether died, but his spirit survives." He assured his listeners that though "the white man's revolution of 1876 is numbered among the past epochs of history, its lessons and experiences remain to be applied to the perplexities and hopes of American life and American ambition in 1916." If one wonders what lessons Henderson had in mind, one need look no further than earlier in his speech where he spoke of the results of the "white man's revolution." "We have lived to see the day," he said, "where the negro, ceasing to be in position to act as a tool for political charlatans, is satisfied with his normal condition, as an equal to the white man in the eye of the law, but not his equal politically or socially."[46]

When the speeches were complete the crowd exited the high school and gathered, their heads uncovered, as female relatives of Meriwether ceremoniously unveiled the monument for the first time. The obelisk itself was twenty-one feet high, made of granite from Winnsboro, South Carolina, and weighed twenty-seven thousand pounds. Inscriptions covered all four sides, each echoing the same theme. One declared the monument dedicated to "Thomas McKie Meriwether, who on 8th of July, 1876, gave his life that the civilization builded by his fathers might be preserved for the children unimpaired." Another offered "forever the grateful remembrance of all who know high and general service in maintaining these civil and social institutions which the men and women of his race had struggled through the centuries to establish in South Carolina." As if these two inscriptions were not clear enough, another side declared, "In life [Meriwether] exemplified the highest ideal of Anglo-Saxon civilization. By his death, he assured to the children of his beloved land the supremacy of that ideal."[47] The dedication of a monument to disseminate and preserve this message marked the victory of the white supremacist memory of the Hamburg Massacre, a remembrance which stood unchallenged for nearly a century.

In recent years, momentum has begun to shift toward a more inclusive memory of the bloodshed at Hamburg. In 2011, the North Augusta Heritage Council, a nonprofit group, sponsored a new historical marker that recalls the details of the massacre. Though it does not name names, it recounts that "after a dispute between whites and a black militia company, about 200 men from local rifle clubs tried to disarm 38 black militiamen and others barricaded in a warehouse. One white was killed and men on each side were wounded before the blacks fled. Two blacks were killed trying to escape. Whites captured 25–30 blacks and executed four of them. 87 whites were charged in the massacre but were never tried for it."[48]

In 2016, the city of North Augusta again memorialized the Hamburg Massacre by erecting a new memorial stone honoring all of those who died. As a goodwill gesture, McKie Meriwether's name is included with the names of the black victims. The ceremony was part of a larger vision of a Hamburg renaissance, which includes plans for a future Hamburg museum. This renewed interest in Hamburg has continued in recent years, with plans for multiple projects currently in the works. The Aiken County Historical Museum has recently received funding to create a film about Hamburg in conjunction with Aiken County schools. The completed project will allow students throughout the state to take a virtual fieldtrip to the now defunct town. The Heritage Council of North Augusta also has received a grant to compile a history of Hamburg, including the massacre.[49]

Yet the trajectory of the memory of the Hamburg Massacre continues to raise uncomfortable questions. Despite all the renewed interest in recognizing the victims of this heinous violence, the obelisk to Meriwether remains, complete with its racially tinged inscriptions. The new historical marker and memorial stone are located several miles away, in a part of North Augusta that was once known as Carrsville. It was here that much of the area's African American community relocated when in 1929 back-to-back floods led to the abandonment of Hamburg. The marker and memorial stone sit in front of the Carrsville Society House, a decaying building made from boards painstakingly moved from Hamburg. The structure is scheduled to be renovated and to eventually house the proposed Hamburg museum. It is here that local historian and activist Wayne O'Bryant hopes to create an African American historical district, likely to be called the Hamburg district.[50]

There is also a more practical reason for placing Hamburg memorials here rather than more prominent locations such as where the massacre occurred or near the Meriwether monument. The Carrsville location offers the best protection from potential vandals. A generic Hamburg historical marker noting the town's growth and decline, placed near the Savannah River in 1963 by the County Historical Commission, vanished in 2004. Some organizers fear that a more prominent monument to the Hamburg Massacre could suffer a similar fate.

Perhaps the most difficult question is what should be done with the Meriwether monument. As cities and towns across the South continue to debate the efficacy of Confederate memorials, one would be hard pressed to find a monument more clearly erected to white supremacy than the Meriwether obelisk. One could also make a sound argument that the monument is an affront to the memory of the African American lives lost during the massacre, as well as to all those who suffered through the decades-long era of segregation and Jim Crow, and therefore should be removed.

In 2017, activist Ken Makin stepped up to the podium at a meeting of the city council and requested the city review and denounce the monument. In response, Mayor Bob Pettit formed an ad hoc committee to investigate and recommend how to proceed.[51] The biggest obstacle to simply removing the monument is South Carolina's Heritage Act, a 2000 law that requires a two-thirds vote in both houses of the state legislature in order to remove a historical monument.[52] To bypass this obstacle, Pettit and his committee have suggested adding to the original obelisk to both honor the African Americans killed in the massacre and educate the public on Reconstruction and the Jim Crow era.[53]

Any such attempt to update the memorial, however, is fraught with difficulty. First, there is a legitimate concern that allowing input from a variety of stakeholders will result in compromises that water down the message and further whitewash the memory of the Hamburg Massacre. Such concerns are not without warrant and have led some activists to reject these plans. Responding to the mayor's announcement, Makin argued that not removing the monument will not "decisively denounce white supremacy," and "sends the wrong message."[54] Such a response is understandable, and if this middle-ground solution fails to present the history of both the Hamburg Massacre and its resulting memorial efforts in all of its white supremacist horror, then removal is clearly the answer. But if the city is truly committed to presenting the Hamburg memorial as an educational opportunity that demonstrates how white supremacists shaped a certain memory of the Civil War and Reconstruction era, and how that ill-conceived version of events continues to influence the historical understanding of many members of the general public, then the effort to reorient the Hamburg monument will serve an important role.

The Meriwether monument is a powerful reminder of how those in power can manipulate commemoration to aid their own agenda and of the pliability of memory in general. Conceivably, an updated memorial that tells the entire history of the evolution of the memory of the Hamburg Massacre would be a greater service to future generations, serving as a cautionary tale of the influences of remembrance and memorialization and potentially providing a blueprint for similar monuments throughout the country.

Notes

1. Rick Hampton, "Confederate Memorials Turn Up Faster Than They Can Be Removed a Year after Charlottesville," *USA Today*, August 16, 2018, https://www.usatoday.com/story/news/nation/2018/08/06/confederate-memorials-list-longer-usa-public-remove/891739002/.

2. Examples of the prominent works on Civil War memory include David W. Blight, *Race and Reunion: The Civil War in American Memory* (Cambridge, MA: Harvard University Press, 2001); Caroline E. Janney, *Remembering the Civil War: Reunion and the Limits of Reconciliation* (Chapel Hill: University of North Carolina Press, 2013); John R. Neff, *Honoring the Civil War Dead: Commemoration and the Problem of Reconciliation* (Lawrence: University Press of Kansas, 2005); Charles Reagan Wilson, *Baptized in Blood: The Religion of the Lost Cause, 1865–1920* (Athens: University of Georgia Press, 1980); Gaines M. Foster, *Ghosts of the Confederacy: Defeat, the Lost Cause, and the Emergence of the New South* (New York: Oxford University Press, 1987); William Blair, *Cities of the Dead: Contesting the Memory of the Civil War in the South, 1865–1914* (Chapel Hill: University of North Carolina Press, 2004); and W. Fitzhugh Brundage, *The Southern Past: A Clash of Race and Memory* (Cambridge, MA: Harvard University Press, 2005).

3. Charles G. Cordle, "Henry Shultz and the Founding of Hamburg, South Carolina," in *Studies in Georgia History and Government*, ed. James C. Bonner and Lucien E. Roberts (Athens: Univer-

sity of Georgia Press, 1940); Rosser H. Taylor, "Hamburg: An Experiment in Town Promotion," *North Carolina Historical Review* 11 (January 1934): 20–38.

4. Henry Getzen's surname is spelled a variety of ways throughout the historical record, sometimes appearing as Getson, Gettson, or Getzon.

5. *Augusta Chronicle*, July 8, 1876; George C. Rable, *But There Was No Peace: The Role of Violence in the Politics of Reconstruction* (Athens: University of Georgia Press, 1984), 166–167; Stephen Budiansky, *The Bloody Shirt: Terror after Appomattox* (New York: Penguin Group, 2008), 226–228; Stephen Kantrowitz, *Ben Tillman and the Reconstruction of White Supremacy* (Chapel Hill: University of North Carolina Press, 2000), 65–66.

6. Kathleen Ann Clark, *Defining Moments: African American Commemoration & Political Culture in the South, 1863–1913* (Chapel Hill: University of North Carolina Press, 2006), 128.

7. *Augusta Chronicle*, July 8, 9, 1876; Kantrowitz, *Ben Tillman*, 67–69; Rable, *But There Was No Peace*, 167; Budiansky, *The Bloody Shirt*, 228–230.

8. Kantrowitz, *Ben Tillman*, 64–71; Clark, *Defining Moments*, 126–127.

9. *Augusta Chronicle*, July 11, 1876; Budiansky, *The Bloody Shirt*, 232–233; Richard Zuczek, *State of Rebellion: Reconstruction in South Carolina* (Columbia: University of South Carolina Press, 1996), 161; Clark, *Defining Moments*, 126–127.

10. *Augusta Chronicle*, July 11, 1876; Budiansky, *The Bloody Shirt*, 233–234; Clark, *Defining Moments*, 126–127.

11. *Augusta Chronicle*, July 11, 1876; Kantrowitz, *Ben Tillman*, 69; Budiansky, *The Bloody Shirt*, 233–234, Clark, *Defining Moments*, 126–127.

12. *Augusta Chronicle*, July 9, 1876; Rable, *But There Was No Peace*, 167; Kantrowitz, *Ben Tillman*, 69; Budiansky, *The Bloody Shirt*, 235–237; Zuczek, *State of Rebellion*, 164; Clark, *Defining Moments*, 126–127. For more on lynching of African Americans in the postbellum South, see William D. Carrigan, ed., *Lynching Reconsidered: New Perspectives in the Study of Mob Violence* (New York: Routledge, 2008); W. Fitzhugh Brundage, *Lynching in the New South: Georgia and Virginia, 1880–1930* (Urbana: University of Illinois, 1993); W. Fitzhugh Brundage, ed., *Under Sentence of Death: Lynching in the South* (Chapel Hill: University of North Carolina, 1997); Edward L. Ayers, *The Promise of the New South: Life after Reconstruction* (New York: Oxford University Press, 1992), 156–157, 495–496; Michael J. Pfeifer, *Rough Justice: Lynching and American Society, 1878–1946* (Urbana: University of Illinois Press, 2004); and Kidada E. Williams, *They Left Great Marks on Me: African American Testimonies of Racial Violence from Emancipation to World War I* (New York: NYU Press, 2012).

13. Congress, House of Representatives, Condition of South Carolina, Views of the Minority, 44th Cong., 2nd Sess., appendix to the *Congressional Record*, 234.

14. *Friends' Intelligencer* (Philadelphia), August 12, 1876.

15. William Stone to Daniel H. Chamberlain, July 12, 1876, Letters Received in Governors' Papers for Daniel H. Chamberlain, South Carolina Department of Archives and History, Columbia, SC, S518004; Kantrowitz, *Ben Tillman*, 70.

16. *Augusta Chronicle*, July 8, 1876; Clark, *Defining Moments*, 128, Kantrowitz, *The Bloody Shirt*, 242–243.

17. *Augusta Chronicle*, July 9, 1876.

18. *Augusta Chronicle*, July 11, 1876.

19. *San Francisco Chronicle*, July 21, 1876.

20. *San Francisco Chronicle*, July 26, 1876.

21. *Hartford Daily Courant*, August 12, July 13, 1876.

22. *Christian Advocate* (Chicago), August 3, 1876.

23. *Chicago Daily Tribune*, July 22, 1876.

24. *New York Times*, July 24, 1876.

25. *Harper's Weekly*, August 12, 1876.

26. *Baltimore Sun*, July 25, 1876; Clark, *Defining Moments*, 127.

27. *Christian Advocate* (Chicago), August 3, 1876.

28. Reprinted in *Augusta Chronicle*, March 24, 1877.

29. In *Race and Reunion*, David Blight identifies three strands of memory that emerged from the Civil War. African Americans and their close allies embraced an emancipationist vision that emphasized slavery's demise and the promise of racial equality as the major results of the Civil War. White supremacists rejected this view, often resorting to violence in order to maintain a racial order where black people were subjugated. Blight's final group encompasses the majority of whites, in both the North and South, who chose to downplay emancipation and racial justice in order to more quickly reconcile the two regions. While several historians have identified weaknesses in Blight's categories, in this case the dominant memory of the events at Hamburg generally fit into Blight's white supremacist strand. Blight, *Race and Reunion*, 1–5.

30. *Press and Daily Dakotian*, February 10, 1881.

31. Kantrowitz, *Ben Tillman*, 161–162.

32. *Edgefield (SC) Advertiser*, December 23, 1914; *Times and Democrat* (Orangeburg, SC), September 11, 1909.

33. *Edgefield (SC) Advertiser*, December 23, 1914; *Times and Democrat* (Orangeburg, SC), September 11, 1909.

34. *Edgefield (SC) Advertiser*, December 23, 1914, *Times and Democrat* (Orangeburg, SC), September 11, 1909.

35. *Abbeville (SC) Press and Banner*, October 6, 1909. Further emphasizing the connection between Hamburg and the American Revolution, the *Abbeville Press and Banner* published the entirety of Tillman's Red Shirt reunion speech under the headline "The Struggle of '76." Most other papers ran the story under the headline "The Dark Days," which was likely the headline of choice for either Tillman or his associates, who distributed the speech for publication. See *Times and Democrat* (Orangeburg, SC), September 11, 1909; *Fort Mill (SC) Times*, September 16, 1909; *Manning (SC) Times*, September 15, 1909.

36. *Augusta Chronicle*, October 12, 1914. For more on the Lost Cause, see Gary W. Gallagher and Alan T. Nolan, eds., *The Myth of the Lost Cause and Civil War History* (Bloomington: Indiana University Press, 2000); Wilson, *Baptized in Blood*; Foster, *Ghosts of the Confederacy*; Blight, *Race and Reunion*, 255–299; and Brundage, *Southern Past*.

37. *Augusta Chronicle*, February 8, 1910.

38. *Anderson (SC) Daily Intelligencer*, February 20, 1914; *Pickens (SC) Sentinel*, March 22, 1914.

39. *Edgefield (SC) Advertiser*, March 11, 1914; *Herald and News* (Newberry, SC), March 10, 1914. For more on southern monument projects and their influence on southern memory, see Brundage, *The Southern Past*, 1–54; Blight, *Race and Reunion*, 80–81, 272–283; Wilson, *Baptized in Blood*, 18–24; Neff, *Honoring the Civil War Dead*, 146–147; Janney, *Remembering the Civil War*, 261–265; and

Cynthia Mills and Pamela H. Simpson, eds., *Monuments to the Lost Cause: Women, Art, and the Landscapes of Southern Memory* (Knoxville: University of Tennessee Press, 2003).

40. *Augusta Chronicle*, December 7, 1914.

41. *Augusta Chronicle*, December 26, 1914.

42. *Bamberg (SC) Herald*, December 24, 1914. For more on the role southern white women played in perpetuating the memory of the Lost Cause, see Caroline E. Janney, *Burying the Dead But Not the Past: Ladies' Memorial Associations and the Lost Cause* (Chapel Hill: University of North Carolina Press, 2008); Karen L. Cox, *Dixie's Daughters: The United Daughters of the Confederacy and the Preservation of Confederate Culture* (Gainesville: University Press of Florida, 2003); Brundage, *The Southern Past*, 1–54; Blight, *Race and Reunion*, 71, 97, 255–256, 272–278; Lesley J. Gordon, "Let the People See the Old Life as It Was: LaSalle Corbell Pickett and the Myth of the Lost Cause," in *The Myth of the Lost Cause and Civil War History*, ed. Gary W. Gallagher and Alan T. Nolan (Bloomington: Indiana University Press, 2000), 170–180; Clark, *Defining Moments*, 53–55, 112–117; and Janney, *Remembering the Civil War*, 9–10, 54, 92–100, 123, 140, 234–235, 238–245, 259, 283–284, 295–301, 304.

43. *Bamberg (SC) Herald*, December 24, 1914.

44. *Edgefield (SC) Advertiser*, May 5, 1915.

45. *Augusta Chronicle*, February 15, 16, 1916; *Edgefield (SC) Advertiser*, January 12, 26, 1916.

46. *Edgefield (SC) Advertiser*, February 23, 1916; *Augusta Chronicle*, February 17, 1916; Budiansky, *The Bloody Shirt*, 280–281.

47. *Edgefield (SC) Advertiser*, January 26, 1916; *Augusta Chronicle*, February 13, 1916.

48. *Aiken (SC) Standard*, February 27, 2011.

49. *Augusta Chronicle*, March 6, 2016; *North Augusta (SC) Star*, July 7, 2017.

50. *Augusta Chronicle*, August 25, 2015.

51. *Aiken (SC) Standard*, November 11, 2018.

52. South Carolina General Assembly, South Carolina Heritage Act of 2000, 113th session, 2000, GB 4895; Kirk Brown, Nathaniel Cary, and Nikie Mayo-Anderson, "Gov. McMaster Doubts Efforts to Remove Confederate Monuments Will Spread to South Carolina," *Independent Mail*, August 14, 2017, https://www.independentmail.com/story/news/local/2017/08/14/s-c-law-protects -confederate-monuments/566472001/.

53. *Augusta Chronicle*, December 2, 2018; "North Augusta Mayor Requests Changes to Monument," WRDW.com, November 13, 2018, https://www.wrdw.com/content/news/North-Augusta -Mayor-Requests-Changes-To-Monument-500431291.html.

54. Dakin Andone, "This South Carolina Mayor Wants to Use a White Supremacist Monument to Teach about Unity," CNN, November 24, 2018, https://www.cnn.com/2018/11/24/us/south -carolina-white-supremacist-monument-trnd/index.html.

ACKNOWLEDGMENTS

Editing this book has been a rewarding journey in many ways: the chance to reflect on George Rable's immense body of work, to read scholarship from his students and colleagues, and to ponder the ways in which our studies interconnect. This volume stands as a testament to George's legacy but also to the historians he has inspired and collaborated with through the years.

The book began as an idea, shared by Laura and Megan, that it would be a fitting retirement present for their advisor. It has turned into so much more than that. Lesley agreed to work on the project during its early stages, bringing valuable editorial experience. This project also would not reach as wide of an audience without her support through the Charles G. Summersell Chair of Southern History endowment.

We have also greatly benefited from the help of others along the way. From the beginning, Mike Parrish, Conflicting Worlds series editor for LSU Press, has been supportive of the project—and even worked with us to keep it a secret. Rand Dotson, along with Mike, provided much guidance as we shaped the essays into a coherent collection. At the University of Alabama, Lisa Lindquist Dorr, Kari Frederickson, Joshua Rothman, Christina Kircharr, Ellen Pledger, and Morta Riggs all provided assistance with the business-related aspects of the project. John Giggie and the University of Alabama's Frances J. Summersell Center for the Study of the South provided additional, much-appreciated financial assistance.

We further benefited from the immense knowledge of our contributors. At different times, both Gary Gallagher and Christian McWhirter made suggestions that vastly improved the collection. Indeed, all of our authors proved overwhelmingly flexible as we moved through this process. We are tremendously grateful for their collegiality. We also thank George for his superb guidance and patience over the years as he shaped and influenced us as students and historians. We dedicate this volume to him.

CONTRIBUTORS

MEGAN L. BEVER is an associate professor of history at Missouri Southern State University. She has published articles in the *Journal of Southern History, Civil War History*, and the *Journal of Sport History*, and has coedited, with Scott A. Suarez, *The Historian behind the History: Conversations with Southern Historians* (2014). She is currently at work on a book-length project exploring the role of alcohol in the Civil War.

GLENN DAVID BRASHER is an instructor of history at the University of Alabama and a former National Park Service interpretive ranger. In 2008 he was a finalist for the Southern Historical Association's C. Vann Woodward Award. In 2013 his book *The Peninsula Campaign & The Necessity of Emancipation* received the Wiley-Silver Award from the Center for Civil War Research at the University of Mississippi. More recently, he has contributed essays to the *Civil War Monitor*, blog postings for the *Journal of the Civil War Era, Daily Beast*, and *Smithsonian*, and book chapters for Oxford University Press and Cambridge University Press.

DANIEL BURGE graduated from the University of Alabama with a PhD in history in August 2017. His dissertation, supervised by George Rable, examined opposition to the ideology of manifest destiny from 1846 to 1871. His most recent article, "Manifest Mirth: The Humorous Critique of Manifest Destiny," was published in the *Western Historical Quarterly*. His research focuses on nineteenth-century expansion and American humor and the ways in which humor was deployed to challenge the rising American empire. He is currently an adjunct professor at the University of Alabama.

RACHEL K. DEALE is an assistant professor of American history at Barton College. Her research examines the southern seizure of federal forts, arsenals, navy yards, customhouses, revenue cutters, courts, and post offices before the firing on Fort Sumter.

Contributors

GARY W. GALLAGHER is the John L. Nau III Professor in the History of the American Civil War Emeritus at the University of Virginia. His most recent books include *The Union War* (2011), *The American War: A History of the Civil War Era* (2015), and *Civil War Writing: New Perspectives on Iconic Texts* (coedited with Stephen Cushman, 2019).

LESLEY J. GORDON is the Charles G. Summersell Chair of Southern History at the University of Alabama. Her publications include *General George E. Pickett in Life and Legend* (1998), *Inside the Confederate Nation: Essays in Honor of Emory M. Thomas* (coedited with John C. Inscoe, 2005), and *A Broken Regiment: The 16th Connecticut's Civil War* (2014). From 2010 to 2015, Gordon was editor of the academic journal *Civil War History*.

A. WILSON GREENE recently retired from a forty-four-year career as a historic site manager, museum director, and battlefield preservationist. He is the author of *A Campaign of Giants: The Battle for Petersburg from the Crossing of the James to the Battle of the Crater* (2018), the first of three volumes on the Petersburg Campaign.

T. ROBERT HART completed his PhD under George Rable in 2004. He currently teaches at the University of North Carolina–Wilmington, where his courses and research focus on southern and environmental history. He was awarded the Jack Temple Kirby Award in 2015 for his article "The Lowcountry Landscape: Politics, Preservation, and the Santee-Cooper Project," published in *Environmental History*.

KEVIN L. HUGHES is a graduate of the University of Alabama, where he studied Reconstruction and the late nineteenth-century South. His dissertation is entitled "The Promise and Perils of Reconstruction: Augusta, Georgia, 1865–1886."

LAWRENCE KREISER JR. is an associate professor of history at Stillman College. He is a coeditor of *The Civil War in Popular Culture: Memory and Meaning* (2014) and author of *Defeating Lee: A History of the Second Corps, Army of the Potomac* (2011) and *Marketing the Blue and Gray: Newspaper Advertising and the American Civil War* (2019).

LAURA MAMMINA is an assistant professor of history at the University of Houston–Victoria, where she teaches courses on gender and sexuality and race and ethnicity in the United States. Her work appears in *Tennessee Women: Their Life and Times,* volume 2 (2015), and *Civil War History.* She is currently working on a book manuscript examining interactions between Union soldiers and southern women during the American Civil War.

JOHN F. MARSZALEK is Giles Distinguished Professor Emeritus of History and executive director of the Ulysses S. Grant Association and Ulysses S. Grant Presidential Library, Mississippi State University. He is the author of numerous books and articles on the Civil War, Jacksonian era, and race relations. He regularly appears on national television and before professional and popular audiences.

CHRISTIAN McWHIRTER is the Lincoln Historian at the Abraham Lincoln Presidential Library and Museum. His work on Civil War culture and memory has appeared in various popular and academic publications. He is the author of *Battle Hymns: The Power and Popularity of Music in the Civil War* (2012).

T. MICHAEL PARRISH is Linden G. Bowers Professor of American History at Baylor University. He is the author of numerous books on the South and the Civil War era, with particular focus on slavery and emancipation, civil-military relations, and the conduct of warfare.

ADAM H. PETTY is a historian and documentary editor with the Joseph Smith Papers. He is the author of *The Battle of the Wilderness in Myth and Memory: Reconsidering Virginia's Most Notorious Civil War Battlefield* (2019). He has published articles in the *Alabama Review, Civil War History,* and the *Journal of Military History.* He specializes in nineteenth-century American history, and his research projects have focused on the Civil War era and the experience of Latter-Day Saints in the southern United States.

LINDSAY RAE PRIVETTE is an assistant professor of history at Anderson University. She is the author of several articles, including "More Than Paper and Ink: Confederate Medical Literature and the Making of the Confederate Army Medical Corps," published in *Civil War History*. Her dissertation, "'Fighting Johnnies, Fevers, and Mosquitoes': A Medical History of the Vicksburg Campaign," examines the way campaigning armies were aided, or hindered, by the capabilities of the Army Medical Corps and the limitations of nineteenth-century medical care.

CHARITY W. RAKESTRAW earned her PhD from the University of Alabama in 2009 under the mentorship of George Rable. She is the author of *Ministers and Masters: Methodism, Manhood, and Honor in the Old South* (2011) and has published several essays and articles on megachurch history and gender and religion. Rakestraw is currently the manager of history faculty at Western Governors University and is working on a book-length study of modern megachurches.

KRISTOPHER A. TETERS received his PhD from the University of Alabama in 2012. His research examines the Union army and the process of emancipation, which is the subject of his book *Practical Liberators: Union Officers in the Western Theater during the Civil War* (2018). He is a course instructor in US history at Western Governors University.

INDEX

abolition movement: antiabolitionist riots caused by drunkenness, 12, 19n21; and black regiments, 23–24, 31; and George E. Stephens, 156; in Lincoln's campaign songs, 63–64; morality of, 10, 16; and temperance reformers, 6, 8, 9, 10–11; Texas Baptists' counterattacks against, 191, 193, 197, 199, 201; and Wilder Dwight, 152, 161

Adams, D. L. "Doc," 251–52, 253, 258

African American citizenship: and black Union regiments, 22–26, 31, 34, 40, 41; and voting rights, 38, 40, 41, 203, 204, 229, 230–31, 253, 254, 255, 260

African American newspapers, 24–25, 27–29, 31

African Americans: agency demonstrated by women, 173, 182n4; civil rights of, 203, 204; David Ross Locke on, 214, 215–16, 218; emancipationist vision of Civil War, 266n29; on Hamburg Massacre, 255; incarceration of, 42; songs portraying Lincoln as emancipator, 6, 67–68; Southern Baptists on inferiority of, 191; in southern legislatures, 224. *See also* black manhood; black Union regiments; black Union soldiers; enslaved African Americans; enslaved men; enslaved women; formerly enslaved African Americans; formerly enslaved African American women; free blacks; freedpeople

Aiken County Historical Museum, 262

Albany Patriot, 86–87

Allison, Joseph, 109

Alva, Duke of, 224–25

American Revolution, 226, 266n35

American Temperance Society, 18n7

American Temperance Union (ATU), 7, 9, 11, 15, 18n7

Anderson, Charles, 90

Anderson, Robert, 84–85

Anderson, Texas, 198

Andrew, John, 23–24, 25, 26, 30

Andrews, Eliza Francis, 228, 229

Anglo-African, 25

Anglo-African Weekly, 39

Anglo-Saxon civilization, 187–88, 250, 261–62

Antietam, Battle of, 50, 51, 151–52

Army of Northern Virginia, 118, 131

Army of the Cumberland, 239, 240

Army of the James, 41, 131

Army of the Potomac, 131

Army of the Tennessee, 100

Attaway, Allan, 252–53

Augusta Chronicle, 252–54, 259, 261

Augusta Democrat, 86

Badeau, Adam, 241, 244

Baines, George Washington, 191, 197

Baines, William M., 197

Baird, Absalom, 184n23

Baird, William, 142

Bancroft, George, 236–37

Banks, Nathaniel P., 184n23

Banner, Matthew Rawley, 104, 111

Baptist church: black Baptist churches, 202–3; and Christian soldiers, 190, 194; and military chaplains, 194–95; "priesthood" of individual believers, 189, 202; and religious liberty, 189–90, 193, 197–98, 202. *See also* Texas Baptists

Baptist Home Mission Society, 201

Index

Barksdale, Andrew S., 141

Barnes, James W., 193

Barnum, P. T., 45–46

Barrier, Rufus A., 141

Barton, Seth, 110

Barton, Thomas, 106

Bates, Delavan, 136

Baugh, William Fielding, 138

Baylor, R. E. B., 196, 199

Baylor University, 190–91, 193–97, 201

Bearss, Edwin, 94n9

Beecham, Robert K., 133–34, 142

Bell, Andrew McIlwaine, 111n6

Bever, Megan L., 5

Bill of Rights, 189

Bishop College, Marshall, Texas, 201–2

Black, James, 10

Black, Jeremiah, 81–83, 85

Black Codes, 223

Blackford, William W., 142

black manhood: and African American citizenship, 23, 24, 26; and black Union regiments, 25–29, 31–32, 34–35, 36, 40, 41; and expression of character in deeds, 157; and ideas of masculinity, 169n33; and stereotypes of black dependency, 23, 35; whites' questioning of, 22

black Union regiments: and black manhood, 25–29, 31–32, 34–35, 36, 40, 41; Lincoln's defense of, 37; northerners' on effectiveness of, 22; public opinion of, 41; and racial equality, 38; recruitment of, 23, 24–26, 31, 32, 34, 38, 41; white officers leading, 24, 26, 142. *See also* 54th Massachusetts Volunteer Infantry

black Union soldiers: character expressed in deeds of, 157–58; Confederates troops' attitude toward, 132–33, 136, 137–38, 140–41, 145n6, 200; debates on, 77; equal pay for, 6, 23, 31–32, 41; massacre of, 77, 134–42, 145n6, 200; and New York Draft riots, 33; as POWs, 32–33, 35, 41, 141–43; southern women's relationships with, 150–51; training of, 133–34; white Union soldiers' attitudes toward, 77, 132, 136, 139, 140, 142–43

Blair, Frank, 238

Blair, Montgomery, 238

Blair, Walter, 208–9, 221n43

Blease, Coleman Livingston, 259

Blight, David, 266n29

Blocker, Jack S., 18n7

Booth, John Wilkes, 53–54, 55, 56, 211

border states, 152, 155

Bostick, J. L., 127

Boston Courier, 26

Boston Daily Advertiser, 25

Boston Herald, 30

Boston Pilot, 26

Boteler, Alexander, 122

Bowen, George A., 119–20

Bowie, Aquila, 105

Bowley, Freeman, 133, 143

Bowman, Samuel M., 240

Boynton, Henry Van Ness, 239–41

Brady, Lisa M., 111n5, 111n6

Bragg, Braxton, 89, 90

Bragg, Elise, 89

Brasher, Glenn David, 6

Brazos River valley, Texas, 190, 192, 202

Brewster, James, 14–15

Brice's Cross Roads, 145n6

Brockett, Linus, 54

Brooks, Preston, 208

Bross, John A., 136–37

Brown, John, 27, 69, 79, 82–83

Brown, Joseph E., 85, 86, 87, 96n40

Browne, Charles Farrar, 209

Browning, Orville, 92–93

Buchanan, James, 81–85, 88–89, 90, 92, 96n40, 210

Buck, Gideon J., 200, 201

Buckingham, William Alfred, 17

Buell, Clarence Clough, 248n25

Buffalo Courier, 35

Burge, Daniel, 187

Burges, William, 197

Burke, Edmund, 226, 227

Burleson, Rufus C., 193–95, 198–99, 201–4

Burlington (IA) Hawkeye, 39

Burmeister, George C., 101, 103, 184n19

Burnside, Ambrose E., 131–35, 139, 144

Bushnell, Douglas, 103

Butler, Benjamin F., 131, 132, 138, 144, 184n23, 232

Butler, Matthew Calbraith, 251–53, 254, 255, 256

Butler, Thomas, 251

Byers, S. H. M., 183n12

Cade, Edward, 102–3, 107, 109

Caldwell, James, 25

Calhoun, John C., 226

Camp, Stephanie M. H., 174, 183n16, 185n48

capitalism, 226

Carney, William, 25, 29, 30, 39–40

Case, Ervin T., 133

Cashin, Joan, 168n26

Castel, Albert, 246–47

Century Magazine, 242–43, 248n25, 248n27

Chamberlain, Daniel H., 253

Champion Hill, Battle of, 104

Chancellorsville, Battle of: assertions of intentional setting of fires for tactical advantage, 117, 118, 126; combat conditions affected by fires, 116, 120, 121–22; and postwar reconciliation, 125–26; soldiers' reactions to fires, 116, 122–25, 126; weather conditions causing fires, 117

Charles L. Webster Company, 237, 243, 245, 246

Charleston, South Carolina, 250, 255

Charleston Courier, 34, 81

Charleston Mercury, 28, 32–33, 81, 231

Charlottesville, Virginia, 250

Chase, Salmon P., 52–53, 175

Chicago Daily Tribune, 254

Chicago Times, 35–36

Chicago Tribune, 36, 37

Chickamauga, Battle of, 117, 126–27

Chickasaw Bayou, Battle of, 103

children, 22, 49

Christian Advocate, 254, 255

Christianity, 11. See also Baptist church; evangelicals; Texas Baptists

Christian paternalism, 189, 191, 195–200, 201, 204–5

Christian Recorder, 29

Christian soldiers, 189, 190, 194, 195–96, 197, 200

Cincinnati Enquirer, 38

Civil Constitution of the Clergy Act, 227

civil liberties, 189–90, 193, 197–98, 227

Civil Rights Bill, 211

Civil War: Christian soldiers in, 189, 190, 195, 197; negotiated peace affected by presence of black Union soldiers, 23; scholarship on, 245, 246, 247, 250; South's seizure of federal forts and arsenals as beginning of, 80, 85, 89–90, 91, 93–94, 94n9; strands of memory emerging from, 264, 266n29; temperance reformers on, 12–13, 14, 16–17, 20n43; Union triumph in, 56; war-related news in newspaper advertisements, 48–49, 50, 52, 57

Civil War music: and anti-Lincoln northern songwriters, 67–71; anti-Lincoln songs of Confederates, 69–70; campaign music, 6, 61–65, 70, 71–72; and Lincoln as great emancipator, 6, 64–67, 72, 73; and Lincoln's assassination, 55, 72–73; and Lincoln's association with the troops, 65–66; and Lincoln's frontier background, 62, 64, 65; and Lincoln's height, 62, 66; and Lincoln's honesty, 61–62; and Lincoln's paternal image, 65, 71; and political culture, 60. See also songs

Clark, Charles Heber, 212

Clay, Henry, 132

Clearfield Republican, 48

Clemens, Samuel L., 242–43, 244, 246

Clemens, Sherrard, 79

Clemens, Will M., 208–9

Cleveland Leader, 240

Cleveland Morning Leader, 30

Clingman, Thomas, 80

Coke, Richard, 204

colonization movement, 201–2, 203

Confederacy: creation of, 80; defeat of, 197; divisions within, 77; David Ross Locke on, 212; and seizure of federal forts and arsenals,

Index

Confederacy (*continued*)
79, 80–84, 85, 86–90, 91, 93–94, 94n7, 94n8, 94n9

Confederate monuments, 250–51, 259–60, 263, 264

Confederates: anti-Lincoln songs of, 69–70; Confederate nationalism and religious faith, 194; former officers on Civil War, 236; and Lost Cause, 197, 201; and prisoner exchanges, 32–33, 34, 35, 41; Reconstruction compared to French Revolution, 2–3, 187, 223, 224, 225–34, 234n1; on soldiers as personifications of selfless white Christian males, 189; veterans' reunions, 201

Confederate troops: access to clean water, 100, 106, 112n7; assertions on intentional setting of fires in battle, 117, 118, 126; attitudes toward black Union soldiers, 132–33, 136, 137–38, 140–41, 145n6, 200; and civil religion, 189; destruction of water supply, 99, 110; enslaved labor used by, 174; environmental factors affecting health of, 100–101; food supply of, 109, 110; and military chaplains, 194–95; and Vicksburg Campaign, 99, 100–101, 108, 109–10

Conkling, Roscoe, 256

Cooke, Chauncey, 102, 103, 104

Cooper, William J., 94n9

Copperhead Minstrel, 67–68

Corden, John, 179

Corinth, Mississippi, Battle of, 195, 196

counterrevolution, of white southerners, 2, 80, 95n10, 187, 233–34

Couse, Elizabeth, 152

Couse, Katherine, 152, 154–55, 157, 161, 163, 166n8

Couse, William, 152

coverture laws, 22

Crater, Battle of the, 134–44

Cristadoro, J., 49

Cromwell, Oliver, 225

Crooke, George, 102

Crossley, Andrew Jackson, 132

Cumming, Alfred, 110

Curtis, George, 45

Cuyler, Theo D., 218

D. Appleton and Company, 237, 246

Daily Hawk-Eye, 53

Daily Palladium, 90

Dana, Charles, 108–9

Darien, Georgia, 27, 39

Davis, Edmund J., 201, 203, 204

Davis, Jefferson, 49, 60, 69, 87

Deale, Rachel K., 77

DeLaughter, J. P., 259

Democratic National Convention, 48, 49

Democratic newspapers: advertisements of, 48, 49, 51, 52–53; on 54th Massachusetts, 27, 28, 32, 34, 35, 37, 40–41; on racial equality, 38–41; on recruitment of black regiments, 25–26; on South's seizure of federal forts and arsenals, 93

Democratic Party: on African American voting rights, 41; and anti-Lincoln northern songwriters, 67–69, 70; David Ross Locke on, 209, 210, 211, 212–15, 218–19, 219n9; on Emancipation Proclamation, 37; and Ku Klux Klan, 202; Lincoln ridiculed by, 6; Matthew Gaines on, 203–4; newspaper advertising used by, 47, 49–52, 57, 58n13; objections to black Union soldiers, 23, 25; perceived moral superiority of, 2, 6; politically themed merchandise of, 47–48; political rhetoric of, 5; and presidential election of 1864, 45; on prohibition, 9; Reconstruction undermined by, 203; return to power, 234; Seba Smith on, 209–10; and secession crisis, 83; and South's seizure of federal forts and arsenals, 91; and temperance reformers, 21n51

Denver *Sunday Post,* 172

Detroit Free Press, 216

Diderot, Denis, 226

domesticity: and boundaries between home front and battlefront, 169n32; cult of, 150, 151, 154, 156; and enslaved women, 150, 159, 165; and gender roles, 150, 151, 165; and masculinity, 157–58, 169–70n33; and middle

class, 150, 156, 159, 165, 169*n*33; and patriarchal control of male heads of household, 165;
racial biases in, 158, 165; struggles within
domestic spaces, 78; and women working
outside home, 156, 168*n*19; and working
class, 170*n*37

Donald, David, 98*n*88

Dorsey, Decatur, 144

Douglas, Stephen A., 62

Douglass, Charles, 25

Douglass, Frederick, 24, 25, 31–32

Douglass, Lewis, 25

Douglass Monthly, 24, 27, 31, 33

Dow, Edwin, 120

Downs, Jim, 175–76

Dred Scott decision (1857), 22, 24

Dwight, Wilder, 151–52, 156–57, 160–61, 166*n*8

Early, Jubal A., 247*n*2

Early Republic period, 171*n*44

economic development: and slavery debates,
13; and social classes, 190; temperance reformers linking slavery and intemperance
to, 14, 15

Eddington, William, 104

Edgefield Advertiser, 259, 260

Edwards, William, 99

emancipation: in Civil War music about
Lincoln, 6, 64–67, 72, 73; Democrats' criticism of, 37, 38; and liberation process, 174;
Lincoln's initial policy on, 84; as Lincoln's
legacy, 64–65, 73; and memory of Civil War,
266*n*29; public opinion of, 41; Republicans'
conception of, 3, 79–80, 94*n*3; and saving
the Union, 8, 22; temperance reformers on,
8, 16–17; and white southerners' historical
allusions to French Revolution, 228, 229

Emancipation Day celebrations, 67

Emancipation Proclamation: Baptist State
Convention of Texas's condemnation of,
200; and black Union soldiers' enlistment,
23; Lincoln's defense of, 37; Lincoln's final issuing of, 174; and politically themed
merchandise, 50; and saving the Union, 8;

temperance reformers on, 15, 16; and Union
officers' use of black women's labor, 184*n*23

Emerson, Luther O., 74*n*8

enslaved African Americans: Christianization
of, 191, 197, 198–99, 201, 204; on enslavement
as state of warfare, 197; and Lost Cause
myth, 258; resistance of, 199, 204–5. *See also*
formerly enslaved African Americans

enslaved men: definitions of being a man,
169*n*31; effect of slavery on, 157; marriage
of, 171*n*47; runaway enslaved men recruited
for black regiments, 23, 25, 34; subsistence
of, 177. *See also* formerly enslaved African
Americans

enslaved women: and cult of domesticity,
150, 159, 165; definitions of being a woman,
169*n*31; effect of slavery on, 156, 157; escap-
ing to Union lines, 172–73, 175; marriage of,
163, 171*n*47; perils faced by, 163; subsistence
strategies of, 177–78; underground network
of, 185*n*48. *See also* formerly enslaved African American women

etiquette rules, 157, 158–59, 162, 170*n*38

evangelicals, 8, 191, 192, 194, 198

Fayetteville Observer, 87

federal authority: and emancipation, 79–80,
84; individual rights versus, 6; Lincoln's
policies on, 84, 91–93; and South's seizure
of federal forts and arsenals, 79, 80–84, 85,
86–88, 90–93

federal forts and arsenals: Buchanan's policies
on, 81–83, 84, 85, 88–89, 90, 92, 96*n*40; John
Brown's seizure of, 82–83; and federal authority, 79, 80–84, 85, 86–88, 90–93; federal
reinforcement of, 80–81, 84, 85, 88, 96*n*40;
Lincoln's policies on, 84, 91–93; South's
seizure of, 80–84, 85, 86–90, 91, 93–94, 94*n*7,
94*n*8, 94*n*9

Federal Writers' Project, 60

Ferguson, Champ, 200

Ferrero, Edward, 132, 133–39, 143, 144

Field, Ann Dagnail, 258–59

Field, S. P. T., 258–59

Index

Fifteenth Amendment, 42

54th Massachusetts Volunteer Infantry: assignments of, 26–27; drunkenness claims by southern newspapers, 34; and film *Glory,* 42; Fort Wagner stormed by, 6, 22, 28–30, 33, 34, 35, 36, 40; marching song of, 67; newspaper coverage of, 25–36, 39–40; pay dispute of, 31, 32, 34, 39–40; recruitment for, 25, 31; treatment as prisoners of war, 32–33, 34, 35, 41

fires, 78. *See also* Wilderness fires

First Confiscation Act, 174

Fisher v. McGirr (1854), 10

Fitzhugh, George, 225, 226

Fleming, Aaron T., 140

Fletcher, Holly Berkeley, 8, 20*n*43

Fletcher, Thomas, 227

Floyd, John B., 80–81, 85

Forbis, James, 108–9

formerly enslaved African Americans: agency of, 173, 182*n*4; and conditions in Union army camps, 175–76, 183–84*n*18, 184*n*19; as contraband, 2, 173, 175, 182*n*5; and enforcement of Reconstruction, 188; Federal Writers' Project interviews of, 60; northerners' treatment of, 180–81; population leaving plantations, 175, 183*n*12; songs honoring Lincoln, 67–68; Union army as protector of, 157, 172, 174–76, 177, 181

formerly enslaved African American women: disguised as soldiers, 78, 173, 177; labor in Union army camps, 176–79, 182; methods of resistance, 173–75; strategies in refugee camps, 78, 172–73, 177–81, 182*n*3; treatment in Union army camps, 176, 177, 178–79, 183–84*n*18, 184*n*19; Union soldiers' raping of, 176, 184*n*21

Fort Gaines, 87, 88, 97*n*60

Fort Jackson, 90

Fort Jefferson, 91

Fort Johnson, 85

Fort Livingston, 90

Fort Macomb, 90

Fort Morgan, 87, 88, 97*n*60

Fort Moultrie, 84–85

Fort Pickens, 91

Fort Pike, 90

Fort Pillow, 133, 136, 141, 145*n*6

Fort Pulaski, 85, 86, 87

Fort St. Philip, 90

Fort Sumter, 27–29, 77, 80, 85, 90–91, 93, 193

Fort Taylor, 91

Fort Wagner, 6, 22, 28–30, 32–36, 40

Foster, Gaines M., 16, 20*n*43

Foster, Stephen, 70

Fourteenth Amendment, 42

free blacks, 25, 150, 159, 165, 169*n*31

Freedmen's Bureau, 224

freedpeople, 223, 224, 229–30, 232, 233, 251–52

Freehling, William, 94*n*7

free-labor society, 14

Freeman, James, 117

Frelinghuysen, Frederick, 55–56

French Enlightenment, 226

French Revolution: Committee of Public Safety, 227, 231, 232; and Jacobins, 3, 225, 226, 229–33; and loyalists in La Vendée, 227–28; radical egalitarianism of, 226, 229; Reconstruction compared to, 2–3, 187, 223, 224, 225–34, 234*n*1; and Reign of Terror, 224, 225, 227–33

Fugitive Slave Law, 80

Gaines, Matthew, 202–4

Galaxy magazine, 237

Gallagher, Gary W., 1, 8

Galwey, Francis, 118

Gardner, Samuel, 56–57

Garfield, James, 175

Garrett, Hosea, 195

Gary, John, 195

Gayle, George Washington, 55, 57

gender roles: and cult of domesticity, 150, 151, 165; familiarity of hierarchy, 2; and men requiring civilizing and moralizing influence of women, 150; and social interactions of soldiers and women, 78, 150–51, 157–58, 165, 169–70n33

gerrymandering, 42

Getzen, Henry, 251, 253

Giddings, Texas, 204

Gilmer, John, 84

Gilmore, Quincy, 40

Glory (film), 42

Glymph, Thavolia, 168n19, 173–74, 183–84n18

Goldfield, David, 18n6

Gooding, James, 25, 27, 28, 31

Goss, Warren Lee, 124, 125–26

Grabeau, Warren, 111n5

Grand Army of the Republic (GAR), 172, 181

Grant, Buck, 242

Grant, Fred, 242, 244, 245

Grant, Jesse, 242

Grant, Julia, 241, 242, 243, 244, 245

Grant, Nellie, 242

Grant, Ulysses S.: and black Union soldiers, 142, 144; and *Century Magazine* Civil War series, 242, 248n27; criticism of memoirs, 245–46; death of, 244, 248n35; financial security of, 241, 242, 243, 246; health problems of, 243–44, 245; and Joseph E. Johnston, 99; and labor programs employing formerly enslaved African Americans, 184n23; and Lincoln on black troops, 41; lower Mississippi River valley and campaign strategy of, 104, 111n5; memoirs of, 188, 237, 241–46, 247; military strategy of, 112n7; and Petersburg Campaign, 131–32, 134–35, 139; as president, 216, 236, 253; Sherman's relationship with, 236, 240, 241

Graves, David, 202

Greenberg, Amy, 169–70n33

Greene, A. Wilson, 77

Greenhow, Rose, 227, 228

Griffin, Clifford, 18n7

Griffin, Simon G., 138

Grinspan, Jon, 219n9

Guerrant, Edward, 200

Gurney, Warren S., 139

Gwin, William, 80

Haco, Dion, 56

Hall, Matthew R., 137, 139–40

Halleck, Henry W., 169n32

Hamburg Massacre: events of, 251–54; evolution of memory of, 251, 254, 255–59, 260, 261, 262–64; historical marker at Carrsville Society House, 262, 263; memorial stone at Carrsville Society House, 262, 263; memorial to S. P. T. and Ann Field, 258–59; memorial to Thomas McKie Meriwether, 250, 259–62, 263, 264; as saving Anglo-Saxon civilization, 187–88, 250, 261–62

Hamlin, A. C., 36–37

Hamlin, Hannibal, 7

Hammond, C. A., 12

Hammond, James Henry, 226

Hammond, William, 103

Hampton, N. J., 126–27

Hampton, Wade, 255–56

Hancock, Winfield S., 119

Hardee, William J., 85

Harper's New Monthly Magazine, 217

Harper's Weekly, 33–34, 35, 255

Harris, George Washington, 211

Harris, R. F., 199

Harris, William H., 133

Harrison, William Henry, 46–47

Hart, T. Robert, 187

Hartford Daily Courant, 254

Haskin, Joseph A., 89

Hawley, J. B., 54

Heg, Hans Christian, 177

Henderson, D. S., 258, 261

Hennessey, John, 128n1

Henry, William Wirt, 132

Heritage Act, 263

Higgins, H. M., 66

Hill, Ambrose Powell, 142

Hill, Benjamin, 231

Hill, Hamlin, 208–9, 221n43

Index

historical memory, 250–51, 256, 264, 266n29

Hitchcock, Henry, 240

Holbrook, Kendall, 230, 231

Holcombe, William H., 229

Holt, David, 141

Holt, Joseph, 85

Holzer, Harold, 46

Hood's Texas Brigade, 192, 196, 197

Hooker, Joseph, 238

Horton, Albert C., 198–99

Houston, Margaret Lea, 194, 196

Houston, Sam, 192–93, 194, 196

Houston, Sam, Jr., 194

Houston *Tri-Weekly Telegraph*, 193

Howe, Julia Ward, 66

Hudson, Frederic, 52

Hughes, Henry, 45

Hughes, Kevin, 187

Hugunin, George, 121

Hurlbut, Stephen A., 175

Hutchinson Family Singers, 61, 63

I. N. Richardson and Company, 208

immigration, 42, 203, 213

Independence, 245

Independence Baptist Church, Texas, 191, 195, 198, 202

industrialization, 226

Insurrection Act of 1807, 81, 82

Jackson, Andrew, 210, 212

Jameson, Robert Edwin, 101–2

Jamieson, Kathleen Hall, 46–47, 58n6

Jamison, David Flavel, 85

Janesville, Wisconsin, *Daily Gazette,* 172

Janney, Caroline, 56

Jefferson, Thomas, 226

Jett, Nancy, 153, 159–60, 164–65, 166n8

Jett, Richard Burch, 153, 164, 167n16

Jim Crow era, 42, 256, 263

Johnson, Andrew, 53, 211, 212, 223, 231–32

Johnson, Charles, 105

Johnson, Francis S., 123

Johnson, Robert Underwood, 248n25

Johnson, William Parker, 179

Johnston, Joseph E., 99, 102, 104, 239

Jones, Josiah, 132

Journal of the American Temperance Union (JATU), 7–9, 11, 12, 14–16, 18n7, 20n36, 20n38

Kansas-Nebraska Act (1854), 10

Kasson, John F., 170n38

Kennesaw Mountain, Battle of, 117, 127

Killgore, Gabriel, 109

Kilmer, George, 140

King, Edward, 153

Knights of the Golden Circle, 56

Kosciuszko, Thaddeus, 225

Kreiser, Lawrence A., Jr., 5, 6

Ku Klux Klan, 201, 202, 224, 233

Landon, William D., 123

Landrum, George W., 178

Largent, John Wesley, 107

laws of war, 158, 169n32

Lawton, Alexander, 85, 86

Leavenworth Daily Conservative, 47

LeConte, Emma, 228

LeConte, Joseph, 228

Ledlie, James, 134–35

Lee, Robert E., 49, 118, 131, 133, 134, 143–44, 220n25

Leftwich, W. M., 227

Lewis, Charles B., 216

Liberty Baptist Church, 202

Lincoln, Abraham: American myth of, 61, 62; American Temperance Union's view of election of, 7; assassination of, 46, 53–54, 57, 72, 211; in children's books, 49; and David Ross Locke, 208, 213, 216, 217; Democratic Party's view of, 6; emancipation policy, 84; and equal pay for black Union soldiers, 6, 31–32; evolution of public image, 64–65, 73; and Federal Writers' Project, 60; humorists on, 211; inaugural addresses of, 53, 92–93, 98n88; inauguration of, 80; Indianapolis address of 1861, 91–92; letter on 54th Massachusetts, 37; Order of Retaliation, 33, 34, 35–36, 38, 39; political journalism used by, 46; politically themed merchandise supporting, 47, 48, 50–51; and presidential election of 1860, 7, 10, 83, 191, 192–93; and presidential election of 1864, 41, 46, 47, 48, 50–51, 52, 53; on reclaiming federal property, 91–92; Reconstruction proposal, 41, 42; and secession crisis, 83, 84, 88, 91–92, 93; as symbol of Union, 72–73; and Union army's complaints of "contraband," 175; and Wilder Dwight, 151. *See also* Civil War music; Emancipation Proclamation

Lincoln, Mary, 69

Lincoln, Robert Todd, 49

Lincoln and Johnson Union Campaign Songster, The, 71

Locke, David Ross: on African Americans, 214, 215–16, 218; as alcoholic, 221n51; critics of, 217–18; on Democratic political figures, 209, 211, 218–19; on Democrats as cowardly, 210, 212–13, 214; on Democrats as ignorant, 213–14, 215; on Democrats as venal spoilsmen, 210, 212; on Democrats' behavior during Civil War, 213, 219n9; on Democrats' intemperance, 214–15, 218; on Democrats' racism, 215–16; as partisan humorist, 208–11, 216, 218–19; Petroleum V. Nasby character of, 209, 210–15, 216, 217, 218, 219, 219n3; and Reconstruction, 208, 213, 219, 219n3; on segregation, 216, 219; writing in dialect, 214, 218, 221n43

Logan, John A., 83–84, 91, 238

Lost Cause myth, 197, 201, 234, 236, 247n2, 258, 260

Louisiana State Register, 238

Louis XVI (king of France), 227, 232

lower class, 194

lower middle class, 194

lower Mississippi River valley, 103–4, 105, 108–9, 111n5, 113n33

Lubbock, Francis, 199

Lubrecht, Charles, 50

McAllister, Robert, 122

McBride, Andrew J., 120

McClellan, George, 45, 47–48, 49, 50–51, 57, 71

McClernand, John A., 238

McClintock, Russell, 94n9

McFarland, J. W., 120, 123

McGee, Hall T., 140

McKie, James B., 259

McParlin, Thomas, 122

McPherson, James B., 239

McPherson, James M.: *Battle Cry of Freedom,* 22, 94n9, 95n10; *For Cause and Comrades,* 94n8

McWhirter, Christian, 5, 6

Mahone, William, 137, 139, 140, 141, 142

Makin, Ken, 263–64

Mammina, Laura, 77–78

Manifest Destiny, 188, 189

Manning, Chandra, 52, 182n4

Marsh, John, 7, 10, 12, 16, 17

Marszalek, John F., 188, 247

Marten, James, 49

masculinity: and domesticity, 157–58, 169–70n33; and virtuous manhood, 190. *See also* black manhood

Mayer, Arno, 95n10

Meade, George G., 131–32, 134, 135, 139, 144

Medlock, G. W., 260–61

Meier, Kathryn Shively, 111–12n6

Memphis, Tennessee, 229–30

Meriwether, Joseph, 257

Meriwether, Thomas McKie, 250, 252, 255, 257, 259–62, 263

Merriam, Leander O., 133

middle class: and cult of domesticity, 150, 156, 159, 165, 169n33; economic rising of, 190; and etiquette, 170n38; ladylike behavior defined by, 156, 165; and marriage within social class, 163; and political sympathies, 162; as proslavery Confederates, 194; and self-control, 160; and white northern women, 155; women of, 155, 160, 161

Military Reconstruction Acts, 224, 225, 231

Militia Act of 1795, 81, 82

Index

Militia Act of 1862, 31

Milledgeville *Federal Union,* 86, 87

millennialist goals, 8, 14, 17, 189

Miller, Charles Dana, 175, 178

Mills, Elon G., 132

Milwaukee News, 35

minstrel shows, 23, 26, 42, 66, 67–68

Mississippi River: as water source, 105, 106, 108. *See also* lower Mississippi River valley

Mitchel, O. M., 184n21

Mobile Tribune, 88

Montgomery, James, 27, 39

Monthly Religious Magazine, 217

Moore, Andrew B., 87–89

Moore, Thomas Overton, 89–90, 94n9

morality: and gender roles, 150, 151; intemperance as sin, 9, 10–11, 14–15, 16, 17; of political compromise, 6; power of state to regulate, 11, 16, 17; slavery as sin, 9, 10, 11, 13, 14–15, 16; slavery causing moral decay, 156; of temperance reformers, 9, 10, 11, 13, 14–16

Morgan, Sarah, 151, 152–54, 158, 160, 161–62, 163, 166n8

Morgan, Sarah Hunt Fowler, 152, 153–54

Morgan, Thomas Gibbes, 152

Morris Island, 27

Mott, Frank Luther, 18n7

Moulton, Charles W., 240, 241

Murphey, Josiah F., 117, 120

Musser, Charles O., 152, 155–56, 162–63, 166n8

Myniart, Albert, 252–53

Nast, Thomas, 218, 255

Neely, Mark, 46

New Bedford Courier, 27, 31

New Bedford Mercury, 25

Newell, Robert Henry, 211, 220n25

New Jersey, election of 1863, 38

New Orleans, Louisiana, 227, 230

newspaper advertisements: Barnum on, 45–46; and election-year merchandise, 46, 47–48, 50–51, 57; and Lincoln's assassination, 46, 53–56, 57; and political culture, 45, 46, 47–50, 52–53, 57; and presidential

election of 1864, 45, 46, 47–52, 53; Samuel Gardner on, 56–57; and war-related news, 48–49, 50, 52, 57

newspapers: on 54th Massachusetts Volunteer Infantry, 25–36, 39–40; on Fort Wagner attack, 22; and humorists, 216–17; partisan nature of, 22, 25–26, 27, 42, 46, 47; readership of, 45–46, 57n2, 234n1; on recruitment for black regiments, 24; on Sherman's memoirs, 237, 238–40. *See also* African American newspapers; Democratic newspapers; northern newspapers; Republican newspapers; southern newspapers

New York Draft riots, 33–34

New York Herald, 28–30, 33, 45, 52, 88, 92, 93–94

New York Journal of Commerce, 27

New York Sun, 51–52

New York Times, 29, 30, 32, 40, 172, 254–55

New-York Tribune, 27–28, 30, 32, 35, 47, 83, 92

New York Witness, 255

New York World, 24, 26

Nichols, C. S., 16

Nichols, John, 172

Nichols, Lucy Higgs: biography of, 181–82; labor for Union troops, 172, 173, 176–77, 181; pension of, 172, 181, 182n1; photograph of, 182n1

Nicolay, John, 88, 91

North: response to South's seizure of federal forts and arsenals, 94n9; white supremacy in political culture of, 2, 38. *See also* Union

North Augusta Civic League, 259–60

North Augusta Heritage Council, 262

northerners: on effectiveness of black regiments, 22; on South's seizure of federal forts and arsenals, 90, 91, 93; treatment of formerly enslaved African Americans, 180–81; white northerners, 9, 22, 23, 26, 150

northern newspapers: on equal pay for black Union soldiers, 31; on federal forts and arsenals, 83, 88, 90, 92, 93–94; on 54th Massachusetts, 27–31, 33, 34–36; on Hamburg Massacre, 254–55; on Lucy Higgs Nichols,

172; readership of, 45; on recruitment for black regiments, 24, 25–26; on Sherman's memoirs, 238–40

Oakes, James, 94n3
O'Bryant, Wayne, 263
Oden, John Piney, 117
Oliver, Amanda, 60
Olustee, Florida, 41
Order of Retaliation, 33, 34, 35–36, 38, 39
Ordronaux, John, 107

Parker, Mrs. A. M., 260
Parks, Moses, 253
Parrish, T. Michael, 188
partisan rancor: David Ross Locke as partisan humorist, 208–11, 216, 218–19; and lack of political compromise, 5, 6; in newspaper coverage, 22, 25–26, 27, 42; Seba Smith as partisan humorist, 210, 220n13
paternalism: Christian paternalism, 189, 191, 195–200, 201, 204–5; of white Union soldiers toward formerly enslaved African American women, 180–81
Patrick, Robert, 99
Peace Democrats, 6, 69
Pegram, Willie, 141
Pemberton, John C., 110
Persons, Warren B., 120
Petersburg Campaign: and Battle of the Crater, 134–44; and Grant, 131–32, 134–35, 139; impact of forest fires on, 78
Pettey, Mattie, 196
Pettey, Tom, 196
Pettey, Virginius E., 196
Pettit, Bob, 263
Petty, Adam H., 78, 111n5
Philadelphia Ledger, 47
Philip II (king of France), 224–25
Phillips, David, 252–53
Phillips, Wendell, 235n16
Pickens, Francis, 85
Pierce, Edward L., 28–31, 35
Pike, Albert, 229–31, 232

Pirtle, Alfred, 150, 152, 155, 158–59, 162, 163, 166n8
Pittsburgh Post, 93
Pleasants, Henry, 131
Poison Spring, Arkansas, Battle of, 200
police brutality, 42
political culture: and Civil War music, 60; and David Ross Locke, 208; of Jim Crow era, 42, 256, 263; and newspaper advertisements, 45, 46, 47–50, 52–53, 57; of Reconstruction, 2, 3, 42, 56, 224; role of political compromise in, 2; role of religion in, 189, 190, 191; white supremacy in North, 2, 38
political power, domesticity tied to, 151, 165
political rhetoric: anti-Lincoln rhetoric, 70; extremism of, 5; and Hamburg Massacre, 254–56; opposition vilified in, 5, 6; of state and local elections of 1863, 37–39; of temperance reformers, 14; and white southerners' historical allusions of Reconstruction, 2–3, 187, 188, 223, 224, 225–34, 234n1
Pomeroy, Mark M., 221–22n61
Porter, David Dixon, 106
Porter, Horace, 124
Port Hudson, Louisiana, 33, 34, 35
Portland Courier, 209
Potter, Robert, 134–35
presidential election of 1840, 46–47, 58n6
presidential election of 1860, 7, 10, 11, 83, 191, 192–93
presidential election of 1864: campaign songs of, 70; and Lincoln, 41, 46, 47, 48, 50–51, 52, 53; newspaper advertisements on, 45, 46, 47–52, 53
Privette, Lindsay Rae, 78
prohibition: as divisive political issue, 9–10; laws on, 9, 10, 12, 13, 15, 16; liquor license laws replacing, 10–11, 12, 13, 15, 16; as moral issue, 9, 10, 11; representative government depending on, 12, 17; temperance reformers on prohibition laws, 9, 12, 13, 15, 16
Prohibition Party, 17
public schools, racial integration of, 203
Puffer, A. F., 184n21

Index

Rable, George: *But There Was No Peace,* 3, 187, 188; *Civil Wars,* 2; on complicated experiences of war, 3, 77; *The Confederate Republic,* 2; *Damn Yankees!,* 2, 3, 233; eclectic interests of, 1, 2; *Fredericksburg! Fredericksburg!,* 1, 2; *God's Almost Chosen Peoples,* 2; legacy of, 1; on partisan rancor, 5, 6; on people as full human beings, 1, 3; on religious terms of Civil War, 18n6

racial equality: backlash against, 3; biracial society, 187; black troops as first step toward, 23; Democratic newspapers on, 38–41; for freedpeople, 230; and Order of Retaliation, 35–36; and pay disparity for black regiments, 32; and political rhetoric, 5; Texas Baptists' rejection of, 201; and treatment of black regiments' prisoners, 22; white supremacy versus, 6

racial hierarchies, 2

racial segregation, 144, 201, 216, 219

racial stereotypes, 6, 23, 35, 47–48

Radical Republicans: and black regiments, 23, 40; and emancipation debates, 79; and impeachment of Johnson, 232; Reconstruction proposals of, 42; Rufus Burleson's opposition to, 201; and white southerners' fears of insurrection, 229–30, 233.

Rakestraw, Charity, 78

Randolph, Ryland, 225, 233

Raymer, Jacob, 120, 123–24

Reconstruction: Confederates showing defiance during, 190; and David Ross Locke, 208, 213, 219, 219n3; Democrats' overthrowing of, 197, 204; failures of, 42, 187; historical allusions describing, 2–3, 187, 188, 223, 224, 225–34, 234n1; Lincoln's first proposal for, 41; memory of, 260; newspaper readership during, 234n1; political culture of, 2, 3, 42, 56, 224; Radical Reconstruction, 201, 203, 230, 232; and Republican Party, 187, 234; testimonies of formerly enslaved African Americans from, 174; violence against blacks during, 202, 223, 233

Redington, Edward S., 180

Redington, Mary, 180

Red Shirts, 251–52, 256, 258, 266n35

Reese, Chauncey Barnes, 88

Reese, Harry, 135

religious liberty, 189–90, 193, 197–98, 227

Renfro, Absalom, 195

Renfro, Henry, 195

Renfro, Summerfield, 195

Reno, Jesse L., 88

Republican Campaign Songster, The, 61–62

Republican newspapers: advertisements of, 48–49; on 54th Massachusetts, 26, 27, 28, 35, 36, 39–40; on Order of Retaliation, 33; silence on unequal pay for black regiments, 32

Republican Party: on black troops, 23, 26; civil rights legislation of, 223–24; and David Ross Locke, 212, 215, 216, 217; and emancipation debates, 3, 79–80, 94n3; and Jefferson, 226; and Lincoln's reelection, 53; and Military Reconstruction Acts, 224; newspaper advertising used by, 47, 52, 57; perceived moral superiority of, 2, 3; politically themed merchandise of, 47–48; political rhetoric of, 5; on prohibition, 10, 11, 12; and racial equality, 38–39; on Reconstruction, 187, 234; and secession crisis, 83; songsters published by, 71–72; and temperance reformers, 7, 11–12, 21n51. *See also* Radical Republicans

Reynolds, Alexander, 110

Rhett, Robert Barnwell, 232, 235n16

Rice, William, 53

Richmond, siege of, 41

Richmond Enquirer, 28, 34

Rigby, William T., 106

Rivers, Prince, 251–52, 253, 260

Robertson, Felix H., 200, 201

Robertson, Jerome B., 192, 200

Robertson, Robert, 117–18

Rock, John S., 24

Roesche, Philip, 101

Rogers, Martha, 196–97

Rogers, William P., 192, 196

Rorabaugh, W. J., 20n32

Rose, Joseph A., 246

Ruffin, Edmund, 80
Russell, George, 54

Sanders, John C. C., 139–40
San Domingo slave revolt, 187, 229, 230, 233
San Francisco Chronicle, 254
Santa Fe Republican, 58*n*7
Savannah Republican, 30, 86
Schultz, Henry, 251
Scott, Reuben, 105
Scott, Winfield, 80–81, 84
secession crisis: Buchanan's policy on, 81–83, 84, 85; Lincoln's policy on, 83, 84, 88, 91–92, 93; and South's seizure of federal forts and arsenals, 80–81, 87, 94*n*9; temperance reformers on, 8, 11–12, 14; Royal T. Wheeler on, 191–92
Second Confiscation Act, 174, 184*n*23
Second Manassas, Battle of, 196
sectional crisis, 7–8, 9, 16, 79–80
Sedgwick, John, 121
Sevitch, Benjamin, 19*n*21
Seward, William, 38, 93, 98*n*91, 211
Shanks, W. F. G., 245–46
Shaw, Robert Gould, 23–24, 25, 27–28, 29, 30, 40
Shepard, James E., 192
Sherman, John, 90–91
Sherman, P. Tecumseh, 237
Sherman, William Tecumseh: and *Century Magazine* Civil War series, 242; criticism of memoirs, 237–41, 245–47; Grant's relationship with, 236, 240, 241; and Joseph E. Johnston, 99; and Louisiana's seizure of federal forts and arsenals, 90; memoirs of, 188, 236–41, 244, 245–47; royalties from memoirs, 237, 246, 247*n*6; on water shortages, 106; white southern women on oppression of, 228
Shiloh, Battle of, 194, 239
Short, Frank, 48
Siddali, Silvana, 94*n*8
Sigfried, Joshua K., 132, 135, 136
Singleton, Otho, 80

slaveholding families, 194
slavery debates: and campaign songs of Lincoln, 63–64; on economic benefits of slavery, 13; on expansion of slavery into territories, 7, 9, 12; temperance reformers and, 6, 7–8, 10, 11, 12, 13–15, 16, 17; Texas Baptists on benefits of slavery for African Americans, 191, 201. *See also* abolition movement
Smith, Channing M., 124
Smith, Charles Henry, 211, 220*n*25
Smith, James West, 108, 109
Smith, Seba, 209–10
Smith, Thad, 99, 108
Smith, William "Sooy," 239
social interactions of soldiers and women: and assessment of appearance, 153, 154, 155, 157; class status affecting, 159, 160, 161; and confirmation of character, 157, 159; courtship and marriage, 163; and formerly enslaved African women, 180; and gender roles, 78, 150–51, 157–58, 165, 169–70*n*33; and language of gentility, 160–61, 162, 170*n*38; and political sympathies, 155, 161, 162–63; and protection of southern women, 160–61; and self-control, 158–60; and sexual intercourse, 164–65
songs: "Abe of Illinois," 63; "Abraham, Our Abraham," 71; "Abraham the Nigger King," 71; "The Assassin's Vision," 72; "The Battle Cry of Freedom," 65; "The Battle Hymn of the Republic," 66; "Bless God, Bless God, for Abram Lincoln's coming," 67; "But Kentucky swore so hard and Old Abe he had his fears," 67; "Canaan," 69; "Come Rally, Freemen Rally," 72; "Come Rouse Ye, Freemen," 71; distribution of songs in songsters, 61; "Dixie," 69; "Emancipation March," 66; from Federal Writers' Project interviews, 60; "Fight for the Nigger," 68; "Five Hundred Thousand More," 70–71; "Get Out de Way, You Little Giant," 63; "Go Down Moses," 67; "Good Old Father Abraham," 65; "Happy Land of Canaan," 69; "He's Gone to the Arms of Abraham," 68; "High Old Abe Shall

songs (*continued*)

Win," 62; "Honest Old Abe," 61; "Hurrah for Lincoln," 61–62; "If you get dar befo' I do," 67; "John Brown's Body," 69, 72; "Kingdom Coming," 66; "Lincoln, The Pride of the Nation," 63–64; "Lincoln," 61; "Lincoln and Liberty," 64; Lincoln's role of emancipator in, 6; "Little Giant," 62; "Little Mac! Little Mac! You're the Very Man," 70; "Little Tad," 72; "Little Willie's Grave," 65; "Live but One Moment," 72; "Marching through Georgia," 73; "Maryland, My Maryland," 69–70, 71; "The Nation is Weeping," 72; "A Nation Weeps," 72; "The Negro Emancipation Song," 66; "Old Abe, The Rail-Splitter," 64; "Old Abe and Old Nick," 69; "Old Abe's Visit to the White House," 61; as reflection of popular perceptions of Lincoln, 60–63; "Shout for the Prairie King," 61; "The Taller Man Well Skinned," 62; "Then Put Away the Wedges and the Maul," 62; "Uncle Abram, Bully for You!," 66; "We Are Coming, Father Abra'am, 300,000 More," 65, 74n8; "We Are Coming, Father Abra'am" parody, 68; "We'll Fight for Uncle Abe," 66–67; "Where Are You Going, Abe Lincoln," 69; "Yankee Doodle" revision, 70; "Year of Jubilee or Kingdom Has Come," 66

Sons of Temperance, 18n7

South: and honor, 167n18; Lincoln's policies toward, 93; military occupation of, 197, 228–29, 231; and Military Reconstruction Acts, 224, 225; and Republican Party's views of emancipation on federal property, 79–80; seizure of federal property, 79, 80–84, 85, 86–90, 91, 93–94, 94n7, 94n8, 94n9; support for prohibition in, 18n9

South Carolina, 84, 85, 224, 259

Southern Historical Society Papers, 245

southern honor, 190

southern newspapers: on black Union soldiers, 137; on enslavement of black POWs, 32–33; on 54th Massachusetts, 27, 28, 30, 32–35; on freedmen, 229–30; on Hamburg Massacre, 253–54, 258, 259; on massacre of black Union soldiers, 141–42; readership of, 45; on Reconstruction compared to French Revolution, 225–26, 230–31, 233; on Sherman's memoirs, 238; on South's seizure of federal forts and arsenals, 86–87, 88; and Winfield Scott's calls for reinforcement of federal forts and arsenals, 81

Spectator, 245

Speight, Joseph W., 193

Spirit of the South, 86

Sprague, J. W., 180

Stampp, Kenneth, 94n9

Stephens, Alexander, 84

Stephens, George E., 39–40, 152, 156, 159, 163–64, 166n8

Stephens, Hampton, 252–53

Stephens, Linton, 231

Stevens, Thaddeus, 79–80, 232

Stinson, Charles F., 135

Strong, George C., 27–28, 29

Strong, Sylvester, 108

Stuart, Jeb, 122

Summers, John, 106, 107–8

Sumner, Charles, 38, 208, 211, 217, 225, 232

Surratt, Mary, 54

Swan, Samuel, 106

Swan, William, 119

Taney, Roger, 24

Taylor, Amy Murrell, 182n3

Taylor, Moses, 51–52

Taylor, Richard, 89

Taylor, Susie King, 151, 153, 154, 157–58, 163, 166n8

temperance reformers: and abolition movement, 6, 8, 9, 10–11; on drunkards, 15, 20n38; on drunkenness as form of slavery, 14–15, 17; on liquor license laws, 11, 12, 13, 14, 15, 19n23; millennialist goals of, 8, 14, 17; nationalistic goals of, 20n43; northern reformers, 7, 9, 13–14; on political compromise, 5, 6; on rum power, 11, 12, 17, 19n23; on slavery debates, 6, 7–8, 10, 11, 12, 13–15, 16, 17; "slave to the habit" phrase used by, 15, 20*n*36; slave trade and rum trade linked by, 14–15, 20*n*32; southern reformers, 7, 18*n*9

Templars' Magazine, 11

tenant farming, 203

Terry, Alfred H., 27

Teters, Kristopher A., 78

Texas Baptist, 191

Texas Baptist Convention, 191, 198, 200, 201

Texas Baptists: as Christian soldiers, 194; foreign mission fields within state, 198; and racial violence, 188, 200; and religious liberty, 193; and secession, 190, 191, 192, 196

Texas Troubles, 191

Thayer, Robert, 49

Thirteenth Amendment, 42, 223

Thomas, George H., 239

Thomas, Henry, 132, 135, 136, 144

Thomas, Mary, 163–64

Thompson, William G., 178–79

Thornhill, Eleazor, 111

Tiffany, John, 121, 123

Tillman, Benjamin, 256–58, 259, 266*n*35

Times (London), 27

"Tippecanoe and Tyler Too" slogan, 46–47

Todd, John, 87, 88

Toussaint l'Ouverture, François-Dominique, 229

Townsend, John, 229

Tracy, Elisha L., 89

Trego, Alfred, 174–75

Trowbridge, C. T., 158

Truth, Sojourner, 25

Turner, Joseph W., 72

Twain, Mark, 208, 216, 237, 242–43

Tyrell, Harrison, 244

Underground Railroad, 199

Union: divisions within, 77; saving, 8, 9, 12, 17, 22, 81–83, 91–92, 152, 192–93

Union army: and African American citizenship, 22; African Americans as laborers for, 23, 31, 40, 41; commanders, on black soldiers in battle, 2, 27; conditions in camps, 77–78, 175–76, 183–84*n*18, 184*n*19; Confederate descriptions of, 197; and formerly enslaved African Americans seeking refuge, 175, 183*n*12; labor programs for formerly enslaved African Americans, 184*n*23; occupation of the South, 227; as protector of formerly enslaved African Americans, 157, 172, 174–76, 177, 181; temperance reformers on effect of alcohol on, 13, 16, 17

Union Association of Churches, 198

Union POWs, 142–43

Union troops: access to clean water, 100, 103–6, 108, 112*n*7; assertions on intentional setting of fires for tactical advantage, 117–18, 126; and civil religion, 189; environmental factors affecting health of, 100–101, 108–9; interpretation of water-dominated landscapes, 100, 111–12*n*6; and *Journal of the American Temperance Union,* 9, 18*n*7; Lincoln's association with, 65; Lucy Higgs Nichols' labor for, 172, 173, 176–77, 181; and politically themed merchandise, 48; and presidential election of 1864, 52, 59*n*20; Vicksburg Campaign, 100–101, 107–8. *See also* black Union soldiers; white Union soldiers

Union University, Tennessee, 200

US Colored Troops: and Battle of the Crater, 134–44; Fort Pillow massacre of, 145*n*6; and Petersburg Campaign, 132, 133; segregation of, 144. *See also* black Union regiments

US Custom House, South Carolina, 85

US House of Representatives, 79–80

upper class: and domesticity, 169*n*33; economic thriving of, 190; and etiquette, 170*n*38; and historical allusions to Reconstruction, 234; men's status as gentlemen, 157, 158, 162, 165, 169*n*31, 169–70*n*33; as proslavery Confederates, 194; women's clothing, 156, 168*n*26; women's status as ladies, 154, 158, 159, 161–62, 165, 168*n*19, 169*n*31

upper middle class: economic strength of, 190; as proslavery Confederates, 194; and status of ladies, 160; and Union sympathies, 152

Index

Upton, Emory, 117, 120

Utley, William, 184n23

Valenčius, Conevery Bolton, 111n6

Vallandigham, Clement, 49–50, 58n13, 211, 212

Van Buren, Martin, 210

Vance, Phillip M., 140

Vanderhurst, Michael Moses, 195

Varon, Elizabeth R., 22, 46

Vicksburg Campaign: environmental factors interpreted as health threats, 101; food shortages of, 100, 109, 110, 111; sanitary conditions of camps, 107–8; water shortages of, 78, 99, 100, 101, 102–10

Voltaire, 226

Waco University, 193, 194, 195, 201

Wainwright, Charles, 122, 123

Walker, Francis, 119

Walker, John, 195

Ward, Ferdinand, 242, 243

Warner, Charles Dudley, 216

Washburne, Elihu, 84

Washington, George, 73

Washington County, Texas, 190–91, 192, 199, 202, 203

Washington *Evening Star*, 34, 49

Washingtonian Movement, 18n7

water: access to clean drinking water, 99, 100, 103–6, 110, 112n6, 112n7, 113n27, 178; collection methods, 100, 104–6, 108, 110; effect on campaigning armies, 99–100, 106, 111n5, 112n6, 112n7; water-borne illnesses, 99, 100, 111n6; water-dominated landscapes, 100, 104, 111–12n6; water shortages, 78, 99, 100, 101, 102–10, 114n64

weather: and battlefield conditions, 99–100, 111n5; dry conditions as cause of fires, 117; and heat as factor in Vicksburg Campaign, 100, 101–3, 108, 109–10; and sunstroke danger, 101–2; and water availability from rainfall, 105

Weekly Anglo-African, 152

Weisiger, David A., 137, 138, 139–40

Weld, Stephen M., 138

westward expansion, 150, 153, 156

Wheeler, Henry, 209

Wheeler, Royal T., 191–92

Whig Party, 9

Whipple, Edwin P., 217

White, Jonathan W., 59n20

Whitehill, James, 101

white northerners: on black regiments, 22, 23; and cult of domesticity, 150; manhood of, 26; as temperance reformers, 9; women as volunteers in Union army camps, 176, 183n16

white southerners: on African Americans in state legislatures, 224; counterrevolution of, 2, 80, 95n10, 187, 233–34; and cult of domesticity, 150; equality among white men, 190; on Hamburg Massacre, 255, 256, 258; historical allusions to Reconstruction, 2–3, 187, 188, 223, 224, 225–34, 234n1; northern temperance reformers chastising, 13, 14; and ownership of public spaces, 251; southern aristocracy compared to nobility of Europe, 224

white southern women: auxiliary clubs organizing Confederate memorial services and monuments, 259–60; and domestic ideology, 2; on invading Union troops, 228; Union soldiers' assessment of, 155, 158–59; Union soldiers socializing with, 78; and upper-class status of ladies, 154, 158, 159, 161–62, 165, 168n19, 169n31

white supremacy: commitment to, 3; David Ross Locke on, 214; and Hamburg Massacre, 250, 256, 257–58, 260, 262, 263, 264; in political culture of North, 2, 38; and political rhetoric, 5, 6; on Reconstruction, 187, 264; and Red Shirts, 251–52, 256, 258, 266n35; restoration of, 233–34; violence employed to maintain, 42, 202, 223, 266n29

white Union soldiers: attitudes toward black soldiers, 77, 132, 136, 139, 140, 142–43; attitudes toward formerly enslaved African Americans, 173, 182n5; racism of, 159, 173, 179, 180; reports of serialized rape of African

American women, 163; southern-born Union soldiers, 155; southern women's relationships with, 150–51, 155

Wide-Awake Vocalist, 61

Wilderness, Battle of: assertions of intentional setting of fires for tactical advantage, 117–18, 126; combat conditions affected by fires, 118–20, 121, 122, 127; and Confederate attack on Union Brock Road, 118–19, 124; fires of, 116, 117; and postwar reconciliation, 126; soldiers' reactions to fires, 123–24, 125, 126

Wilderness fires: accidental causes of, 116, 117; assertions of intentional setting for tactical advantage, 117–18, 126; as cause of soldiers' deaths, 121–22; combat conditions affected by, 116, 118–20, 121; and postwar reconciliation, 116–17, 125–26, 127; soldiers' reactions of, 116, 122–25, 126, 127

Wilke, Franc B., 238

Wilkeson, Frank, 121, 124–25

Willcox, Orlando, 134–35

Williams, Alpheus S., 179–80, 238

Williamson, William W., 123

Willison, Charles, 107

Wilson, Douglas, 98n91

Wilson, Henry, 36

Winn, David R., 117, 121–22

Winner, Septimus, 68

Winters, Harold, 111n5

Wise, Henry A., 133

women: as dependent under coverture laws, 22; and ideas of ladylike behavior, 155, 156, 161; as teachers at Baylor University, 194. *See also* enslaved women; formerly enslaved African American women; social interactions of soldiers and women; white southern women

Wood, Fernando, 212

Woods, Joseph Thatcher, 105

Woodworth, Steven, 195–96

Work, Henry Clay, 66

working class: and domesticity, 170n37; and etiquette, 170n38; and masculinity, 169n33; men's views of women, 164; middle-class contempt for poor white women, 156; slavery as degrading to, 156, 159; Union soldiers' violence, 159–60

Yaggy, Job, 106

Yazoo River, 105, 113n32

yeomen class, 150, 159, 164, 165, 169n31, 170n37

CPSIA information can be obtained
at www.ICGtesting.com
Printed in the USA
LVHW110149020520
654850LV00015B/409